THE PULL OF POLITICS

THE PULL OF POLITICS

STEINBECK, WRIGHT, HEMINGWAY, AND THE LEFT IN THE LATE 1930s

MILTON A. COHEN

UNIVERSITY OF MISSOURI PRESS
Columbia

Library of Congress Cataloging-in-Publication Data

Names: Cohen, Milton A., author.
Title: The pull of politics : Steinbeck, Wright, Hemingway and the left in
   the late 1930s / Milton A. Cohen.
Description: Columbia : University of Missouri Press, [2018] | Includes
   bibliographical references and index. |
Identifiers: LCCN 2018014592 (print) | LCCN 2018019620 (ebook) | ISBN
   9780826274151 (e-book) | ISBN 9780826221636 (hardcover : alk. paper)
Subjects: LCSH: Novelists, American--20th century--Political and social
   views. | Politics and literature--United States--History--20th century. |
   Politics in literature. | Right and left (Political science) in
   literature. | Steinbeck, John, 1902-1968. Grapes of wrath. | Wright,
   Richard, 1908-1960. Native son. | Hemingway, Ernest, 1899-1961. For whom
   the bell tolls. | Steinbeck, John, 1902-1968.--Political and social views.
   | Wright, Richard, 1908-1960.--Political and social views. | Hemingway,
   Ernest, 1899-1961--Political and social views.
Classification: LCC PS374.P6 (ebook) | LCC PS374.P6 C75 2018 (print) | DDC
   813/.5209358--dc23
LC record available at https://lccn.loc.gov/2018014592

Typeface: Trump Mediaeval

for Florence

Contents

Acknowledgments

A Special Faculty Development Assignment from the University of Texas at Dallas facilitated the completion of this book.

I wish to thank Dr. Alex Vernon for reading the Hemingway chapter (chapter 3) and Gary Kass, of the University of Missouri Press, for his careful editing and cogent suggestions. Interlibrary Loan at McDermott Library, University of Texas at Dallas, was especially helpful in obtaining materials expeditiously. And, as always, I thank my wife, Florence, for her tireless efforts in reading and editing the many drafts of this book.

THE PULL OF POLITICS

Introduction

CULMINATING A TUMULTUOUS decade, the years 1939 to 1940 witnessed the publication of three major novels that achieved the distinction of being both popular and critical successes: *The Grapes
of Wrath* (1939), *Native Son* (1940), and *For Whom the Bell Tolls*
(1940). All three were runaway best-sellers; all three were made
into films; two (*For Whom the Bell Tolls* and, remarkably, *Native
Son*) were Book-of-the-Month Club selections; and *The Grapes of
Wrath* won the Pulitzer Prize in 1940 and the National Book Award
in 1939.[1]

Although set in different locales and addressing different sociopolitical issues—the plight of migrant farmers in Oklahoma and
California, a black man's killing of a white woman in Chicago, and
Loyalist *partizans* fighting in the Spanish Civil War—these novels
and their authors share important similarities, which, in turn, tell
us something about American literature and politics at the end of
the 1930s. All three novels have highly political themes and slants
that, in their individual contexts, can be construed as leftist.[2] *The
Grapes of Wrath* strongly empathizes with displaced migrant farmers and explicitly condemns the combination of large landowners
(the Associated Farmers, Inc.), landowning banks, and hired deputies that repress these migrants; moreover, the novel affirms that
the migrants must organize and take action collectively. Although
Bigger Thomas, the protagonist of *Native Son*, is in many respects
unsympathetic and his crimes repulsive, Richard Wright's novel clearly delineates the overwhelming racism he experiences his

3

entire life. The only people willing to help him are communists or fellow travelers. The Spanish Civil War was of course explicitly political, as the fascist Rebels (or Nationalists) led by General Franco and supported by Nazi Germany and Fascist Italy attacked a democratically elected coalition of leftist groups (the Republicans or Loyalists), whose military leadership and matériel came mostly from the Soviet Union. The independent protagonist of *For Whom the Bell Tolls*, Robert Jordan, like Tom Joad in *Grapes*, learns the value of collective action by working with a group of Loyalist partizans to carry out his mission. But he also deals directly with, and gives his allegiance to, the covert Soviet leadership in Spain, which has imported Stalinist tactics.

The Pull of Politics situates each novel within the political development of its author: the personal and historical events that awakened his commitment to a leftist cause; his earlier literary works reflecting stages of that commitment; and, following analysis of his major novel, the biographical and historical events that ultimately severed that commitment.

Despite their shared move toward various kinds of leftism, the authors' political views and history would seem to make them an anomalous grouping. Two—John Steinbeck and Ernest Hemingway—were relatively apolitical before they encountered the issues that pulled them to the left.[3] Neither author was a "joiner" by nature, and both chose relatively independent modes of political involvement. Richard Wright, on the other hand, joined the Communist Party (CP-USA) in 1934 and, despite a rocky relationship with the Party thereafter, was committed to it for several years. When examined more closely, however, these three writers share important similarities that argue for their being studied together. First, as noted, they produced major novels with leftist themes—indeed, the most important American novels regardless of politics—on the cusp between the 1930s and 1940s. This historical confluence in itself precludes consideration here of other major political authors, such as John Dos Passos and James T. Farrell, who produced their major trilogies, *U.S.A.* and the Studs Lonigan novels, several years earlier, and who had repudiated the Communist Party by 1936/37. By contrast, the political conflicts experienced by Steinbeck, Wright, and Hemingway came at the end of the decade and reflect, in varying ways, a larger crisis in the Left at precisely this period.

Another important quality linking the three writers is that all were attracted to the Left by one or two particular appeals rather than by a broad-based ideological agreement with communist doctrine. For Steinbeck and Hemingway, these appeals were the issues depicted in their novels: the mistreatment of the migrant farmers and the Spanish Loyalists' struggle against fascism. For Wright, also, the central issue that kept him in the Communist Party was not communist ideology in general but the CP-USA's actions to improve the status of blacks in America.

Two of these writers were also drawn left by self-interest. The personal benefit to Wright was obvious: the Chicago John Reed Club[4] gave him his start as a writer, encouraged him, and provided a sympathetic audience and publishing venues in leftist literary magazines. To hold office in the club, he had to join the CP-USA. The benefits Hemingway received in gravitating to the Left were less obvious, but nonetheless distinct: leftist critics who had lambasted his indifference to the Depression and hostility to the Left in *Death in the Afternoon* (1932), *The Green Hills of Africa* (1935), and in his *Esquire* magazine articles now celebrated his political commitment to Loyalist Spain. Even before that war began, Hemingway made quiet overtures to the Left while still proclaiming his political independence.

The three authors shared other political ties to the Left. All three published—or attempted to publish—articles in communist newspapers: the San Francisco *People's World* for Steinbeck; *Pravda* for Hemingway; and the *Daily Worker* for Wright, who, as its Harlem "editor" (actually, a reporter) in 1937, published hundreds of brief articles there. Hemingway and Wright also published works in *The New Masses*, the CP-USA's literary magazine and, for most of the 1930s, the most influential journal of the American Left. Further, in their journalistic work, both Wright and Hemingway supported Stalinist positions (Wright generally, Hemingway regarding the Soviet Union's political priorities in the Spanish Civil War). All three authors joined the League of American Writers, a group created by the American Writers' Congress in 1935 (both groups, in turn, fronting the CP-USA). Steinbeck joined in 1937, was elected to the

National Executive Council that year and served as a vice president from 1939 to 1940. Hemingway also joined in 1937 and gave an electrifying keynote speech at the 1937 Congress. Like Steinbeck, he held the largely honorific position of vice president from 1939 to 1940. Wright joined at the League's inception in 1935, was elected to the National Council that year and from 1939 to 1941, became a member of the League's executive committee in 1938, vice president in 1941, and was a prominent speaker at the 1941 Congress. All three became interested for a time in the documentary genre with a leftist or progressivist slant: Hemingway worked hard in 1937 on a propaganda film supporting the Loyalist cause, *The Spanish Earth*; Steinbeck worked briefly with the great documentary filmmaker Pare Lorentz and then helped make a film in 1939, *The Forgotten Village*, about the need for modern medicine in Mexico; Wright collaborated with the photographer Edwin Rosskam in 1941 on a book about African-American history, *12 Million Black Voices*. Finally, all three writers were under FBI surveillance in the late 1930s and early 1940s for their leftist activities.[5]

They were far from being true believers, however, for each author held conflicted attitudes that complicated his pull to the Left. Despite believing that collectivism would enable the migrants to prevail over the big landowners, Steinbeck had long distrusted group thinking and behavior (which he termed "the phalanx") and admired the detached observer and the migrants' individualism. Wright's burgeoning identity as an independent author, needing time to write and express his own themes, conflicted with the Communist Party's rigid expectations of its authors and its directives commanding their time. Hemingway's characteristic need for independent thought and action did not cohere with his support of authoritarian Soviet leadership in Spain and even less with his decision to parrot the Party line in his journalism and early fiction about the war. All of these topics will occupy part 1 of this book (chapters 1 through 3), as it traces each author's gravitation to the Left, followed by a brief synthesis (chapter 4).

Just as these authors experienced dissonance in their attraction to a form of leftism, so their great novels ending the 1930s reflect these tensions in thematic fissures and unresolved contradictions. In *The Grapes of Wrath*, where the contradictions remain submerged, Steinbeck never successfully reconciles his admiration for the migrant farmers' tough individualism with the collectivism that he feels is essential to overcome the power conglomerate of the large landowners, banks, and police. Though the communists in *Native Son*, particularly Bigger's defense attorney, Boris Max, are presented sympathetically, their ideological appeals to Bigger do not speak to his existential sense of himself. Lastly, Hemingway's Robert Jordan hopes (in a "true book" he will write after the war) to reconcile contradictions he has come to recognize in his values and in the war itself, such as his belief in democratic freedom and his support of Russian terror and authoritarian control. Though never written, the "true book" he envisions becomes Hemingway's attempt to set the record straight after two years of defending Soviet actions and lies in Spain. Part 2 (chapters 5 through 7) will examine political themes, tensions, and contradictions in each novel.

These political tensions in the fiction anticipate each author's movement away from the Left after his major novel was published. This falling away occurred immediately for Steinbeck and Hemingway, and after sixteen months for Wright. Essentially, the issues that had drawn them to the Left were overridden either by personal factors (Steinbeck's exhaustion and need to escape the firestorm his novel had created), or by dissolution of the "pull" itself: for Hemingway, the Spanish Loyalists' defeat; for Wright, the Communist Party's refusal to actively oppose racism after June 1941—a betrayal, in his eyes. The Party's attacks on *For Whom the Bell Tolls* and *Native Son* further repelled their authors.

Internationally, the Soviet Union's abrupt reversals of its foreign policies in these years also alienated these writers from Russia and the Communist Party. The Nazi-Soviet Non-Aggression Pact of August 1939, which reversed the Soviets' much-proclaimed antifascist position (the "Popular Front"), and especially Russia's invasion of Finland, angered Steinbeck and Hemingway. Though Wright, as a loyal Party member, supported these actions, he was dumbfounded when, after Germany invaded Russia, the Communist Party reversed its opposition to involvement in the "imperialist" war and now urged military aid for the Allies. Wright had recently published "Not My People's War" and was infuriated when the Party forced him to reverse his position. The falling away of each author thus varied in difficulty: for Steinbeck and Hemingway, whose political roots had not gone deep, it was relatively painless; for Wright, it involved a divorce from the Party full of mutual recriminations when it went public in 1944. Part 3 (chapter 8) traces these separations and disaffiliations, noting in two cases the authors' subsequent political positions in their next novels. The conclusion synthesizes the separate stories of these disaffections and places them in a broader context of American literary-political history.

In examining the political odysseys of Steinbeck, Wright, and Hemingway, I have not tried to discover new facts about the writers, but rather new ways of comparatively understanding the factors that attracted them to and repelled them from the Left, and to trace tensions in their political beliefs and in their great novels. Accordingly, for the biographical aspects of parts 1 and 3, I have relied heavily on the superb biographies that exist for each writer—Jackson Benson's *John Steinbeck, Writer*, Michel Fabre's *The Unfinished Quest of Richard Wright*, and Carlos Baker's *Hemingway: A Life Story*—augmented, of course, by other biographies, by the authors' letters, articles, and other literary works, and by secondary criticism.

One question that arises in a selective comparison of this sort is to what degree is the story of these three authors representative of other writers in the 1930s and early 1940s? Were the authors' experiences typical or idiosyncratic? I would argue that they were both. The pull to the Left that they responded to pervaded the 1930s, affecting numerous writers and artists, beginning with the Great Depression and overlapped by the rise of fascism. These three authors missed—or ignored—the first large wave of leftist attraction in the early thirties, when writers responded to the Depression with the belief that capitalism was finished and communism was a viable replacement.[6] By the mid-1930s, with Roosevelt's New Deal precluding the likelihood of (and, for many, the necessity for) an economic revolution in the United States, concern with aggressive fascism became, in effect, the second wave of leftist appeal, significantly furthered by the Soviet Comintern's new policy in 1935 of the Popular Front against fascism. Anti-fascism drew even larger numbers to the Left as fellow travelers if not as party members. The approximately fifty thousand international volunteers who went to Spain to oppose fascism (three thousand from the United States) dramatize this intensifying concern. Even among leftists who did not volunteer, virtually all supported the Spanish Republic, as the 1938 survey documented in *Writers Take Sides* makes clear.[7]

The authors in this study responded to differing aspects of fascism. Hemingway directly opposed it from the front lines of the Spanish Civil War, and his articles warned about the inevitability of another world war if fascism wasn't stopped in Spain. Steinbeck worried about home-grown fascism and, in his journalism, accused Associated Farmers, Inc. and its police cohorts of using "fascistic methods" against the migrants. Later, he simply called hired vigilantes "fascists."[8] Wright believed that disaffected blacks like Bigger Thomas could easily become fascists.[9]

For Steinbeck and Wright, however, international fascism was not the main issue. Their concerns were more localized, though no less political for that. Steinbeck did not attribute the Okies' migration to dust storms and drought so much as to the bank-landowners' consolidation of small farms into big ones. This hunger for profits literally pushed the small farmers off their land and exploited them as cheap labor to work the mega-farms of California. It was this unchecked agricultural capitalism—and its terroristic apparatus in the Associated Farmers and police—that Steinbeck felt must be opposed and overcome by collective action. For Wright, ubiquitous American racism was the enemy. The Communist Party—and specifically the hope it offered to oppressed blacks of joining forces with the white working class—promised the best means of overcoming this racism. For both authors, then, their particular pulls to leftism were tangential to the main currents of the time.

What, then, do the histories of these three authors and their novels tell us about the Left in the latter half of the 1930s? First, they show how diverse the appeals of leftism were, not only geographically, spanning the continent from Chicago to Key West to California, but politically in opposing different forms of oppression: racism against black Americans, exploitation of small farmers migrating from the Plains, and a fascist war to destroy democracy in Spain. These diverse situations, however, share a common denominator of powerful forces—the white race, agribusiness, and fascism—exploiting and oppressing weaker ones. The Left's appeal in each case was its support, actual or potential, for the underdog. And the strength of that pull was sufficient to shake two of the writers in this study—Steinbeck and Hemingway—out of their apolitical indifference and bring them into differing orbits of the Left.

The conflictedness these authors experienced as leftists can also be seen as a microcosm of the Left in the late 1930s. The Moscow Trials and Stalinist purges, Russia's authoritarian and terroristic control of the Spanish Loyalists, its murderous obsession with Trotsky and Trotskyism, and finally the Nazi-Soviet Pact and Russia's invasion of Finland, all helped fissure the Left in these years into pro- and anti-Stalinist camps, as represented by the two most influential leftist journals in America: *New Masses* and *Partisan Review.* Devotion to Soviet communism became increasingly problematic for many leftists in this period: cognitive dissonance was rife, requiring many Party members and fellow travelers to turn an increasingly blind eye to Russia's anti-democratic actions. In the turmoil of factions and issues arising from these divisions, each month seemed to bring new petitions and counter-petitions in leftist magazines.[10] Although the political conflicts experienced by Steinbeck, Wright, and Hemingway were particular to each writer, centering on differing forms of individualism against the demands of collectivism and the Party's cynical actions, the *fact* of the authors' conflictedness was characteristic of a divided Left—a Left in crisis—in the late thirties.

Finally, the writers' abandonment of leftism, again for reasons specific to their own situations, was nonetheless typical of the time. Just as the issues that pulled these three writers to the Left were focused rather than broadly ideological, so too was the appeal of the Popular Front's anti-fascism for many other writers and artists. And in both the individual and general contexts, that narrow appeal became vulnerable and tenuous. When the Spanish Loyalists were defeated in 1939 and the CP-USA stopped fighting racism in 1941/42, Hemingway and Wright lost their chief justification for being leftist; even Steinbeck's enthusiastic support of the migrants' cause could not withstand his physical and psychological exhaustion after *Grapes* was published. Analogously, when the antifascists' champion, Soviet Russia, betrayed its Popular Front ideology by colluding with the enemy (signing the Non-Aggression Pact) and by emulating fascism's international aggression by occupying eastern Poland and the Baltic countries and invading Finland, many who had been drawn to the Left in the later 1930s also felt cut off and adrift, resulting in numerous disaffections by communists and fellow travelers following the Pact.

Thus, the odysseys of these three authors to and from the Left were both individual and a reflection of the larger leftist appeals and dilemmas of the late 1930s, as the idealism of attraction ultimately withered, for so many, into the disillusionment of separation, a disillusion acidly expressed on the day World War II began in W. H. Auden's depiction of the time as "a low dishonest decade."[11]

PART 1

Steinbeck

1934–1939

GAUGING JOHN STEINBECK's political views in the mid-1930s is tricky: such words as "contradictory" and even "paradoxical" come to mind, and certainly "drastically changing." Steinbeck scholars reflect this ambiguity in their sharply contrasting depictions of his politics then. Was he drawn to the "communist movement," forging an "alliance" with it in the 1930s? Alan Wald would have it so.[1] Was he, rather, essentially apolitical, at most a "New Deal Democrat?" This is the view of Steinbeck scholar and biographer Jackson Benson: "Steinbeck [while writing *In Dubious Battle*] really did not like or trust politics, particularly mass movement politics, because he saw that it often used man rather than served man. . . . He also saw particular political phenomena as rather minor events within the whole course of natural history."[2] Susan Shillinglaw, another distinguished Steinbeck scholar, states that he was, by nature, a loner, not a joiner.[3]

Yet in 1934/35, Steinbeck and his spouse, Carol, were virtually inundated by leftist politics close to home. Agricultural workers struggled for something better than their pitifully low wages in the fertile Central Valley; leftists and communists attempted to organize these workers. On the other side, the big growers and their powerful cohorts—the Associated Farmers,[4] sheriffs, and vigilantes—combined to break the strikes and harass and jail the organizers. Most important, friends and associates of the Steinbecks expressed strong sympathy for these organizing efforts and for the Left generally. Out of Steinbeck's contacts with workers, strikers, organizers, and supporters came his labor novel of 1936 *In Dubious Battle*. In 1937, he joined the communist-organized League of American Writers—an uncharacteristic act for someone who was not a "joiner."

Steinbeck's contacts with the Left in these years came primarily through two liaisons, both of whom lived in Carmel, close to the Steinbeck home in Pacific Grove. The well-known author and socialist Lincoln Steffens and his radical spouse, Ella Winter, were themselves the hub of a group of young radicals. Steinbeck met Steffens in late 1933, and often visited the Steffens-Winter home to talk politics, even though Steffens's views were far more radical than his own (Benson, *Steinbeck, Writer*, 294–96). When Steffens urged Steinbeck to write about labor conditions in California, instead of dismissing the idea out of hand, Steinbeck was interested. According to Carol Steinbeck, the young radicals who congregated at the Steffens-Winter home were "members of either The John Reed Club or the Young Communist League" (or both) and "started dropping by the Steinbeck cottage in Pacific Grove on almost a regular basis. They came to talk and be fed." And "[t]hey glowed with a spirit of holy mission . . . . [Steinbeck] did more listening than talking" to their absolutist views (*Steinbeck, Writer*, 294). Sometimes they were accompanied by Ella Winter, sometimes by Anna Louise Strong and Mike Gold.[5] Even though Steinbeck was far less leftist than these fervent radicals, he must have gotten an earful from their vociferous advocacy of communism.

Another source also worked on Steinbeck's political sensibility: Francis Whitaker, a metal sculptor and a leader of the local John Reed Club. He and his wife "worked hard during the early and mid-thirties to convert John and Carol to a socialist point of view. . . . [but] Steinbeck remained skeptical of Whitaker's politics" (Benson, *Steinbeck, Writer*, 225). Whitaker did persuade the Steinbecks to attend some John Reed Club meetings, where Steinbeck was "a meticulous observer."[6] More important, Whitaker helped Steinbeck meet two union organizers who, in 1934, were hiding from the law—meetings that would lead directly to Steinbeck's next novel. One of these organizers, Cecil McKiddy, a migrant from Oklahoma, had helped organize the peach and cotton strikes that same year, and had much information to share with Steinbeck about labor organizing in general and these strikes in particular. Sympathetic to the men's destitution, Steinbeck offered to buy their story to help them—and help himself: he planned to use McKiddy's knowledge to write a first-person narrative, an autobiography in diary form, of an experienced labor organizer, based on the man who had mentored McKiddy, Pat Chambers. Chambers and McKiddy would become models for the labor organizers of *In Dubious Battle*, Mac McLeod and Jim Nolan. Steinbeck met with McKiddy often for several weeks, "questioning him in great detail." He also visited labor camps in the Salinas area to gain more experience listening to workers (*Steinbeck, Writer*, 298).

On the advice of one of his agents, however, Steinbeck turned this pseudo-autobiography into a novel narrated from a conventional third-person limited point of view. But other aspects of the novel were quite unconventional for the time. Here was the literary Left's favorite topic of the 1930s: oppressed workers taking action and organizing a strike; proletarian novels and plays employing this theme are too numerous to mention. But Steinbeck did not intend to write a proletarian novel. Instead of focusing on the oppressed workers, the novel limits itself to the organizers' perspective, particularly their strategies and schemes for organizing—and manipulating— the workers. The novel's emotional tone is cool, its stance toward both the organizers and the strikers is detached rather than sympathetic. Steinbeck was much more interested in studying the behavior of the organized workers as a distinct unit—a "phalanx" as he called it—than in advocating their cause; his perspective was sociological, rather than political and leftist.

This approach to a highly political subject suggests that, despite Steinbeck's continuous exposure to the radical Left's advocacy of these strikes, he was not won over to its point of view. As Benson observes, "although surrounded by the genuine concern of many near him for the misery of the farm worker and migrant, Steinbeck remained emotionally uninvolved" (296).[7] Yet questions remain. Did he listen to the young radicals and go to the meetings of the John Reed Club just to gather material and study their mindsets? Why did he focus on communist organizers and oppressed workers in *In*

Dubious Battle, rather than on the big growers, local police, and vigilantes, who had also organized themselves to fight the workers? Or why not focus on both sides equally? Clearly, he wanted to observe, to study how people behave in groups, but is it coincidental that the groups, like his two protagonists, were leftist? Did nothing of their devotion rub off on Steinbeck's "objective" sensibility? He had recently published his first successful novel, *Tortilla Flat* (1935), on a group of Mexican-American *paisanos* living together, but their wine-soaked misadventures were clearly apolitical. Now, political organizing itself was the issue, and Steinbeck was clearly curious about these passionate organizers and their selfless devotion to this cause, devotion that often landed them in jail or in a ditch badly beaten or worse. At what point does curiosity—and its satisfaction in extensive knowledge—edge into sympathy? Were seeds being planted now that grew so impressively just a few years later? Certainly, detachment from and curiosity about the Left were both at work in Steinbeck's complex sensibility—and perhaps the beginnings of something more.

The Phalanx

That detachment was an increasingly rare commodity for writers in the mid-1930s. The Popular Front had been attracting increasing numbers of formerly apolitical authors, publishers, and book reviewers to the left, but Steinbeck's intellectual interests since the early 1930s focused on a blend of science and sociology rather than politics. In 1930, living in Pacific Grove, California, he met Ed Ricketts, who, having studied biology and ecology in college, had constructed and operated his own biological lab on the Monterey coast, where he collected and sold biological samples to local schools. Ricketts was Steinbeck's intellectual mentor and close friend in these years; Steinbeck and Carol even worked for a time in Ricketts's lab, and Steinbeck went there often—nearly every day for a time—for good conversation, drink, and good music.[8] Ricketts's impact on Steinbeck's ideas and writing was, in Benson's view, "unquestioned" (*Steinbeck, Writer,* 183); critics and biographers disagree only on the degree, but nearly all would concur that the influence was profound, especially in the early 1930s when they lived nearby, and again after the publication of *The Grapes of*

Wrath. From Ricketts, Steinbeck developed not only a love of scientific investigation, but also a way of seeing human struggles in a broader biological context. A few years later, Steinbeck recalled their discussions in general terms:

> Very many conclusions Ed and I worked out together through endless discussion and reading and observation and experiment. We worked together, and so closely that I do not know in some cases who started which line of speculation since the end thought was the product of both minds.[9]

From these experiences evolved Steinbeck's own socio-biological interest in studying human behavior in the context of groups, or "phalanxes." He summarizes this theory in a letter to a friend, "Dook" Sheffield (21 June 1933). The key hypothesis is that people in groups behave differently than they do as individuals. The group operates with a will of its own:

> When acting as a group, men do not partake of their ordinary natures at all. The group can change its nature. It can later alter the birth rate, diminish the number of its units, control states of mind, alter appearance, physically and spiritually. . . . [Thus,] the group is an individual as boundaried, as *diagnosable*, as dependent on its units and as independent of its units' individual natures, as the human unit, or man, is dependent on his cells and yet is independent of them.[10]

Again, Steinbeck's attitude towards the phalanx was detached—"scientific"—as a biologist would examine a colony of microbes under a microscope. The behavior of phalanxes deserved study, not admiration or fear: "[A]s individual humans we are far superior in our functions to anything the world has born—in our groups we are not only not superior but in fact are remarkably like those most perfect groups, the ants and bees" (*Steinbeck: A Life in Letters*, 76).

By 1934/35, there was no shortage of phalanxes to observe: the goose-stepping Nazis and Italian fascists, the invading Japanese armies sworn to the code of Bushido, the communists' rigid conformity to Marxist-Leninist doctrine in their worldwide fight against capitalism, and the many smaller causes and their followers. But, as noted above, the group issue that most interested Steinbeck at the time—an issue that was currently being played out all around him in the fertile fields of the Central Valley, as well as in the dockyards of San Francisco—was the organizing of self-interested workers into a group with a common purpose to receive higher wages and better treatment from the "bosses"—the big growers and corporate owners—and, if necessary, to strike for those collective improvements. *Could* the workers be organized? If so, by what techniques? How could the group mentality be maintained; how long would it hold together? And how would the workers' behavior as a group differ from their individual behaviors?

In Dubious Battle: "I'm not interested in ranting about justice and oppression . . ."

These are clearly the questions that *In Dubious Battle* explores. Its point of view is revealing, following in third person not the exploited workers but the two communist organizers: Mac, the experienced mentor, and his protégé, Jim, who has just joined the Party. Rather than experience the workers' exploitation firsthand, which could elicit empathy, the reader learns of it from a distance, only after Mac and Jim arrive on the scene. Throughout, the narrative focuses on the two organizers' plans and intentions; the workers are merely the objects of these plans. In Mac's many decisions and statements, once he and Jim arrive at the apple orchards, it is clear that he cares *only* for organizing the men successfully: whatever furthers their coherence as a group is good; whatever impedes it is bad. About their individual welfare, he is indifferent. Numerous instances reveal his views and strategies. After he single-handedly and successfully organizes an effort to deliver an indigent girl's baby, even pretending to have medical experience, he reveals to Jim that he didn't care about her welfare:

That was a lucky break. We simply had to take it. 'Course it was nice to help the girl, but hell, even if it killed her—we've got to use anything [that comes to us]. . . . With one night's work we've got the confidence of the men . . . we made the men work for themselves, in their own defense, as a group. That's what we're out here for anyway, to teach them to fight in a bunch. (48)

When Old Dan's fall from a tree galvanizes the pickers, Mac comments, "The old buzzard was worth something after all. . . . He tipped the thing off. We can use him now" (79). Using people or situations to further his ends is all that matters to Mac. When Jim admits to liking Anderson, an old farmer who allows the strikers to camp on his land, Mac corrects him: "Don't you go liking people, Jim. We can't waste time liking people" (90). Even the murder of a comrade, Joy, elicits no sympathy from Mac; instead, he exploits the murder by displaying Joy's body on a platform to work up the group. When Anderson suffers grievously for his generosity to the strikers, Mac tells Doc, "I can't take time to think about the feelings of one man . . . . I'm too busy with big bunches of men" (158). Nor is he averse to seeing his own men killed by the police: "Suppose they do kill some of our men? That helps our side. For every man they kill ten new ones come over to us" (253). About the strike itself he is pessimistic. When questioned by Jim, he admits that "we don't have a chance to win," but "some day—it'll work" (121). Thus, the strikers are merely pawns of a much larger struggle; their personal suffering during the strike doesn't matter: "It doesn't make any difference if we lose. Here's nearly a thousand men who've learned how to strike" (222). One of the strike leaders perfectly sums up Mac: "You're a cold-blooded bastard" (129), a label Mac indirectly confirms when he praises Jim's emerging coldness: "You're turning into a proper son-of-a-bitch. Everybody's going to hate you, but you'll be a good Party man" (208).

Because the point of view remains strictly with Mac and Jim, their enemies—the landowners and the police and vigilantes whom the landowners have skillfully organized—remain distant, impersonal forces. Steinbeck inserts only two face-to-face encounters: a perfunctory "get back to work" demand from the superintendent and a meeting with the landowners' representative, who is atypically oily in trying to smooth over the deep divisions between the owners and workers. The strikers—and thus the readers—experience the repressive actions of the owners, but never really see their faces.

The one character in *In Dubious Battle* who stands at right angles to the novel's dual struggles (between organizers and workers, and between both and the power-conglomerate) is Doc, a genuine doctor who works tirelessly to treat the strikers' wounds and keep the temporary camp sanitary, until he mysteriously disappears. Unlike Mac's narrowly pragmatic nature, Doc is philosophical, speculative, and more interested in observing and understanding the dynamics of these conflicts than in committing himself ideologically. "I don't believe in the cause," he tells Mac, "but I believe in men" (153). Unlike the organizers, Doc sees ironies and paradoxes of the "us versus them" mentality. He tells Jim, "[I]n my little experience the end is never very different in its nature from the means. . . . [Y]ou can only build a violent thing with violence" (199). Benson is spot on when he asserts that Doc is clearly Steinbeck's surrogate[11]—as when Doc declares, "I want to see the whole picture—as nearly as I can. I don't want to put on the blinders of 'good' and 'bad' and limit my vision" (113). Doc virtually paraphrases Steinbeck's letter (quoted above) in describing the "group-men" the strikers are becoming:

> I want to watch these group-men, for they seem to me to be a new individual, not at all like single men. A man in a group isn't himself at all, he's a cell in an organism that isn't like him any more than the cells in your body are like you. . . . [Group man's] nature, his ends, his desires. . . . [are not] the same as ours. (104–5)

Opposing Doc's desire to study this phenomenon scientifically, Mac is the anti-intellectual man of action: "If you see too darn much, you don't get anything done" (114). For Doc, lack of a larger vision produces only "wild-eyed confusion and bewilderment" (115). In the rage that Mac and Jim try to work up in the men, Doc sees futility: "It all seems meaningless to me, brutal and meaningless" (198). Yet he continues to work for the strike's success.

Through Mac's strategies and Doc's observations, Steinbeck develops his phalanx theory, dramatizing the elements that spark the group to action: food, anger, and, most chillingly, blood. Mac's prediction that "What they need is blood. A mob's got to kill something" (244) proves true when London, the strikers' elected leader, breaks an accuser's jaw. Blood flows copiously, and the crowd is now eager to charge the police barricades (247). Descriptions of the group are typically animalistic—"the angry crowd-roar, a bellow like an animal in fury" (199); "'it was just one big—animal, going down the road'" (249). At least twice the strikers are referred to as sheep. The strikers' wives, when mentioned at all, come off even worse: "The women crawled like rodents from the tents and followed" (197). Even Mac comes to accept Doc's group man analysis with a sense of foreboding: "It *is* a big animal. It's different from the men in it. And it's stronger than all the men put together. It doesn't want the same things men want—it's like Doc said—and we don't know what it'll do" (249).

The ruthlessness of the owners and their henchmen turn the strike into a series of disasters: Joy is shot by a sniper; Anderson's barn and crop are burned; his son's lunch wagon is destroyed and the son badly beaten; Doc goes missing; and finally, Jim (who was previously shot) is murdered when he and Mac are lured away from the camp. Although Steinbeck ends the novel before the strike's conclusion plays out,[12] there are strong hints that it will fail, as Mac predicted. But from the organizers' perspective, that failure doesn't matter: "We done what we came to do," Mac says. "The thing goes right on . . ." (259).

The novel's title, drawn from Milton's *Paradise Lost*, clearly reflects Steinbeck's narrative distance from the issues and participants of the strike. All sides are at fault: the greedy owners, their ruthless henchmen, the manipulative organizers, the easily manipulated sheeplike workers. All are, to the author, no more than microbes squirming under his microscope, tidal forces that wax and wane. So as not to deflect his study with ethnic prejudices of his characters and readers, Steinbeck even simplified the microscopic sample, making them all white, instead of Mexican (who made up three-quarters of those in the peach and cotton strikes) or recent migrants from the Dust Bowl. He saw them, instead, as an abstraction—not individuals, but "man"—and studied their reactions *en masse*. As he wrote his friend, George Albee, he simply used the strike as

a symbol of man's eternal, bitter warfare with himself. I am not interested in strike as a means of raising men's wages, and I'm not interested in ranting about justice and oppression, mere outcroppings which indicate the condition. But man hates something in himself. He has been able to defeat every natural obstacle but himself he cannot win over unless he kills the individual. And this self-hate which goes so closely in hand with self-love is what I wrote about. The book is brutal. I wanted merely to be a recording consciousness, judging nothing, simply putting things down. (15 Jan. 1935, *Life in Letters*, 98)

If, as Jay Parini claims, "he sympathized deeply with the plight of workers and admired the idealism that lay, in theory, behind communism," he certainly doesn't show it in this novel.[13] Benson's conclusion seems more accurate: "If Steinbeck's organizers are cold, it is because the author was cold" (*Steinbeck, Writer*, 304).

Fortunately for Steinbeck—or perhaps unfortunately, considering his near-reclusive hatred of public attention—critics and reviewers of the novel were not equally cold toward the novel, and, much to Steinbeck's surprise, most—even those on the left—liked it, though some complained about the novel's violence. *New York Times* reviewer Fred T. Marsh, for example, called it "courageous and desperately honest . . . . the best labor and strike novel to come out of our contemporary economic and social unrest."[14]

There were two noteworthy exceptions to these positive reviews, and these grated on Steinbeck. The first almost caused Covici-Friede not to publish the novel. A communist editor there, Harry Black, read and rejected the manuscript, writing Steinbeck's agent, "The book is totally inaccurate. . . . It is sure to offend people on the right as well as the left."[15] Black's rejection enraged Steinbeck, who complained about some "drawing room" communist in New York doubting his accuracy (13 May 1935, *Life in Letters*, 110). Pat Covici, however, later overruled Black's rejection of the novel and fired him.

Mary McCarthy, reviewing *In Dubious Battle* for *The Nation*, also panned it for not living up to its "proletarian" acclaim and for consistently subordinating "legitimately dramatic incidents" to "ponderous" observations, such as how crowds behave, which McCarthy dismissed as "infantile."[16] Her criticism hit home and "generated a life-long enmity between her and Steinbeck."[17] Steinbeck scholars tend to dismiss these negative, leftist criticisms as smugly ideological. Benson writes, "[The two reviewers] had the cocksure certainty of the parlor theoretician who never got his hands dirty" (*Steinbeck, Writer*, 324).

Ideological these reviews certainly were, but then so was Steinbeck's novel, only in a different direction. As these critics charged, he *had* changed facts about his source material—the strike's participants and organizers—to suit his theoretical ends. Two actual organizers of those strikes, Pat Chambers and Caroline Decker, were, as Benson notes, far more sympathetic to the workers they organized than were Mac and Jim in the novel (*Steinbeck, Writer*, 303). In suggesting the strike's futility, he ignored that his models—the peach and cotton strikes—were actually successful. And in showing leaders on both sides of the strike at fault, the book *did* seem likely to offend readers on all political sides, as Black claimed. Steinbeck himself anticipated the novel's offensiveness when he called it "brutal," and told one of his agents "I hardly expect you to like the book. I don't like it."[18] Finally, McCarthy's charge that he subordinated "legitimately dramatic incidents of the strike" to his theorizing is valid. But if these ideological rejections "soured the author's attitude towards party members," as Keith Windschuttle avers, they did not prevent his politics from moving much further to the left in the next few years.

Turning Point: "The Harvest Gypsies" and the Salinas Lettuce Strike

The same year that *In Dubious Battle* was published, 1936, two events in California shattered Steinbeck's quasi-scientific detachment towards the big landowners and crop workers. The first event was huge and had been building for several years, the sort of epochal, group phenomenon that appealed to Steinbeck's socio-biological musings: the migration to California of hundreds of thousands of people from the Plains: Kansas, Oklahoma, Nebraska, Texas, Colorado, and Missouri. What drove them west—California's promise of a better life—was certainly not a new belief, and people had been moving there since the gold rush. But with the severe drought of the early 1930s in the Plains, affecting both farms and the small towns that depended on them, the numbers of migrants increased dramatically.[19] Social historians have documented that this migration included more people from towns and cities than from farms, and that many migrants moved to California's big cities in search of service or industrial jobs.[20] But Steinbeck's interest in and connection to this migration focused on the plight of migrant farmworkers.

That he had grown up in Salinas, at the very center of California's agribusiness, and had just published a novel on farm workers (albeit, with the "migrant" dimension intentionally omitted) obviously predisposed Steinbeck toward an interest in the Plains migrants. Moreover, like his novel's inaccurate characterization of the fruit pickers, these migrants were predominantly white—which intensified Steinbeck's interest in their American roots.[21] Because Steinbeck's novel established him as someone knowledgeable about labor conflicts in farming, the editor of the liberal *San Francisco News*, George West, asked the author to write a series of investigative articles on the growing migrant problem. West had already met Steinbeck at the home of Lincoln Steffens (*Steinbeck, Writer*, 295), and the locale of their meeting, like the political slant of the newspaper, is significant. Quite possibly, West shared some of Steffens's radical views and may well have communicated to Steinbeck sympathy for the migrants and antipathy to the large growers.

But why did Steinbeck take on this assignment? He certainly had enough on his plate at the time without adding journalistic duties that required time-consuming research and field observation. When West proposed the idea at the beginning of August 1936, Steinbeck was working frenetically to finish revising his novella, *Of Mice and Men*. He finished the book shortly thereafter, typically exhausted and in need of a rest. As Steinbeck well realized, the novella could easily be converted to a play, a likely follow-up project. Then, too, he and Carol had just moved into their new home near Los Gatos. The house still lacked electricity and the couple "camped out" there, Steinbeck sometimes writing by kerosene lamp (*Steinbeck, Writer*, 330). Handy with tools, he could easily have spent the next few months with Carol, making the house livable and taking a much-needed break from writing. Money was no longer an issue: royalties from *In Dubious Battle* and *Tortilla Flat* were coming in regularly, and Paramount had bought the film rights to the latter (*Steinbeck, Writer*, 323). The journalistic assignment West proposed would pay a pittance. Moreover, having already written a novel about farm labor conditions, Steinbeck could reasonably feel that he was through with the subject. Thus, taking on a new, open-ended job that required considerable research, travel, and working in an entirely different medium seemed to make no sense.

Benson explains Steinbeck's decision as professional: "Steinbeck had gone [to investigate migrant conditions] to get away from his own preoccupations, to get ideas, and to find new material. Previously he had no idea what his [next] major project, the 'big book,' was going to be about. Now, whatever he wrote, it was somehow going to be about this [migrant] family" (i.e., the one later described in "The Harvest Gypsies," 333).[22] But besides not considering why Steinbeck chose *this* venture to find "new material," Benson's explanation excludes a different motivation: that Steinbeck's experience researching and writing *In Dubious Battle* in 1934/35 had sensitized him to the problems of farm laborers. Though he had approached the problems then with scientific detachment does not mean he felt the same way in 1936, when, with the massive influx of migrants, the farm labor problem had changed and grown so much more severe. Quite possibly (as noted above), George West had dramatized the conditions of the migrants in trying to sell Steinbeck on the assignment. And for Steinbeck to investigate and describe the conditions of individual families required a different mentality than to examine the hypothetical (that is, imagined) workings of semi-abstract groups and phalanxes. I believe that Steinbeck's "cold," "scientific" detachment was giving way—gradually, even imperceptibly—to the beginnings of a new empathy for these migrant farmworkers, and correspondingly, a new concern for, and even anger at, the way they were being treated in California. Their conditions could no longer be considered "outcroppings" of the central issue. They *were* the central issue.

So he agreed to investigate and write up the conditions of the migrant workers: the kind of life and conditions they left in the Plains; what they were seeking in California; what kind of reception they experienced from California authorities; their working and living conditions in California; what the federal government was doing for the migrants through Roosevelt's Resettlement Administration (RA); and what it all boded for the future if Steinbeck's recommendations were or weren't followed. When he returned from his travels researching migrant conditions for these articles, he was a different person.

But not entirely different. The need to understand and analyze a phenomenon objectively carried over from his days writing *In Dubious Battle*. Accordingly, his first stop was San Francisco to discuss his assignment with editors at the *San Francisco News* and to gather background (including statistical data) on the problem from federal officials of the RA. This source was central to Steinbeck's investigation. Part of his assignment was to describe how the RA was addressing housing and sanitation problems of indigent migrants by providing "sanitary camps" for them. Concerned about receiving good publicity (to counter much local hostility to the RA camps), the RA not only provided Steinbeck information and data, but its representatives accompanied him on his travels, profoundly influencing not only what he saw but also how he would understand the migrant problems in the years following.

Accompanied by Eric Thomsen, an RA regional manager for the San Joaquin Valley, Steinbeck travelled south to the area around Bakersfield for about the last two weeks of August to study migrant living and working conditions. There, he observed two strikingly different types of living conditions for the migrants: squalid roadside and farm camps, typically without decent sanitation, and two clean, well-organized camps built by the RA to house a tiny number of the migrant influx.[23] At one of these government camps in Arvin called "Weedpatch," he met Tom Collins, the camp supervisor, whose influence on Steinbeck in the next three years would be enormous, and who would largely—if temporarily—eclipse Ed Ricketts as Steinbeck's mentor. Collins accompanied Steinbeck on the remainder of his investigation, and the two became good friends. Collins, moreover, provided Steinbeck with detailed data from reports he prepared for the government, data and anecdotes on the migrants' habits and behavior in the camps he managed—information Steinbeck depended on both in his articles and in his later fictional treatment of the camp in *The Grapes of Wrath*. The camp's order, sanitation, and especially, the fact that the migrants themselves ran most of its functions as an example of self-governance deeply impressed him.[24] But accommodating about two hundred families each, the camps could scarcely begin to address the enormity of the migrants' housing crisis. Several new camps were planned, but the proposals faced intense local resistance, spurred by the landowners who considered them breeding grounds for political agitation and strikes (Benson, *Steinbeck, Writer*, 337).

Already, Steinbeck was observing a pattern: the migrants' desire to find a better life and their capacity to be responsible citizens if given the chance versus the well-organized efforts of the big land-owners, through the Associated Farmers, local police, and aroused townspeople, to repress the migrants in every way possible—to keep them moving, keep them away from government benefits for the indigent, and most of all prevent them from organizing. Significantly, Steinbeck felt he had to get "down and dirty" to understand the migrants' situation. As Collins later recalled, Steinbeck "sat in the ditches with the migrant workers, lived and ate with them. . . . We ate fried dough and sow belly, worked with the sick and the hungry, listened to complaints and little triumphs."[25] The experience profoundly affected Steinbeck and changed not only his views of the farm labor problems in California, but his quasi-scientific detachment toward them. Parini uses such phrases as "unprepared for the starkness of what he saw" and "everywhere he was stunned by the magnitude of the problem."[26]

When he returned to Los Gatos, Steinbeck wrote Collins, "I want to thank you for one of the very fine experiences of a life. But I think you know exactly how I feel about it. I hope I can be of some kind of help. On the other hand, I don't want to be presumptuous. In the articles I shall be very careful to try to do some good and no harm" (Benson, *Steinbeck, Writer,* 347). Just how did he feel about it? Benson offers this: "His trips to the Valley had made him an impassioned advocate of labor,[27] but also a man so certain of his cause, on the basis of his firsthand experience, that he could not tolerate disagreement" (350). From detached scientist-observer to impassioned advocate almost overnight? The transformation seems too abrupt and would have been implausible as fiction. Or had the ice already been melting? Note his concern now is to *help,* "do some good" for the migrants, not merely to report with detachment.[28] Yet, he realized that his articles could not be merely a passionate plea if he were to win over skeptical readers; they would need proof: facts and first-person accounts.

"The Harvest Gypsies"

Steinbeck wrote seven articles about the migrants, published under the title "The Harvest Gypsies" in October 1936.[29] The articles are very much in the style of documentary reportage, a journalistic genre that had become popular during the Depression to dramatize the destitution of particular groups and locales.[30] That is, the articles are an amalgam of factual reporting, using case studies, facts, and statistics "calm[ly] and carefully presented," much as a social worker or sociologist might do, combined with what Benson calls "advocacy reporting" in more emotionally tinged language to convey how the migrants have been brutalized by the California landowners and authorities.[31] For example, "The inhabitants of the [Arvin] camp came there beaten, sullen and destitute" ("Harvest Gypsies," 40). "They arrive in California . . . bewildered and beaten, and usually in a state of semi-starvation" (21). Steinbeck describes how the migrants have been systematically exploited by the large landowners; how they are intimidated and bullied by gun-toting sheriffs; are prevented from organizing politically; are kept from settling in any one place (and are thus ineligible for public assistance and schooling for their children);[32] and, finally, how they continually struggle with hunger, disease, filth, and intimidation. But the new migrants are tough, "their blood is strong": "They have weathered the thing, and can weather much more . . ." (22).

"Weathering" is a long-term prediction, however; it does not alleviate their immediate suffering, which Steinbeck describes vividly in a typical family in his article on "Squatters' Camps":

> Here, in the faces of the husband and his wife, you begin to see an expression you will notice on every face; not worry, but absolute terror of the starvation that crowds in against the borders of the camp. . . .
>
> The dullness shows in the faces of this family, and in addition there is a sullenness that makes them taciturn. Sometimes they still start the older children off to school, but the ragged little things will not go; they hide themselves in ditches or wander off by themselves until it is time to go back to the tent, because they are scorned in the school. . . .
>
> Somewhere the family has found a big piece of old carpet. It is on the ground. To go to bed the members of the family lie on the ground and fold the carpet up over them.
>
> The three year old child has a gunny sack tied about his middle for clothing. He has the swollen belly caused by malnutrition.
>
> He sits on the ground in the sun in front of the house and the little black fruit flies buzz in circles and land on his closed eyes and crawl up his nose until he weakly brushes them away. (27, 29–30)

Against the emotional phrasing of "ragged little things," the prose becomes coldly matter-of-fact about their chances to survive: "He [the three-year-old] will die in a very short time. The older children may survive. Four nights ago the mother had a baby in the tent, on the dirty carpet. It was born dead, which was just as well because she could not have fed it at the breast; her own diet will not produce milk" (30).

Steinbeck applies this same specificity to the enemies of these migrants in the third article (which he entitled "Corporation Farming" in the Lubin edition). He identifies the chief culprit, the Associated Farmers, Inc., whose board members include "officials of banks, publishers of newspapers, and politicians; and through close association with the State Chamber of Commerce they have interlocking associations with shipowners' associations, public utilities corporations and transportation companies" (33). Specifically, he identifies "the tremendous Bank of America" as being one of the largest landholders in the San Joaquin Valley (33). Working together, these large groups are "able to impose their policies on a great number of small farms," which might otherwise treat migrants more decently (34). Finally, at the point of contact between migrants and representatives of the absentee landowner, brute force and threat are always present:

> The will of the ranch owner, then, is law; for these deputies [his employees] are always on hand, their guns conspicuous. A disagreement constitutes resisting an officer. A glance at the list of migrants shot during a single year in California for "resisting an officer" will give a fair idea of the casualness of these "officers" in shooting workers. . . .
>
> The worker sees himself surrounded by force. He knows that he can be murdered without fear on the part of the employer and he has little recourse to law. (35–36)

In day-and-night contrast to this systematic repression and destitution of migrants, the Resettlement Administration's camps are a model of decent treatment:

> [T]he intent of the management has been to restore the dignity and decency that has been kicked out of the migrants by their intolerable

mode of life. . . . The people in the [Arvin] camp are encouraged to govern themselves, and they have responded with simple and workable democracy. . . . [T]here has not been any need for outside police. (39–40)

Steinbeck's description of the migrants' background and motive for migrating contains two statements that he would significantly alter two years later as his political involvement intensified. The first passage attributes the migration to the drought gripping the Plains states:

The drouth in the middle west has driven the agricultural populations of Oklahoma, Nebraska and parts of Kansas and Texas westward. Their lands are destroyed and they can never go back to them. . . . They are resourceful and intelligent Americans who have gone through the hell of the drouth, have seen their lands wither and die and the top soil blow away; and this, to a man who has *owned* his land, is a curious and terrible pain. (21–22, emphasis added)

There is no mention of banks pushing tenants off their land in order to consolidate small farms, as happens in *The Grapes of Wrath*.

The second statement suggests that the migrants' concept of farming was out of date and simply incompatible with the modern, industrialized farming that they found in California:

And they are strangely anachronistic in one way: Having been brought up in the prairies where industrialization never penetrated, they have jumped with no transition from the old agrarian, self-contained farm . . . to a system of agriculture so industrialized that the man who plants a crop does not often see, let alone harvest, the fruit of his planting . . . (23)

The articles therefore imply that, like the drought that drives them from their land, the migrants' incompatibility with the new industrial farming cannot be helped. It is tragic, but not remediable. The tone here sounds more like the Steinbeck of *In Dubious Battle*: detached and empirical, though the author romanticizes the preindustrial mentality of these "simple agrarian folk." When Steinbeck reprinted these articles in 1938 as *Their Blood Is Strong*, and when he dramatized the Joads being "tractored out" in *Grapes*, he would give the banks and mechanized farming far more prominence and menace in causing the migrants' woes—a problem that could be remedied.

In the last article, Steinbeck offers suggestions for change: "From almost daily news stories, [and] from a great number of Government reports . . . it becomes apparent that some plan must be contrived to take care of the problem of the migrants" (58). This plan should include a state migratory labor board, with labor representatives. The board, working with labor unions, should regulate the demand for and supply of labor to prevent the intentionally created oversupply of labor at particular farms, which drives down wages. Steinbeck also proposes something more radical: "Agricultural workers should be encouraged and helped to *organize* both for their own protection, for the intelligent distribution of labor and for their self-government . . ." (60, emphasis added). And vigilante terrorism must go—"[It] is the disgrace of California"—"[Criminal syndicalism] laws have been used only against workers. Let them be equally used on the more deadly *fascistic* groups which preach and act the overthrow of our form of government by force of arms" (61, emphasis added). Steinbeck might be accused of letting the local problem blind his larger perspective when he claims, "California democracy is rapidly dwindling away. Fascistic methods are more numerous, more powerfully applied and more openly practiced in California than any other place in the United States" (61). Richard Wright, for one, could have proposed an entire *group* of states—the South—that outdid California in systematically applying "fascistic methods" to enforce Jim Crow laws.

If California ignores these suggestions and maintains the status quo, Steinbeck predicts a grim future: "[Migrant] wages will continue to be depressed and living conditions will grow increasingly impossible until from pain, hunger and despair the whole mass of labor will revolt." Threatened with "peonage" and starvation, "they can [become] an army driven by suffering and hatred to take what they need" (61–62). (Steinbeck would make a similar, more nuanced prophecy in *The Grapes of Wrath*.) And California itself risks losing its democracy, which is incompatible with the exploitive and fascistic methods practiced by big agriculture.

These outcomes need not be the future, however, if Californians recognize that the migrants have the potential to be good, constructive citizens: "The new migrants to California from the dust bowl are here to stay. They are of the best American stock, intelligent, resourceful; and, if given a chance, socially responsible. . . . They can be citizens of the highest type . . ." (62).

Here, Steinbeck makes an unfortunate—but at the time standard—distinction between the "American" white migrants from the Plains and previous groups of foreign-born migrants: Chinese, Japanese, Mexican, and Filipino. (The sixth article traces the history of the "Foreign Migrant.") Some scholars have accused Steinbeck of racism, particularly in his assumption that the foreign migrants' "lower standard of living" led them to accept lower wages than white labor would work for and in his praise of the "American" values and origins of the white migrants.[33] This criticism is valid, but Steinbeck also shows how the foreign-born laborers "have been subjected to racial discrimination"; how they were exploited by the big growers who wanted a "peon" class; and how they suffered the same "vigilante terrorism" if they dared to organize (54).

In sum, the tone and method of these articles mix objective description of the migrants' conditions, analysis of causes of the problems, protest at their brutal treatment and exploitation, and, in the conclusion, strong advocacy for change, combined with prophetic warnings of dire outcomes if change does not occur. While traces are evident of Steinbeck's earlier persona of detached observer of social groups, a new identity has largely replaced it: Steinbeck as outraged critic of agribusiness methods and advocate of the oppressed migrant. Strengthening the impact of these articles were Dorothea Lange's photographs of the migrants and their conditions, beginning with the soon-to-be-famous "migrant mother," Florence Owens Thompson.[34] Together, the articles and photographs presented an indictment powerful enough to infuriate California's large landowners and the Associated Farmers, marking Steinbeck as their enemy.

One source of criticism surprised Steinbeck. He heard that some migrant workers resented the word "Gypsies" in the title—it *was* an unfortunate choice with its connotation at the time of rootless wandering and irresponsibility. Disturbed, he quickly declared in a letter to the *San Francisco News* (20 Oct. 1936), "Certainly I had no intention of insulting a people who are already insulted beyond endurance." A response printed in the same newspaper by the migrants' "Camp Central Committee" must have assuaged his embarrassment: "We think you did a fine job for us and we thank you. [T]his is a big battle which cannot be won by ourselves, we need friends like you."[35]

The second event that deeply affected Steinbeck in 1936 was a lettuce strike in his hometown of Salinas in the autumn. It was brutally crushed by vigilantes, acting as an impromptu local militia, and using tear gas, beatings, illegal roundups, incarceration, and arson. As Benson summarizes,

> The major growers had conspired with local officials to place the town's police and judicial powers in the hands of a retired army officer, who declared his own version of martial law and formed a local militia to resist the strike and scatter the strikers. Civil rights were voided and an internment camp was set up, and neither county nor state government interfered to any significant extent in one of the largest vigilante actions ever to take place in California. (*Steinbeck, Writer*, 346–47)

According to one news account,

> at the height of the strike all male residents between 18 and 45 were mobilized under penalty of arrest, were deputized and armed. Beatings, tear gas attacks, wholesale arrests, threats to lynch San Francisco newspapermen if they didn't leave town, and machine guns and barbed wire all [figured] into the month-long struggle which finally broke the strike and destroyed the union.

Another report, from a Salinas resident at the time, recalls

> a group of maybe two dozen men, local merchants and members of the Rotary went marching out there to the camp outside town with

clubs and rifle butts. They wanted to bash some heads in. . . . The troublemakers were put in a barn under armed guard, the kingpins were sent away. Nobody was allowed to walk the streets after dark for over a month. The police just stayed out of it.[36]

This wasn't the first time vigilantes had struck in Salinas. In "The Harvest Gypsies," Steinbeck describes how a Filipino bunkhouse was burned down and all the residents' possessions destroyed because they had dared to organize (56). Now, however, the repression was far more comprehensive and systematic.

Steinbeck went to Salinas while the strike was still going on and was appalled and depressed by what he saw and later learned. "This isn't the place I knew as a boy," he wrote a friend.[37] To his agent, Elizabeth Otis, he wrote soon after, "I just returned yesterday from the strike area of Salinas and from my migrants in Bakersfield. This thing is dangerous. Maybe it will be patched up for a while, but I look for the lid to blow off in a few weeks. Issues are very sharp here now."[38]

For Steinbeck, the legalized lawlessness of Salinas demonstrated exactly what he warned of in "The Harvest Gypsies": domestic fascism overriding democratic processes. He said as much the following year, in responding to a survey by the League of American Writers of how writers felt about the Spanish Civil War. Steinbeck compared these California vigilantes to Franco's fascists: "We have our own fascist groups out here. They haven't bombed open towns yet but in Salinas last year tear gas was thrown in a Union Hall and through the windows of workingmen's houses."[39] In a year, he had already moved from calling the growers' *methods* of repressing the migrants "fascistic" in "The Harvest Gypsies" to directly calling the growers' henchmen "fascist."

Experiencing these two events, Steinbeck had come a long way from the detached stance regarding labor-landowner conflict he had taken in *In Dubious Battle*. True, the desire to understand and inform in "The Harvest Gypsies" still reflects Steinbeck the scientist and sociologist. But his firsthand experience with migrant conditions engaged his sympathies (notice he refers to "my migrants" in his letter to Otis)[40], made him more a partisan for social change than a detached observer. It was one thing to *imagine* vigilantes acting lawlessly in *In Dubious Battle*, quite another to see them doing it in real life to the lettuce workers in his hometown and to the migrants living in squalid camps. As his involvement in these issues intensified over the next two years and his anger against the big growers and their cohorts flared ever larger, Steinbeck's politics had moved from liberalism towards radicalism, from being an individual observer to becoming a champion of collective action.

1936–38: Engaged and Enraged

The next two years were remarkably crowded for Steinbeck and witnessed his deepening involvement with the migrant issue—and his growing radicalism regarding it. At the same time, his creative writing not only continued, but flourished in the novella and play *Of Mice and Men*. Steinbeck finished the book in August 1936, just before beginning his journalistic investigation of the migrants. Perhaps because the writing occurred in this transition period, it resembles neither *In Dubious Battle* nor the later *Grapes*. The two protagonists are not simply exploited members of a phalanx but "two lost souls," as Parini calls them.[41] Except in their shared— and hopeless—dream of owning their own plot of land,[42] Lenny and George are virtual foils, and even the bunkhouse cowboys are distinct characters. Moreover, Steinbeck's feeling toward them is empathetic, rather than either detached or passionate; the novel's tone is tragic, not angry. Published in February 1937, the book was a huge success, chosen as a Book-of-the-Month Club Selection. Realizing from the start its dramatic quality, Steinbeck permitted the leftist Theatre Union to dramatize it in San Francisco (21 May 1937), following the novel's text closely.[43] He then worked with George S. Kaufman in the spring and fall of 1937 to convert the novella fully to play form. Directed by Kaufman, it opened in New York on 23 November 1937, was an immediate hit, and earned the New York Drama Critics' Circle Award.

Four successes in a row—*Tortilla Flat*, *In Dubious Battle*, and *Of Mice and Men* as both novella and play—firmly established Steinbeck's popular and critical reputation by 1937 and created considerable anticipation for his next novel. Financial security from these successes provided the time he needed to work on it. Steinbeck had already decided that that novel would directly address the migrant issue he had investigated the year before. It would be "a big book," a broad treatment of the problem on several levels. "The subject is so huge that it scares me to death," he wrote Elizabeth Otis. "And I'm not going to rush it. It must be worked out with great care" (27 Jan. 1937, *Life in Letters*, 134).

Before settling down to write it—before he even started actively collaborating with Kaufman on the stage version of *Of Mice and Men*, Steinbeck and his wife travelled to Europe for a vacation— an "escape," Steinbeck called it.[44] Their itinerary was northern: Sweden, Denmark, Finland—and Russia (Leningrad and Moscow). The last country, given its political significance in the 1930s, raises some provocative questions about the Steinbecks' motives. Of course, since the late 1920s, visiting Russia—making a pilgrimage to the new holy land—had been almost a duty for devout leftists (as well as a source of curiosity for non-leftists like E. E. Cummings). Steinbeck's neighbor Lincoln Steffens had gone there early—in 1919—and famously declared on returning, "I have the seen the future, and it works!" Very likely, he had urged Steinbeck to see this glorious future for himself, just as he had urged him to write about labor issues in California. Other writers also made the journey. Dos Passos went in 1928, Cummings in 1931, Edmund Wilson in 1935. Yet Steinbeck, while increasingly drawn to the Left by 1937, was no camp follower and still considered himself an independent thinker. Most likely, he just wanted to see the place for himself—at least, its biggest cities—as he had the migrants' conditions in California. And the destinations weren't so very far from Finland.

Curiously, he left no direct record of the visit that might have explained his aim and given his impressions. His biographers and critics are puzzled or laconic. Shillinglaw describes his purpose as "unrevealed." Alan Wald concurs: "No one has satisfactorily explained Steinbeck's complete silence about his 1937 trip to the Soviet Union . . ." Benson devotes a sentence to the visit: "Their time in Russia was too brief for them to get any clear impressions except a general sense of poverty and backwardness and suspicion." Parini deduces Steinbeck's impressions from brief comparisons he made in his 1947 visit and journal (*A Russian Journal*): the streets [in 1937] were "muddy and dirty"; districts of old Moscow were "narrow [and] dirty"—all much improved by the time of the second visit. Parini adds, without providing documentation, that "Steinbeck had hoped for some time to write about the Soviet Union perhaps in fictional form" but was disheartened because the Russians lacked a "firm sense of individual identity."[45]

Whatever Steinbeck hoped to find in Russia—inspiration? encouragement to move even further left? evidence to test the glowing descriptions of radicals like Steffens?—he would have to rely on his own understanding of his subject, the migrants in California, for the motivation to write the "big book." First, though, he needed more material, more data, more direct contact with the migrants. Once again, he arranged to visit migrant camps, this time for an entire month (October–November 1937). He wrote Collins, "I've got to get the smell of drawing rooms out of my nose. A squatter's camp is a wonderful place for that" (Benson, *Steinbeck, Writer*, 359). His plan was to travel first to the new government camp at Gridley (which Collins now supervised), then to Stockton, and on to Needles—almost the reverse of the California part of the Joads' migrations.[46]

Once again, Tom Collins accompanied him: "[T]he two went out together for several days in the Gridley area to work in the fields and to stay the night on a ranch and then in a squatters' camp" (Benson, *Steinbeck, Writer*, 362). Steinbeck wrote a friend, while sitting in a ditch, "I'm out working—may go south to pick a little cotton. . . . migrants are going south now and I'll probably go with them. I enjoy it a lot" (ibid., 362). The upbeat tone expressed in these letters suggests two things: first, that Steinbeck was eagerly anticipating turning his research into fiction; he was not merely studying conditions for a newspaper assignment as he had in 1936. Second, what he saw did not shock him as much as his journalistic investigation had a year earlier. He was psychologically prepared and liked working alongside the migrants to experience this part of their lives firsthand.

Returning home, Steinbeck launched into his novel, which he had decided to call "The Oklahomans." It would focus, he told a journalist in January 1938, on "the salutary, irrepressible character of the migrants. . . . 'The Oklahoman knows just exactly what he wants. He wants a piece of land. And he goes after it and gets it.'"[47] That Steinbeck admired them is clear from his comments elsewhere: "[T]hey are kind, humorous and wise" and in their strength and resilience, he predicted, they would create "a new system and a new life [in California] which will be better than anything we have had before."[48]

In early 1938, however, not only was "the Oklahoman" not getting his piece of land, he and many of his fellow migrants were starving. Conditions had so worsened for the migrants that Steinbeck had to rethink his optimistic (and simplistic) view and pay more attention to what was now threatening the migrants' very survival: not only the opposition of the large landowners, but a new factor: the weather. If drought had, in part, driven the farmers from their land, now floods plagued them as migrants. As Steinbeck describes in his letters, California was hit by continuous rain in January and February 1938: "It is the longest and wettest rain I remember and it has sealed us in the house" (*Life in Letters*, 157). He soon learned from Collins and from Fred Soule, Information Officer for the Farm Security Administration, that floods were devastating migrants living in tents, particularly in two camps: Visalia and Nipomo, California. Steinbeck was so moved that, as he explains to Elizabeth Otis in February, he felt duty-bound to put aside his writing and aid the stricken migrants in this life-or-death situation:

> I must go over to the interior valleys. There are about five thousand families starving to death over there, not just hungry but actually starving.[49] The government is trying to feed them and get medical attention to them with the fascist group of utilities and banks and huge growers sabotaging the thing all along the line . . . In one tent there are twenty people quarantined for smallpox and two of the women are to have babies in that tent this week. I've tied into the thing from the first and I must get help down there and see it and see if I can't do something to help knock these murderers on the heads. Do you know what they're afraid of? They think that if these people are allowed to live in [government] camps with sanitary facilities, they will organize

and that is the bugbear of the large landowner and the corporation farmer. The states and counties will give [the migrants] nothing because they are outsiders. . . . I'm pretty mad about it." . . . (47, 158)

In a follow-up letter, dated 14 February 1938, Steinbeck describes one way he could help:

This is the 19th day of rain. . . . The resettlement administration of the government asked me to write some news stories. The newspapers won't touch the stuff but they will under my byline. The locals are fighting the government bringing in food and medicine. I'm going to try to break the story hard enough so that food and drugs can get moving. Shame and a hatred of publicity will do the job to the miserable local bankers. . . . Talk about Spanish children. The death of children by starvation in our valleys is simply staggering. I've got to do it. If I can sell the articles, I'll use the proceeds for serum and such. . . . Of course no individual effort [alone] will help. Ten thousand people are affected in one area. Anyway, I'll do what I can. (ibid., 159)

One thing he did besides writing about it was distribute food he had bought to the families he worked with—over fifty of them. He even threatened to castigate FSA officials in his articles if they did not provide food to these families immediately.[50] He also got *Life* Magazine to commission a photo-text article and agree to donate his fee for the text to relief funds for the migrants (ibid., 161).[51] As the floodwaters rose, Steinbeck and Collins threw themselves into helping the migrants move their belongings to higher ground. Collins later recalled their exhausting labors:

For forty-eight hours, and without food or sleep, we worked among the sick and the half-starved people, dragging some from under trees to a different sort of shelter, dragging others from torn and ragged tents, floored with inches of water, stagnant water, to the questionable shelter of a higher piece of ground.

Collins goes on to describe Steinbeck and himself sleeping exhausted in the mud and the next day feeding a family: "We sat there [on the dirt floor] and the five of us ate the food which John had obtained from the little store some muddy distance away. . . . a bite that was a banquet."[52]

But such "banquets" were the exception. Steinbeck described to Elizabeth Otis his feeling of helplessness:

[T]he water is a foot deep in the tents and the children are up on the beds and there is no food and no fire, and the county has taken off all the nurses because "the problem is so great that we can't do anything about it." So they do nothing.

. . . It is the most heartbreaking thing in the world. . . . I break myself every time I go out because the argument that one person's effort can't really do anything doesn't seem to apply when you come on a bunch of starving children and you have a little money. I can't rationalize it for myself anyway. . . . I want to put a tag of shame on the greedy bastards who are responsible for this but I can best do it through newspapers. . . . I was in mud for three days and nights. . . . I am hectic and angry. (7 March 1938, *Life in Letters*, 161–62)

This was Steinbeck's moment of maximal involvement in the cause of the migrant farmers. He was far beyond merely observing, no longer just writing about their problems, but fighting to alleviate them with every tool at his command including his pen, his money, and his physical strength. His emotional commitment was also at its peak, not only in support of the migrants, but in hatred of the human forces that had caused their destitution and were now trying to starve them: the power complex of big landowners, the Associated Farmers, banks and utilities, local government, police, and vigilantes. Even before he left for Visalia, that is, before he saw the starvation and suffering firsthand, he had branded this group in his letter to Otis as "fascist" and "murderers." His tone was even angrier when he returned from the experience. A few months later, when rest and comfort provided him a chance to cool down, his anger and commitment had not. As he described himself to a journalist trying to organize a supposedly "non-partisan" forum aimed at ending labor strikes,

I am completely partisan. Every effort I can bring to bear is and has been at the call of the common working people to the end that they may eat what they raise, wear what they weave, use what they produce . . . And the reverse is also true. I am actively opposed to any man or group who, through financial or political control of means of production and distribution, is able to control and dominate the lives of workers.[53]

When he wrote this letter, he was hard at work on *The Grapes of Wrath.*

"Starvation Under the Orange Trees" and *Their Blood Is Strong*

Steinbeck's writing from this point, whether journalistic or fictional, would now identify the migrants' suffering and their tormentors with no holds barred. As he had told Otis, "I want to put a tag of shame on the greedy bastards who are responsible for this" (*Life in Letters*, 162). The newspaper articles he planned were to be an indictment. He completed only one of these articles, "Starvation Under the Orange Trees" (February 1938), but it powerfully conveyed the misery and death Steinbeck had just observed in Visalia: the migrants' complete destitution; their starvation (while "the orange trees are loaded"); their children dying of diseases—pneumonia, measles, tuberculosis—and of starvation itself. Far more than he had done in "The Harvest Gypsies," Steinbeck documents individual examples of this suffering in first person:

I talked to a man last week who lost two children in ten days with pneumonia. His face was hard and fierce and he didn't talk much. I talked to a girl with a baby and offered her a cigarette. She took two puffs and vomited in the street. She was ashamed. She shouldn't have tried to smoke, she said, for she hadn't eaten in two days. . . . I heard a man tell in a monotone how he couldn't get a doctor while his oldest boy died of pneumonia but that a doctor came right away after it was dead.[54]

He even challenges the reader: "If you don't believe this [that the migrant cannot support his family on his earnings], go out in the cotton fields next year. Work all day and see if you have made thirty-five cents. A good picker makes more, of course, but you can't" ("Starvation," 32–33). Sarcasm curdles his anger when he describes his bête noir, the Associated Farmers, "which is made up of such earth stained toilers as chain banks, public utilities, railroad companies, and those huge corporations called land companies . . ." (ibid., 31).

The themes he would develop in *The Grapes of Wrath* are already present: California treats the American migrants as it did the foreign workers before them: "to keep them segregated, to herd them about like animals, and if there were any complaints, to deport or to imprison the leaders. . . . The moment the crop is picked, the locals begin to try to get rid of the . . . [migrants]. They want to run them out, move them on. The county hospitals are closed to them. They are not eligible to relief" ("Starvation," 32–33).

Finally, in place of the moderate proposals that concluded "The Harvest Gypsies," Steinbeck ends this article with an angry and prophetic rhetorical question:

> Is it possible that this state is so stupid, so vicious and so greedy that it cannot feed and clothe the men and women who help to make it the richest area in the world? Must the hunger become anger and the anger fury before anything will be done? ("Starvation," 33)

Given the inflammatory accusations of the article, it is not surprising that the Scripps-Howard chain of newspapers rejected Steinbeck's proposal to syndicate this and future articles.[55] Then he went to the other extreme and sent it to *People's World*, San Francisco's communist newspaper, not caring that "association with this paper would mark him as a radical."[56] Finally, in what must have seemed a humiliating comedown, the small local newspaper *The Monterey Trader* first published "Starvation" on 15 April 1938.

About this time, the Simon J. Lubin Society, a private advocacy group for migrant laborers, approached Steinbeck for permission to reprint "The Harvest Gypsies" articles as a pamphlet to raise money for the migrants. Steinbeck agreed, added "Starvation" as "Epilogue: 1938," and made other changes. Five Lange photographs were reproduced, including a soon-to-be-famous one on the front cover of a nursing mother staring defiantly at the camera. The new title Steinbeck gave the pamphlet reflects his changed thinking

since 1936. In place of the ill-chosen "Gypsies," with its connotation of irresponsibility, "Their Blood Is Strong" directly communi-
cates Steinbeck's admiration for the resilient migrants.

With "Starvation" as its stinging conclusion, however, *Their
Blood Is Strong* was more than just a reprint of "The Harvest
Gypsies." Differences between the two texts reveal telling signs
of Steinbeck's changed views. Take the matter of what caused the
small farmers to migrate. In "The Harvest Gypsies," drought is
the culprit that has "driven the agricultural populations . . . westward." The farmers "have seen their lands wither and die and the
top soil blow away" (*Their Blood*, 2–3). The Epilogue of *Their Blood
Is Strong* adds a new cause:

> But then the dust *and the tractors* began displacing the sharecroppers
> of Oklahoma, Texas, Kansas and Arkansas. Families who had lived for
> many years on the little "cropper lands" were dispossessed because
> the land was in the hands of the banks and the finance companies and
> because the owners found that one man with a tractor could do the
> work of ten sharecropper families. (*Their Blood*, 32, emphasis added)

Readers of *The Grapes of Wrath* will recall this same duality: Chapter 1 describes the dust-covered land (but, significantly, that dust
does not send the farmers packing). Chapter 5 dramatizes a family like the Joads being pushed off their land by the tractors working for "the bank." The difference between the two causes of the
exodus is startling: nature's drought, which in the short term one
cannot fight, versus banks, land consolidation, and tractors—all
human-created causes that people can fight. *Their Blood Is Strong*
also makes the migrant farmer more vulnerable by identifying him
as a sharecropper (ibid., 32), who can be easily dispossessed by the
landowner and bank, where "Harvest Gypsies" had described him
as one "who owned the land."[57]

A more subtle difference between the articles and the later pamphlet appears in the way mechanized farming affects the migrant
farmers. In "Harvest Gypsies," Steinbeck states that the migrants'
type of farming was anachronistic and incompatible with the modern, industrialized farming that they found in California. Like the
drought, not much can be done about these incompatible types

of farming. In *Their Blood Is Strong*, tractors are "displacing" the tenant farmers, physically pushing them off their land. They are the mechanical means of "dispossessing" the farmers of their land, sent by "the banks and finance companies" to consolidate the small farms. Moreover, as the passage quoted above makes clear, profit, resulting from land consolidation, is the owners' single motive: "the owners found that one man with a tractor could do the work of ten sharecropper families." In *The Grapes of Wrath*, Steinbeck would dramatize this "tractoring out" of the Joads, giving it far more thematic weight than the drought. The epilogue also anticipates *Grapes* in describing what the migrants would encounter in California: the big owners' "fascistic" means of maintaining their profits and control by repressing the migrants; the sheriff's club and shotgun and the vigilante's gas can. These differences between "Harvest Gypsies" and *Their Blood Is Strong* reveal how much Steinbeck's thinking—and political involvement—had changed in just two years.

"The Oklahomans," "L'Affaire Lettuceberg," and Writing *The Grapes of Wrath*

Except for "Starvation Under the Orange Trees" and *Their Blood Is Strong*, Steinbeck devoted his writing in the spring of 1938 to the large novel he envisioned to tell the migrants' story—and to arouse in readers the same anger he now felt, the same belief in the need for radical change, in the inevitability of that change. That effort was not going well. *The Oklahomans* now seemed too optimistic, its focus too narrow; it would take more than the tough individualism of these migrants to overcome the forces so well organized against them. He put aside this attempt (it was subsequently lost), and turned to an entirely different approach: a scathing satire of his hometown, Salinas, for its brutal treatment of the striking lettuce workers in 1936.[58] But in addition to having a precious title, "L'Affaire Lettuceberg," it was, in Steinbeck's words, "a vicious, mean book" written when he felt "so ferocious about the thing that I won't have much critical insight."[59] Clearly, the anger Steinbeck felt about his Visalia visit went directly into "Lettuceberg" and marks the peak of his radicalism. But he realized the book was too strong, too much of a rant, "a bad book and I must get rid of it."[60]

He did so in mid-May and returned to the plan of telling the migrants' story. Now, however, he aimed to make the story a saga, to give it an epic scope that functioned simultaneously on several levels. At the narrowest and most individual level would be the story of one extended migrant family and of the distinct individuals that compose it. But that family's journey would ripple into expanding circles of meaning. In chapters that would alternate with the Joads' story, Steinbeck planned to include what he had learned about the migrants as a group and to dramatize their typical experiences: being pushed off their small farms, stopping each night by the roadside, meeting other migrants along the way, and so forth. These "general" chapters, as Steinbeck called them, which presented the migrants' traits and values, would contrast sharply with general chapters that sketched in broad strokes the history and mentality of the migrants' nemesis: the big landowners. For their culpability in causing the migrants' misery, Steinbeck would bring the full weight of judgment and prophecy. He also hoped to suggest epic parallels between the migrants' journeys and other mass migrations of the past: the land-hungry pioneers moving ever-westwards, the African-Americans' liberation from slavery, and the Exodus story of the children of Israel. Diametrically opposed to this epic scale were vignettes of types that the migrants would typically encounter: the used car salesman, a diner waitress and cook, a car parts salesman, etc. A few chapters would diverge from the plot to convey an evocative scene, such as the Joads' abandoned cabin, or to symbolize larger themes.

To capture these multiple levels, Steinbeck would employ a wide array of styles. The Joads' story, of course, would be narrated realistically; their abandoned cabin would be rendered imagistically; the soon-to-be-famous turtle chapter would read like a fable or allegory, while the chapter depicting the used car salesman would be presented entirely in the con artist's voice and thoughts. The general chapters featuring the migrants would recall Steinbeck the detached sociologist, examining the workings of a phalanx; but in the general chapters depicting the big owners, he gave vent to his anger, rumbling in the certitudes of an Old Testament prophet.

Thus, while the themes in *The Grapes of Wrath* are just as partisan as in Steinbeck's angrier, intensely politicized writing, he now gives them a complex, many-sided scope and significance, a sense of inevitability, rendered in an impressive diversity of tone and style. Fortunately, in this array of levels and styles, Steinbeck the superb storyteller remains dominant. In mid-May 1938, he began writing *The Grapes of Wrath* and he did not stop until the novel was finished in October.

Conclusion

Steinbeck's journey from detached observer of labor conflicts, circa 1934/35, to passionately engaged partisan by 1938, would appear to be quite individual and even isolated, resulting from his personal encounters with the migrant farmers' increasingly desperate situation in the makeshift camps of California. But although he was still essentially not a "joiner," several aspects of his journey towards his own kind of radicalism link him to the larger leftist movement of writers and intellectuals in the latter half of the 1930s. By 1934, he had already met with communist labor organizers on several occasions to gather material for *In Dubious Battle*. Though his portrayal of these organizers in that novel was certainly not flattering, he continued to have dealings with the Communist Party and its various organizations. He sends "Starvation Under the Orange Trees" to a communist newspaper, for example. He and Carol visit the Soviet Union in 1937. That same year, he joins the communist-sponsored League of American Writers, is elected to its National Executive Council that year, and would hold the largely honorific position of vice president in 1939/40. Certainly, he was not oblivious to the central political issue that concerned the Left at this time: standing up to German and Italian fascism. Presumably, this was why he joined the League in the first place. As his anger grew against the California power complex of large landowners, banks, sheriffs, and vigilantes, he began calling first their tactics "fascistic" and then the groups themselves "fascist." His point was telling: Fascism was not just a political system other countries have adopted; it could also be a set of tactics that aimed to intimidate people and deny them their basic rights, tactics that could be—and were—employed in this country, now. Richard Wright, for one, would have heartily agreed with this view.

When Steinbeck compared the starving migrant children in California to the hungry children in Spain (*Life in Letters*, 159, quoted above), he directly linked the Spanish Civil War to the undeclared war being fought in California—a war in which he was on the front lines. The linkage also points toward his growing political sympathy with the Loyalist struggle in Spain—he donated money for that cause—and his seeing both struggles as a fight against fascism. His response to the League of American Writers survey about Spain ("We have our own fascist groups out here") conveys this antifascist solidarity. Without intending to jump on the antifascist bandwagon, Steinbeck nonetheless came to the same political point of view by his own route: Visalia and Nipomo were his Madrid and Guernica.

Nonetheless, the battle he chose to fight as a writer against California fascism was, except for the help of Tom Collins, individual, almost quixotic. *He* would expose "the greedy bastards who are responsible for this," and his weapons were his journalism and especially his new novel. In numerous letters written while he is completing the novel or just after, he conveys a kind of eagerness for battle, a knowledge that this book would be incendiary and would, he hoped, make important people furious. Earlier, when he urged Fred Soule to try to syndicate "Starvation Under the Orange Trees," he added, "[I]t might not be a bad idea to try to make a few other people angry about it."[61] Once his new novel hit the streets, his enemies would *really* have something to howl about; so he predicts to his agent, Elizabeth Otis, "It pulls no punches at all and may get us all into trouble but if so—so. . . . Think I'll print a forward [*sic*] warning sensitive people to let it alone" (July 1938, *Life in Letters*, 167). To his publisher, Pat Covici, he predicts (wrongly), "I am sure it will not be a popular book. . . . I think to the large numbers of readers it will be an outrageous book" (Oct. 1938, ibid., 172); he even advised Covici to print a small first edition so as not to lose money on it (173). Another expression of his aggressive aim is even stronger: "I am not writing a satisfying story. I've done my damndest to rip a reader's nerves to rags, I don't want him satisfied" (16 Jan. 1939, ibid., 178). How closely this desire to provoke resembles Richard Wright's aim for *his* big novel: to write it "so hard and deep" that bankers' daughters wouldn't have the luxury of the tears they shed over his previous book; this time "they would have to face it" ("How 'Bigger' Was Born," 454).

Steinbeck knew, of course, that some of those readers—the novel's targets—would do more than just squirm: they would strike back, using every tool at their disposal: editorial denunciations, smear campaigns, even physical threats. He had, after all, experienced some of this abuse before. When he described to Elizabeth Otis his intent to go to Visalia, he cautioned, "No word of this outside because when I have finished my job the jolly old associated farmers will be after my scalp again" (*Life in Letters*, 158).[62] "Again" shows that his fears were not imaginary. He had already received hate mail for "The Harvest Gypsies," so much that his friend George Albee feared for his physical safety there—a fear Steinbeck dismissed (ibid., 133–34). Now, in response to the far stronger indictment of the novel, he expected his enemies to take stronger retaliatory measures (letter to Pat Covici, 1 Jan. 1939, ibid., 174).

Steinbeck was enormously pleased with the proposed title that his wife, Carol, had drawn from "The Battle Hymn of the Republic" because it pointed to "our own revolutionary tradition."[63] "Wrath," of course, captured his own anger against the "murderers" exploiting and starving the migrants. But far more important, it expressed the fictional migrants' growing anger, which had begun to "ferment" in response to their treatment (*Grapes*, 284), particularly as they saw the big landowners destroying crops to keep prices up, while they, the migrants and their children, were starving: "and in the eyes of the hungry there is a growing wrath. In the souls of the people the grapes of wrath are filling and growing heavy, growing heavy for the vintage" (ibid., 349). Steinbeck may have distinguished *his* "revolutionary" book, with its American setting, title, and history (*Life in Letters*, 174), from communist revolutionary literature, but in the chapter about burning the oranges he borrows a powerful Marxian argument, which American communists had asserted years earlier—that the destruction of crops while people go hungry during the Depression demonstrates the failure of the capitalist system.

He knew he was writing a revolutionary novel that predicted a profound change coming in American social and economic relations, a novel intended to disturb readers. But in anticipating the response to this novel, he badly underestimated the intensity of both the novel's popularity and the hatred and abuse it would arouse. Nor did he foresee the profound effects these responses would have on his physical well-being and mental outlook.

Wright

1933–1939

READERS WHO TRY to understand Richard Wright's association with the Communist Party-USA only by reading his autobiographical narratives are bound to be confused because those narratives end in Chicago around 1937.[1] Moreover, they appear to end with the termination of Wright's membership in the Party, an evolving decision made first by Wright himself, when he asks to be removed from the Party rolls, and then by the Party cell, formally expelling him to save face.[2] In fact, these narratives end dramatically with Chicago Party members refusing to let him march in a May Day parade and physically hurling him out of the line of marchers—a neat, if obvious, metaphor for his larger expulsion.

The only problem with these narratives of Party membership is that they are distorted, unreliable, and misleading. Wright's relationship with the CP-USA did not end in Chicago in 1936/37. It continued, even flourished for a time, after he moved (in late May 1937) to New York, where he was welcomed by the New York City branch of the CP-USA and made a reporter at the Harlem bureau of the *Daily Worker*.[3] Thus, what his physical expulsion from the May Day march really ended was Wright's association with the *Chicago* cell of the Party and its narrow-minded attitude toward his creative writing. That Wright misremembers the date of his May Day expulsion as 1936—it was really 1937—points to a problem of the narrative's reliability that goes beyond mere chronology. Since he wrote this narrative in 1943, after he had privately broken from the Party (see chapter 8) and long after his departure from the Chicago cell, he may well have attributed later doubts and disillusions retroactively to the earlier years of his Party membership.[4] Nonetheless, his autobiographical narratives are the primary source of his political experiences in Chicago—particularly in describing his ambitions and feelings about the Party's actions. His major biographers—Michel Fabre and Hazel Rowley, for example—rely heavily on his narratives, and I shall too.

Clearly, Wright's move from Chicago to New York was a major turning point in his experience as a communist, but, more important, in his history as a creative writer. In Chicago, he published strongly ideological poetry in several leftist magazines, but could not place his early novels. When he turned to short stories about racial conflict in the Jim Crow South, he began to experience success the year before moving to New York. That success soared meteorically when his story "Fire and Cloud" won the *Story* magazine prize, which led to publication of a book of his stories, *Uncle Tom's Children*, by Harper & Brothers in 1938. National recognition of *Uncle Tom's Children*, in turn, established his career as a fiction writer. Put simply, Chicago emblemizes his relationship with the Communist Party—initially idealistic and enthusiastic, then difficult and conflictual, finally alienated—and his fledgling, often-failing career as a writer. New York represents a renewed Party affiliation and a string of literary successes marking Wright as a major author. These very different New York successes, however, began increasingly to interfere with each other. As Wright sought more time for his creative writing, his Party responsibilities and obligations, such as grinding out articles for the Harlem branch of the *Daily Worker*, came to appear increasingly onerous and intrusive. A conflict with the Party similar to what he experienced in Chicago loomed on the horizon.

Several questions about Wright's New York years must be addressed: If he was as alienated from the Party as he claims in "I Tried," why did he renew that relationship in New York? And why did the New York branch not only accept him readily, ignoring his history with the Chicago cell, but also give him a secure Party position as reporter? How did Wright attempt to reconcile his two careers in the early New York years (1937–40)?

Before we can address these questions, however, we need to review his Chicago years to answer equally important questions: What attracted Wright to the Communist Party in the first place? What did he hope to gain by joining and by becoming executive secretary of the local John Reed Club? What did the club gain by accepting him as a member? How did the Party's treatment of him differ from what he experienced in the John Reed Club? And how did his literary career evolve in Chicago even as his relationship with the Chicago cell of the Party soured?

I. The Chicago Years, 1933–37

The young man who attended his first John Reed Club meeting in the fall of 1933 just to observe (precisely as Steinbeck did the following year in Monterey, California) probably never dreamed that it marked the beginning of the most important social and political relationship in his life. There, in a shabby room littered with pamphlets and cigarette butts, he encountered young artists and writers who were all politically radical—many were members of the CP-USA—all militantly idealistic, and, especially telling for this would-be writer, all committed to the arts. Wright recalls, "The members were fervent, democratic, restless, eager, self-sacrificing" ("I Tried," pt. 1, 63). Most important, they were genuinely friendly and welcoming to Wright, a far cry from the hostile or at best condescending responses from whites he was accustomed to. The club members were interested in his ambitions as a writer; in fact, they invited him to sit in on an editorial meeting of their literary magazine, *Left Front*. For a young man who had experienced only intellectual alienation from both the white and black worlds up to this time, the impact of this friendly welcome cannot be overstated. For once, his race did not seem to matter; his ideas—and his potential as a writer—did.

In fact, however, both his race and his literary future mattered. The John Reed Clubs, like the CP-USA itself to which they were connected, needed and wanted more black members. As Michel Fabre notes, even Wright's friend and fellow postal worker Abe Aaron, who had invited him to that first meeting, "was acting according to a plan adopted during the summer of 1933 to deliberately enlist black members." At the time there were only two in this chapter, both painters (Fabre, *Unfinished Quest*, 96, 540n1). These dual motives—considering Wright's race as well as the aesthetic or political quality of his work—would also affect the decisions of leftist magazines in accepting his poetry.

At the time, however, Wright sensed nothing to diminish his exhilaration over finding, at last, an intellectual and artistic home for himself. Eagerly, he read the pamphlets he had been given, and he began to see—another revelation—that he was not alone in either his racial or intellectual feelings of isolation: "I was amazed to find that there did exist in this world an organized search for the truth of the lives of the oppressed and the isolated" ("I Tried," pt. 1, 62). But beyond promising an intellectual and artistic home for himself, these literary-political affiliations spoke directly to Wright's racial identity as one of the "oppressed":

> The revolutionary words leaped from the printed page and struck me with tremendous force. It was not the economics of Communism, nor the great power of trade unions, nor the excitement of underground politics that claimed me; my attention was caught by the similarity of the experience of workers in other lands, by the possibility of uniting scattered but kindred peoples into a whole. It seemed to me that here, at last, in the realm of revolutionary expression, Negro experience could find a home, a functioning value and role. (ibid.)

With his own painful racial experience, he realized immediately that he was perfectly situated to reveal this new home and hope to black people. But in his post-facto narrative, he frames that new role in terms of the communists' previous failure to reach black people, indeed the masses generally, whereas *he* could represent their experience: "The Communists, I felt, had oversimplified the experience of those whom they sought to lead. In their efforts to recruit masses, they had missed the meaning of the lives of the masses, had conceived of people in too abstract a manner" (ibid., 63). Although it is possible that Wright had already reached this conclusion from hearing communist speakers in public parks, he had had few direct contacts at the time with communists and had not previously read their literature. The passage thus sounds like a conclusion he reached later and made retroactive to his feelings in those early days. In any case, he saw in a revelatory moment how he could make a real contribution to the Party by using his own experience to bridge that gap: "I would try to put some of that meaning back. I would tell Communists how common people felt, and I would tell common people of the self-sacrifice of Communists who strove for unity among them" (ibid., 63). Fabre is right to call this ambition "naïve" (*Unfinished Quest*, 98); it is also more than a little presumptuous. But such often are one's early enthusiasms, and for Wright this realization went far beyond "enthusiasm" to become a conversion experience and give his life new meaning and direction.

Wright's Proletarian Poetry

Political poems began pouring out of him, the first and one of his best, "I Have Seen Black Hands," coming that very first night, according to his memoirs. This poem made it to the top leftist journal: the CP-USA's *New Masses*, which published it the following June 1934. Eighteen more poems followed in the 1930s, nearly all appearing in leftist magazines between 1934 and 1937. His first two published ones—"Rest for the Weary" and "A Red Love Note"— appeared in *Left Front* (Jan.–Feb. 1934). Jack Conroy's proletarian magazine, *The Anvil*, published "Strength" and "Child of the Dead and Forgotten Gods" the following month; the prestigious *Partisan Review* took "Between the World and Me" (July–Aug. 1935); and *International Literature*, the monthly of the International Union of Revolutionary Writers, published Wright's most ambitious poem, "Transcontinental," in its January 1936 issue. *New Masses*, in fact, took so many of Wright's poems—"Red Leaves of Red Books" (30 April 1935), "Spread Your Sunrise" (2 July 1935), "Hearst Headline Blues" (12 May 1936), "Old Habit and New Love" (15 Dec. 1936), and "We of the Streets" (13 April 1937)—that Wright's status there approximated E. E. Cummings's prominent position at *The Dial* a decade earlier.[5]

But beginning with Wright's own assessment of his poetry as "crude," critics have routinely dismissed these poems with the same adjective, as merely "agitprop" poems that preach to the choir.[6] Without question, these poems are crude and usually unsubtle, but it seems unfair to expect the highest achievement from these first attempts in a new medium, composed by a young writer driven far more by his newfound revolutionary zeal than by a desire to master the intricacies of his art. Rather than dismiss them out of hand, we can discover in them the themes and images that resonated for Wright in this earliest and most devoted allegiance to communism, themes and images he would develop more fully in his fiction.

"Black Hands," his first effort, is a powerful poem because Wright based it—as he did all his best work—on his racial experience. Through vivid imagery, the poem traces the stages of black life from infancy (nursing on "black nipples"), through childhood (candy, balls and bat), schooling (pens and books), adolescent rebellion (dice, cigarettes), work (the startling masturbatory image of hands "jerked up and down at the throbbing machines"), unemployment, theft from desperation, imprisonment, and—a grim staple in Wright's work—lynching. Only in the poem's concluding section does Wright superimpose his hopeful vision (just as he would later do in the story "Fire and Cloud") of black hands, now "raised in fists of revolt, side by side with the white fists of white workers /. . . On some red day . . . on a new horizon!" Significantly, the speaker says of this vision, "it is only this which sustains me." The poem's chantlike repetition beginning each section ("I am black and I have seen black hands, millions and millions of them—"), deriving from Sandburg and Whitman, also contributes to its cumulative urgency.

Several aspects of this poem appear in Wright's other political poems. Most obvious, of course, is its racial focus that encompasses both the innocence of childhood and the horror of lynching. The latter would become, as Wright called it in the title of another poem, an "Obsession" (*Midland Left*, Sept. 1935), and references to lynching appear not only in "Obsession" but also in "Between the World and Me," "Hearst Headline Blues," and "Transcontinental." This ever-looming reality, and what it said about the status and vulnerability of black people, not just in the South but in the entire country, never diminished in Wright's sensibility throughout the 1930s, as is gruesomely apparent in his first story of *Uncle Tom's Children*, "Big Boy Leaves Home."

The identity and perspective in these poems, however, are dual: class-based as well as racial, expressing the sensibility of struggling workers as well as oppressed blacks. The two poems published in the September 1935 issue of *Midland Left* perfectly exemplify this dual identity: "Rise and Live" captures, in a blueslike repetition, the despair of unemployed workers who have seen their lives consumed and discarded by the capitalism they helped build:

> They tell us we're human—
> Tell us we're human beings—
> They tell us that our lives in this world mean something!
> Where are our days gone? . . .
> Towering above our heads are the granaries we built!

"Obsession," as noted, makes the black speaker's dread of inevitable lynching ("no other way out") the central fact of his identity, "The deep rock on which I stand to face the world!" The dual identities in these poems were Wright's own and at the time presented no conflict in priority. Collective, radical resistance was the solution to them both: "Comrades, let's rise and slay this monstrous irony!" ("Rise and Live"). This solidarity, versus the ineffectuality of individual action, is the most important theme in the political poems. "Strength" contrasts the "gentle breeze" of a "lone comrade" with the "raging hurricane" that results "when [he is] united with millions and millions / of other lives, steeped in the sense / of an historic mission."

The triumphant vision of the coming workers' revolution that concludes "Black Hands" is also a staple of these poems. It sometimes appears merely as a premonition—"all the folks talkin' 'bout something's going to break" in the dialect poem "Ah Feels it in Mah Bones"—or as the "printed hope" of a book's "red leaves" that causes the "calloused hands that grip you" to become "hardened to the steel of unretractable purpose!" ("Red Leaves of Red Books"). More often, the poems confidently prophesize the revolution itself that will overwhelm the capitalistic "guardians of gold":

> soon our brawny hands shall
> relieve you of your burdens!
>
> it'll be all over before you know it! . . .
> it'll be a red clap of thunder rising from the very depths of hell!
> ("Rest for the Weary," "A Red Love Note," *Left Front,* Jan.–Feb. 1934)

Only a few of these poems end pessimistically, typically those with racial perspectives and lynching themes: the above-described "Obsession" and "Between the World and Me," in which the speaker, having stumbled on the remains of a lynching and recreating the brutal images in his mind, now becomes the "dry bones and stony skull." Against the implacable white racism and violence of the South, Wright's personal experience was steeped in a realism that trumped the programmatically hopeful outcomes expected of proletarian poetry. Several poems, however, return this violence in envisioning revolutionary outcomes, when the shoe is on the other foot. His first published poems, "Rest for the Weary" and "A Red Love Note," gloat over the forthcoming day when "the claws of history / have stripped from your tawdry lives the tinseled pretense" ("Rest"), while "Love Note" coos to its capitalistic victim with menacing terms of endearment: "darling . . . sugarpie," etc. "Transcontinental" envisions this violence graphically. As Keneth Kinnamon observes, "Destructive violence recurs over and over in Wright's early poetry and remains a dominant motif throughout his entire writing career. At times the violence is masochistic, as in 'Rise and Live' . . . . More often the violence is aggressive."[7]

Wright's most ambitious poem in length and scope is "Transcontinental," which runs 243 lines and depicts, as the title suggests, a journey taking in all of America. It begins from a perspective Wright knew well from his travel to and from the 1935 American Writers' Congress in New York: that of a hitchhiker. In this Marxian "Song of the Open Road," the drivers who speed by the speaker in their big Packards and Chryslers—"Their lips are tight jaws set eyes straight ahead"—represent the indifferent, white America of plenty, which the first refrains question: "America who built this dream," "who owns this wonderland," "why turn your face away." But the narrative quickly shifts to the speaker's fantasy of role reversal when "America is ours / This car is commandeered . . . We'll drive and let you be the hitch-hiker."

A dialogue of sorts follows in which an imagined white adversary (the driver?) invokes clichés to defend capitalism, some of which the speaker punctures:

America's a free country

Did you say Negroes

Oh I don't mean NEEEGROOOES

After all

Isn't there a limit to everything
You wouldn't want your daughter . . .

In the ensuing refrain *"UNITEDFRONT-SSSTRIKE,"* the repeated
S's cleverly capture the hissing tires on the highway, and "UNIT-
EDFRONT" evokes the new Popular Front against fascism, introduced by the Comintern in 1934/35. The speaker envisions the car
overwhelming the enemies of radicalism—"Hurdling desks of Con-
gressmen Fascist flesh sticking to our tires . . . carbon monoxide for
the President . . . Plunging the radiator into the lynch-mob"—and
taking aboard the disenfranchised: ("sharecroppers / Come on You
Negroes . . . There's room / Not in the back but front seat"), and
"WOORKERSWOORKERS" in Wright's own Chicago.

As in Wright's other proletarian poems, the future is not just rosy
but red: "We're heading for the highway of Self-Determination . . .
We're speeding on wheels of revolution . . . Cities breed soviets . . .
Plains sprout collective farms." And the poem ends with fragments
of the Communist "Internationale": "Arise, ye prisoners . . . Arise
ye wretched . . . For Justice . . . Thunders," as the car races "Ever
Faster" toward the inevitable triumph.

Amidst this lengthy and predictable catalogue of clichés and
stereotypes, Wright's talent shows in precise images and sound
patterns—"Yanking tired thumbs at glazed faces"—and in the all-
too-rare glimmers of sardonic humor: "The lights flash red Comrades let's go."

In sum, these poems may not impress many readers with Wright's
talent at a poet. But biographically, they represent his primary creative effort in 1933 to 1935. He had published two short stories several years earlier—which Kinnamon dismisses as "adolescent"[8]—and
he was working on a novel in 1935 (subsequently titled *Lawd Today!*) that was continuously rejected by publishers and would never

see print during his life. By contrast, his publishing successes in poetry—perhaps coming too easily in leftist magazines eager for material and especially from a black poet—encouraged him to think of himself primarily as a poet, just as Ernest Hemingway did in the early 1920s. Collectively, these poems have a raw energy and convey Wright's wholehearted, if naïve, enthusiasm for communism at the time, and an almost schizoid sensibility of revolutionary hope and racial despair. Further, they anticipate aspects of his future fiction: themes of violence (by whites against blacks, but also the reverse), of rebellion and collective action bridging the chasm between black and white; images of red, black, and white marching or burning; and "self-determination," even if it is achieved with a hatchet or a brick.

Finally, the poetry—and Wright's success in publishing it—raises a question about the sincerity of his political commitment to the John Reed Club. As he himself noted, "Many young writers joined the club because of their hope of publishing in *Left Front*" ("I Tried," pt. 1, 63)—a hope intensified by the bleak publishing prospects elsewhere during the Depression. Was Wright describing himself here? Surely it was a pleasure to see his poems receive a warm reception among his peers in the club and prompt publication. But to assume a purely opportunistic motive for Wright's belonging to the John Reed Club, we would have to discount all of his descriptions, such as those quoted above, of what joining the club meant to his identity as a painfully isolated black man and intellectual, as well as the new convert's unbridled enthusiasm for communism in the poems themselves.

Rising in the John Reed Club and Joining the Party

Though Wright's enthusiasm was strong, it was also narrowly focused and partially self-interested. Despite the poetry's boilerplate images and rhetoric about the workers' triumph over capitalism, Wright's chief concerns at the time were—and remained—to advance his race and to develop his nascent career as a writer. What the Communist Party and the John Reed Club had already done and could do for blacks was his constant criterion for gauging their ideology and his commitment to it. His contrasting responses to that first club meeting perfectly reflect this standard. Initially, he was skeptical: "I felt that Communists could not possibly have a sincere interest in Negroes" ("I Tried," pt. 1, 61). But when enthusiasm replaced doubt, race was still the measure: "It seemed to me that here at last, in the realm of revolutionary expression, Negro experience could find a home, a functioning value and role" (ibid., 62). In the flush of this new enthusiasm, it is not surprising that he vastly overestimated the Party's commitment to "Negro equality" as "one of the main tenets of Communism" (ibid., 63). Discovering this overestimation would take years, but he would quickly realize the Party's coldness to his literary ambitions once he left the welcoming shelter of the club.

For the time being, however, Wright basked in the club's warm welcome and encouragement. In short order, he joined the editorial board of *Left Front* and in early 1934, just a few months after attending his first meeting, he was elected executive secretary of the club.[9] As Fabre describes, Wright poured the same energy and enthusiasm into running the club that he did into his poetry. He organized weekly Tuesday meetings and a Saturday night lecture series, featuring prominent speakers that he recruited from nearby universities. He himself gave a lecture and led a discussion on "Negro Culture in a Marxist Perspective." He lectured at other John Reed Clubs in the region. Shortly after becoming executive secretary, Wright was informed he would have to join the Communist Party if he wanted to hold this position—an index of how closely the John Reed Club was tied to the Party, which had organized these clubs. He writes in "I Tried" about his interview with Party officials: "I stated that I favored a policy that allowed for the development of writers and artists. My policy was accepted. I signed the membership card" ("I Tried," pt. 1, 64).[10] Self-interest, of course, was certainly a factor in his decisions here. The local club was divided between artists and writers. The more radical artists supported the demands of the local Party cell for money for political activities. The writers, including Wright, wanted to keep the money in-house to support their literary magazine. Hence Wright's policy favoring the "development of writers and artists." Then, too, joining the Party at this point must have seemed like the next logical step in his political evolution.

The CP-USA indirectly resolved the feud between the artists and writers of the local John Reed Club, but not the way Wright wanted. In mid-1934, following the dictates of the Soviet Comintern, the Party decided to close all the John Reed Clubs, beginning with their magazines. In place of the clubs, which catered to young, unrecognized writers and artists, the Party aimed to recruit prominent writers to national congresses to be held biennially, beginning in 1935, out of which would come the League of American Writers. What occasioned this major decision was an even larger reorientation of Comintern policy away from the sectarian infighting of the past five years (the so-called Third Period) and toward an alliance with other leftist groups and liberal intellectuals called the "Popular Front" against fascism. Bourgeois writers and artists, formerly scorned, were now welcomed; their reputations would, it was hoped, increase the status of the CP-USA and its leftist affiliates. But in seeking the fame of established writers, the CP-USA foolishly severed a conduit of youthful supporters in the John Reed Clubs.

Wright was appalled: "I asked [at the national John Reed Club congress] what was to become of the young writers whom the Communist Party has implored to join the clubs and who were ineligible for the new group, and there was no answer . . ." ("I Tried," pt. 1, 69). He protested again, belatedly, the following year, at the first American Writers' Congress and again received cold silence (ibid., 70). Such protests did not go down well with the Party.[11] Once decisions were made and handed down, they were to be accepted and obeyed without question: "Members of the party do not violate the party's decisions" he was told on another occasion (ibid., 68).

Cut off from the group that had welcomed and inspired him, Wright had only the local cell of the CP-USA as the external link between his new political and creative lives. But in the Party cell, he encountered problems foreign to his club experience. Party members of this South Side cell, though predominantly black, were not sympathetic to Wright's needs as a developing writer. They followed Party dictates obediently and expected him to participate unquestioningly in typical and time-consuming Party activities of organizing, researching, and attending meetings. Wright, accustomed to the club's understanding and encouragement, was shocked when the cell responded coldly to his requests for exclusion from these activities in order to devote his limited free time to his writing. Worse, Party members, reflecting the general attitude of the CP-USA, distrusted his intellectualism—his vocabulary was definitely not working class, nor of the South Side black belt. These suspicions bred larger ones: What were his motives? Was he merely a bourgeois intellectual dabbling in the Party for his own ends? He had already shown himself willing to challenge the Party decisions to close *Left Front* and the John Reed Clubs. Had the Party mistakenly recruited a renegade?

Wright also began having doubts. About the time the John Reed Club Congress announced the closings (September 1934), he concluded,

> I . . . tried to make up my mind to stand alone, write alone. I was already afraid that the stories I had written would not fit into the new, official mood. Must I discard my plot ideas and seek new ones? My writing was my way of seeing, my way of living, my way of feeling, and who could change his sight, his sense of direction, his senses? ("I Tried," pt. 1, 69)

Although the "stand alone" statement sounds superimposed from his later attitudes, the rest of the passage rings true. Wright was beginning to write fiction in 1934/35: he was working on a novel and short stories. Both types of fiction focused specifically on the experiences of black men, a Chicago postal worker in the novel, Southern blacks in the stories. Yet the Party now called for a deemphasis on racial consciousness—"We Communists don't dramatize Negro nationalism" he was told ("I Tried," pt. 2, 49)—in favor of the larger *inter*national philosophy of the Popular Front, merging antifascists from all classes, races, and nations. For that matter, the Party had always considered race as a subset of class: it was the working class that would make the revolution. Accordingly, Party leaders "severely criticized the novel and tried to prevent Wright from getting it published"—discouragement that he resented.[12]

Wright also resented being told with whom he could and could not associate. In late 1934, he had contemplated writing biographical sketches of black communists under the putative title "Heroes, Red and Black," embodying his aim to act as an interpretive liaison between the communist and black communities. But the man he chose for his first sketch was as much an anarchist as a communist and was already in trouble with the Party. Wright was told peremptorily to drop the project, indeed drop all contact with this anarchist, and associate in future only with orthodox communists. As Fabre summarizes,

> In Wright's eyes, the dilemma was insoluble: either he would have to conform to the Party directive and sacrifice his integrity as a writer, or he would once again be cut off and isolated. For the time being he tried to stall in order to remain part of the cultural organization of the Left without becoming a mere political tool. (*Unfinished Quest*, 107)

These doubts, however, intermingled with political achievements. Although he was scarcely the equal of the prominent writers invited to the first American Writers' Congress, Wright was appointed a delegate, even though he had to hitchhike to and from New York to attend. At the Congress, though he had publicly challenged the decision to close the John Reed Clubs, he was nonetheless elected to the national council of the League of American Writers, joining thirty-eight other writers. The experience of meeting and interacting with established writers in New York, as well as his election to the council even *after* he had protested a Party decision, suggested to him that New York's radical literary atmosphere was more exciting and encouraging than Chicago's, that its political climate was more tolerant. Here, one could be both literary *and* militantly political; and one might dare to think for oneself. Chicago began to look provincial.

The slurs he received in Chicago from one prominent black communist—"petty bourgeois degenerate," "bastard intellectual," "incipient Trotskyite" ("I Tried," pt. 2, 48, 51)—further poisoned his relationship with the Chicago cell. Such abuse seems fantastic, especially coming from a political organization that was not suffering from a surplus of members, but the same sort of slurs are mentioned in numerous other accounts of "official" efforts to put down dissenters. Wright asserts that Party members began spying on him at social events and reporting on his behavior, a claim confirmed by Fabre (*Unfinished Quest*, 137). But the nub of his conflict with the Chicago cell was in his determination to be "my kind of Communist," "to shape people's feelings, awaken their hearts" through his writing ("I Tried," pt. 2, 50)—and to reserve for his writing the little free time his daytime jobs permitted. When local Party leaders rejected his impassioned pleas to fulfill these aims and, instead, assigned him mundane and time-consuming research tasks, such as researching the cost of living and the housing crisis in Chicago to prepare for a protest, Wright contemplated quitting the Party, but temporized. Meanwhile, he was assigned several tasks for an upcoming National Negro Congress to be held February 1936 in Chicago: to preside over a session on black history and culture; to write a foreword to the delegates' program; and to report on it to *New Masses* (Fabre, *Unfinished Quest*, 126). He complied. But when he proposed organizing a South Side literary group to replace the defunct John Reed Club, he was turned down flat.

Trouble at the Federal Theatre Project
and Federal Writers' Project

In an entirely different realm—the Federal Theatre Project (FTP) and Federal Writers' Project (FWP) of the WPA—Wright alleges that Party members made serious trouble for him. In late 1935, Wright left his job at the South Side Youth Club, where he had worked since late 1934, to join the FWP as a researcher for its American Guide series. In March 1936, he transferred to the Negro Theatre Unit of the Chicago FTP, where he handled publicity. Characteristically, Wright threw himself headlong into the unit's operations and politics. He was appalled by the practice of the white director, "an elderly missionary type" ("I Tried," pt. 2, 52), to convert "white" plays to black characters and settings, often "African,"[13] while rejecting as too controversial "[c]ontemporary plays dealing realistically with Negro life" (ibid., 52). Through his connections in the WPA, Wright successfully worked to have her replaced by someone more receptive to contemporary black drama, Charles De Sheim. But when Wright and De Sheim presented to the black company their first project, Paul Green's *Hymn to the Rising Sun*, a "grim . . . powerful one-acter dealing with chain-gang conditions in the South" (ibid., 52), rebellion ensued. The company refused to perform it, and, according to Wright, the men directly threatened him with knives, forcing both De Sheim and Wright to leave the unit. Though Wright eventually transferred back to the FWP, trouble followed him. After a few months, when he had been made acting supervisor of essays, there were calls for his removal. He learned from the project's administrator that these calls came from "my erstwhile comrades" (ibid., 55), who had also, allegedly, been behind the rebellion and threats that drove him from the Negro Theater Unit. This time, the comrades failed, but Wright never forgot that they had tried "to take the bread out of my mouth" (ibid.).

Developing His Literary Career

Undaunted by the Communist Party's indifference to his literary goals, Wright helped to organize the South Side group of writers and artists in the spring of 1936, comprising Arna Bontemps, Theodore Ward, Frank Marshall Davis, Margaret Walker, and others. He later wrote that the group's aim was "to render the life of their race in social and realistic terms" and he added with some hyperbole: "For the first time in Negro history, problems such as nationalism in literature, perspective, the relation of the Negro writer to politics and social movements were formulated and discussed."[14] More than ever now, Wright needed this literary group to provide constructive criticism and encouragement for the fiction he was writing. His literary ambitions had moved beyond writing Party-line poetry in leftist magazines (though he was still publishing plenty of that in 1936–37) to fiction that would appeal to a more general and less politicized readership. Successes, however, were still problematic. Several prominent publishers had rejected his novel, originally titled "Cesspool." Now he was furiously revising it and had given it a less offensive title: "Lawd Today!" Wright's real breakthrough, however, occurred in the short stories he began writing in 1935 about oppressed, rebellious blacks in the Jim Crow South. The first of this group, "Big Boy Leaves Home," he had read to an approving Chicago literary soirée and, of course, to his South Side literary group. In January 1936, the editors of *The New Caravan*, an anthology of contemporary writing, accepted the story. It appeared in November and attracted attention and praise from critics of all stripes, leftist and non-leftist, white and black. That success had two immediate results. It decided Wright finally on fiction rather than poetry (Fabre, *Unfinished Quest*, 134), and it gained him a "supervisory" position in the Chicago FWP, providing him more time to write.

More short stories of the same ilk soon followed: "Down by the Riverside," "Long Black Song" (completed July 1936), "Fire and Cloud," "Bright and Morning Star"—all the stories that would make up *Uncle Tom's Children*—as well as "Silt" and "Almos' a Man." The novel form, however, still proved problematic: both the revised *Lawd Today!* and a second novel, "Tarbaby's Dawn," were rejected by publishers.[15] Still, the progress Wright had made in short fiction in such a brief period was remarkable, and the completion of these stories *and* novels in this same period shows that he was writing at a frenetic pace.

Conflict and Rupture with the Party

Clearly, this pace could not be maintained if he were to carry out the duties assigned him by the Party, while also working during the day. He had already stopped attending cell meetings. Matters came to a head when he declined the chance to visit Switzerland and the Soviet Union as a communist delegate to a Youth Congress—no doubt, a high honor. Wright explained that he could not abandon his writing at this point. Insulted for making this decision, he finally decided to break with the Party—"This is good-bye" ("I Tried," pt. 2, 51)—and at the next cell meeting he formally requested that his name be dropped from Party rolls, declaring "I simply do not wish to be bound any longer by the party's decisions" (ibid.). Then he learned about the Party's refusal to accept resignations, converting them to expulsions, often buttressed by false charges.

Wright began to hedge his bets. He had taken the civil service exam for the Post Office, achieved a near-perfect score, and was offered a permanent clerkship at a salary of $2100 a year. Accepting that position would solve his financial problems, but not those with the Party. He inquired at the Chicago FWP about transferring to the New York branch and received an encouraging response, but was told the transfer would take several months.

According to "I Tried," the culminating event in Wright's break with the Chicago cell of the CP-USA occurred at the May Day parade, 1937 (which he misdates as 1936), when he was prevented from marching with the communists and roughly hurled from the line. This physical expulsion seems almost too neat—too metaphorical—a culmination. But it did occur in Chicago, and it did end his relationship with the Chicago cell. Wright effectively concludes this passage in "I Tried" by juxtaposing the visionary lyrics of "The Internationale" being sung by the marchers with the blindness of his communist adversaries (pt. 2, 56). Less than a month later, he moved to New York. Though this was the symbolic break, his relationship with the Chicago cell had effectively ended when it turned down his request to have his name removed from the rolls. Apparently, he had thought this exit meant leaving the Party altogether, not just the Chicago cell, for in a letter dated 9 February 1937, James T. Farrell (who himself had recently broken with the Party) congratulates Wright: "I'm glad to hear you left the Party . . ." (Fabre, *Unfinished Quest*, 138). The New York branch, however, "reinstated" him, offering him a position in the Harlem office of the *Daily Worker*. And, as noted, Wright felt that the Party there would be "more liberal and intelligent."[16]

The Chicago years had witnessed Wright's simultaneous discovery of radical politics and a literary voice to express it. The two discoveries were inseparable: he was not merely a writer who had opportunistically latched on to leftism for the audience and publishing opportunities it provided. In discovering a community of radical writers and artists—a surrogate family—he simultaneously discovered his métier, his subjects, and a political ideology he could believe in. More, he fashioned for himself a purpose in establishing a vital link between black oppression in the United States and a radically political response to it. In the John Reed Club, Wright found a home that valued his intellect and creative potential, and in that welcoming climate his creativity soared. Joining the Communist Party seemed the logical next step in the progress of his political development. But the Party's attitude in Chicago was hostile to his creative growth, and Wright's determination to develop as a writer, combined with his growing self-confidence, inevitably clashed with the cell's narrow-minded and rigid definition of his role. As it turned out, his Chicago experience with the Party emulated, in miniature, his lifetime relationship with the Party: involvement, disagreements over his creative work and ideology, and withdrawal. But his feelings about the Chicago cell in 1937 did not equal his feelings about communism itself or its potential and already proven contribution to the plight of black people in America. New York promised a better climate for his writing and a better relationship with the Party.

II. New York: 1937–39

In moving to New York at the end of May 1937, Wright made a decision that profoundly affected his dual lives as writer and communist. He had decided to forgo a financially secure job at the Post Office—the first in his and his family's time in Chicago—for the uncertain future of his writing. As he put it to friends at the time, "I thought I ought to give myself a chance, and that's what I did" (Fabre, *Unfinished Quest,* 139). More practically, in New York, he would be close to the major commercial publishers and could directly promote his submitted novels, instead of relying on an agent whom he suspected of apathy.

He had thrown off the burden of supporting his family—his younger brother's WPA job could now do that—and the unfeeling demands of the Chicago cell of the CP-USA. But he still needed to support himself, and the promised transfer to the New York City branch of the Federal Writers' Project would not take effect until December. The New York branch of the CP-USA interceded to help him by appointing him a reporter for the Harlem office of the *Daily Worker*—not a well-paying job, but enough to support him.

Why did the New York branch welcome him and give him this position when the Chicago cell had virtually expelled him? Fabre's view that Wright's battles with the Chicago cell "had been kept a secret" (*Unfinished Quest,* 147) is implausible given the Party's assiduous information-gathering on its members. Far more likely, the New York branch, itself composed of many prominent writers and artists, recognized Wright's talent, growing reputation, and potential contribution to the Party. Here was an asset to be developed, not stifled.

Wright's acceptance of the Harlem position, in turn, showed that, in striking contrast to his autobiography, he was certainly not through with the Communist Party. Despite his disillusioning experience in Chicago, he still admired the Party's active opposition to the oppression of blacks in America, still shared its analysis of capitalism and its striving to organize and unite the oppressed worldwide, still supported the Popular Front against fascism (even though the Popular Front had indirectly resulted in the closing of the John Reed Clubs and in the discouragement of "negro nationalism"). Wright still believed he had much to contribute to the Party—but in his own way, through his writing, not by beating the pavement carrying picket signs or petitions.

His first acts in New York were to attend, again as a delegate, the 1937 American Writers' Congress and to collaborate with Dorothy West and Marian Minus on a new black literature quarterly. The 1937 Writers' Congress reflected the Popular Front appeal to liberals as well as to committed leftists and devoted more time than had the 1935 congress to writers' professional problems, such as balancing creative freedom with a commitment to Party goals. In his own participation at the congress, Wright felt far more self-assured than he had at the 1935 congress and spoke persuasively on the writer's obligation not to sacrifice artistic integrity to political expectations. One delegate described him as "the clearest and hardest of the minds present" at a session attended by novelists (Fabre, *Unfinished Quest*, 141). At the congress, Wright met such prominent writers as Malcolm Cowley and Kenneth Burke and heard Ernest Hemingway, just back from Spain, deliver an antifascist keynote address that brought down the house. Significantly, Wright presided over part of one session, where he introduced the director of the Federal Writers' Project, Henry Alsberg.

As for the black literary quarterly, *New Challenge*, Wright not only contributed a major ideological article, but also largely wrote the lead editorial, which argues for the creation of social realist literature that fuses the current condition of blacks in the United States with "the struggle against war and fascism." The language is clearly Party-line, though the Communist Party did not underwrite the quarterly. Perhaps for this reason, the magazine folded after the first issue, the editors quarreling about its future direction. But Wright's essay remains important as a major statement on the relationship between racial and political imperatives for black writers. And it reveals how closely tied to Party ideology he was in 1937.

"Blueprint for Negro Writing"

Wright's essay urges black writers to ally themselves ("shoulder to shoulder") with black workers, the one class of African-Americans capable of organizing "forms of struggle to better their lot. Lacking the [petit-bourgeois] handicaps of false ambitions and property, thcy have access to a wide social vision and a deep social consciousness" (99, 98). In forging this alliance, black writers must ignore their previous audiences, the black and white middle classes, neither of which is genuinely interested in or capable of improving conditions for blacks. Having identified their audience, black writers must work toward "molding the lives and consciousness of those [negro] masses towards new goals" (99). Clearly, that consciousness must become revolutionary because "at the moment when a people begins to realize a *meaning* in their suffering, the civilization that engenders that suffering is doomed" (100, Wright's emphasis).[17] Specifically, that civilization is "capitalist America" (101). Thus, for black writers merely to create "simple literary realism . . . devoid of wider social connotations, devoid of the revolutionary significance of these [negro] nationalist tendencies, must do a rank injustice to the Negro people and alienate their possible allies [i.e., white workers and the radical Left] in the struggle for freedom" (101). Curiously, Wright here seems to be rejecting the naturalistic style of his previous novel, *Lawd Today!*, a style that emphasized "literary realism" to a fault and was devoid of any "revolutionary significance."

In writing specifically for a *racial* working class, however, black writers had to be wary of catering to "Negro nationalism," a sectarianism the Party now considered reactionary and discouraged.[18] The solution, Wright argued, was to "accept the nationalist implications of [negro] lives, not in order to encourage them, but in order to change and transcend them" (101)—a neat solution, but one that had questionable relevance to Wright's own fiction, past and future.

Wright also addresses the black writer's beliefs:

[I]n the lives of Negro writers must be found those materials and experiences which will create a meaningful picture of the world today. Many young writers have grown to believe that a Marxist analysis of society presents such a picture. It creates a picture which, when placed before the eyes of the writer, should unify his personality, organize his emotions, buttress him with a tense and obdurate will to change the world.

And, in turn, this changed world will dialectically change the writer. Hence, it is through a Marxist conception of reality and society that the maximum degree of freedom in thought and feeling can be gained for the Negro writer. (102)

All the hallmarks of Marxian social realism are present in Wright's essay: Writers must ally themselves with and write for the working class (the only class capable of revolutionary change) to help it realize its revolutionary potential. In turn, writers themselves are transformed by the response of their audience. The racial dimension ("Negro nationalism") will ultimately be transcended. Even Wright's diction is replete with words and phrases like "parasitic and mannered . . . petty bourgeois"; "the emergence of a new culture in the shell of the old"; "dialectically"; "change the world"; and so forth—stock phrases from communist pamphlets. Although one may conclude that he was merely parroting the Party line, it seems likelier that he sincerely believed these social realist axioms. But making his fiction conform to them—especially in avoiding an exclusively realistic focus on black life and conditions—would prove difficult indeed. Several stories in *Uncle Tom's Children* could be (and were) accused of expressing negro nationalism, as well as the new novel he was already working on, *Native Son*. Their "reactionary" slant, however, points not to intentional hypocrisy on Wright's part, but to his being guided by his deepest, most personal understanding of racial issues rather than by Party doctrine.

Wright's prose at times shows another quality typical of radical journals of the day: a kind of baroque stridency. The opening paragraph of "Blueprint" describes earlier black writers as they "entered the Court of American Public Opinion dressed in the knee-pants of servility, curtsying to show that the Negro was not inferior, . . . [T]hese artistic ambassadors were received as though they were French poodles who do clever tricks" (97). The same scorn was leveled at Harlem Renaissance writers who glorified black primitivism and exoticism. Zora Neale Hurston's *Their Eyes Were Watching God* came in for particular abuse in his *New Masses* review of the novel, "Between Laughter and Tears." With "no theme, no message, no thought," her novel voluntarily continues "the minstrel technique that makes the 'white folks' laugh" at "quaint . . . Negro life" (25). Wright's harsh language echoes, perhaps emulates, editor Mike Gold's abusive reviews, which had become a model for *New Masses* reviewers.[19] Wright had already become one of the communist magazine's prized poets. Now, he was publishing fiction there—"Silt" appeared in the 24 August 1937 issue—and criticism. The following year, he joined its editorial board.

Although *New Challenge* folded after a single issue and Wright's early novels were in limbo, his literary career was nonetheless advancing rapidly. One of the short stories that he had completed in Chicago, "Big Boy Leaves Home," had already been published to considerable acclaim. Now, in mid-December 1937, another story, "Fire and Cloud," won first prize out of some six hundred competitors in *Story* magazine's National Fiction Contest for FWP members. Not only did Wright receive a much-needed award of five hundred dollars, but also popular notice and critical praise. He was interviewed by major newspapers, and now the big publishers were paying attention. The *Story* prize created the biggest breakthrough of his career: Harper & Brothers decided to publish as a collection the four stories Wright had submitted to *Story*.[20] Wright came up with a brilliant title for this collection set in the South: "Uncle Tom's Children." Wisely, he acquired a new agent at the same time, the prominent Paul Reynolds Company.

The book's Southern setting also informed a personal narrative, "The Ethics of Living Jim Crow—An Autobiographical Sketch," which Wright published in a 1937 anthology of FWP creative work called *American Stuff*. So closely related were "Ethics" and the stories of *Uncle Tom's Children* in setting and theme that "Ethics" was included in the book's second edition as a kind of introduction. There, the fiction and autobiographical sketch function as a two-pronged attack on Southern racism and violence against blacks, actual and threatened. As Richard Yarborough observes, the memoir's lived experience helped verify the stories' authenticity.[21]

Like the later *Black Boy*, "Ethics" is a kind of bildungsroman, in which the narrator learns from a series of painful experiences what it means to be a young black man growing up in the South: the two sets of rules in kids' fights (we use cinders; *they* use broken bottles); the two types of housing (their houses have lawns and hedges; ours have neither); etc. Most of all, the narrator learns through his work experiences his place and expected behavior in this society. His naïve social mistakes—wanting to advance in a company by learning the business, and not saying "sir" to a white man, for example—are punished with white threats, white betrayals, white violence. He learns to look the other way, defer his glance, not to do or say anything that whites would consider threatening. If another black man is punished—as one is castrated for being caught in bed with a white prostitute—it is because he hasn't learned. Finally, the narrator learns more advanced coping mechanisms: "I learned to lie, to steal, to dissemble. I learned to play that dual role which every Negro must play if he wants to eat and live" (*Uncle Tom's Children*, 13). He illustrates this dissembling with his clever ploy at the library for checking out books that would otherwise be denied to blacks by pretending they are for whites. The memoir's conclusion, however, points in a different direction than simply coping with white oppression. The narrator quotes a black friend: "Ef it wuzn't fer them polices 'n' them ol' lynch-mobs, there wouldn't be nothin' but uproar down here!" The message couldn't be clearer: the ever-present threat of violence that supports white racism can barely suppress the deep resentment, simmering rebellion, and even counterviolence that it breeds.

Fighting Back: *Uncle Tom's Children*

The stories of *Uncle Tom's Children* convey themes similar to "The Ethics of Living Jim Crow," except that the menace of white violence for the narrator of "Ethics" now becomes actual: black men and women are verbally abused, cheated, beaten, raped, shot, and burned to death by whites. The most startlingly effective dramatization of this violence occurs in the opening story, "Big Boy

Leaves Home." Deceptively, it begins as an idyll with young black men playing hooky from school, horsing around on a summer's day, and deciding to go skinny-dipping. That the swimming hole is on a white man's property, forbidden to them, is barely considered, rather like a distant rumble of thunder. Suddenly and without warning the storm blows up as a young white woman not only sees the boys swimming naked but inadvertently stands between them and their clothing. A scene that would otherwise be hilarious—her exaggerated distress (she screams repeatedly), their intense embarrassment and inability to get to their clothing—here turns deadly serious: showing themselves naked to a white woman is tantamount to rape. Her fiancé, an army officer, comes running, carrying a rifle. The reader, seeing events from the boys' perspective, is as shocked as they are. Harmless fun has now become a racial transgression, a crime punishable—and punished—by death. What scene more vividly portrays the fragile, volatile condition of Southern blacks, in which the slightest mistake can result in their murder?

The stories of *Uncle Tom's Children*, however, go beyond "Ethics" in one crucial element: the black "uproar" threatened at the end of "Ethics" has arrived, either as individual acts of counterviolence or as collective protest. In all but one of the five stories, the black protagonists do not passively accept white violence against them but respond with devastating violence of their own. After the white army officer, Jim Harvey, kills two of Big Boy's black friends, Big Boy grabs Harvey's rifle and beats him with it, knocking his teeth in. When the white man comes at him and lunges for the rifle, Big Boy shoots and kills him. In "Down by the Riverside," Mann fires his gun in self-defense at a white man who has fired at him for allegedly stealing the white man's rowboat; as in "Big Boy Leaves Home," the black man kills the white. In "Long Black Song," Silas, a black farmer, first horsewhips, then shoots the white salesman who has raped his wife. Finally, Sue, in "Bright and Morning Star," prevents Booker from betraying the names of Party members to the police by shooting him. Only in "Fire and Cloud" does the protagonist, a man of the cloth, not resort to violence, though suffering it himself. Instead, Reverend Taylor lends his influential presence to a protest march against hunger, an action far more productive than the shootings and more threatening to white hegemony. The consequences of these acts of black violence against whites are predictable, and Wright is too much a realist to soften them. Three of the black protagonists who shoot whites—Mann, Silas, and Sue—pay with their lives. Indeed, in Silas's case, he knows he will die and is determined to take as many whites with him as he can: "Ahm gonna be hard like they is! So hep me, Gawd, Ah'm gonna be *hard*! When they come fer me Ah'm gonna *be* here! . . . Ef Gawd lets me live Ahm gonna make em *feel* it!" (152–53). Only Big Boy escapes—significantly, to Chicago—but not before witnessing the hideous death of his innocent friend, Bobo, who is burned alive by a white mob.

It is difficult to overestimate the radical implications of these violent black responses. First, no writer—black or white—had ever depicted in fiction to that time black people fighting back, turning the weapons of oppression against their white oppressors. Although in each case, Wright is careful to justify these acts as self-defense (Big Boy, Mann), or retaliation for rape (Silas), or, in Sue's case, defense of her son and his comrades who will likely be killed if their names are revealed, these justifications can scarcely have mattered to Southern white readers. And even to other white readers, safely removed from the South, the prospect of black people picking up guns and firing at whites must have been unsettling. Eleanor Roosevelt spoke for many when she declared that the vividness of the stories had given her "a most unhappy time."[22] These stories announce, albeit prematurely, that the era of black people passively accepting white violence is over. Clearly, the characters behave as Wright would like to see Southern blacks act: fighting back.

But these acts of individual black violence and rebellion are doomed to futility—even Sue's martyrdom in "Bright and Morning Star" cannot save her son, Johnny-Boy, though it may save the other communists. Wright, however, was too sympathetic to social realism, too committed to Party ideology at the time to limit his perspective of Southern racial conflict to pessimistic determinism. Accordingly, "Fire and Cloud" stands out from the other stories in featuring collective action and an upbeat ending. It is also by far the richest and most nuanced of the five stories in presenting a thoroughly believable and sympathetic protagonist, Reverend Taylor, who is torn among conflicting forces: the demand of younger radicals that he lead (or at least sanction) a hunger march through the town; the cajoling and threats of white town leaders anxious to prevent the march; the devious efforts of a black church elder to undermine Taylor's standing; and finally, Taylor's own initial desire to stick to his ministry and stay out of politics. That all of these contesting forces appear physically in Taylor's home at virtually the same time, as Taylor desperately tries to keep them separate and unknown to each other, is both comical and patently implausible. But ultimately this flaw does not diminish the story's power, which rests on the necessity of this influential leader to reach a decision and take a stand.

But it is more than just a decision. In choosing to march with his people, despite his deep misgivings and against his previous inclination, Taylor has undergone a kind of conversion experience from professional detachment to social activism, from believing that "The good Lawds gonna clean up this ol worl some day!" to realizing that "somethings *gotta* be done" in *this* world and now (159, 160). White racists provide the catalytic experience—the sign Taylor has been seeking—brutally whipping him until he reaches the same realization that Silas does in "Long Black Song": that since he's going to die whether or not he fights back, he might as well go out fighting. It is then that he shifts from demeaning himself ("Yyyyessuh") to calling his oppressors "white trash cowards" (200–201). More important, when he returns home, he prevents his son from taking personal revenge for the beating—the non-solution of the first three stories—and instead teaches him the collective truth he has so painfully learned: "Yuh cant do nothing *erlone*, Jimmy! . . . We gotta git wid the *people* son. . . . Gawds wid the people!" (209–10).

As in Wright's political poems, this epiphany is purely Marxist: collective action, not individual retaliation, is the solution; action now to achieve results in this world, not in a heaven by and by. In the march itself, Wright pushes the communist message even further, as the marchers no longer need someone to lead them:"'Ain nobody leadin us nowhere!!' 'We goin ourselves!'" (215). When the mayor seeks Taylor out to represent the marchers, the latter refuses to speak for them—the "state" has withered away! But he does preach his new understanding to the crowd. The sign he had previously pleaded of God ("Show us the sign n well ack!") is now the fire he felt in the lacerating whip (symbolizing all white violence against blacks) and in his anger and determination to resist intimidation—a fire that can only be borne through collective action ("Ah cant bear this fire erlone! Ah knows now whut t do! Wes gotta get close t one ernother! . . . Now its fer us t ack." (218). The fire and cloud that guided the children of Israel in their exodus from slavery is now the fire of pain converted into determined action. Wright cannot resist including a final Marxist article of faith, even though it runs directly counter to Southern reality at the time: poor whites join the poor blacks in the march: "He looked ahead [and behind] and saw black and white marching"—and singing. Thus class trumps race. Perhaps in New York, but not in Dixie in 1937! Social realist aesthetics demands an upbeat ending, and Wright provides one: the mayor easily (and implausibly) caves and promises food for the marchers. Taylor, now baptized in his activist and collectivistic faith, concludes—and as it is the story's closing line, Wright clearly intends us to conclude as well—that "Freedom belongs to the strong!"

It is significant that "Fire and Cloud" concluded the original *Uncle Tom's Children*, for it seems to point to a progression in Wright's literary aesthetics. The first three stories follow a pattern of white violence against blacks, individual acts of black self-defense, retaliation or resistance, and the inevitable punishment these acts provoke. In its pessimistic outcome and sense of inevitability, the pattern of these three stories is essentially naturalistic—a genre that strongly influenced Wright's intellectual and literary development.[23] Not so "Fire and Cloud," in which Wright consciously incorporates the social realist aesthetics of social awakening and collective action to produce a successful outcome. The later "Bright and Morning Star," however, straddles both genres. Like Taylor, Sue converts, albeit too easily, from religious to social belief: "The wrongs and suffering of black men had taken the place of Him nailed to the Cross; the meager beginnings of the Party had become another Resurrection . . ." (225). But her desperate act to save her son and his communist friends results in her death. And, in contrast to her son's Party-line insistence of class over race ("Ah cant see white n Ah cant see black. . . . Ah sees rich men and Ah sees po men"—234), Sue's commitment is as much to her race and family (protecting Johnny-Boy) as to her newfound political religion (preventing Booker from revealing the names of his comrades). It is still the white man who beats her, betrays her trust, and finally kills her and her son. Fabre feels that the story's "fundamental hesitation between the ethnic and the Marxist perspectives certainly reflects Wright's own ambivalence at the time of composition, in spite of his firm propagandistic intentions" (*Unfinished Quest,* 164).[24] Considering that the first three stories in *Uncle Tom's Children* are written exclusively from a racial perspective and that the last—"Bright and Morning Star"—presents race and ideology in an uncertain balance, Wright's "ambivalence" applies to the entire book.[25] In practice, his fiction could not easily transcend the racial focus that he condemned so formulaically in "Blueprint for Negro Writing." That ambivalence would deepen into a fissure with his next novel.

When it was published in March 1938, *Uncle Tom's Children* established Richard Wright's popular and critical reputation: "[I]t brought Wright to the attention of white critics and readers, many of whom had never encountered a black text that so moved and challenged them . . ."[26] Non-Southern white readers might have been able to shunt aside the predominant racism as regional, not representative of the entire country, and the book's violence as typical of Southern Gothic literature. But Richard Yarborough is correct when he calls the book "the most unrelenting and rage-fueled critique of white racism ever to surface in fiction written by blacks directed toward a mainstream American readership."[27] Wright's narrative power made it impossible to elude the book's ominous themes.

Rather like the critical responses to Hemingway's first major book of stories, *In Our Time,* thirteen years earlier, reviews of *Uncle Tom's Children* concurred that the book marked the appearance of a major new fiction writer, an event all the more significant because he was black. Lewis Gannett, one of the judges in the *Story* competition, described why he chose the book for the Book Union's April 1938 selection: "Here was the voice of a new generation of black America; a hard fresh voice in which one could still detect something of the melody of the old spirituals. Here, in Richard Wright, was not merely a prize-winner but a new American writer."[28] Fred T. Marsh, writing in the *New York Herald Tribune*, felt that three of the stories "are as fine . . . as any of modern times" and recommended the book for the Pulitzer Prize.[29] Marxist critics loved the book (though its negro nationalism might have given them pause). Granville Hicks, one of the most discerning leftist critics, enthused, "the literature of the left has been immeasurably strengthened" and "the revolutionary movement has given birth to another first-rate writer."[30] Wright's friend James T. Farrell was also enthusiastic: "[It is] a true and powerful work by a new American writer. . . . It is not merely a book of promise. It is a genuine literary achievement."[31]

Other critics, even those on the left, had more mixed feelings about the book's handling of racial conflict. Malcolm Cowley, reviewing it for the *New Republic*, felt that the stories, though "heartening as evidence of a vigorous new talent," were also "terrifying as the expression of racial hatred that has never ceased to grow and gets no chance to die." Robert Van Gelder, similarly, considered Wright's theme "highly inflammatory." Charles Poore praised Wright's ability to create memorable scenes, but was put off by the one-dimensional depiction of white Southerners. One anonymous reviewer in a Southern paper (the *Jackson* [Mississippi] *Daily News*) went much further than Poore in damning the book's supposed narrowness of focus, titling the review "A GARBAGE CAN BOOK." The reviewer, who apparently only bothered to read "Big Boy Leaves Home" since he or she does not refer to any other story, writes, "The book is nothing more or less than a squawk against lynching . . . . [and contains] plenty of writing about the lynching of a negro and a burning at the stake." Asserting that the book was "obviously written as propaganda" for the NAACP (in its campaign for an anti-lynching law?), the reviewer complains that there is "[n]ot a word in the volume about the millions of white and negro people who dwell together in the South in peace and harmony . . ." The review concludes that Harper's only possible motive for publishing "such slush, slop and drivel" was to make money. Black reviewers, with the notable exception of Zora Neale Hurston, admired the book. Alain Locke, editor of *The New Negro*, a central text of the Harlem Renaissance, saw it as the beginning of "a major literary career."[32] The challenge for Wright was now to build on that beginning.

Wright as Journalist

The widespread praise for *Uncle Tom's Children* was no doubt exhilarating to Wright, but it didn't pay the rent. Until his transfer to the New York branch of the FWP took effect, the Communist Party provided his only source of income by assigning him to the Harlem bureau of the *Daily Worker*, a position he assumed shortly after arriving in New York.[33] According to Earle Bryant, he produced over two hundred articles, mostly unsigned, interspersed with about forty longer articles with a byline.[34] That total equals about one article for every day of Wright's seven months with the *Daily Worker*—an output that obviously demanded most of Wright's time and energy. Given his junior status, Wright had to "submit his articles to other editors who would censure, change or print them, with or without a by-line" (Fabre, *Unfinished Quest*, 147).

Wright wrote about conditions, events, and people in Harlem and also how Harlem responded to national and world events, particularly the fascist aggressions in Europe and the Far East. Having already researched such everyday topics as food prices in Chicago for the local cell there, and having lived in slum apartments there with his family, he was familiar with the specific problems that Harlem blacks faced: substandard housing, inflated rents, landlord evictions and rent strikes, price-gouging merchants, dealing with the Emergency Relief Bureau (ERB), etc. It was a matter of applying this experience to the specific geography, socio-political structure, and current events of Harlem. Here, for example, is an excerpt from a long article (8 Oct. 1937) about the opening of the Harlem River Houses, a federally built and subsidized apartment project. To provide context for these new apartments for "574 Negro families," he writes,

> Harlem is New York's shame spot when it comes to housing. . . .
> Residential segregation has caused Negroes to live as many as 620 to the acre in houses 85 percent of which were built over 35 years ago. On many streets garbage is piled on sidewalks; as many as 15 to

20 percent of the residences have been branded as "unlivable." No electric facilities. No hot water. Violations of the Multiple Dwelling Law are widespread.

With these conditions as a background, it can be seen that the 56,157 Negro families who live in Harlem are not adequately helped when 574 of their number are allowed to live in the Harlem River Houses. (Wright, *Byline*, 50, 53–54)

Other sections of the articles zero in on specific families, contrasting their old and new living conditions. The statistics in the passage above show that Wright did his homework; his perspective is radical. These apartments, while certainly better than the status quo, are merely a drop in the bucket and do not address the more fundamental racial issues of housing, such as "residential segregation," which forces blacks to live in slum housing.

In a story about the "Sheffield-Borden Milk Trust" raising the price of milk by one cent per quart,[35] Wright uses the fictional techniques of a first-person perspective, present-tense narrative to show how this seemingly minor price increase affects a large family on relief:

> Mount the steps at 14 E. 120th St. and knock. The door opens and you hear the shouts of children. Mr. and Mrs. Adolphus Green stand in the center of the front room and ask you what you want. You tell them that you are representing the *Daily Worker* and you want to know how the rise in the price of milk will affect their living. They ask you to come in and sit down; and then they begin to talk.
>
> Here is a family of ten, the mother, father, and eight children . . . .
>
> They have been on relief for more than two years. The children, including the mother and father, are undernourished. . . . Mrs. Green declared timidly:
>
> "I'm always ashamed to tell people how old my children are, they are so small. They simply don't get enough to eat." (33–34)

Wright then provides the grim budgetary statistics for the Green family, noting that although "dieticians of the ERB have instructed Mrs. Green to use eight and a half quarts of milk per day for her children," they provide the destitute family only three quarts daily. The family can only afford two additional quarts daily from their "$63 monthly living allowance." Wright calculates that the price increase will cost them 60 cents per month, "and many a day that 60 cents will mean the difference between stark hunger and [a] skimpy meal for ten people. It means that her children's weight will decrease; it means that during the coming winter they will be targets for rickets and tuberculosis" (34).

Like his approach to economics, Wright's articles on Harlem's responses to international events reflect, as one would expect, the positions of the CP-USA, particularly its anti-fascism. Typical topics include picketing of the Italian and Japanese consulates; Harlem rallies supporting China in its war against Japan; Harlem boycotts of "fascist goods"; and especially articles about Harlem rallies or black volunteers in support of Loyalist Spain. It is noteworthy that Wright replicates the Party line on such controversial and partially concealed issues as the progress of the war that fall 1937, the nature of Soviet involvement in Spain, and the reasons why the Caballero government fell and the Negrín regime replaced it. For example, in a lengthy article on Ralph Bates, an English novelist who had volunteered for the International Brigade and was now on a lecture tour of America, Wright reports Bates's explanations without questioning or challenging them. Thus, the role of the Communist Party of Spain (presumably meaning the Soviets since the local Communist Party of Spain was quite ineffectual) was as "an awakener and organizer of the masses" and it "made the will of the people articulate." Under Communist influence, "[f]rom below there rose companies, then battalions, then brigades, and finally army corps." Moreover, "demands of the People's Front led to the downfall of the Caballero Government. This downfall came in May after the disgraceful uprising in Barcelona." The "Negrín Government is the political expression of the Spanish people's will to win."[36]

As chapter 3 will show, all of these claims are dubious or blatantly false: the Soviet presence, once established, organized and ran the Loyalist military units from above, staffing them with communist generals trained in Russia; the Soviets engineered the fall of Francisco Largo Caballero, who had been resisting Soviet influence, and replaced him with the thoroughly compliant Juan Negrín; and the "disgraceful uprising" in Barcelona—the pretext for removing

Caballero—was also instigated by Soviets in order to purge two anti-Soviet parties: the POUM and the Anarcho-Syndicalists. Finally, the communists' aim to express "the will of the people" was among the least important concerns for the Soviets in Spain. Whether Bates knew his assertions were distortions and lies is not the issue; they simply embodied the Party line on Spain. What matters is that Wright printed them as given. Since he had not been to Spain himself and probably had no access to those who knew the partially hidden truths about the Soviet presence there, he would have no reason to challenge Bates's explanations. And even going to Spain was no guarantee of challenging Soviet myths, as Hemingway demonstrated (see chapter 3). Then, too, on foreign matters, Wright was quite willing to accept and repeat the Party line.

The style of most of these articles is smoothly competent and occasionally, as in the milk article quoted above, quite engaging when it employs fictional techniques to create immediacy and involve the reader more viscerally. Two of Wright's friends from Chicago, however, found his *Daily Worker* pieces forced, perfunctory, and indifferently written. Both Abe Aaron, who had introduced Wright to the John Reed Club in 1933, and Herbert Caro assumed that their supposed mediocrity resulted from Wright's being "less than interested" in his job and being asked to produce when you're not in the mood . . . when you're hungry, worried, down at the heel and down in the mouth. Uncertain of the future . . ."[37] Although their intuitions about Wright's attitude toward his job and his resulting moods are not off the mark, their critiques of his *Daily Worker* articles seem rather harsh in my view. On the other hand, Earle Bryant, who has taken the trouble to collect these *Daily Worker* pieces, is understandably a bit enthusiastic in describing them as "disciplined, sculptured prose." Bryant is more accurate in characterizing them as "well researched and smoothly written."[38] In Fabre's view, "[Wright] was not a particularly brilliant journalist . . ." (*Unfinished Quest*, 151). But if his friends were correct about his lack of enthusiasm—and evidence cited below shows that they were—then the professional quality he gave these articles is all the more impressive, especially considering that he had no previous journalistic experience.

When the subject inspired him, moreover, Wright's journalism rose above professional competency. His articles on Joe Louis's championship victories show both literary skill and social insight. The first of these, "Joe Louis Uncovers Dynamite," published in *New Masses* (8 Oct. 1935), depicts the electrifying effect that Louis's knockout of Max Baer had on the black community of Chicago. Describing how crowds of joyous blacks poured into the streets, blocked streetcars and traffic, and even jumped on running boards of passing cars demanding to know which fighter the driver had favored, Wright captures the crowds' identification with Louis's triumph over a white man. The article imagines a response to an imaginary white fan of Baer: "Didn't think that we had it in us, did you? Thought Joe Louis was scared, didn't you? Scared because Max talked loud and made boasts. We ain't scared either. We'll fight too when the time comes. We'll win too."

But beyond describing this euphoric identification, Wright analyzes what Louis's victory had really released:

> Something had popped loose, all right. And it had come from deep down. . . . Four centuries of oppression, of frustrated hopes, of black bitterness, felt even in the bones of the bewildered young, were rising to the surface. Yes, unconsciously they had imputed to the brawny image of Joe Louis all the balked dreams of revenge, all the secretly visualized moments of retaliation, and He Had Won! . . . . Joe was the concentrated essence of black triumph over white. . . . [of] long-nourished hate vicariously gratified . . . . They stepped out of the mire of hesitation and irresolution and were free! Invincible! A merciless victor over a fallen foe! (*New Masses Anthology*, 162–63)

As Wright would later dramatize in his fiction, the "dynamite" uncovered by Louis's victory and compounded by centuries of white oppression was not pretty: pride, yes, but also "revenge," "hate," and basking in a "merciless" victory.

Three years later, on the occasion of another huge triumph by Louis—his knockout of Max Schmeling in one round for the 1938 heavyweight championship—Wright's analysis of the fight's symbolism delved deeper.[39] Now, he saw both Louis and Schmeling not merely as symbols, but "puppets," their significance vastly expanded and manipulated by publicists and their respective minions to become microcosms of political forces, democracy and fascism, egalitarianism and Aryan supremacy (Schmeling espoused Hitler's racial beliefs), battling on a world stage. Wright himself participates in this expansion of symbolic meaning, reading Louis's triumph as a victory for "proletarian aspiration" (Wright, *Byline,* 161). Although he published other articles on this prizefight in the *Daily Worker,* the venue for this one, *New Masses,* may have inspired a more profound analysis, just as it did for his 1935 "Joe Louis Uncovers Dynamite."

Wright had mixed feelings about writing for the *Daily Worker.* As Hazel Rowley observes, the job did provide him extensive knowledge of Harlem and contemporary black issues, and he rather enjoyed bringing these issues to national (at least nationally communist) attention.[40] But just as he had resented in Chicago having to divert time from his creative writing to mundane Party duties, so he did here too, except now the time demands were virtually all-consuming, the routine more exhausting. To the poet Sterling Brown he complained in October 1937, "This newspaper work leaves me absolutely no time at all for anything else and it's ephemeral" (quoted in Wright, *Byline,* 8). He said much the same thing to Ralph Ellison: "It was not for this that I came to NYC. I'm working from 9 A.M. to 9 and 10 P.M. and it's a hard, hard grind. Can't do any [creative] work, haven't the time. I am thinking definitely in terms of leaving here, but I don't know when."[41]

If Rowley is correct that he also "resented having to write [Party] propaganda . . . and hated toeing the Party line," his articles certainly don't show it.[42] Indeed, Wright's willingness to accept communist orthodoxy was never stronger than when he supported the Stalinist position on the Moscow Trials, signing the "Statement of American Intellectuals" in 1938, which declared that the accused Party members were guilty Trotskyists and constituted a real danger to the Soviet Union.[43] It would therefore be more accurate to say that his willing conformity to the Party's political positions created dissonance with his need for creative freedom and for determining his own leftist identity as an artist. Certainly he was mindful of his debts to the Party. As he stated in the *Daily Worker* (with hyperbole that sounds dutiful), "I owe my literary development to the

Communist Party and its influence which has shaped my thought and creative growth. It gave me my first full-bodied vision of Negro life in America."[44] In this same statement, he still believes that he can integrate his communist ideology and the racial focus of his fiction: "I'm trying to express the Negro's struggles, not as an isolated movement, but as part of the American working class." But if the two foci should diverge (as they did in most of *Uncle Tom's Children*)—or if the Party should try to intrude on his literary priorities, Wright knew which side he was on. He would continue to accept the Party's authority on political issues, not only because it was expected of him as a Party member, but because he actively supported those positions, especially on Stalinism and fascism. But no one could tell him how to construe the status of black people in America or interfere with his literary imagination. Those were *his* bailiwicks, his and his alone.

Writing for the *Daily Worker* produced another conflict that echoed Wright's experience in Chicago: other editors at the Harlem branch resented Wright's literary ambitions and intellectuality. Ralph Ellison describes the atmosphere based on his frequent visits to the Harlem office:

[H]is comrades [at the office] looked upon Wright as an intruder. He was distrusted not only as an "intellectual" and thus a potential traitor, but as a possible "dark horse" in the race for the Harlem party leadership, a "ringer" who had been sent from Chicago to cause them trouble. Wright had little sense of humor about their undisguised hostility and this led, as would be expected, to touchy relationships. Despite his obvious organizational and journalistic abilities . . . the members of the Communist rank and file sneered at his intellectuality, ridiculed his writings, and dismissed his concern with literature and culture as an affectation. In brief, they thought him too ambitious, and therefore a threat to their own ambitions as possible party functionaries.[45]

The writing career that his *Daily Worker* colleagues sneered at suddenly took off, when, on one golden day in mid-December 1937, he learned he had won *Story* magazine's national competition and award and that a prominent publisher would bring out a book of his stories.[46] At this crucial launching point of Wright's career as a fiction writer, his drudgery at the *Daily Worker* must have seemed intolerable, and what he had been contemplating in November—throwing it up—had now become a necessity. One final and decisive factor—alternative income—solidified the decision to leave: the transfer to the New York branch of the FWP had finally come through in mid-December. The advantages were immediate. The pay was adequate. More important, recognized writers such as Wright were not required to put in more than a few hours a day; better yet, they could work at home, checking in at the office only once a week. And he could also apply his newly gained knowledge of Harlem to his work. For an FWP book entitled *New York Panorama*, he handled the chapter on Harlem, researching its history, economy, social structure, and artistic life (Fabre, *Unfinished Quest*, 165). Best of all, he now had time to work on his next big project, a novel he had already started, set in Chicago, but far more sensational than *Lawd Today!* had been.

Writing *Native Son*: 1938–39

Though his *Daily Worker* colleagues may have muttered about Wright's early exit and special status at the FWP, the New York branch of the Communist Party celebrated his new literary achievement and fêted him as one their own. In March 1938, the month *Uncle Tom's Children* appeared, he was guest of honor at the annual ball given for *New Masses*; three months later, he joined its editorial board. Also, in June, a communist reception in Harlem was held in his honor, where he was hailed as "our new comet." His book was translated into Russian, published in *International Literature*, and favorably reviewed in *Pravda*.[47] He was even invited by *International Literature* to spend a year and a half in Russia editing the English language version of the journal. He declined.

March 1938 was momentous for Wright in several ways: *Uncle Tom's Children* was published; he moved from Harlem to Brooklyn, where he lived in the home of friends and fellow-Marxists Herbert and Jane Newton; and he began work seriously on his new novel, soon to be titled *Native Son*. He had known the Newtons in Chicago and respected Jane's literary judgment. In fact, as he completed pages of his manuscript, he submitted them to her for criticism and suggestions. That month, he sent an outline to his editor at Harper's, Edward Aswell, and set right to work. Like Steinbeck, who was writing *The Grapes of Wrath* that same spring and summer, Wright worked intensively, and sent the first completed draft to Harper's in October. Harper's gave him a four-hundred-dollar advance.

Set in Chicago, the novel drew on several sources: Wright's personal experience living in the South Side slums; his work at the South Side Youth Club; the experiences of several young black men he had known growing up in the Deep South (as a composite model for his protagonist, Bigger Thomas); a sensational trial in Chicago of a young black man accused of murdering a white woman; and one influence that critics have not noticed: Joe Louis's boxing triumphs and their effect on the black community. About his Youth Club experience, he wrote, "The Communists [in Chicago] who doubted my motives [in taking this job] did not know these boys, their twisted dreams, their all too clear destinies; and I doubted if I should ever be able to convey to them the tragedy I saw here" ("I Tried," pt. 1, 68). Those same tragic destinies tormented the real-life models of Bigger Thomas. As Wright described in "How 'Bigger' Was Born," the explanatory essay he converted from lectures after the novel was published, "They were shot, hanged, maimed, lynched, and generally hounded until they were either dead or their spirits broken" (437). Those fates sound very similar to those of the black characters in *Uncle Tom's Children* who dared answer white violence with violence of their own. But just as he had moved the setting of his novel to the North—an all-important change from the two-dimensional Jim Crow ethos of hate in the stories—Wright had a different, more complex fate in mind for his protagonist. Neither deterministic doom nor social realist triumph would suffice this time. Finally, the murder trial of Robert Nixon, which occurred when Wright was halfway through his first draft, provided him a shocking example of the racist legal proceedings and sensationalist journalistic treatment of a black killer in the supposedly more tolerant North. To get a thorough background on the murder and trial, he had his Chicago friend, the poet Margaret Walker, send him details of the trial and newspaper articles. Later, he would go to Chicago (just as Joyce had returned to Dublin) to check street names and locations and further research the Nixon trial. He later worked into his novel actual headlines and quotations from the *Chicago Tribune*'s coverage. South Side slums, the blighted futures of young black men, a black murderer caught in the implacable gears of a racist white community and judicial system, with only a few communists attempting to aid him—here were the makings of another *American Tragedy*, a tragedy in black, white, and red. But Wright was not willing to limit the novel's implications to deterministic—and predictable—tragedy; he had another dimension of Bigger Thomas in mind that would utterly transform the story's meaning and make it one of the most profoundly disturbing novels ever written.

About the time he sent off the first draft of *Native Son*, Wright applied for a Guggenheim Fellowship, another index of his expanding self-confidence. Several prominent writers and critics wrote on his behalf, including Granville Hicks and Lewis Gannett. And it didn't hurt his case to have a supportive letter from the First Lady, Eleanor Roosevelt. In March 1939, he learned that he had won the coveted fellowship. For a year, then, he would be able to devote himself entirely to writing and revising and not worry about income.

Meanwhile, he struggled over revising his novel. His most astute readers—Jane Newton and Edward Aswell—were especially critical of book 3 (Bigger's incarceration and trial) and the communist attorney's long plea in particular. But Wright dug in his heels; as will be discussed in chapter 6, he had particular reasons for keeping that speech intact, and he was willing to sacrifice the reader's patience if necessary. In fact, he was not particularly concerned about having readers like his novel or its characters. To Margaret Walker he confided, "I think it will shock people, and I love to shock people."[48] In "How 'Bigger' Was Born," he famously expressed one reason for making his novel a difficult experience for white readers:

When the reviews of [*Uncle Tom's Children*] began to appear, I realized that I had made an awfully naïve mistake. I found that I had written a book which even bankers' daughters could read and weep over and feel good about. I swore to myself that if I ever wrote another book, no one would weep over it; that it would be so hard and deep that they would have to face it without the consolation of tears. (454)

Exactly as Steinbeck intended in *his* big novel, Wright wanted this book to be a bitter pill for white readers' sensibilities, an in-your-face assault in its depiction of contemporary racial conditions in the North. To that end, he daringly created a protagonist who was antipathetic, whose crimes were gruesome, even sociopathic, and, in effect, challenged readers to follow Bigger's limited thinking and violent actions. On 11 June 1939, he sent in the revised manuscript.

Then came a surprise which delayed the novel's publication, but guaranteed huge sales and recognition. The Book-of-the-Month Club had selected it for its readers—a quite remarkable decision considering the novel's inflammatory content. But there was a catch: its editors insisted that certain offensive scenes be deleted or changed. Curiously, the editors did not object to Bigger cutting off the head of a white woman and stuffing her body into a furnace, but to his masturbating with a friend at the movies and to the white woman, Mary, coming on to Bigger. Black violence was acceptable; black-white sexuality was not. Wright complied with those requirements, which seems contradictory, if not hypocritical, to his earlier insistence on retaining off-putting passages and on not courting the reader's empathy. But he must have felt that the changes the Book-of-the-Month Club wanted did not significantly compromise the novel. Doubtless, too, he wanted those huge sales and national promise—even unlikable books can make money. But the revisions took time, and the Book-of-the-Month Club then delayed publication several times, from September 1939 to March 1940. In retrospect, this delay probably increased the novel's sales, for if it had appeared in September 1939, it would have been competing directly with the hugely popular *The Grapes of Wrath*. In March 1940, that novel's sales were falling and another major novel, Hemingway's *For Whom the Bell Tolls*, would not appear until October 1940. *Native Son* thus fit neatly into the interim.

Conclusion

In the years from late 1933 to 1939, Richard Wright made three life-altering discoveries: communist ideology, particularly its relevance to oppressed peoples such as his own; an intellectual and artistic home for himself in the Chicago John Reed Club; and, most important, his calling as a creative writer. His career made astonishing progress in these six years. In late 1933, he was unknown as a writer—even to himself—and barely supporting his family in Chicago. By 1939, he was a nationally known and celebrated writer, the most promising black author of his age, and on the verge of publishing a novel that would confirm this promise and become a landmark in American literature. Truly, he was the comet the Party had called him.

Initially, Wright fused his newfound Marxist ideology and creative writing, acting as an intermediary, as he called it, between the communists and the black community, neither of which, he felt, understood the other. Poetry became his primary medium in the years from 1933 to 1935, encouraged and published exclusively by leftist magazines. Explicitly Marxist, the poems expressed Wright's newfound enthusiasm for Party ideology more than they showed mastery of the craft. Nonetheless, several poems, such as "Transcontinental," conveyed programmatic themes in vivid images and often violent motifs, pointing toward Wright's literary gifts and thematic proclivities.

As he turned from poetry to short fiction in 1935 and 1936, however, Wright's focus also shifted from imaginary black workers raising clenched fists of communist solidarity to real blacks oppressed in the Jim Crow South and fighting back. Literary naturalism influenced these stories as much or more than did social realism, but the two styles did not cohere well in Wright's fiction. Neither did Marxist emphasis on working class solidarity align with Wright's focus on American racism and black self-awareness. In "Blueprint for Negro Writing," Wright held to the Party dictum that negro nationalism must be subordinated to *class* awareness, but his stories still emphasized the former. That same problem would trouble his new novel, which dramatized a young black man's consciousness twisted and stunted by Northern racism. But by now, Wright seemed less concerned with heeding Party priorities. He was no longer writing just to reinforce the beliefs of fellow radicals, but to forcibly enlighten a white readership nationwide.

Practically and intellectually, Wright's relations with the Communist Party, which he joined in 1934, were divided. His support of Party ideology and policy had not flagged by 1939, as shown in "Blueprint" and in his support of Party-line positions such as the

Moscow Trials. Other leftists were beginning to doubt Stalin's actions: his persecution of artists and intellectuals, his terrorizing purges, the highly questionable Moscow Trials. In fact, the prominent leftist magazine *Partisan Review* became a rallying point for the anti-Stalinist Left. But Wright still stuck to the Party line and, like Hemingway in Spain, accepted the Party's increasingly dubious claims about its actions in Spain and elsewhere. Moreover, Wright still believed that social realist aesthetics *could* be given a racial focus because he saw the black working class as potentially the most revolutionary in America.

But his personal relations with the Communist Party were rocky and depended on his Party cell's receptiveness to his needs as a writer. In Chicago, where that sensitivity was conspicuously absent once the John Reed Club closed, his relationship with the local Party quickly deteriorated. New York promised a more receptive environment, but Wright still fought to free himself from Party responsibilities, such as writing for the *Daily Worker*. The Federal Writers' Project and his literary successes enabled him to do so, and as his fame grew, he needed the Party less than the Party needed him. He especially resisted what he considered restraints on his creative expression. In all of these regards, *Native Son* would prove a watershed.

Hemingway

1932–1939

I. The Two Hemingways: 1932–36

THE PERSONA THAT Ernest Hemingway projected to the public in the early 1930s—in his books, stories, and magazine articles in *Esquire*, and in the increasing publicity he attracted—was that of a man who seemed to have everything: immense success as a writer, wealth (the largest home in Key West, Florida, a yacht), an exciting sportsman's life, and, perhaps most important from Hemingway's own perspective, creative independence from—and indeed defiance of—the prevailing leftward shift of his fellow writers and critics. Here was a man's man, who lived the kind of life *he* wanted despite the crippling economic Depression around him—deepsea fishing on his yacht in the Gulf, big-game hunting in Africa and Wyoming—but who could still write the stories that had made him, by the end of the 1920s, the premier fiction writer in America. True, he seemed to have abandoned the novel after *A Farewell to Arms* for nonfictional prose. *Death in the Afternoon* (1932) was a study of bullfighting in Spain; *The Green Hills of Africa* (1935) narrated an African safari Hemingway and his wife, Pauline, had taken.[1] If these subjects were not to everyone's taste and remote to Americans standing in breadlines, they certainly addressed *Hemingway's* interests, as did the hunting and fishing articles he began publishing in 1933 for a new slick magazine, *Esquire*. Moreover, such stories as "A Clean Well-Lighted Place" (1933), "The Gambler, the Nun, and the Radio" (1933), and "The Short Happy Life of Francis Macomber" (1936) ranked with the best he had written in the twenties, and showed that he still had the stuff. And unlike so many of his fellow writers, he was not jumping on the leftist band-wagon because it was the fashion of the times—so he proudly (and repeatedly) declared in his *Esquire* articles and his private letters. He was too busy having a good time to bother with politics; as he boasted in *Green Hills*, "I have my life which I enjoy and which is a damned good life" (25). He simply valued his creative independence too highly to "truckle," as he put it, to the New York reviewers who all seemed infected by the virus of leftist politics.[2]

But as in negatives of old photographs that invert all lights to darks, all of these "positives" had a dark underside in Hemingway's life that disturbed him deeply. The components of this underside do not require psychoanalytical speculation to ferret out; Hemingway made them clear, sometimes in his books and articles and more often in his letters, sometimes directly but more often in the trans-parent disguise of protesting too much—too loudly and too often—that the contrary was true. His writing, his comfortable home life and sportsman's excitements, and most of all his vaunted creative independence from the political times—all of these were sources of gnawing discontent.

Hemingway's home and sporting life is not the subject of this study, which will therefore confine itself to a few observations. In these years of breadlines and Hoovervilles, with millions out of work, out of their homes, out of hope, one wonders if Hemingway ever felt uneasy with his comfortable lifestyle, much of which was financed by his wife's wealthy family. Scott Donaldson writes that he was "troubled by the poverty and misery of the Depression,"[3] but his comments in his letters appear callous. In the summer of 1932, en route to a Wyoming vacation ranch in his new Ford V-8, he was surprised at seeing so many people on the roads looking for work; his comment in one letter is both misleading and defensive: "[N]ow they are all broke where before [in the boom] they were lousy with cash. . . . On the other hand we didn't participate in the boom." In the next sentence, he boasts of getting a dollar a word ($2,693 total) for a story he sold to *Cosmopolitan*: "Think of that in this time of Depression . . . Well well well this depression is hell."[4]

Without question, Hemingway hugely enjoyed his sporting life and especially the African safari that he undertook with Pauline in

1933/34. But in a letter he sends the Russian critic Ivan Kashkin, traces of another emotion may be present: "Being on the sea; the work in catching a very big fish; fighting, fornication, the elation of drinking; a storm; and enjoyment of danger can all . . . give you such a physical enjoyment of life that you can be ashamed of being so happy when most people have no enjoyment" (12 Jan. 1936, *Selected Letters*, 431). As with his brusque dismissal of the widespread poverty around him, was there just a trace of guilt beneath all this publicly declared happiness? And did the good life conceal dangers beyond physical harm? According to Matthew Josephson, who saw Hemingway several times in Key West in early 1937, Hemingway stated, "I could stay on here [fishing at Key West] forever, but it's a soft life. Nothing's really happening to me here and I've got to get out."[5] More important for a creative writer, in making his sporting life the subject of his writing—not just in a book, but in the articles he easily churned out for *Esquire* from 1933 to 1936—was he taking the easy way and selling out his talent? He denied as much to his *Esquire* editor, Arnold Gingrich: "Am probably the only living son of a bitch who is universally believed to have sold out and who did not sell out nor get any dough for it."[6]

The one document that most undermines Hemingway's many declarations of complete satisfaction with his comfortable sporting life is fictional and must therefore be approached with the standard caveat that even in autobiographical fiction, authors can and do invent away from their lives. And those creative divergences are certainly present in "The Snows of Kilimanjaro" (1936). Harry, the protagonist, is not Hemingway, but rather the author's warning to himself of what he easily could become: corrupted by the easy, monied life, having sold out his talent as a writer. This undercurrent of dissatisfaction in Hemingway's life helps explain why, when the opportunity arose in late 1936 to temporarily abandon his easy life at Key West for a dangerous, uncomfortable one in a Spain riven by civil war, Hemingway took it. But two other factors also pushed him: his long-standing feelings about Spain and its beleaguered democracy now under attack, and his personal war with leftist critics in America.

The issue that most bothered Hemingway in the early and mid-thirties—and about which his denials were, correspondingly, the strongest—was how the leftward shift of writers in the early 1930s affected his literary standing with critics and reviewers. Why should Hemingway have cared about this leftward shift? What were his politics then? Repeatedly, he tells his correspondents that he is no communist:

> To John Dos Passos: "I can't be a Communist because I hate tyranny and, I suppose, government. . . . I can't stand *any* bloody government I suppose." (30 May 1932, *Selected Letters*, 360)

> To Ivan Kashkin: "I cannot be a communist now because I believe in only one thing: liberty. . . . [T]he state I care nothing for. . . . I believe in the absolute minimum of government." (19 Aug. 1935, *Selected Letters*, 419)

As these letters suggest, Hemingway's political stance was a kind of Jeffersonian libertarianism, and in one letter to Dos Passos he elaborates: "I suppose I am an anarchist . . . I don't believe and can't believe in too much government—no matter what good is the end. To hell with the Church when it becomes a State and the hell with the State when it becomes a church" (14 Oct. 1932, *Selected Letters*, 375).

Although as a young man, Hemingway had voted for the socialist Eugene Debs,[7] he was no longer impressed with socialists, referring to Norman Thomas in 1932 as "The Sentimental Reformer" (*Selected Letters*, 373). Throughout his life, however, Hemingway sympathized with underdogs and the disenfranchised and opposed dictators and fascism. When the despotic Cuban leader Gerardo Machado was challenged by a general strike in 1933, Hemingway hoped the "lousy tyrant" would be deposed (letter to Max Perkins, 10 Aug. 1933, *Only Thing*, 196). He was. As will be discussed below, Hemingway also cheered the Spanish revolution in 1931, favoring the landless people over the wealthy landowners and the Catholic Church. But he was skeptical in both revolutions that idealistic aims could be translated into an effective government, cynical that corruption was contagious; and when he himself dramatized a version of the Cuban revolution in *To Have and Have Not* (1937), he depicted all but one of the revolutionaries as common murderers.

Hemingway also characterized himself in some letters as disillusioned with politics in general, having witnessed as a journalist in the early 1920s his hopes for a better world dissolve into squabbling and selfish statesmen, amidst rising new dictatorships on the right and left. The new radicals of the 1930s, he asserts, were oblivious to—or too young to understand—these world events of the twenties. He writes to Paul Romaine in 1932, "[T]hey [the current leftists] never even heard of the events that produced the heat of rage, hatred, indignation, and disillusion that formed or forged what they call [my] indifference" (6 July 1932, *Selected Letters*, 363).[8] Being challenged, even attacked, for this political indifference and for his sportsman's life was what most rankled Hemingway. He was not alone among modernists in feeling this political pressure, which had become widespread by 1931/32;[9] but that didn't make it any less irksome.

The pressure expressed itself as carrots of encouragement to write about social (and preferably leftist) topics, combined with sticks of increasingly negative reviews of his three books in the early thirties. His public responses to both were typically declarations of independence, threats to the reviewers, and insults about their status and motives. Privately—and increasingly—he worried about his diminishing literary reputation and discussed with his editor, Max Perkins, how he could restore his standing with the leftist "New York critics."

Repeatedly in the early thirties, correspondents, respectful critics, and friends asked Hemingway why he kept writing about hunting, fishing, and bullfighting, about brutality and sudden death, instead of social subjects; why his heroes, like Frederic Henry and Jake Barnes, were always "isolatoes." Wasn't it time to forget about the Lost Generation and recognize a new one with a new sense of "brotherly purpose," portraying the sufferings of men "bound together in belief"? Wasn't it time to join the "leftward swing" in American writing? How about a novel addressing a strike?[10] Leftist friends approached the prickly writer cautiously: Matthew Josephson wrote to Kenneth Burke from Key West that "he had to 'go slow in bringing Hemingway around.'"[11] Hemingway's responses to these appeals varied, perhaps depending on his mood, the way in which the appeal was couched, and who made it. Generally, he complained to his editors about the "'chickenshit communists' who wanted him to write about labor strife."[12] But his declarations of writerly independence and belligerent threats seem stronger in the early thirties (1932–33) and softened somewhat later on. To Paul Romaine, whose "presumptuous" tone angered the writer, he shot back,

> As for your hoping the Leftward Swing etc. has a very definite significance for me that is so much horseshit. I do not follow the fashions in politics, letters, religion etc. If the boys swing to the left in literature you may make a small bet the next swing will be to the right and some of the yellow bastards will swing both ways. There is no left and right in writing. There is only good and bad writing. (6 July 1932, *Selected Letters*, 363)

To Clifton Fadiman, he boasted that he would continue writing "so well and steadily that he would end by ruining each and all of the reviewers. Every two years he would break one 'lousy critic's jaw,' starting with [Max] Eastman and drawing his other victims by lot."[13]

Once might simply attribute these threats to the bully in Hemingway, a side of him that was becoming ever more prominent in the 1930s. But swagger doesn't explain why he felt compelled to make these threats in the first place, instead of simply ignoring the letters. Similarly, his repeated need to declare to correspondents and reviewers his independence of political movements suggests that these well-intentioned suggestions had struck a nerve. At the very least, his responses show his discomfiting awareness of how out of step he was with the political trend of his times.

He was not always belligerent, however. To Charles Strauss, who had hoped Hemingway's future work after his 1935 *New Masses* article "Who Murdered the Vets?" might be infused with a new sense of "brotherly purpose," Hemingway politely replied that "he would like to get the concept of human brotherhood into his work. But if a man was capable of writing 'truly,' he did not have to take sides overtly."[14] This response, too, is revealing: it refers to the new novel Hemingway was working on then, *To Have and Have Not*, which would indeed mark a political shift in his literary subject matter.

If these letters encouraged Hemingway to change, the reviews of his books in the early thirties slapped him for not changing, growing increasingly harsh with each new volume that ignored the social and political times and dwelled, instead, on Hemingway's favorite subjects. The reviews of *Death in the Afternoon* were more puzzled than disrespectful; this was, after all, Hemingway's first book after his highly acclaimed *A Farewell to Arms*, and in 1932 his reputation was still riding that wave of critical adulation. Still, as Carlos Baker notes, the reviews were "mixed." Granville Hicks and Malcolm Cowley faulted Hemingway's interests for being parochial and not living up to the book's concluding advice to see the world clearly and as a whole if one wants to save it.[15] Others complained about "its endless preoccupation with fatality" and its "he-mannish posturing." The most inflammatory review was Max Eastman's "Bull in the Afternoon," which, in attacking Hemingway's *macho* literary style (akin to "wearing false hair on the chest"), dared to attack the author's manhood: "The fact is Hemingway lacks the serene confidence that he was a full-sized man."[16]

The collection of stories that followed in 1933, *Winner Take Nothing*, also received mixed reviews. Some were now edged with impatience since it was clear from these stories that Hemingway's indifference to the times in *Death in the Afternoon* was not an anomaly and that the author had not at all changed his themes and focus from the 1920s—themes such as existential despair that did not speak to the Depression thirties. Since the short story was a Hemingway specialty, the mixed reviews stung even more than those of the bullfight book, suggesting either that something was amiss with the fundamentals of Hemingway's writing, or, as he preferred to believe, that the critics were just out to get him for not conforming to the times.[17]

The reviews of *Green Hills of Africa* accelerated the plummet of Hemingway's critical standing. John Chamberlain spoke for several reviewers:

[T]his cult of blind action, this glorification of the dangerous life of hunting and fishing, is keeping Hemingway . . . from writing about the life of his times. His animus against "New York literary men" is part of a general animus against ideas. He is fretful when his contemporaries get interested in the underlying aspects, the fundamental meaning, of the human comedy—or tragedy. His book is all attitude, all Byronic posturing.[18]

Probably the negative review that most bothered Hemingway was from the critic he most respected, Edmund Wilson. In his "Letter to the Russians about Hemingway," Wilson, writing an invited response to the Russian critic Ivan Kashkin's assessment of Hemingway, rated *Green Hills* as "far and away his weakest book" and "a great disappointment." The book's foregrounding of Hemingway's freewheeling opinions on life, letters, and New York critics especially irritated Wilson:

> [S]omething frightful seems to happen to Hemingway as soon as he begins to write in the first person. . . . [H]e seems to lose all his capacity for self-criticism and is likely to become fatuous or maudlin. . . . When he expounds . . . in his own character of Ernest Hemingway, the Old Master of Key West, he has a way of sounding silly. . . . [H]e is certainly his own worst-drawn character and . . . his own worst commentator.[19]

Though Wilson was certainly a leftist at the time, he did not conveniently fit Hemingway's stereotype of a critic hoping to "put him out of business." In fact, Wilson's high esteem for the writer's earlier fiction in the same review intensifies by contrast his disappointment with *Green Hills*.

Finally, Granville Hicks, writing in *New Masses*, discerned something in Hemingway's attitudes that other critics had not: "He is very bitter about the critics and very bold in asserting his independence of them, so bitter and so bold that one detects signs of a bad conscience."[20]

In these negative reviews, one senses not merely disapproval but exasperation with Hemingway's assumptions that the American public of 1935—still staggering under a worldwide economic depression, and now confronting the rise of Nazism and the aggression of Italian fascism—would thrill to the expensive adventures of this sportsman in a far-off land and eagerly devour his most casually delivered pontifications on American literature and letters. To the economic and political issues of the day, the book is serenely indifferent—except to the leftist critics who have dared to criticize the author. Leftism had continued to intensify since the early 1930s, and by several markers, reached a high point in 1935;[21] critics and reviewers in its sway had grown correspondingly intolerant of unreconstructed modernists like Hemingway. And despite his disclaimers in *Green Hills*, their attacks were hitting home. Matthew Josephson described his state in early 1937 in terms of the bullfight Hemingway so loved: "They [American communist critics] have certainly gored and maddened him."[22]

Hemingway, however, was never one to take a punch without giving two back, and his published attacks on leftist critics matched their own rising chorus of complaint. *Green Hills* took some shots at both leftist writers and critics: the New York writers are "[a]ll angleworms in a bottle . . . afraid to be alone in their beliefs." And the critics whose praise these writers seek are the "lice who crawl on literature" (21, 109). His December 1934 article in *Esquire*, "Old Newsman Writes," also heaped scorn on "the literary revolution boys," who are making "a nice career . . . by espousing a political cause . . . [I]f it wins [they] will be very well placed." Any writer, he declares, "is cheating who takes politics as a way out. It is too easy." And he advises, "[D]on't let them suck you in to start writing about the proletariat if you don't come from the proletariat, just to please the recently politically enlightened critics" (reprinted in Hemingway, *By-Line*, 183–84).

A more personal—and paranoid—motive for his attacks on the leftist critics also appears in this article:

> Of course the boys are all wishing you luck and that helps a lot. (Watch how they wish you luck after the first one.) . . . All the critics who could not make their reputations by discovering you are hoping to make them by predicting hopefully your approaching impotence, failure and general drying up of natural juices. (ibid., 184–85)

While the latter quotation refers directly to Max Eastman's inflammatory review of *Death in the Afternoon* (and comically anticipates

General Jack D. Ripper of the film *Dr. Strangelove*), the paranoia in both statements—that the leftist critics want Hemingway to fail, his genius to dry up—completely undermines the author's pose of serenity at the conclusion of the article. After reading over his new book (*Green Hills*) and seeing it is "good . . . [and] truly written," the author concludes, "you can let the boys yip and the noise will have that pleasant sound coyotes make on a very cold night when they are out in the snow and you are in your own cabin that you built and paid for with your work" (ibid., 185).

The anxiety that this conclusion fails to conceal is the underside of Hemingway's threats and attacks on leftist critics, and his repeated assertions of authorial independence. His letters, especially to his editor, Max Perkins, increasingly express concern about how unpopular his writing is with leftist (aka "New York") critics, often followed by defiance:

> [T]here is a time in every man's life, if he is worth a damn, when he has to be unpopular. . . . I am against and outside of this present damned YMCA [i.e., communist] economic hurrah business and you will find, when it is over, that I will be neither old fashioned, nor behind the times. I will be the same as always, only better . . . (letter to Max Perkins, 17 Jan. 1934, *Only Thing*, 205)

> With the critics hating my gut[s] the way they do [I] could bring out Hamlet new and they would see no good in it. (letter to Max Perkins, 30 Dec. 1935, *Only Thing*, 232)

This concern even verges on anxiety—dare we call it fear?—about how these critics would respond to his new books, combined with vindictive fantasies in besting these critics:

> Am not very hot about mixing in articles and stories [in a new edition], Max. That just gives them the opportunity to dismiss it all . . . as the trash I write for that Men's Clothing Trade magazine [*Esquire*]. . . . [It would be] damned as a hybrid book and cursed by all that N.Y. outfit that foam at the mouth at the mention of fishing or shooting or the idea that I ever have any fun or any right to have any fun. (19 April 1936, *Only Thing*, 242)

> I will survive this unpopularity and with one more good book of sto-
> ries . . . and one good novel you are in a place where they will all have
> to come around and eat shit again. (7 Sept. 1935, *Selected Letters*, 423)

Even the fear of personal ostracism for his refusal to go left appears in his letters, though again by way of denial. He writes to Ivan Kashkin in 1935,

> Everyone tries to frighten you now by saying or writing that if one
> does not become a communist or have a Marxian viewpoint one will
> have no friends and will be alone. They seem to think that to be alone
> is something dreadful; or that to not have friends is to be feared. I
> would rather have one honest enemy than most of the friends that I
> have known. (*Selected Letters*, 418–19)

Hemingway was not exaggerating this threat. E. E. Cummings, for example, whose early 1930s writing also challenged the leftward movement, wrote of being shunned by former friends in this period.[23] Though Hemingway posed as a proud loner, his letters in this period often contain lonely pleas to friends (e.g., Fitzgerald, Dos Passos, MacLeish) to visit him at Key West (e.g., see *Selected Letters*, 425–28). He was human; he needed friends.

The question then became what to do about his unpopularity with leftist critics, how to make them "eat shit" or, better, how to win them over. The last aim may seem antithetical to Hemingway's professed values. Indeed, he declares to Max Perkins in April 1936,

> They can't tell literature from shit, and I have no more illusions on
> that score, nor any of fairness, nor any idea but what they want to put
> me out of business. Nor will I ever again notice them, mention them,
> pay any attention to them, nor read them. Nor will I kiss their asses,
> make friends with them, nor truckle to them. (*Only Thing*, 243)

But more than anything, he wanted to be number one again, to regain the heavyweight crown from the much-praised John Dos Passos,[24] and that meant winning over these influential critics. And by the time he had made these suspiciously excessive resolutions to Perkins, he had already begun his new strategy of courting leftist critics.

Overtures to the Left

The first effort in this strategy was public, an article published in the premier leftist magazine at the time, *New Masses*, entitled "Who Murdered the Vets?"[25] In early September 1935, immediately following a devastating hurricane, Hemingway traveled to nearby Matecumbe Key, which had taken a direct hit. There, he and two friends provided aid to survivors and undertook the ghastly work of retrieving the corpses of local people and several hundred World War I veterans who had been caught there working on a CCC railroad project. Back at Key West, he received a telegram from Joe North, editor of *New Masses*, asking for an article about the disaster. Given his earlier encounters with *New Masses*, what it represented as the Communist Party-USA's literary magazine, and his expressed contempt for the "comrades," Hemingway had every reason for rejecting the offer. After all, he had once called the magazine, on its revival in 1926, "the most puerile and shitty house organ I've ever seen" (*Selected Letters*, 216). *New Masses* had slammed his 1920s novels and had rejected two of his stories in the mid-twenties.[26] In 1928 its editor, Mike Gold, had called him "heartless" and "too bourgeois to accept the labor world."[27] A few years later, a *New Masses* editor, Isador Schneider, had criticized the "baby talk" simplifications of the so-called "Hemingway school."[28] And more recently, a *New Masses* reviewer, Robert Forsythe, had gotten under his skin by writing in 1934 about "his extreme sensitivity to criticism" and "the suspicion that Mr. Hemingway may have slipped slightly south of genius . . . ."[29] Hemingway responded—typically—by threatening to break the critic's jaw. Thus, he might well have responded to North's cable with the epithet he once expressed to Ezra Pound: "FUCK the new masses and their revolution."[30] Moreover, Hemingway had an alternative venue at hand: *Esquire* magazine was printing everything he sent them and would certainly pay more money for an article than *New Masses* could afford. Why, then, did Hemingway accept North's proposal?

The most plausible explanation is that the article provided an approach to the Left—an overture for which Hemingway would receive leftist recognition—without making it appear as if he were simply caving in to the prevailing pressure to go left.[31] His article expressed rage and made accusations not against capitalism (though it does take a swipe at "the millionaires" who visited the island in winter), but against the federal government for placing these hapless veterans in harm's way and then bungling their evacuation even when weather forecasters knew a hurricane was coming: "Who advised against sending the train from Miami to evacuate the veterans until four-thirty o'clock on Monday so that it was blown off the tracks before it ever reached the lower camps?" (*New Masses Anthology*, 184). This bungling, in Hemingway's eyes, amounted to negligent homicide hundreds of times over. His article concludes,

> You're dead now, brother, but who left you there in the hurricane months on the Keys where a thousand men died before you when they were building the road that's now washed out?
>
> Who left you there? And what's the punishment for manslaughter now? (ibid., 187)

Hemingway wasn't pleased when the *New Masses* editors changed his original title—"Who Killed These Men?"—to the more lurid "Who Murdered the Vets?" without his permission.[32] Still, the article attracted widespread attention from leftists, as Hemingway had intended; it was reprinted in the *Daily Worker* and translated into Russian for *International Literature*, which called it "one of the most important documents of the development of revolutionary literature in America."[33] Granville Hicks, probably the most respected *New Masses* critic of the time, said of the article, "[it] had a quality that had been disastrously absent from his previous work. . . . [It] suggested that Hemingway was going somewhere . . ."[34] James Mellow probably overstates its effect when he writes, "Marxist critics viewed it as Hemingway's coming-out as a political writer opposed to the villainy of capitalism."[35] But it was a start. And in choosing the government and not capitalism as the target of his wrath, Hemingway was safe from charges that he had betrayed his earlier anti-leftist declarations. Michael Reynolds's assertion, therefore, that Hemingway's "anger got the better of his judgment" in choosing *New Masses* is incorrect; Hemingway knew precisely what he was doing.[36]

Three months earlier, June 1935, he had been invited to attend the International Congress of Writers in Paris, organized by the Soviet Comintern as part of the new Popular Front strategy. That the organizers invited him, given his public hostility to leftist politics, seems to reflect their hope of catching a big fish. More surprising still was that, in lieu of attending, Hemingway cabled them greetings.[37] He did the same thing the following year, sending a congratulatory telegram to *New Masses* on the occasion of its twenty-fifth anniversary. In it, Hemingway apologized(!) for not writing a longer tribute, explaining that he was busy working on his novel. He then writes, "Congratulations twenty-fifth anniversary will send you a good story for the fiftieth."[38] As with the article about the vets, the editors had solicited these messages from writers. But no one forced Hemingway to send the wire to a political magazine he had once scorned, or to make it cordial. Though slight, these gestures were signals of his new rapprochement with the Left.

Then there was his statement to a leftist critic, John Weaver, in April 1936, that among the three novels he planned to write was a "study in the mechanics of revolution."[39] By the time Hemingway wrote this, he was well into his next novel, *To Have and Have Not*, which certainly did treat the subject of political revolution, though not in a way that revolutionaries of any ilk would likely approve. Still, the very fact that Hemingway was considering a subject that his previous books had shunned[40] and which he had claimed publicly was not his concern shows how far he was moving towards political engagement. But once again, Hemingway devised a clever way to bring off this new political overture to the Left without exposing himself to sneers that he had expediently abandoned his tough guy go-it-alone persona as writer and iconoclast.

To Have and Have Not

Beginning with its title, *To Have and Have Not* proclaims itself something new in Hemingway's fiction. The protagonist, Harry Morgan, operates a fishing boat for any way he can make money: smuggling liquor and undocumented immigrants, and, as the novel opens, chartering the boat for wealthy fishermen. He is not successful in any of these enterprises, barely making enough money to feed his wife and two daughters. In no previous Hemingway novel does the protagonist worry about money: Jake Barnes makes enough as a correspondent (work that occupies little fictional space) to have a good time; if Frederic Henry needs money, he simply wires his family and presto!—a draft appears. Significantly, neither Barnes nor Henry is married; in fact, Hemingway ends *A Farewell to Arms* by removing the very factors, a future wife and child, that would force Henry to think about things like work and income. Harry Morgan *is* married and worries often about how he'll feed his family in these Depression years. He tells his friend Albert, "[M]y kids ain't going to have their bellies hurt and I ain't going to dig sewers for the government for less money than will feed them" (96). He doesn't attend bullfights in Spain. He doesn't go on African safaris. He scrambles for a living and has real responsibilities.

But if Morgan is a have-not, he still possesses the signal qualities of a Hemingway protagonist: he is tough, resourceful, proudly independent, and knowledgeable and skillful at his trade. Though he loses an arm in a liquor-smuggling shootout, he makes do with one—even uses the stump effectively in making love to his wife— and refuses to feel sorry for himself. As Albert observes, "[S]ince he was a boy he never had no pity for nobody. But he never had no pity for himself either" (98). Hemingway, however, introduces something new by pushing toughness into brutality and, in effect, making Morgan an antihero. He is often and deservedly called a bully, and the way he murders Mr. Sing (after taking his money for supposedly smuggling a group of Chinese to America) shows both his homicidal sadism and his author's virtually pornographic fascination with violence.[41]

In contrast to Morgan's working both sides of the law, his friend Albert plays it straight, takes WPA ditch-digging jobs to try to support *his* family and cannot. Morgan pointedly reminds him, "You're making seven dollars and a half a week. You got three kids in school that are hungry at noon. You got a family that their bellies hurt . . ." (95). Rounding out these portraits of have-nots are the other conchs on Key West—small-boat operators like Captain Willie (who greets Harry as "brother")—and a group of World War I veterans working for the CCC, shunted from island to island in the Florida Keys and presently at Key West—the fictional personas of the future hurricane victims.

In obvious contrast to the have-nots are the haves: the rich whose yachts are tied up at Havana and Key West. Hemingway paints them with a broad brush: they are all decadent, weak, sexually perverse (as Hemingway would construe "perverse"), or, in Helène Bradley's case, sexually predatory. And dishonest, as when Mr. Johnson skips town without paying Morgan the hundreds he owes him for the fishing charter and loss of tackle. In case we miss the point of these contrasts of rich and poor, Hemingway helpfully provides reminders: "The money on which it was not worth while for [Henry Carpenter] to live was one hundred and seventy dollars more a month than the fisherman Albert Tracy had been supporting his family on . . ." (233).

Morgan's desperation to feed his family—the government has impounded his boat—compels him to accept what he realizes is an almost suicidal job of running bank-robbing revolutionaries to Cuba. When his plan to shoot them all fails, his dying words *seem* to make him a proletarian hero: "No matter how, a man alone ain't got no bloody fucking chance." The narrator adds, "It had taken him a long time to get it out and it had taken him all of his life to learn it" (225). Thus rugged individualism is no longer enough. The clear implication—although Morgan does not state it and, given his values, would be unlikely to accept it—is that only when working men band together do they *have* a chance: "Working men, unite and fight!"

If this précis were all the novel offered, leftist critics (the less discerning ones, anyway) would have welcomed it with "hurrahs!" for it would have the components of a proletarian novel: corrupt rich versus hard-working poor; good guy is poor; good guy learns that individualism doesn't work and (nearly) discovers that solidarity is the key. But Hemingway would also have exposed himself to ridicule from non-leftist critics for abandoning his apolitical, independent stance and blatantly currying favor with the Left. Precisely to avoid these accusations while still positioning himself to receive leftist approval, Hemingway complicated these simplistic oppositions to make the novel appear more politically balanced and objective.

Virtually all of these complications appear on the "proletarian" side. First, as noted above, Harry Morgan is only partly admirable, having a murderously cruel and bullying side to his personality. The vets on the island—true proletarians—are even less admirable: with one exception, they are a collection of punch-drunk and rum-drunk vagabonds, making them less than satisfactory subjects for the proletarian writer Richard Gordon. The novel's ridicule of this writer, moreover, is nothing less than obsessive. He fails in *everything* he tries: his novels are "shit," the one reflective vet tells him; he completely misconstrues the meaning of Marie, Morgan's wife, imagining Morgan's sexual indifference to her when the opposite is true. Gordon humiliates himself in his attempted affair with Helène Bradley; he imagines a hackneyed and ludicrous scenario of Morgan's love for the "young, firm-breasted, full-lipped little Jewess" leftist; Gordon's wife tells him off and leaves him; etc. Hemingway's trashing of this character is reminiscent of his treatment of Robert Cohn in *The Sun Also Rises*, and in both cases, the characters were modeled on real people whom Hemingway was determined to "get."[42] Richard Gordon's model was clearly John Dos Passos, and Hemingway had (in his own mind) several justifications for this savage attack: Dos Passos's successful *U.S.A.* novels, his leftist sympathies, and, most recently, their run-in in Spain. In any case, the novel's satire of Gordon precludes it from being taken as proletarian.

Finally, the *professional* revolutionaries in the novel, the Cubans who rob a bank and charter, then commandeer Morgan's boat to get to Cuba, are, with one significant exception, murderous thugs. The worst of the group, Roberto, gratuitously murders Albert and plans to murder Morgan too. Following Morgan's conversation with the one exception, a young and naïve idealist, Morgan thinks,

What do I care about his revolution. F— his revolution. To help the working man he robs a bank and kills a fellow works with him [the lawyer who recruited Morgan] and then kills that poor damned Albert that never did any harm. That's a working man he kills. He never thinks of that. With a family. (168)

By ridiculing the proletarian novelist and demeaning the professional revolutionaries, Hemingway complicates reading the novel as leftist. Likewise, his mixing of hard-working have-nots like Morgan and Albert with the drunken, mind-shattered veterans avoids a "proletarian" label. And to his credit, in virtually all of these groups (except the rich), Hemingway includes exceptions and mixtures: the "nice kid" among the Cuban revolutionaries, the thoughtful veteran, Morgan's mixed qualities. In sum, by establishing a new focus on rich and poor, loafers and workers, and by creating empathy for some of the have-nots, Hemingway has approached the ranks of leftist writers in the 1930s—but from a distance. For in separating Morgan from the indifferent rich, the murderous Cuban revolutionaries, the officious New Deal bureaucrats, the ridiculous Richard Gordon, and the drunken vets, the novel's political stance is slippery and too idiosyncratic to be deemed anything more than proto-leftist. And despite Morgan's final realization, which some would argue is out of character, he never quits *acting* like the tough, independent Hemingway hero. Thus the novelist could not be accused of abandoning Hemingway's earlier values for fashionable leftism.

But it was leftist *enough* to please politically oriented critics and signal to them that Hemingway was finally beginning to come around. Malcolm Cowley, for example, saw the novel as evidence that "he was just beginning a new career" because Harry Morgan evolves from "a tough guy capable of killing people in cold blood . . . [to] a sort of proletarian hero." Alfred Kazin, likewise, spoke of Hemingway as "a promising young novelist" "who has worked his way out of a cult of tiresome defeatism." Phillip Rahv, writing in *Partisan Review*, went even further, referring to the author as having "succumbed to the social muse," and called his "surrender, after nearly a decade of being wooed and reviled by the critics of the Left . . . an important literary event." Interestingly, he sees in Morgan's death Hemingway's farewell to his own past, a death that "may presage Hemingway's social birth." Though words like "succumb" and "surrender" are not compliments and suggest that Hemingway's strategy failed, Rahv's tone is hortatory rather than dismissive, lecturing the new convert on the need to educate his social "consciousness."[43]

To be sure, reviewers of all political stripes noted the novel's many flaws, especially its disjointedness. Its jumping from narrator to narrator (à la Faulkner's *As I Lay Dying*) and between first person and third sometimes obscures who is narrating. A more interesting inconsistency is that, as the novel progresses, it becomes more political. Not only does Morgan's momentous realization come near the end, but so also do the caricatures of the rich, the satire of Gordon, and the Cuban revolutionaries. The novel's intermittent creation accounts for both its disjointedness and its intensifying political themes. Hemingway began it in autumn 1933, well before he began making overtures to the Left. In the first section, originally titled "One Trip Across," Morgan is the brutal individualist, albeit one who is stiffed by the rich Mr. Johnson. The second section, originally called "The Tradesman Returns," was not completed until December 1935—after Hemingway wrote "Who Murdered the Vets?"[44] By the end of this section, one sees a glimmer of solidarity among the have-nots, as Captain Willie helps Morgan avoid arrest and hails him as "brother."

The novel was far from finished in the summer of 1936, when civil war broke out in Spain between those who supported the Spanish Republic (the Loyalists or Republicans) and the fascists who sought to overthrow it, led by General Francisco Franco. Hemingway became actively involved, interrupting his novel and moving much further to the left. It was not until May/June, 1937—after he returned from his first trip to Spain (and after his blowup with John Dos Passos)—that he finished rewriting the novel, inserting Morgan's dying words (chap. 23), the vignettes of the rich on their yachts (chap. 24), and quite possibly the sections (in chaps. 21 and 22) skewering Richard Gordon.[45] The Hemingway who wrote these politically charged sections was not the same Hemingway who had begun the novel nearly four years earlier.

II. Hemingway and Spain 1937–39:
From Libertarian to Stalinist

Hemingway's experience with the Spanish Civil War was intense, prolonged, and complicated. Over the span of twenty months, from March 1937 to October 1938, he made four trips to Spain: two in 1937 (mid-March to early May, and early September through late

December), and two in 1938 (the end of March to the end of May, and September to October)—a huge investment of time, effort, expense, and personal risk for a professional fiction writer who had been living comfortably in Key West. In Spain—and in the brief respites back in the States with his family—he produced a considerable amount of war-related prose: thirty-one journalistic dispatches for the NANA consortium (North American Newspaper Alliance) and at least eighteen magazine pieces, mostly for the new political magazine *Ken*. In addition, he played a major role in producing a propaganda film, *The Spanish Earth*, that supported the Loyalists. Without question, until he began *For Whom the Bell Tolls*, his creative writing in this period suffered from the time and effort he devoted to this prose and to covering the war. As he complained once to Arnold Gingrich, publisher of *Ken* and *Esquire*, "I was really going nuts with [having to write journalistic pieces]. Every time I would get going [with my fiction] I would have to interrupt" (22 Oct. 1938, *Selected Letters*, 472). Nonetheless, he managed to write about the war in a play (*The Fifth Column*, 1937) and five stories in 1938 and 1939. Between his first and second trips, he finished revising *To Have and Have Not*, and well after his last trip (October 1938), he started on *For Whom the Bell Tolls*.[46]

Crucial to understanding all of these works—the journalism, film, articles, fiction, and drama—Hemingway's political attitudes towards the war, towards the Left generally, and towards the Russian communists' role in the war specifically, underwent remarkable changes in these few years. Before Spain, his political views (as he described them himself) were essentially libertarian: the less government the better. In Spain, he became not just a leftist but a staunch supporter of the Soviets' covert and brutal control of the Republican side: a Stalinist.

These changes, in turn, transformed his intentions and purpose in writing about the war: from an incongruous blend of a supposedly objective observer and Loyalist supporter, to engaged writer and propagandist for the Loyalist cause, to staunch defender of the Soviets' role in Spain, and finally to a *somewhat* more independent writer of the play and short stories set in Spain. Tracing and explaining these changes is a complex business, not least because Hemingway's views were seldom single-minded in a war so politically complicated, and his public statements often concealed quite different private opinions. Audience mattered. For example, he presented his purpose in going to Spain to his Catholic, anticommunist in-laws, the Pfeiffers, as to be a neutral, antiwar observer, but he had already quietly donated thousands of dollars to pay for ambulances for the Loyalist side and to pay transport for some Loyalist volunteers.

His deeply felt, emotional views often concealed uncertainties (which Hemingway was never one to admit), such as the need for political sophistication in a man who previously prided himself on being indifferent, if not hostile, to politics. In turn, his political commitment affected his personal friendships, most notably the ugly breakup of his friendship with John Dos Passos and secondarily with Edmund Wilson. Hemingway's erratic behavior in the Dos Passos split has been much discussed by biographers and memoirists, but even he later alluded to it ruefully in a 1943 letter to Archibald MacLeish:

> [If you come down] I promise absolutely not to be self righteous, no good and bastardly as in my great 37–38 epoch when [I] alienated all my friends (who I miss like hell) . . . . I was *awful* for a whole period of years. Too awful for anybody to stand. (4 April 1943, 5 May 1943, in *Selected Letters*, 544, 545)

Finally, Hemingway's marriage to Pauline Pfeiffer was falling apart at the time, and he was carrying on a barely concealed affair in Spain with the author and journalist Martha Gellhorn—conditions that intensified his emotional turmoil.

July 1936 to March 1937:
Neutral Observer or Partisan?

Although the Civil War began in late July 1936, Hemingway was in no hurry to see it. At its outbreak, in fact, he seemed indifferent. According to the journalist S. L. A. Marshall, who fished with him that summer, "[We] talked the whole thing over several times. Hemingway was quite disinterested. He said, 'It means nothing to me; I have good friends on both sides.'"[47] When he did leave Key West that summer, it was to go to Wyoming for hunting. He also had a novel to finish, and by September he felt he was only about three-fourths done with it (*Selected Letters*, 451). Nevertheless, the war grated on his conscience (ibid., 457) and by September he had decided to report on it as a journalist, arranging a well-paying contract with NANA.[48] But even then, he delayed. Though he told Max Perkins in December, "I've *got* to go to Spain," he immediately added, "But there's no great hurry. They'll be fighting for a long time and it's cold as hell around Madrid now!" (15 Dec. 1936, *Selected Letters*, 455).

His motives for going were mixed. Spain, and particularly its bullfights, held special meaning for him, of course, from the time of his first visits there in the early 1920s; and he closely followed the political travails of its recently created republic. Key West was losing its charm: as noted above, he had complained to Matthew Josephson in 1937 about the soft life he was leading there and the need for a change. War had always been one of his specialties as a writer; it certainly provided a more profound subject than fishing and hunting, one which centralized and compressed issues of life and death. Moreover, Hemingway thrived on the danger it promised and anticipated again sharing what he called "the pleasant, comforting stench of comrades" (*Green Hills*, 148). And this was not a meaningless war: it addressed (as World War I had not) basic issues of democracy and fascism, rich and poor, the many and the few, as well as national sovereignty and foreign intervention.

Another reason for Hemingway to go to Spain—a major one in my view—was to dramatically extend his overtures to the American Left, which he had begun with his 1935 diatribe "Who Murdered the Vets?" and was developing in his novel-in-progress, *To Have and Have Not*. Spain had quickly become *the* leftist issue of the mid-1930s for those who supported the Popular Front against fascism, a kind of litmus test of one's sincerity and commitment. As Hemingway himself eloquently put it in *For Whom the Bell Tolls*, "[Volunteering] gave you a part in something that you could believe in wholly and completely and in which you felt an absolute brotherhood with the others who were engaged in it. . . . But the best thing was there was something you could do about this feeling and this necessity too. You could fight" (251). By going to Spain to support the Loyalist cause, Hemingway knew he would win over leftist critics like Cowley and Hicks, who had attacked his political indifference. Even if he approached the war idiosyncratically, they would recognize that he was on the right side, that he had joined the struggle. His explanation to journalist George Seldes provides the strongest evidence for this motive. Seldes recalls him saying, "I had to ('go to Spain' or 'do this' . . . meaning commit himself to the loyalists) before you liberal bastards would believe I was on your side."[49]

Spain and a new war also provided, as Alex Vernon points out, "new stories and people for his fiction. His writing needed it. . . . The war in Spain came along at just the right time." Moreover, Hemingway had a reputation to maintain. As fellow journalist Josephine Herbst noted, "He had answered a definite call when he came to Spain. He wanted to be *the* war writer of his age . . ."[50] Entangled and inseparable, all of these motives drove Hemingway to Spain: the idealistic (saving Spain and opposing fascism)[51], the careerist (winning over leftist critics), the personal (getting away from the soft Key West life, courting danger), even the romantic in pursuing his interest in Martha Gellhorn. Even had he wanted to, it's doubtful that Hemingway himself could have sorted out these reasons.

But on what terms would he go and report the war, as a Loyalist supporter and propagandist or as a neutral observer? The former would earn him plaudits from the Left but the latter might make his journalistic dispatches more convincing and marketable to a disengaged American public and would maintain the fiction of his "above-politics" persona. Could one be neutral in reporting this war? How did he see his purpose? What did he really believe?

The evidence, again, is mixed and suggests that Hemingway held divided, if not contradictory, views. His *actions* before he left show that he clearly supported the Spanish Republic and opposed the fascist rebellion. From as far back as the summer of 1931, when he was in Madrid researching for his bullfighting book—and when the new Spanish republic replaced the monarchy—Hemingway, who had renewed his friendship with the artist Luis Quintanilla, an ardent republican, was "euphoric" about the new democracy. So Quintanilla's son, Paul, writes (possibly with a touch of hyperbole), as he quotes and paraphrases his father's memoir: "[Hemingway] hoped the new government would finally rectify the numerous abuses the Spanish people had endured for centuries."[52] A few years later, when Luis Quintanilla was arrested and imprisoned by a right-wing government, Hemingway (and Dos Passos) supported an exhibition of Quintanilla's art to raise money to free him: they both wrote pieces for the catalogue, and Hemingway donated money. Incredible as it sounds, according to Alex Vernon, Hemingway also helped organize a picket line in front of the Spanish consulate that may have attracted hundreds of marchers and, with prominent American leftist writers, signed a petition for Quintanilla's release intended for President Zamora of Spain.[53] Finally, and most tellingly, in mid-December 1936, Hemingway donated three thousand dollars (a large part borrowed) to the Medical Bureau of the American Friends of Spanish Democracy to buy ambulances for the Loyalist side.[54] The American Friends named him chairman of a committee to send an ambulance corps to Spain. His explanation of this support to his friend Harry Sylvester captures what seems Hemingway's bedrock political view: "[M]y sympathies are always for exploited working people against absentee landlords even if I drink with the landlords and shoot pigeons with them."[55] And, after all, "[t]he rebels have plenty of good Italian ambulances."

Yet, in this same letter to Sylvester (an anti-Republican Catholic), Hemingway also takes a more balanced, non-partisan position: "The Spanish war is a bad war, Harry, and *nobody is right*. All I care about is human beings and alleviating their suffering which is why [I] back ambulances and hospitals. . . . It's none of my business and I'm not making it mine . . ." [emphasis added]. As he notes fascist atrocities (bombing hospitals and the working quarter of Madrid), he also recognizes pro-Republican crimes: "I know they've shot priests and bishops but why was the church in politics on the side of the oppressors instead of for the people—or instead of not being in politics at all?" He ends this letter with another telling remark: "I think that's a dirty outfit in Russia now but I don't like any governments" (*Selected Letters*, 456–57).

Very likely, Hemingway took into account Sylvester's strongly anticommunist views. The same can be said for a letter he wrote a few days later to Pauline's family: "The Reds may be as bad as they say but they are the people of the country versus the absentee landlords, the moors, the italians, and the Germans. . . . I would like to have a look at the others to see how it lines up on a basis of humanity." He adds another reason for going, which would become almost a leitmotif in his public statements: "This [war] is the dress rehearsal for the inevitable European war and I would like to try to write anti-war war correspondence that would help to keep us out of it when it comes" (9 Feb 1937, *Selected Letters*, 458). He maintained the same anti-war persona in public statements, such as his dockside statement to the press when he sailed for Europe on 27 February 1937. The new wars, he warned, were total and would not spare civilians. Clearly, Hemingway saw his job as making this brutality against civilians so vivid that Americans would resolutely stay out of the next war: "[I]f enough people get fear-knots tied into their guts, then we just are not going to get into the next war."[56]

Thus, Hemingway's public persona (and his stance in some private letters) was as an essentially neutral and determinedly antiwar observer, evaluating the humanity of *both* sides. But his acknowledgements of "Red" atrocities in his letters are always undercut by noting atrocities on the right and by his clear-cut sympathy for the "people" and against the church and the absentee landlords, i.e., the supporters of Franco's fascists. Though his views and role in Spain were to change markedly in a very short time, one position did not change: his determination to keep America out of the next war.

Getting the Faith: The Influence of Joris Ivens, Mikhail Koltsov, and Gustav Regler

During his first trip to Spain (mid-March to early May 1937), Hemingway worked on two projects concurrently: writing journalistic dispatches for NANA and helping to make the propaganda film *The Spanish Earth*. Regarding the latter, while still in the States, he had been asked by Archibald MacLeish in January 1937 to participate with other distinguished writers in making a film to present the Loyalist side of the civil war. The writers included MacLeish (the group's organizer and treasurer), John Dos Passos, Lillian Hellman, and Clifford Odets; they called themselves "Contemporary Historians, Inc." Hemingway not only agreed to serve, he quietly put up four thousand dollars to help finance the project.[57] This was not his first involvement in filmmaking on the war. In late 1936 and early

1937, he had helped write the captions for a propaganda documentary entitled *Spain in Flames*.[58] That film was "intended as a kind of stop-gap rebuttal to the commercial newsreels on the war" in American movie theatres: "It would make the case for Republican Spain until Contemporary Historians could present their own films . . ."[59] Supervising both films, *Spain in Flames* and *The Spanish Earth*, was the Dutch filmmaker Joris Ivens.

When Hemingway arrived in Paris in mid-March, he spent a few days in Ivens's company before both traveled to Valencia, Spain. Ivens's influence on Hemingway's politics in Paris and Spain has recently drawn much attention, especially when Ivens's biographer, Hans Shoots, revealed that he was not merely a communist but in close contact with (and perhaps a member of) the Soviet Comintern, and that he had spent almost two years in Russia before moving to the United States to study documentary filmmaking.[60] In his memoirs, Ivens boasted about having converted Hemingway to a strongly pro-Loyalist and pro-communist view of the war. Critics and biographers disagree about the precise degree to which Ivens influenced Hemingway, but no one disputes that his influence was significant.

That Ivens worked closely with the Comintern before making *The Spanish Earth* is clear. From the United States, he had to report regularly on his activities to Mezhrabpom, the Russian-German film studio that made revolutionary films; to the head of the Soviet film industry; and to Amkino, the Soviet film distribution company in New York.[61] When he learned that Hemingway was coming to Spain and had been asked to participate in the new film project, evidence suggests that he lengthened his stay in Paris to spend time with the writer.[62] Indeed, since he was taking orders from the Comintern at the time, he may well have been following Comintern instructions aimed at landing this "big fish" for the Loyalist-communist side, as Stephen Koch asserts.[63] While in Paris, Ivens introduced Hemingway to prominent communists, and he and Hemingway probably discussed, among other things, fascist atrocities in Spain, the factional confusion on the Loyalist side, the disastrous consequences of the non-interventionist policy of the United States, France, and England, and of course their upcoming filming. In his first book of memoirs, *The Camera and I*, Ivens portrayed Hemingway's initial political knowledge of the war as naïve: "[H]e saw no particularly deep implications in this war and was pretty skeptical when I described it as the first test of fascism in Europe, fascism on its first battlefield."[64] Critics Alex Vernon and William Watson are rightly skeptical of this self-aggrandizing narrative, noting Hemingway's pro-Loyalist, antifascist actions *before* he left for Europe.[65] But there is little doubt that Ivens pushed Hemingway's pro-Loyalist sympathy much further and may indeed have seen "converting" Hemingway to a pro-Soviet view as his mission by emphasizing the need for strong control of the Loyalist factions.

In a 1982 interview with William Watson, however, Ivens' claims were more modest: "I set the task to make Hemingway understand the anti-fascist cause. I felt he would be an asset to our cause because he wrote such good articles."[66] Baker called Ivens Hemingway's "Political Commissar," and Watson goes so far as to depict him as a kind of "case officer" charged (by himself or the Comintern) with "recruiting" Hemingway "in order that he would become a contributor, witting or unwitting to the propaganda objectives of the Comintern."[67] Significantly, when Hemingway flew to Valencia on 16 March to begin his war coverage for NANA, Ivens met him there, and the two drove to Madrid a few days later.

To those ends, Ivens not only worked closely with Hemingway on the filming of *The Spanish Earth*, but, perhaps more important, introduced him to prominent Soviet operatives in Madrid, whose presence will be discussed further on. A journalist who wanted special privileges—cars, drivers and gasoline, access to battlefields off-limits to other journalists, better food and liquor than was otherwise available, and most important, the "true gen" on the war— would obviously benefit from cozying up to these Russian leaders. Hemingway could trade on his famous name to establish such a relationship, and Joris Ivens became the intermediary for the newly arrived journalist, providing the crucial contacts.

Ivens handled these introductions carefully. He recalled, "I had a plan for Hemingway and I think I used the right tactics. . . . I didn't introduce him to the Russians when he first asked me. But after four weeks [of our working closely together], I thought, now, he is ready to make that step, and it worked." Ivens continued,

> I knew, for example, [Mikhail] Koltsov of Pravda and some of the Russians. They were living in the Gaylord Hotel and I introduced Hemingway to them so that he would know some other communists. That gave him an edge and with it came more confidence, which for him was very important, because other correspondents did not have this access. So through me he was able to get accurate, first-hand information. I didn't keep any secrets from him. "Yes, here are the Russians," [I said]. For many people the Gaylord Hotel was some kind of secret center.[68]

Two details should be noted in these important passages. First, according to Ivens, Hemingway *asked* to be introduced to the Russians well before Ivens did so, undermining the image of Hemingway as a naïve dupe. Second, the edge these introductions gave him was psychological as well as material and professional: "with it came more confidence, which for him was very important, because other correspondents did not have this access." Hemingway was always intensely competitive, so, in part, these introductions and the relationships they created enabled him to scoop other journalists. But I believe that the confidence Ivens describes also implies Hemingway's insecurity when he arrived in *not* knowing the ins and outs of this complicated and concealed politics. Ivens, and especially Mikhail Koltsov and Gustav Regler, provided Hemingway that "insider" information he could obtain in no other way.

The Russian journalist and propagandist Mikhail Koltsov, who wrote for *Pravda* and *Izvestia*, was close to the center of Russian operations in Spain and thought to have reported directly to Stalin: "Stalin's eyes and ears on the spot," Martha Gellhorn called him.[69] He was even suspected of ordering a major execution of government prisoners in the fall of 1936, the "Model Prison" executions.[70] Years later, Hemingway described his relationship with Koltsov: "He knew I was not a Communist and never would be one. But because he believed in me as a writer he tried to show me how everything was run so that I could give a true account of it."[71] In *For Whom the Bell Tolls*, the Russian journalist Karkov (a thinly disguised Koltsov even in the similarity of their names) plays a major role in keeping the protagonist, Robert Jordan, well-informed with inside information on various battles and intelligence operations. For example, Jordan learns from Karkov that political executions were practiced "very very extensively" (261). Precisely what Hemingway learned from Koltsov is not known, but Donaldson surmises, "He learned . . . that Russian communists were taking charge of the political and military structure of the Spanish Republic" and also that the Kremlin "did not want it known that there were Russians in Spain." Not coincidentally, Hemingway's journalism and early fiction about the war denied Soviet presence. Like Joris Ivens, Koltsov saw Hemingway as an important "asset,"[72] yet a novice whose views could be molded. In turn, Hemingway considered him "the most intelligent man I have ever met"[73]—precisely what Robert Jordan says of Karkov (247).

Hemingway's third tutor was Gustav Regler, the political commissar of the Twelfth International Brigade. Hemingway became good friends with Regler and accompanied him several times on tours of battlefields near Madrid. Like Koltsov, Regler considered Hemingway a kind of novitiate-friend and shared confidential information with him. As Regler recalled, during the spring of 1937,

> I told him the inside stories of operations and crises which I had witnessed earlier. I let him know our losses and gave him advance information whenever I could, feeling certain that he could really understand what it was all about. I gave him secret material relating to the Party, which he respected, because it was fighting more actively than any other body . . .[74]

Regler also joined Hemingway and Koltsov at the Gaylord. Of this troika of tutors, Stephen Koch describes Koltsov as the leader, mentor to both Ivens and Regler.[75]

Armed with his new knowledge and orientation about the war—from the Soviet perspective—Hemingway was able to restore the persona so important to him as the "master" of a particular subject, be it war, bullfighting, big-game hunting, deep-sea fishing, and now the tangled politics of Loyalist Spain. From the beginning of his time in Spain, he also took advantage of the other privileges (described above) that his high status and Russian contacts provided.[76] Other journalists living at the Florida Hotel, for example Josie Herbst, wrote about the good smells often wafting from Hemingway's room. To his credit, he generously shared some of these goodies, though this largesse, of course, redounded to his prominence. As he became working friends with the correspondents Herbert Matthews and Delbert Sifton, he provided them transport in his car to various locales. And he made his rooms at the Florida Hotel readily available to any International Brigade volunteer who wanted a hot shower, good food and liquor, or a chance to listen to Chopin on a record player or nap on a comfortable bed. Hemingway's letters and short fiction (e.g., "Night Before Battle") describe the hive of activity and "crashing" his room had become for these volunteers. Perhaps he felt guilty about his privileges. In his play, *The Fifth Column*, he projects this soft living onto Dorothy Bridges, but in *For Whom the Bell Tolls*, Robert Jordan recalls ruefully that, regarding his access to Russian-controlled privileges at the Gaylord Hotel, "I corrupted very easily" (245).

Though he was never required to "pay" for these advantages in his writing about the war, Hemingway voluntarily adopted and staunchly defended the Russian-communist view of the war: its actions and depictions of other Loyalist groups. As Watson summarizes,

> He supported their campaign to get rid of the politically based militias and to reorganize the military under a unified command. He joined them in their attacks on the anarchists and the anti-Stalinist Communists [the POUM] as Gestapo-infiltrated traitors. He saw the war, as they did, as an international conflict—a war of resistance against foreign invasion, a war against international fascism—and virtually ignored, even denied, the social and political conflicts in Spain itself that had provoked it and now fueled its most bitter passions.[77]

In one important sense, Hemingway didn't need to be indoctrinated—or lured by rewards—to take the side of the Russian communists. Despite—or perhaps because of—their brutal methods, the Russian leadership, he believed, promised the best and likeliest chance of a Loyalist victory in the chaotic situation of diverse and squabbling pro-Loyalist groups, each with its own agenda, leadership, possibly a militia, and questionable ability to work with other groups and the government. Add to this chaos the infusion of tens of thousands of foreign volunteers—the International Brigades—and the argument for a single, authoritarian leadership becomes even stronger, even when its methods directly contradicted much of what Republican Spain stood for. Hemingway never changed this view, adopted early on, that authoritarian Russian leadership was essential for the Loyalists to win. In *For Whom the Bell Tolls* (178), Robert Jordan makes the case succinctly that the communist discipline he fought under "offered the best discipline and soundest and sanest for the prosecution of the war" (see chapter 7). What Jordan does not comment on is the painfully ironic paradox of this logic: In resorting to brutal means to prevail over the fascists, Republicans must abandon democratic values—the very values on which the government was formed—and use quasi-fascistic methods.

Thus were Ivens, Koltsov, and Regler successful in winning Hemingway to the communist position on the war. As Watson summarizes: "it is doubtful that without their efforts to bring his views into alignment with those of the Communist International, Hemingway would have become, not just a champion of the Loyalist cause, but a defender and supporter of the Communists in their political campaigns as well."[78]

The Spanish Earth

After Hemingway spent a few days reporting on battle fronts near Madrid for NANA, while Ivens and cameraman John Ferno were in Valdesas, the film crew reassembled in Madrid, and in late March through early April they shot scenes on the Madrid front: at Casa del Campo, Morata de Tajuña, and the Arganda Bridge. Hemingway actively participated in the filming, scouting shooting locations and sharing the very real danger involved in working close to the front lines. Ivens recalled that Hemingway pitched right in, "carrying anything that had to be carried," "taking orders willingly," and using his knowledge of combat to make suggestions about filming the battles. Ivens wanted more than help, however; in Watson's view, by having Hemingway participate, he aimed "to integrate him into a network of contacts, experiences, and even friendships that would gradually bring Hemingway into the framework of the Comintern propaganda apparatus . . ."[79] The filming experience also strengthened their friendship and mutual trust as they shared dangers like war comrades. Ivens comments, "You know yourself that if you are on the front line with a man even for one day, you come to know who he is. We saw each other and we held each other in high regard. . . . So this friendship grew out of mutual respect . . ."[80] By the end of their work together in Madrid, Ivens trusted Hemingway's judgment enough to leave him in charge of Ferno and Sydney Franklin when Ivens left to film in Fuentedueña.[81]

The film crew—Ivens, Hemingway, Ferno, Franklin, and often Gellhorn—faced nearly the same dangers, dirt, fatigue, and fear as the front-line soldiers they filmed. Hemingway captured these experiences vividly in an article he wrote for *Verve* magazine the following year. Because they had moved into the danger zone and received several shots from a rebel sniper, the crew hurriedly moved back to a safer location in an abandoned house overlooking the front line. Hemingway writes,

> [Y]ou ran with cameras, sweating, taking cover in the folds of the terrain on the bare hills. There was dust in your nose, and dust in your hair and in your eyes, and you had the great thirst for water, the real dry-mouth that only battle brings. Because you had seen a little of war when you were young you knew that Ivens and Ferno would be killed if they kept on because they took too many chances. ("The Heat and the Cold," 46)

Thus, it was Hemingway who advised them to pull back. He then adds a remarkably candid admission: "And your moral problem was to get clear how much you were holding them back from necessary and just prudence based on experience, and how much was simply the not so pretty prudence of the burnt monkey who dreads the hot soup" (46).

Dos Passos soon joined the group, and a disagreement with Hemingway either began or renewed itself about what to film—the war (Hemingway) or struggles of the Spanish peasants (Dos Passos). A compromise was reached: The film would show both the war and the civilian sides of the struggle. The split with Dos Passos went much deeper than differing conceptions of the film, however. Their bitter falling out over the José Robles affair occurred at this time. Dos Passos and Ivens soon left to film the village of Fuentedueña and the peasants' struggle there to build their own irrigation system for the first time. After more filming of Casa del Campo with Ferno, Hemingway left with Gellhorn for a ten-day trip into the Guadarrama Mountains.

Ivens, Hemingway, and Gellhorn left Spain about the beginning of May 1937. After a few days in Paris, all returned to the United States. Gellhorn and Ivens stayed in New York editing the film and adding sound effects. Marc Blitzstein composed and Virgil Thomson arranged a music score, using Spanish folk songs. Hemingway returned to Bimini and Key West, but made several trips to New York to help with the editing. Several weeks later, after Orson Welles's narration proved unsatisfactory, Hemingway re-recorded the voice-over narrative. In the meantime, the American Writers' Congress was holding its second biennial meeting of writers (including Richard Wright) in early June 1937. *The Spanish Earth* was shown, sans narration, on 4 June at Carnegie Hall, with Ivens providing a running commentary. Hemingway was invited to give the keynote speech. To a packed house of 3,500 (with many more turned away), Hemingway spoke briefly about the fundamental incompatibility of fascism—"a lie told by bullies"—with any kind of truthful writing. By all accounts, he brought down the house. In the much-quoted recollection of Paul Romaine, "It was magnificent. As if everyone had taken him into their arms—truly a companion in arms in the fight against fascism. How could this fight be lost now, with Hemingway on our side?"[82] One might be tempted to discount Romaine's recollection as swollen by nostalgia. But an article appeared the following year in the *Partisan Review*, entitled "Substitution at Left Tackle: Hemingway for Dos Passos," noting not only Hemingway's rise in standing with the Left, but Dos Passos's corresponding decline. If, as I believe, one major reason for Hemingway's Spanish involvement was to regain the esteem of fellow writers and critics who had gone left, esteem that he had enjoyed in the 1920s but lost in the first half of the thirties, he had clearly succeeded.

Less successful was the film's impact on President Roosevelt. Through her friendship with Eleanor Roosevelt, Gellhorn obtained an invitation to show the film at the White House on 8 July, hoping of course to change the government's policy of non-intervention. Ivens and Hemingway accompanied her and the latter was impressed by neither the president—"very Harvard charming and sexless and womanly" (*Selected Letters*, 460)—nor the dinner they were served. In turn, the Roosevelts were only mildly supportive of the film, suggesting that it needed to make the Loyalist cause clearer to an uninvolved American public and to emphasize more the peasants' struggle to cultivate their land as an underlying cause of the conflict—just what Hemingway did not want to hear. In any case, the film effected no change in American foreign policy.

From there, the film went to Hollywood, with Hemingway, Pauline (subbing for Martha?), and Ivens flying there and showing the film at several private parties and one public event. At one of the private parties Scott Fitzgerald was present—he had also heard the Hemingway speech and the resulting adulation at Carnegie Hall. His telegram to Hemingway expressed uncritical admiration: "The picture was beyond praise and so was your attitude." To Max Perkins, their mutual editor, however, he was more discerning: "I felt he was in a state of nervous tensity, that there was something almost religious about it."[83] The film's showings in Hollywood were hugely successful in raising tens of thousands of dollars for medical supplies and ambulances. But otherwise, it was preaching to the choir. It failed to get widespread distribution—distributors were leery of its propaganda—and played in only few big-city theatres. When it opened in New York, Hemingway was already en route for Spain again.

How successful was the film as propaganda and as a quality documentary in a decade of documentary films, photos, and literature? It may have enlightened some viewers—how many is impossible to say—about the issues in Spain and converted some to the Loyalist side, and it certainly strengthened the pro-Loyalist sympathies of those already predisposed towards the Spanish Republic. One reviewer—John T. McManus of the *New York Times*—shared the Roosevelts' view that the scenes showing the peasants struggling, "not for broad principles of Muscovite Marxism, but for the right to the productivity of a land denied them through years of absentee landlordship" were the most effective in the movie. But in a second review the next day, McManus also criticized the producers' emphasis on propaganda: "They have used [the film] as a violent outcry against fascism. Ivens might have made it lasting art as well."[84]

McManus's criticism should be considered in the context of the extremely limited resources available in making the film. Overall, it has both the benefits and shortcomings of what looks like an amateurish production. The hand-held cameras filming the marching troops and the jerky movements of filming under fire at the front lines convey authenticity; and the scenes depicting the bombing of civilians in Madrid are an unforgettable image of civilian fear in a total war. But the abrupt cutting back and forth between the war and civilian scenes is jerky, the land-cultivating scenes themselves border on tedious. The voice-over narrative is mostly prosaic and redundant, but at the end Hemingway's prose achieves simple eloquence as he describes—and the film simultaneously shows—the Loyalists fighting to hold the Arganda bridge: "Six men were five. Then four were three, but these three stayed, dug in and held the ground. Along with all the other fours and threes and twos that started out as sixes. The bridge is ours. The road is saved."

What is most grindingly monotonous are the crude sound effects—the unrelenting (and false-sounding) tapping for machine-gunning, for example—and the music, comprising Spanish folk songs. The shrieking winds sound like chalk perpetually squeaking on blackboards. The problem with the film, then, is not that it is propaganda—that is a given considering its purpose and focus—it's that the propaganda is often crudely accomplished.

The NANA Dispatches

Hemingway wrote thirty-one dispatches for NANA over his first three trips to Spain; he did not represent the syndicate on his last trip. Twenty-eight of these dispatches were printed. (He destroyed one, about the battle of Teruel, and two others remain in manuscript.) The published dispatches were widely circulated, printed in sixty newspapers throughout North America and Europe, and several were reprinted by *New Republic, Time,* and the British magazine *Fact.* Nine were later reprinted in *By-Line: Ernest Hemingway* (1967).[85] William White's view is thoroughly plausible that Jack Wheeler, general manager for NANA, hired Hemingway "because [he] was a celebrity and a name that could sell NANA's syndicated services. . . . Wheeler wanted color and drama and the personal adventures of the celebrated writer."[86] In turn, the dispatches provided Hemingway high fees and the opportunity to increase his public recognition, just as his *Esquire* articles had earlier in the thirties. As in those articles, he could again present himself as an expert on a particular subject, in this case war and military strategy. But the dispatches also provided a means to win support for the Spanish Loyalists, that is, to serve as propaganda for the side Hemingway had supported all along. The persona of "neutral antiwar observer" who would investigate both sides "on the basis of humanity" was gone by the time Hemingway arrived in Spain in March 1937, if indeed it had ever existed.

As Watson notes, the dispatches encompass a range of types and styles, including a few human interest stories; depictions of war's brutality in the bombing of civilians (though oddly omitting the Guernica bombing); gruesome close-ups of dead Italian soldiers (accompanied by stills of same taken by Hemingway); and, very occasionally, an explicitly political appeal for Loyalist support and against the non-intervention policy of England, France, and the United States. As an example of the last, Dispatch 2 (15 March 1937, *By-Line,* 14–15) indirectly ridicules the policy by describing the "12,000 Italian troops" that had no trouble entering Spain (bringing the total number to "88,000" Italians and "16,000–20,000" Germans in Spain). Meanwhile, "the French border is closed up and airtight" for anyone else wanting to enter Spain. Political topics were subject to two forms of censorship (three, including self-censorship). First, the Republican government strictly censored every journalist's dispatches for anything it considered anti-Loyalist or likely to reduce support for the cause abroad. NANA editors also exerted a kind of censorship in limiting Hemingway to the colorful stories it wanted, often by explicitly ordering him to stop dispatches that diverged from that aim. Controversial topics were to be avoided. As Virginia Cowles, another journalist in Spain, recalled, "The International Brigades were not allowed to be publicized; no reference could be made to Russian armaments . . ."[87] And if Russian armaments couldn't be mentioned, Russian leadership surely could not be. Thus, not only do Hemingway's dispatches exclude any instances of Russian or Spanish governmental repression, they don't mention Soviet operatives and generals at all! Nor do they mention, except in one elliptical instance, the International Brigades that fought for the Loyalists.[88] Thus, Phillip Knightley's harsh criticism of Hemingway's journalism for not mentioning examples of Russian brutality seems unfair as applied to the NANA dispatches.[89] (Hemingway's silence in the *Ken* articles, however, where he had almost carte blanche to say what he wished, is quite a different matter and will be discussed below.)

Given these dual forms of censorship, and prudently considering his limited experience in the labyrinthine complications of Spanish politics, Hemingway chose to devote most of his dispatches to two closely related subjects about which he had considerable knowledge and experience: close-up accounts of individual battles and military tactics, strategy, and prognoses.

In describing particular battles, Hemingway was at his best, applying the fictional techniques of precise and vivid imagery for which he was famous. We get the exact sound—or as close as onomatopoeia can come to it—of shells flying overhead or landing close by:

> Our shells were going overhead sounding like downcurving aerial subway trains with a boom at the end. (Dispatch 6, 9 Apr. 1937, *By-Line*, 24)

> (at this moment while writing this back in the hotel a shell just came in on the roof of a building just behind the hotel, exploding with a great whoom . . .) (Dispatch 5, 26 March 1937, *By-Line*, 21)

> Or rifle shots: "*tacrong, carong, craang, tacrong . . .*" (Dispatch 8, 18–19 Apr. 1937, *By-Line*, 30)

Though at times he gets the combat second-hand (as in some of the Guadalajara battles around Madrid, which he arrived too late to see), the battles he does witness have an unmistakable sense of authenticity:

> We went forward on a path through the heavy green-moss-trunked trees of the old royal hunting lodge with shells bursting around us in the heavy woods. The only one that came with that authentic personal final rush of splitting air that you flatten to without choice or pride hit a big linden tree twenty yards away and splintered new spring-sapped wood and steel fragments ripped out together. We were stopped within three hundred yards of the front line . . . (Dispatch 6, 9 Apr. 1937, *By-Line*, 24)[90]

These close-up narratives also bolster an image that Hemingway had carefully cultivated for years: that of a brave man who, despite the dry-mouthed fear that came with being under fire, performed courageously and competently. This was not merely an image, however; by the accounts of those who worked with him, Hemingway did his various jobs with a conspicuous indifference to danger. A famous photograph by Robert Capa shows him lying down at the front lines at the battle of Teruel (December 1937), helping a Loyalist soldier with his rifle. Hemingway describes the experience briefly in Dispatch 18: "[T]he soldier I was lying next to was having trouble with his rifle. It jammed after every shot and I showed him to knock the bolt open with a rock" (21 Dec. 1937, *By-Line*, 65).

At times, his descriptions of feeling fear sound like ill-concealed boasting:

> Your correspondent entered Lérida today. It is not very hard to do. All you have to do is keep your legs moving steadily and control a slight tickling sensation between your shoulder blades and the base of your neck as you cross a railway yard and come under machine gun fire from a tower 500 yards away (Dispatch 27, 29 Apr. 1938, *By-Line*, 85)

But far more often, that dry-mouthed fear he often refers to sounds like a candid admission, and in one exceptional instance (described above in the retreat to a safer filming location) Hemingway even wonders if fear has caused his prudence.

As a military analyst, Hemingway used his considerable knowledge of tactics, strategy (sometimes even referring to Clausewitz), and skills in reading maps and terrain to explain with detailed precision and insight the unfolding of particular battles. Watson's mild criticism that the technicality of some of these passages make them better suited for a war college is valid, but Hemingway's command of his subject here is nonetheless impressive.[91] He coupled these analytical skills with frequent predictions about what each side would likely do—or have to do—in the near future. He also made longer-range predictions about what direction the war would take a year or more out. The accuracy of these predictions and assessments varied considerably. Generally, the closer his predictions were to the present, the more accurate they were. As early as his fourth dispatch, he writes, "To win the war Franco must either encircle Madrid and cut the line of communications to the coast from Teruel, thus separating Barcelona from Valencia, or come up the coast and take Valencia." Eventually, Franco did both. Yet, in the very next paragraph, Hemingway grossly overestimates the significance of the Loyalist victory over Italian troops at Guadalajara: "It looks as though the turn in the fortunes of this war came when the supposed invincible Italian mechanized columns were defeated . . ." (22 March 1937, *By-Line*, 20). This overestimation might be explained by the newly arrived Hemingway's callow enthusiasm for the Loyalists. His estimates of this battle's importance are even more ludicrous in his next dispatch: "It is impossible to overemphasize the importance of this battle . . . . [T]he battle of Brihuega will take its place in military history with the other decisive battles of the world" (Dispatch 5, 26 March 1937, *By-Line*, 22).

His commitment to the Loyalists and his ever-present awareness that what he wrote might influence attitudes in the United States—nobody likes backing a loser—deeply impaired his long-term military assessments and predictions, especially those written during his third trip in spring 1938, when Franco's forces had made large gains in the north and Loyalist victories were few.

Repeatedly, Hemingway falls back on optimistic scenarios of the future, when the Loyalists will have successfully trained and organized their forces:

> [T]ime is working for the Government in that every day that Bilbao holds out they are training a new army which will have 600,000 men in the field by this fall. (Dispatch 11, 9 May 1937, *By-Line*, 42)

> [Regarding the government's "nibbling offensive in the extreme north of Aragon"]: They can fight on this way indefinitely, improving their positions while they forge their troops into an attacking army . . . for operations on a grand plan. (Dispatch 16, 6 Oct. 1937, *By-Line*, 58)

In both the NANA dispatches and the *Ken* articles of 1938, he repeats the hopeful prediction that, given the Loyalists' demonstrated ability to resist fascist attacks and regroup, the war won't end anytime soon, indeed will still be going on a year from "now." As Franco's drive to the sea forced the Loyalists into a massive retreat, Hemingway, while conceding the retreat, holds tightly to a beleaguered optimism:

> [S]eeing the fight being made for Tortosa today, you see the extent and seriousness of the Government resistance. It is not over yet by a long shot, and one thing that has been learned in this Spanish war is that anything can happen and the experts are always wrong. (Dispatch 21, 5 Apr. 1938, *By-Line*, 75)

By 1 May 1938, his tone becomes extreme and belligerent: "Anyone who thinks the war is over in Spain is a fool or a coward" (Dispatch 28, *By-Line*, 88).[92] Hemingway continued publishing these predictions right up to his last dispatch on 10 May 1938—"[T]here is a year of war clearly ahead . . ."—*after* he had privately expressed concern to the U.S. Ambassador to Spain for the safety of American medical volunteers once the fascists prevail. In fact, the war ended on 28 March 1939, when Madrid fell to the fascists, only a few months before Hemingway's prediction.

If his unduly optimistic assessments can be construed as propaganda for the Loyalists, Hemingway's attacks on the Spanish anarchists and the POUM party (the anti-Stalinist communists) in both the NANA and *Ken* articles more narrowly reflect his full support of the Soviet position in Spain. In discussing the battle of Belchite, for example, he directly attacks the "noncombativity of the Anarchist and P.O.U.M. troops":

> The P.O.U.M. troops have boasted they have never lost a foot of ground on the Aragon front, but they omitted to state that they hadn't lost a man either in six months of so-called fighting nor ever gained a yard. (Dispatch 13, 13 Sept. 1937, *By-Line*, 50)

> [T]he Anarchist columns . . . had so much respect for the problem [of attack that] they had avoided all contact with the enemy. . . . [Their] only contact . . . was on the purest friendly basis, . . . when the Anarchists would issue invitations to the Rebel forces for football matches. (Dispatch 14, 23 Sept. 1937, *By-Line*, 52–53)

Though they bear Hemingway's name, these dispatches sound as if they came directly from Mikhail Koltsov's propaganda machine. Indeed, they provide post-facto justification for the Soviet-Loyalist purge of both groups in May and June 1937. At times, in fact, Hemingway coyly alludes to his special "insider" status with the Russians: "[A]ccording to official figures released exclusively to me today . . ." (Dispatch 10, 30 Apr. 1937, *By-Line*, 37). As Watson summarizes about Hemingway's political stance in his journalism,

> What must have struck many close observers of Hemingway's political conduct in the spring and summer of 1938 was how often and consistently he seemed to agree with the Communists' position on many issues. He . . . condoned the use of force to get rid of [the militias], knowing full well that these units belonged to the political enemies of the Communists. Hemingway consistently disparaged the Anarchists and the POUM . . . . He appeared to agree with the Communist-promoted purges of Largo Caballero and Prieto from the Spanish Government . . . [and] blamed the alleged Gestapo-infiltrated Anarchists and POUM for the Republican defeats in Aragon . . .[93]

The *Ken* Articles and Other Pieces

During and after Hemingway's third trip to Spain (31 March to late May 1938), he began submitting articles to a new magazine, *Ken*, published by his friend Arnold Gingrich and David Smart. Like Gingrich's *Esquire*, *Ken* was to be a mass-circulation magazine, but political: "one step left of center" and specifically antifascist. As with his arrangement with *Esquire*, Hemingway had virtual carte blanche to write whatever he chose, and Gingrich encouraged him to make the pieces "strongly-worded." That suited him perfectly, as did the one thousand shares of *Esquire* stock (worth about $16,000) that the publishers gave him.[94] He published thirteen pieces in *Ken*, twelve articles and one very short story ("Old Man at the Bridge"). The articles, with three exceptions,[95] all address issues concerning the Spanish Civil War, but, unlike the dispatches, they generally avoid discussing battles and military strategies in detail.

Considering the latitude Hemingway now enjoyed to write what he wished in these articles,[96] one might have expected them to present not only a more expansive persona of the author, but also a more candid analysis of the war, particularly of political issues blocked by government censorship of the dispatches. The expansiveness is certainly present in Hemingway's penchant for editorializing and firing broadsides at various targets, but not the candor. As a group, the articles are disappointing and seem self-indulgent, often trivial, as Hemingway allows himself to "unload" on topics that interested him. And, as will be shown, two of the articles—"Treachery in the Aragon" (30 June 1938) and "Fresh Air on an Inside Story" (22 Sept. 1938)—reinforce his adoption of the Soviet-Loyalist government line, when he claims that he knew no one who was disappeared and that no terror existed in Madrid in April 1937.

The most common theme is that America's non-intervention policy is morally wrong, ill-advised, and will backfire in its aim to keep America out of war. He declares in "Dying Well or Badly,"

> If the democratic nations allow Spain to be overrun by the fascists through their refusal to allow the legal Spanish government to buy and import arms . . . . history will label their actions in 1936 and 1937, when they refused to allow Spain to arm herself to fight their enemies [i.e., Italy and Germany], as criminal stupidity. (68)

Variants of this theme also appear in this article: that a fascist defeat in Spain would delay or even prevent an otherwise inevitable European war by breaking the Berlin-Rome-Tokyo axis; that "[t]he fascist nations act [and grow stronger] while the democratic nations talk, vacillate, connive and betray." Even as late as 8 September 1938, when Franco's fascists had just about won the war, Hemingway was still declaring, in "False News to the President," "It is still not too late to lift the arms embargo and allow the legal Spanish government to buy arms to defend itself against German and Italian invasion" (18).

One curious offshoot of his attacks on American policy is Hemingway's repeated assertion that the American State Department is riddled with fascists, who, taking their cues from fascists in the British foreign service, want to see Loyalist Spain lose, and therefore mislead their superiors to that end:

[T]he fascists in the U.S. State Department have done their level, crooked, Roman, British-aping, disgusting, efficient best to end [the war] by denying the Spanish government the right to buy arms to defend itself against the German and Italian aggression ("His Majesty's Loyal State Department," 36).

[State Department personnel] have for two years consistently, as all events now show, supplied their President with false information on the status of and conduct of civil war in Spain. . . . They should be fired. ("False News to the President," 17)

Substitute communists for fascists, and these charges eerily anticipate Senator Joseph McCarthy's claims that the State Department of the early 1950s was also infiltrated.

As in the long-range predictions in his dispatches of Loyalist endurance when the fascists were consolidating their hold on Spain, Hemingway's crystal ball in these articles is clouded by propaganda. Even in August 1938, "there will be war in Spain for a long time" ("A Program for U.S. Realism," 3, reprinted in *By-Line*, 291). Yet this same article accurately predicts, "War is due in Europe by next summer at the latest." Right on the mark!

Hemingway's ties with *Ken* ended in 1939, when the magazine folded.

The *Pravda* Article

Hemingway's role of propagandist for Loyalist Spain and the Soviets reaches its extreme in an article he published in *Pravda*, "The Barbarism of Fascist Interventionists in Spain," 1 August 1938 (reprinted in "Humanity," 114–18). Though the article was solicited by M. J. Olgin (American correspondent for *Pravda*), whom Hemingway did not know, it is likely that Mikhail Koltsov urged him to write the propaganda piece (and probably urged Olgin to solicit it). As Watson points out in his introduction,[97] Hemingway had declined many such requests from leftist magazines, Soviet and American, so why did he accept this one? Koltsov's influence seems the likeliest explanation, and in accepting, Hemingway asked Olgin to pass along his regards to Koltsov.[98] Why he was solicited is no mystery. He was "Hemingway, the great American writer," whom Comintern agents had been cultivating ever since his arrival in Europe in 1937. He had no rival in their eyes, now that they had written off Dos Passos. In any case, he put aside all his other projects to meet the *Pravda* deadline.[99]

The article straightforwardly contrasts two targets of fascist bombing and strafing: military (in which Hemingway includes himself as journalist on the front lines) and civilian. The former doesn't anger the author, even though the fascist planes have aimed directly at him; the latter does: "There is no bitterness when the Fascists try to kill you. Because they have a right to. Even by mistake. But you have anger and hatred when you see them do murder [i.e., bomb civilians]. . . . every day" ("Humanity," 117). The article predicts that these atrocities will not only intensify the Spanish people's "hatred of the Fascist invaders," but also "raise the world against [fascism]." Conversely, the Loyalists' humanity is plain to see:

> You went with the infantry in the assault on Teruel and entered the city with the first troops, and during the fighting in the town, you saw the government troops gently carrying children, helping old men and women to evacuate the town. *You did not see one act of brutality nor of barbarism.* (ibid., 118, emphasis added)

Of course, in a piece intended for *Pravda*, to expect mention of Loyalist, much less communist, atrocities is absurd.[100] Still, regardless of what Hemingway did or did not see in Teruel, the ghosts of Andrés Nin and José Robles must have smiled grimly at his bald assertion.

Hemingway's bravado has never been more extreme than in this article: "A man observing this same war and writing of it cares for nothing for his life . . . if he believes in the necessity of what he is doing. He cares only to write the truth" ("Humanity," 116).[101] Thus, when a Messerschmidt strafes him and misses, "you laugh at the plane because you are alive" (ibid., 116). No base fear intrudes, not even the dry mouth Hemingway mentions so often in his dispatches.

The José Robles Murder
and the Blowup with Dos Passos

One of the strangest echoes of the communist party line in Hemingway's journalism occurs in Dispatch 9 (20 April 1937), but to understand it requires background on a particularly ugly and controversial episode in Hemingway's years in Spain, his blowup with John Dos Passos over the execution of José Robles.

Many biographers and critics have written about the Hemingway-Dos Passos falling out and the mystery of Robles's execution; in fact, it is the core of Stephen Koch's book *The Breaking Point: Hemingway, Dos Passos, and the Murder of José Robles*. A brief review of facts and reasonable surmises includes the following: José Robles, a Johns Hopkins professor of Spanish, was Dos Passos's translator and friend. Visiting Spain at the outbreak of the war, Robles, an ardent Republican, volunteered his services to the Loyalists. Since he was fluent in Russian, he was assigned to a Russian general as a translator-interpreter and liaison to the government.[102] In March 1937, Robles was arrested, briefly held in prison, and executed. Precisely who arrested him, the Spanish government, the Russian NKVD, or another group, is not known; nor is there any record of his trial, if he had one. And why he was executed remains to this day a mystery.[103]

When he arrived in Spain, Dos Passos, on learning only that Robles had been arrested, began making inquiries on his behalf in Valencia (the government seat) and then in Madrid, where he was to help with filming *The Spanish Earth*. There, he met Pepé

Quintanilla, head of counterintelligence in Madrid. According to Dos Passos, Quintanilla told him Robles had been executed by a "'special section' (which I gathered was under the control of the Communist Party). He [Quintanilla] added that in his opinion the execution had been a mistake and that it was too bad."[104] When Dos Passos expressed his anguish about Robles's fate to Hemingway, the latter warned him strongly against pursuing the inquiry further, saying, in effect, "This is war." Hemingway also expressed complete confidence that Robles would receive—or did receive—a fair trial. When Robles's execution was confirmed, Hemingway again echoed the official line that Robles must have been guilty of treason as accused.

Hemingway's response to Dos Passos's concern—high-handed, condescending, and didactic—by itself would have been enough to destroy their friendship. But that friendship was already fraying well before the Robles affair. In the late 1920s, Hemingway acknowledged envying Dos Passos;[105] and the latter's critical success in his *U.S.A.* trilogy only heightened Hemingway's resentment when contrasted with the negative reviews his own 1930s work had been receiving. While they were still nominally friends in 1936, Hemingway mocked Dos Passos to Matthew Josephson as one whose heart bled for the proletariat while he himself stayed in first-class hotels.[106] The two writers also disagreed sharply on the direction *The Spanish Earth* should take, as noted above.

Before leaving Spain, Dos Passos travelled to Valencia, where he attempted to intercede with the government on behalf of Robles's widow, and to Barcelona, where he spoke openly with the leader of the POUM party, Andrés Nin, and with George Orwell, who, as an ally of the POUM, had undergone his own disillusionment with the Russian communists in Spain, which he later expressed in his memoir *Homage to Catalonia*.[107] For Dos Passos to be seen openly consorting with Nin, someone whom the Stalinists now labeled a Trotskyite, was, for the communists, tantamount to betrayal; and that is precisely how Joris Ivens characterized the meeting in letters to Hemingway: "I still get angry when I think of the fact that Dos after being with us went into the POUM office in Barcelona—it [was] . . . dirty disloyal to all of us."[108] Dos Passos was to be expelled from their circle and—as Ivens later arranged matters at the American Writers' Congress—prevented from speaking to the membership when *The Spanish Earth* was presented.

But Hemingway had his own incentive for breaking with Dos Passos. Possibly in Madrid and certainly when the two met briefly in Paris in May 1937, Dos Passos told Hemingway that he intended to write an article expressing his disillusionment with Soviet Communism and its repressive actions in Spain.[109] In publishing this article, however, he knew he was now bucking the leftist tide. This is precisely what Hemingway told him in Paris, when Dos Passos's wife, Katy, was present. But it was the way Hemingway warned him—and the response Hemingway received—that are so revealing. William L. White, editor of the *Emporia Gazette*, describes the scene based on what Dos Passos told him years later.[110] When Dos Passos spoke of his intent to write this article, Hemingway responded, "'You do that and the New York reviewers will kill you. They will demolish you forever.' Katy fired back, 'Why Ernest I have never heard anything so despicably opportunistic in my life!'"[111] Here is direct confirmation that Hemingway deeply cared what leftist critics thought about his writing and acted accordingly. That Katy Dos Passos had had the temerity to point this out and condemn Hemingway's opportunism was unforgiveable in Hemingway's eyes.

There was a deeper reason, however, for Hemingway's anger than being squelched so effectively—and by a woman! If Dos Passos was correct in his charges—that Robles had been murdered; that the Russian communists in Spain had a significant presence and were using terror tactics against the other leftist groups—then Hemingway would appear to be a naïve, gullible dupe to accept the assurances of government officials about Robles at face value. Rather than admit such a possibility—and given Hemingway's ego, this would have been impossible—he launched a campaign to refute Dos Passos's claims about the Russians in Spain and to publicly humiliate him in his journalism and in his novel *To Have and Have Not*.

The first reference was that odd inclusion in Dispatch 9, dated 20 April 1937—approximately the same day as the Hemingway-Dos Passos encounter about Robles in Hemingway's room. The dispatch discusses the fascists' continuous and "indiscriminate bombardment" of non-military targets in Madrid, purely to harm and terrorize civilians. In the middle of it appears this paragraph:

> The bombardment is puzzling since it either means the Fascists are shooting up available ammunition, hoping to kill all the supposedly Red population of Madrid (where not one friend of this correspondent from the old days when I lived here, regardless of politics or religion, has been executed or is missing in this war, except for those killed fighting at the front, and this includes newspapermen, bull fighters, hotel keepers, painters, antique dealers, doctors, engineers, store keepers and bar keepers with whom I have met and passed the time of day recently), or [they] seek through the bombardment of Madrid to terrorize . . . (*By-Line*, 34–35)

The parenthetical inclusion is a complete non sequitur: the subject was fascist bombing, not government executions or abductions. Its presence suggests that Hemingway, upset and very likely drunk[112] when he wrote this, was responding to Dos Passos's charge with a categorical denial.[113]

The following year, after an undeterred Dos Passos published his article "Farewell to Europe!" in *Common Sense* (July 1937),[114] Hemingway devoted an article in *Ken* to what can only be called character assassination. "Treachery in Aragon" (*Ken*, 30 June 1938, 26) begins by attributing the fascists' breakthrough on the Aragon front in March to "treachery" instigated by the Gestapo; the Spanish government, Hemingway adds (in a curious anticipation of McCarthy tactics), cannot yet list the "traitors." Quickly, he transitions to "some very politically naïve people in America who do not believe that there is such a thing as treachery. Any time anyone is shot for treachery they are certain it is for some other reason. . . . [They] will hold up their hands in horror and call it a reign of terror when it is simply a military punishment for a military offense." The article gradually narrows "politically naïve people" to "American liberals" and follows with an example of "an American writer [further on, he is "an American novelist"] who was a very good friend of mine . . . . His main preoccupation was to locate a friend and former translator of his whom he had heard was being held in prison." Dialogue follows in which the friend is made to sound ridiculous, mindlessly repeating "absolutely" to reveal his lack of judgment and objectivity: "I absolutely guarantee him. . . . I know he is absolutely loyal to the government and I guarantee him personally. Absolutely and without reservations." Hemingway portrays himself as coolly objective, bringing out through questions that his friend hasn't seen the translator for over a year, and asking, "How do you know that he is still loyal . . . ?" Then, Hemingway fills in the narrative with his superior knowledge, while assuming a sympathetic attitude: "This all made me feel rather badly because I happened to know this man had been shot two weeks before as a spy after a long and careful trial in which all the charges against him had been proven."

On learning that the translator was shot, the "friend" now considers him a "martyr." Hemingway concludes, "This is as good an example as any of the good hearted naïveté of a typical American liberal attitude. . . . Perhaps it is just old Harvard loyalty." As a corrective, Hemingway then narrates an unrelated example of disloyalty in a commissar whom Hemingway had once thought "a very good fellow," so that the American novelist, on reading this example, "may admit the possibility of his friend and translator being [a traitor]." He then resumes his posture of superior experience and wisdom: "But we who have seen this war for a long time have learned that there are all sorts of treachery . . ." The smugness in Hemingway's tone would be laughable if it weren't so outrageous.

A later article in *Ken*, "Fresh Air on an Inside Story" (reprinted in *By-Line*, 294–95) reiterates the same scenario with a different goat. A journalist in Madrid declares repeatedly "There is a terror here," while Hemingway questions him to reveal the man has no concrete evidence. Although Hemingway acknowledges that "three people had been shot for espionage that month," he nonetheless concludes emphatically that for months Madrid has been . . . free of any terror . . . But that was too dull for [the journalist]."

In contrast to this "great man" writing for a "truly great newspaper," Hemingway includes himself in a group of "hard-working, non-political, straight-shooting correspondents who risked their lives daily working in Madrid and *who had been denying there was a terror in Madrid ever since the government had taken control of the situation and stopped all terror*" (*By-Line*, 296, emphasis added).

Of course, this description—self-righteous and unintentionally comical in using the trite westernism "straight-shooting"—refers to only one journalist who felt he had to "deny" the terror in Madrid.

The parallels of this article to the "Treachery" article are striking, almost formulaic: both "other" writers make extreme claims about victims of government oppression, claims that are made to look foolish under Hemingway's objective questioning. Both articles rebut the charges with Hemingway's privileged information: "I happened to know . . ." ("Treachery"); "I had friends in Seguridad that I had known from the old days and could trust . . ." ("Fresh Air"). Both articles either deny terror existed in Madrid at the time or assert that a suspected instance of terror (the Robles execution) was a justifiable punishment for treason. The journalist in "Fresh Air" even looks like Dos Passos: tall, balding, and near-sighted.[115]

The question remains of why Hemingway felt such an obsessive need not just to refute charges of terrorism, but to ridicule both the claims and claimants. In the case of Dos Passos, professional jealousy does not suffice as an answer. By the time of the two *Ken* articles, Hemingway had reestablished his standing with the Left, while Dos Passos was on their blacklist with the publication of his *Common Sense* article. Two sentences in "Fresh Air" hint at a deeper reason: "The [journalist's] dispatch [claiming that terror prevailed in Madrid] was a lie. . . . It made liars out of every honest correspondent in Madrid." Equating himself with "every honest correspondent," Hemingway reveals that, if the reporter's claims were valid, then Hemingway's denials were at best naïve (making him look foolish in uncritically accepting and parroting the government's denial of terror) or, worse, mendacious (if he denied what he knew to be true through his insider contacts).[116]

This apparent need to overcompensate for his uncertainty regarding the Soviets and terror reached an extreme in an ugly letter he sent Dos Passos about 26 March 1938,[117] before he published the *Ken* articles discussed above. Responding to Dos Passos's article in *Redbook* about a luncheon for the Fifteenth Brigade that he (Dos Passos) attended in 1937,[118] Hemingway fires off several "corrections." First, he lists several Loyalist generals that Dos Passos supposedly identified as Russian (in fact, he had named only one, General Walter). Describing their non-Russian backgrounds,

Hemingway concludes, "I'm sorry, Dos, but you didn't meet any Russian generals." As several historians point out, however, the generals Hemingway lists (including Walter), though born outside of Russia, belonged to or were trained by the Red Army and were "fully under its discipline"; moreover, Stalin strove to conceal their Russian connections.[119] Second, Hemingway assumes that Dos Passos's point is that it is a "communist run war . . . . imposed on the will of the people" (a claim Dos Passos never makes in the article). Hemingway responds, "[T]his hasn't been a communist run war for a long time" (*Selected Letters*, 463–64). He follows these "corrections" with a far more egregious mistake about the former leader of the POUM, Andrés Nin, whose death Dos Passos mentions in a separate article.[120] Hemingway writes, "Then there is Nin. Do you know where Nin is now? You ought to find that out before you write about his death" (ibid., 464). Apparently, Hemingway swallowed one of the stories spread by the NKVD about the missing Nin, either that he had been kidnapped by the Anarchists, or that he had escaped to Paris.[121] In fact, he had been dead since June 1937, executed by the NKVD.

Hemingway's "corrections" reveal that either he was badly misinformed about—and probably by—the Russians in Spain, or he knowingly repeated, with obvious desperation, their official myths about their generals and Nin's disappearance. Probably both alternatives were partially true. But unlike the flat-out denials in his articles, he concedes indirectly that it had once been "a communist-run war." Still, the factual basis of his disagreement with Dos Passos needs closer examination. Specifically, how widespread *was* the Russian presence in Spain in these years? Did Soviet operatives and their allies in the Spanish government conduct instances of political disappearance, torture, and murder not only against fascist spies but against leftists putatively on their side? And, most important for this study, what were Hemingway's connections to the alleged practitioners of this terror? How much could he have known?

The Soviet Presence in Spain, the Counterespionage Apparatus, and Hemingway's Links to Loyalist Terror

Even before it shipped arms to the Loyalists, the Soviet Union sent numerous "advisers" to Republican Spain beginning in the summer of 1936, including military leaders and technicians, propaganda and public relations specialists (principally Mikhail Koltsov), and NKVD organizers and operatives, led by Alexandr Orlov.[122] Although the total number of Soviets in Spain never exceeded more than three thousand, they exerted disproportionate influence on both the military and civilian sides of the Republican government. Militarily, Red Army officers (e.g., Kléber, Lukacs, Gall, and Walter) took control of most of the original brigades. Although, as Hemingway pointed out to Dos Passos, none of these generals was a native Russian, they—and Spaniards like Enrique Líster and Gustavo Durán—were trained by the Red Army. As Payne states, they were disguised as foreign volunteers to conceal the Russian presence in Spain. By May 1937, a Soviet operative boasted that "Communists or sympathizers make up nine-tenths of the officers in the central [Madrid front] army"—a claim Payne calls "nearly correct."[123]

The Soviets also reorganized security and counter-intelligence operations. Orlov, as head of the NKVD in Spain, had prisons built to house fifth columnists, foreigners (e.g., members of the International Brigades), Spanish political dissidents, and increasingly, members of rival political parties that the Comintern had resolved to squelch. Crematoria were also built to dispose of the bodies of those executed.[124] In addition, Orlov manufactured forged documents showing the disloyalty of the accused, and, as in the case of Andrés Nin, creating false evidence about his whereabouts after his murder. Orlov also planted agents to act as spies and provocateurs in targeted political parties like POUM.

Finally, the Soviets put steadily increasing pressure on the civilian government to carry out its aims, through directives from Moscow (including personal instructions from Stalin), through Soviet personnel in Spain, and through communist members of the ruling cabinet and the Spanish Communist Party (PCE). Though they initially supported the appointment of Francisco Largo Caballero as prime minister in 1936, the Soviets grew increasingly dissatisfied with him as he began to resist the expansion of Soviet influence. For example, in mid-April 1937, Caballero declared that all Russian-installed political commissars appointed to military units without his approval would shortly be removed. Infuriated, the Comintern sent orders to the PCE to "precipitate a governmental crisis that would remove Caballero as minister of war."[125]

The planned crisis also aimed at destroying the two parties that Moscow most hated: the anti-Stalinist POUM[126] and the Anarcho-Syndicalists, both based in Barcelona. When a group of Socialists attempted to take over the telephone exchange in Barcelona, provoking open warfare among the various leftist groups—the "May Days" of 1937—the Republican government had its justification to intervene, close down their targeted groups and arrest almost a thousand members, including the POUM leader, Andrés Nin. In the ensuing political crisis, the government of Largo Caballero fell, and he was replaced as prime minister by a cabinet minister, Juan Negrín, who, in Payne's words, was "ultra pro-Soviet."[127] His first order of business was to carry out Stalin's direct order to dispose of Nin, who was removed to an NKVD prison, tortured, and then executed, with a cover story planted by Orlov that he had been kidnapped by the Anarchists. In 1938, seeing that the war was essentially lost, Stalin began to withdraw his advisers and sharply reduce the flow of armaments to Spain.

As he closed in on Madrid in 1936, a fascist general infamously boasted that, along with his four columns of troops, a fifth column, comprised of spies and informers, artillery spotters and saboteurs, secretly resided in Madrid. To counter these espionage efforts, the Republican government created two counterespionage agencies in spring and summer of 1937: Dirección General de Seguridad (which Hemingway shortened to Seguridad) and SIM (Servicio de Inteligencia Military). According to historian Hugh Thomas, "the SIM employed all the odious tortures of the NKVD" and became "the bureaucratic instrument . . . through which the Communist Party murdered its enemies." Donaldson adds, "the SIM did much of its deadliest work not against actual fascist spies but against factions on the left threatening the dominance of the Russian Stalinists in Spain. Hemingway knew about these activities but chose not to write about them."[128]

Madrid in particular, with its close proximity to the front lines, was a hotbed of both spies and counterintelligence actions. In its restaurants and cafés, paranoia intermingled with rational fear of enemy snooping and government eavesdropping. In both his dispatches and fiction, Hemingway describes the charged atmosphere of bars like Chicotes, where patrons might talk indiscreetly but were also aware that anything they said might be picked up by fifth columnists—and by government counterespionage agents quick to arrest loose-lipped Loyalists. As Virginia Cowles, an eyewitness, summarizes,

> Madrid was honeycombed with Fifth Columnists and spies, and the Republicans had a large secret police force working to combat the leakage of information. Dossiers were kept on thousands of suspects, including the entire foreign press, and garish posters pasted on the buildings warned the population of the dangers of spies even among friends . . .
>
> None of us [journalists] knew the full activities of the secret police or what went on behind the prison walls of Madrid. There is no doubt, however, that the Government was waging a desperate struggle against Fifth Columnists who were supplying the enemy with a steady stream of information by radio and courier."[129]

But in seeking out fascist spies—and in trying to terrorize Loyalists to keep their mouths shut and not question the government line—counterespionage agents were prone to make mistakes and arrest loyal citizens. Secret informers and denunciations were at work, sometimes driven (as Dos Passos surmised in his *New Republic* letter) by personal grudges, thus intensifying both paranoia and the inaccuracy of identifications. Cowles continues, "There is no doubt, either, that many thousands of innocent persons were dragged from their beds and shot without trial."[130] As Alex Vernon writes, "Everyone knew that these events [executions and disappearances] happened."[131] Hemingway must have known it too, as early as his first trip to Spain in March and April 1937—well before he slammed Dos Passos in his *Ken* article and letter.

His knowledge was even more likely because, through his friendship with Joris Ivens, he met and became friendly with the Spanish and Russian leaders of counterintelligence with links to the NKVD. He spoke familiarly, for example, of Vittorio Vidali, a Comintern "adviser on paramilitary and other subversive activities."[132] Journalist Herbert Matthews describes Vidali's practice of briefly interrogating prisoners brought before him, and, when he decided, as he almost always did, that they were fifth columnists, he would shoot them in the back of the head with his revolver. Ernest Hemingway told me that he heard that Vidali (aka 'Carlos') fired so often that the skin between the thumb and index finger of his right hand was badly burned.[133]

Another journalist, George Seldes, writing to Hemingway's first biographer, Carlos Baker, stated, "I do not doubt that the communist leaders in the International Brigade, notably [André] Marty, did commit crimes. . . . Now Hemingway knew these facts much better than I did."[134]

He also knew another prominent killer, Pepé Quintanilla, head of counterintelligence in Madrid, whom Hemingway himself called "the chief executioner of Madrid."[135] Hemingway, in fact, boasted to Josie Herbst of his close ties to Quintanilla (whose brother, Luis, was the painter Hemingway had long known and aided when imprisoned). "[Pepé] Quintanilla was a swell guy," Hemingway told her; she "ought to get to know him."[136] In fact, through Hemingway, she did meet and have lunch with him at about the time the fate of José Robles was revealed. Both Herbst and Virginia Cowles, who was also present, describe the tense lunch they had with Hemingway and Quintanilla, during which they were forced to sit through a fascist shelling while Quintanilla regaled them with stories. Responding to Hemingway's probing questions, Quintanilla admitted to making "mistakes."

> [Hemingway:] "How many people have died in Madrid?"
> [Quintanilla:] "A revolution is always hasty."
> [H]: "And have there been many mistakes?"
> [Q]: "Mistakes? It is only human to err."
> [H]: "And the mistakes—how did they die?"
> [Q]: "On the whole, considering they were mistakes, . . . very well indeed; in fact *magnifico!*"[137]

Hemingway directly refers to Quintanilla by his first name in the story "The Denunciation" and thinly fictionalizes him—and this dialogue—in the play *The Fifth Column*. While the play and stories will be examined below, here we should note Hemingway's apparent sense of impunity in referring to this much-feared counterintelligence chief by name and virtually quoting Quintanilla's breezy acknowledgment of "mistakes." Knowing that counterintelligence made mistakes in arresting and summarily executing innocent people—many thousands, according to Cowles—did not prevent Hemingway from categorically denying José Robles's innocence or from asserting that he, Hemingway, never knew of anyone who had been disappeared.

The only communist counterintelligence agent with a notoriously bloody record whom Hemingway consistently disparaged in his fiction (but not in his journalism) was the French commissar of the International Brigades, André Marty, who was reputedly responsible for shooting five hundred international volunteers as spies[138] and was thought to be quite mad. That is precisely how Hemingway depicts him—by name—in *For Whom the Bell Tolls*.

From Hemingway's extensive contacts with these Russian and Spanish leaders in police and counterintelligence, as well as from his fictionalizing of these same connections, there can be little doubt that he knew, better than other foreign journalists, the evidence of torture, murder, and disappearances conducted by representatives and secret operatives of the Loyalist government. Whether or not he knew of the Robles execution before declaring in Dispatch 9 that he knew of no one who had been disappeared is really not the issue; he must have heard of many other such cases. Indeed, in his "Fresh Air" *Ken* article, Hemingway admits to knowing that three people had been shot for espionage that month (April 1937), but he still asserts that there was no terror in Madrid then. Perhaps he was just unwilling to label these executions and the other evidence he had learned of as "terror." To Milton Wolff, a captain in the Abraham Lincoln Brigade, he called the tortures and executions "playing dirty"—just as the fascists did.[139]

For a writer who placed such a high premium on "truth," Hemingway's refusal in his journalistic dispatches and magazine articles to reveal Loyalist instances of atrocities, political torture, and execution (regardless of whether one defines them as "terror")—indeed, his flat-out denial of their existence—does not stand to his credit. William Watson puts the matter succinctly: "He suppressed certain realities he knew to be true and he promoted as realities things he must have known to be false, all in the name of winning a war whose character the Communists had largely defined."[140] His reluctance to discuss instances of terror stems from several sources, as have been discussed: censorship, journalistic restrictions (though he certainly had freedom to opine in his *Ken* articles), fear of harming the Loyalist cause with negative stories (the same reason he exaggerates shards of hope on the battlefield and dismisses the almost certain Fascist victory), and a desire to believe in what the government officials told him, though he almost certainly knew better from some of these same officials. Phillip Knightley has suggested one more reason, which subsequent evidence strongly supports: Hemingway was saving for his fiction and drama the *real* story, the story he felt he could not—or would not—tell in his nonfiction.[141] Whether his motive was this self-serving, or whether, as he later portrayed it more nobly, he held back so as not to hurt the cause,[142] is an open question. In any case, the "carnival of treachery and rotten-ness" he had known about almost from the beginning would find its way into his art.[143] In fact, it had already begun leaking into his Spanish Civil War stories and play even before the war ended.

III. *The Fifth Column* and the
Spanish Civil War Stories: 1937–39

During his second trip to Spain, in autumn 1937, while he waited out a lull in the war in Madrid, Hemingway completed the first draft of a play, *The Fifth Column*, which he revised over the following winter. The play was published with his collected short stories (*The Fifth Column and the First Forty-Nine Stories*) in October 1938 and performed on Broadway in 1940. During 1938, he finished four stories about the war and completed another in January 1939. In contrast to the novel that he largely wrote *after* the war ended, when he had time to consider the issues at greater distance, both the play and stories were written hurriedly, while the turmoil of the war (lulls notwithstanding) still engulfed him, and while his ideological fervor for the Loyalists and communists was at its height. This lack of detachment goes a long way to explaining their mediocrity, but does not account for their glimpses of unpleasant truths that he had refused to recognize in his journalism.

The Fifth Column

Hemingway's contacts with Spanish and Russian counterintelligence agents in 1937 must have fired his imagination, for he projected himself into that role—a kind of James Bond figure before its time—in the play he wrote in Madrid that autumn, *The Fifth Column.* Considering that he had never before written a full-length play,[144] this venture into a new medium is curious and might have been admirable if the results were not so dismal.

The play is essentially a melodrama that pits good guys—Philip Rawlings and his disfigured fellow agent, Max—against the baddies: fascist spies, assassins, and artillery spotters in Madrid. The good guys—all two of them—successfully raid a spotters post manned by many more armed bad guys and capture the key figures—an easy and implausible victory. Complicating the plot, Philip poses as an American journalist, a cover that completely deceives his girlfriend, Dorothy Bridges. Since many others seem to know Philip's secret work, Dorothy's obtuseness—she complains about his mysterious absences and muddy shoes when he returns from a mission—provides comic relief. Besides serving as a passing love interest for Philip, Dorothy also represents an alternative future for him: the easy, hedonistic life she and Philip can enjoy together once he abandons his political commitment:

> Philip: And will we have the *Continental Daily Mail* for breakfast and *brioches* and fresh strawberry jam?
> Dorothy: Darling we'll have œufs au jambon and you can have the *Morning Post* if you like. And every one will say Messieur-Dame. (23)

This soft civilian life—similar to the one Hemingway temporarily left behind with Pauline—is all the more appealing to this burned out counterespionage agent when he considers the spartan rigors ahead if he continues fighting against fascism. Hence, the play's second conflict.

The play's autobiographical roots (and fantasy projection) are obvious. As in his Spanish Civil War story "Night Before Battle," much of the play's action is set in a hotel room similar to Hemingway's (even the hotel's name and his room number are the same), where other antifascists come for R&R and which Philip uses as a command post. Dorothy's features strongly resemble Martha Gellhorn's, and each possesses a fur coat, symbolizing (in Dorothy's case) her self-indulgence and obliviousness to the suffering of the Spanish people. Dorothy also has some of Pauline Hemingway in her. When Philip cruelly presents a future scenario of all the places they could go together, knowing he will shortly break off with her, he recalls Harry's cruelty to Helen in "The Snows of Kilimanjaro," and approximates the exotic and comfortable life Hemingway enjoyed with Pauline. Considering how negatively Dorothy is portrayed—at one point Philip says to her "You're uneducated, you're useless, you're a fool. And you're lazy" (83)—it is remarkable that Gellhorn didn't break off with Hemingway when she read the play.

Though the play consistently privileges Philip's insider knowledge against Dorothy's naïve shallowness, it avoids any serious analysis of the war itself and never questions the Loyalist cause. The only rationale for fighting comes in Max's generically egalitarian speech (he is a Marxist), which sounds almost like a brief for the New Deal: "You [fight] so *every one* will have a good breakfast . . . You do it so *no one* will ever be hungry. You do it so men will not have to fear ill health or old age; so they can live and work in dignity and not as slaves." When a child is wounded nearby by a fascist artillery shell, Max adds, "You do it to stop *that* forever" (67–68).

If he ignores the war's larger issues, Hemingway does confront the ugliness of one of its actions: the torturing and executing of suspected spies—a subject he carefully avoided in his dispatches and articles. Philip's job requires him to interrogate fifth columnists, who are often tortured to elicit information. Although the play is ambiguous about whether Philip himself tortures them, he has often been present during their torture. In sharp contrast to Max, who cannot stand to watch their new captive being tortured and leaves beforehand, Philip "stayed all through it. Every bit of it," as he tells Max afterwards (79). Hemingway even reproduces his own luncheon conversation with Pepé Quintanilla about "mistakes" in identifying and killing suspected fifth columnists and has Philip's superior, Antonio, acknowledge them, just as Quintanilla did (see above), followed by the same discussion of how these mistakes died: "All very well" (38).

What softens—or is intended to soften—this portrait of Philip as willing participant in torture and murder is that he is now burned out, fed up with his role in these acts. He confides to Antonio, "I don't like to see them die. It's O.K. I guess if you like to see it. But I don't like it.[145] Sometimes I don't know how you stick it" (37). Philip feels *he* can no longer stick it—"I'm very tired, see, and I'm also disgusted with my job" (39). He's also tired of killing: "You know what I'd like? I'd like to never kill another son-of-a-bitch, I don't care who or for what, as long as I live" (38). But this disgust does not keep him (and Max) from shooting one of their new captives following their raid when the latter turns recalcitrant. Nor does it keep Philip from watching Antonio work over the other prisoner for hours.

Philip is thus made to look tough and heroic when, ignoring his existential fatigue, he chooses this harder, dangerous life and leaves Dorothy and the soft life behind—"Where I go now I go alone, or with others who go there for the same reason I go"—because "We're in for fifty years of undeclared wars and I've signed up for the duration" (90). Philip's bravado, in his tough-guy willingness to participate in torture and murder of fifth columnists, is uncomfortably close to Harry Morgan's guiltless sadism in killing the Chinese smuggler in *To Have and Have Not*—another instance of the antihero. But at the same time, Philip's refusal to abandon the "cause" marks a 180 degree turn from Frederic Henry's desertion from a cause he no longer believes in. As would be developed much more fully in *For Whom the Bell Tolls*, the Hemingway hero now has something real to fight for.

Despite the cheap heroics of the action and the two-dimensional dilemmas, *The Fifth Column* does at least deal with a subject Hemingway had either ignored or denied in his journalism: Republican torture and murder of both fifth columnists and those "mistakenly" suspected of being fifth columnists. It excludes, however, any mention of Soviet involvement in these acts except for one facetious reference;[146] and it ignores the persecution of rival political parties on the left, or, like José Robles, individuals who knew too much. For these omissions, the play has been sharply criticized.[147]

Such omissions were not oversights, however. It is telling that, when Hemingway discussed the revision of the play with Benjamin F. Glazer, who was hired to make it performable, Hemingway stipulated in the contract that "the new version should contain no adverse criticism of the Spanish government or the Communist Party."[148] Glazer complied, but his revisions were no improvement. Not surprisingly, as the Spanish war quickly faded in the American public's consciousness, the play, which opened on Broadway in March 1940, ran for only about three months.

The Spanish Civil War Stories

In all, Hemingway published five short stories about the Spanish Civil War.[149] One, "Old Man at the Bridge," was a two-page vignette he dashed off while observing the civilian and troop retreat across the Ebro River during his third trip to Spain (late March to May 1938). This he sent to *Ken* magazine (published 19 May 1938) and also published it in *The Fifth Column and the First Forty-Nine Stories* (1938). He wrote four fully developed stories—"The Denunciation," "The Butterfly and the Tank," "Night Before Battle," and "Under the Ridge"—during his last trip to Spain (September to October 1938), when, with no NANA assignment, he had more free time. These four would join the play in a posthumous edition, *The Fifth Column and Four Unpublished Stories of the Spanish Civil War* (1969).

None of these stories represents Hemingway at his best, but they are interesting both for their views of the war and for what they exclude. These perspectives, whether of the battlefield or of behind-the-lines Madrid, are what Hemingway had always specialized in: close-up depictions of how people—both soldiers and civilians—behave under stress and danger, how they talk and how they handle tension and fear. The first three stories—"The Denunciation," "The Butterfly and the Tank," and "Night Before Battle"—are set in the Madrid locations Hemingway frequented as a foreign correspondent: Chicotes bar, the Gran Via restaurant, and his hotel room; in fact, he referred to the three as his "Chicote" stories (*Selected Letters*, 472). "Under the Ridge," though set on the battlefield, is, like "Night Before Battle," narrated by a civilian who is shooting a film about the war. Only the slightest of the five stories—the "Old Man at the Bridge" sketch—lacks this obviously autobiographical element. Hemingway's view of the war was still narrow, limited to his own experiences as a foreigner; he was not yet ready to characterize with convincing specificity the Spanish people of this Spanish war.[150] But the scenes he does portray are rendered with authority, especially through the technique of juxtaposition. They are an eerie amalgam of military and civilian life within walking distance of each other in Madrid: the frenetic gaiety and tension hanging like a cloud of cigarette smoke in Chicotes; the wildly diverse moods of morbid fatalism, drunken celebration, fear, and indifference among the various characters of "Night Before Battle"; the contrasting responses to battlefield fear in "Under the Ridge."

"Night Before Battle," at almost three times the length of the other stories, is the most ambitious—and most loosely written—of these studies in contrast. As the title indicates, the story is set the night before a major Loyalist attack and moves back and forth between Chicotes bar, the narrator Henry's hotel room, and the Gran Via restaurant. In these crowded milieus, the differing situations and mentalities of several international Loyalists play out: Al Wagner, a tank commander who has just fought in one failed action and is certain that the next morning's attack, which his tanks will lead, will also fail and kill him; a drunken, elated pilot ("Baldy") who is celebrating downing a German bomber; crapshooters in Henry's room who are oblivious to everything but their game; a young Spanish woman without papers who fears she'll be arrested as a fascist spy; a Hungarian who listens to Henry's phonograph records of Chopin; Henry himself, who is shooting a film about the war; and finally, a mysteriously important patron of the bar and restaurant. The story also juxtaposes the diverse motives and rewards for fighting: the hired pilots are very well paid, while Al, a volunteer, is not; idealism, not money, motivates him. When Al and Henry finally part, they try to conceal the pessimism they share about Al's chances in the morning, and, in Hemingway's typically understated manner, the narrator concludes, "You get angry about a lot of things and you, yourself, dying uselessly is one of them" (139).

At Chicotes, Henry and Al discuss the failed attack that day and encounter the mysterious civilian, who is not afraid to loudly blame the current prime minister, Largo Caballero, for the attack's failure and who also predicts the next day's attack will fail. His lack of discretion worries Al, who warns him, "If anyone around here speaks English you're liable to get shot Comrade." The man is not only undeterred, he bluntly asks Al his unit, if he is a Communist Party member, and reveals that he already knows "all about Comrade Henry," specifically that he is not a Party member. Finally, he declares, "[W]e'll get rid of Largo Caballero . . . right after his offensive" (113–15). The man's certainty about his own safety, his knowledge of Henry's politics, and the "we" in his prediction of getting rid of Caballero all suggest that he's a high-ranking intelligence operative, probably Russian. His importance is later confirmed when Al and Henry see him at the Gran Via restaurant "talking with some people I knew were very big shots indeed" (127). One other noteworthy detail of this scene: when Al wonders aloud about the identity of this man, Henry responds, "I don't know, . . . but I'm going to find out"—suggesting that Henry, too, has contacts in the government.

This aura of uncertainty, fear, and dread continues in Henry's room when a young Spanish woman, Manolita, confides to Henry her fear of imminent arrest because she lacks papers and is suspected of being a fascist spy. Henry's response closely resembles Hemingway's about José Robles: "Nothing will happen to you if you're all right"—this, even though Manolita's fiancé, a policeman, was shot "by accident." Once again, Henry reveals he has contacts. Though he refuses to let Manolita stay with him—he can't be sure she's "all right"—he tells her to call him if she gets arrested, implying he has clout with counterintelligence officers in Madrid.

This same mysterious connectedness of the narrator appears in "The Denunciation." Its plot, however, is far more focused, and less rambling and loquacious than that of "Night Before Battle." The narrator, Henry Emmunds (or Edmonds),[151] a writer, is approached by a waiter in Chicotes who has spotted a prominent fascist, Luis Delgado, an old-time customer whom they both know—Emmunds had once shot pigeons and gambled with him before the war. The fascist is sitting with new Loyalist pilots who don't know him; worse, he is wearing a Loyalist uniform. Should he be denounced (which will inevitably lead to his arrest and execution)? And if so, by whom? The waiter expects the narrator to do the dirty work.

Emmunds refuses, but on being prodded, gives the waiter a special phone number for Seguridad headquarters and tells him to "[a]sk for Pepé," an undisguised reference to Pepé Quintanilla, head of Madrid counterintelligence. The police soon arrive to make the arrest, which Emmunds safely observes from outside the bar. But he feels guilty about his part in denouncing a former friend, especially about having the waiter do the dirty work: it was "one of those excesses of impartiality, righteousness and Pontius Pilatry, and the always-dirty desire to see how people act under an emotional conflict, that makes writers such attractive friends" (97). To make amends, he himself calls Pepé and asks that Delgado be told that he, Mr. Emmunds, denounced him, not the waiter. What partially mitigates Emmunds's guilt, however, is that Delgado is definitely a fascist spy in false uniform—an offense for which capital punishment is standard in many countries. If Delgado's politics and appearance had been more ambiguous, the morality of denouncing would have correspondingly been more uncertain—and closer to situations of those thousands whom Virginia Cowles describes as being falsely arrested. As it is, Mr. Emmunds "felt very badly" about his role in the affair, which shows in his description of Pepé's voice: "It was a strange and very deadly voice and I never got used to hearing it . . ." Yet, he feels "much better" after calling Pepé. Tellingly, their conversation shifts from Emmunds's request to their plans to meet for lunch tomorrow, when they anticipate having "some meat." The moral ambivalence of the ending is prominent, as are the narrator's mysterious connections to the most-feared powers of Madrid.

In only one of these stories, "Under the Ridge," is the Russian presence in Spain mentioned, but it is asserted by an unreliable Spanish soldier who hates all foreigners and calls them Russian, including the narrator, an American. When the narrator asks him why he hates the Russians, the soldier replies, "Because they are the representatives of tyranny and I hate their faces." The first half of the answer sounds canned (even if it proved true), while the second half merely reiterates the soldier's prejudice and destroys his credibility. By contrast, the narrator carefully identifies a *Polish* officer who shows the narrator and his camera crew the positions that Polish volunteers had just captured. The implied contrast here—blindly tagging every foreigner as Russian versus carefully identifying non-Russian foreigners—echoes Hemingway's angry letter to Dos Passos accusing him of misidentifying and not meeting any Russian officers in Spain. As in the letter, the story never considers that the Polish officer may have direct links to the Soviets.

The narrator then observes a middle-aged French soldier, an International Brigader, calmly walk away from his position and "out of the war" (144). The deserter is soon pursued by two men in leather coats and civilian caps, carrying Mauser pistols. As soon as they spot the deserter, they shoot him. The shooting of those thought to be deserters was practiced by many countries in wartime—it nearly happens, by mistake, to Hemingway's Frederic Henry in *A Farewell to Arms*. But the executioners in this case are police agents attached to the military (the story calls them "battle police"). Only the unreliable Spanish soldier, however, identifies the police as Russian. In fact, though, the Soviets staffed the International Brigades (which they had created) with commissars who policed these units—Hemingway's friend Gustav Regler was one such commissar who was trained in Russia. Yet the story undermines the Russian identity of the battle police, just as *The Fifth Column* undermines Russian presence in Max's facetious remark.

The narrator's response to the execution reveals much about Hemingway's complex attitude towards soldiers in war. Rather than simply condemn the man, the narrator expresses sympathy with what may have motivated his desertion: "I understood how a man might suddenly, seeing clearly the stupidity of dying in an unsuccessful attack; . . . seeing its hopelessness, seeing its idiocy, seeing how it really was, simply get back and walk away from it as the Frenchman had done. He could walk out of it not from cowardice, but simply from seeing too clearly; knowing suddenly he had to leave it; knowing there was no other thing to do" (147). Yet, the narrator concludes that "In war it is necessary to have discipline." Hemingway said approximately the same thing to Dos Passos to stifle the latter's concern for José Robles. Russian discipline, even administered by men in leather coats carrying Mauser pistols, was something he felt necessary to win the war. Though he understood what motivates a man to simply give up and walk away from an attack that is bound to fail, and though he shows no empathy for the "hunting dogs" who track down the deserter, Hemingway's real empathy was with those, like Al Wagner in "Night Before Battle", who do not quit, even when they know "the hopelessness" and "idiocy" of dying in a doomed attack.

Taken together, the play and stories mark a transitional stage in Hemingway's evolving attitude towards the war. Unlike his dispatches and magazine pieces—some written at the same time as the drama and fiction—the play and stories acknowledge *some* of the uglier realities on the Loyalist side that complicate any understanding of the war as a simplistic good guy-bad guy affair. The play illustrates what Hemingway allegedly told Milton Wolff: "They play dirty. We play dirty." The Loyalists torture and execute without trial suspected fifth columnists and "sometimes" make mistakes, and the protagonist is a close party to these tortures and murders. Although the stories avoid what happens in the back rooms and courtyards of counterintelligence centers, they capture the aura of fear and dread these actions create. The men in leather coats are ever-present to shoot deserters and arrest suspected spies, even if they are innocent; fifth columnists lurk even in Loyalist bars; and among the real power brokers, there are wheels within wheels that know in advance an attack will fail—perhaps *want* it to fail to further their larger machinations. Like Hemingway, the narrator of "The Denunciation" knows "the chief executioner of Madrid" by his first name. The stories reveal one other depressing fact left out of the journalism: the Loyalist attacks are often bungled by inept leadership, cowardice of key players (e.g., some of Al's tankers), and inadequate armaments ("There were only four batteries down there, when there should have been forty, and they were firing two guns at a time," 141).

The two realities that Hemingway was not yet ready to acknowledge were the early Loyalist atrocities against priests and profascists and the Soviet presence on the battlefield and in manipulating the government. Both the play and stories *allude* to the Russian presence, but always unreliably. It would take another year—and the Loyalists' final defeat—before Hemingway could deal with that reality. Still, his short fiction and drama about the war suggest a writer struggling to throw off the distorted views of it that he promulgated in his journalism—and insisted upon in his irrational attacks on former friends. Perhaps this evolution reflects

Hemingway's differing valuations of his media. If one views the war from one side only, journalism—whether newspaper dispatches or magazine articles—has an ineradicable taint of propaganda. To the extent that such journalism *is* propaganda, it may shade, distort, or repress the truth, if doing so furthers the cause. But for Hemingway, his art was on a higher plane; intentionally distorting *that* was criminal, a betrayal of self. Thus, if *The Fifth Column* still dealt in good guys and bad guys, that oversimplification probably issued from Hemingway's own simplistic conception of the war at that early stage of his encounter with it. But both the play and stories had made a start in recognizing the unsavory facts that undermined that very conception of the war.

Conclusion

Hemingway's political veer to the left in the 1930s was sharp but uneven. Well before the outbreak of the Spanish Civil War, he had begun making overtures beneath a smoke screen of disdain for leftist critics and repeated declarations of authorial independence and political indifference. By 1935, intensifying criticism of his recent work—along with years of cajoling by correspondents and critics—had finally pushed him to this new direction. But if winning over leftist critics were his only political aim, he could have declared victory in 1937, when he scored such a success with his keynote speech at the American Writers' Congress, received recognition in Hollywood for supporting the Loyalist cause, and was praised for his new political awareness by the leftist reviewers of *To Have and Have Not*. The perfect index of his new standing with the Left was the February 1938 *Partisan Review* article "Substitution at Left Tackle: Hemingway for Dos Passos," which declared that Hemingway had replaced Dos Passos as the Left's favorite writer. But all these markers are predicated, directly or indirectly, on his 1937 involvement with the Spanish Civil War, that litmus test of antifascist commitment, which Hemingway obviously passed with good colors (pink, not red). Having achieved this new standing with the Left, then, why did he continue his involvement with Spain, returning once more in 1937 and twice more in 1938? The answer appears to be that beyond any function Spain may have served in his domestic calculus, the war took on a meaning of its own for

Hemingway, drew him in, and turned his vague involvement with the Left into an intense commitment to Loyalist Spain—and to the Russian communists in Spain.

Thus, the Spanish war did not originate but vastly accelerated and advanced his movement left. His initial stance—as both quiet supporter of the Loyalist war effort and self-proclaimed neutral and antiwar observer—was obviously contradictory and insupportable, with the latter persona falling away as soon as he arrived in Europe. That he supported the Loyalists was consistent with his lifelong attitude towards Spain and towards the right of common people everywhere to self-governance. What was surprising was that, among the many factions on the Loyalist left, Hemingway aligned himself with the Soviet communists. Several factors conspired in this choice. The communists—in the persons of Joris Ivens, Mikhail Koltsov, and Gustav Regler—actively cultivated him, orienting him toward their internationalist and increasingly dominant position in the war effort, and providing him privileges, comforts, and, most important, the insider status he always sought and which was unavailable to other journalists.

But Hemingway was not the dupe of these handlers, though his benighted assertions to Dos Passos made him seem like one. How could he have been, with his insider knowledge of the disappearances and assassinations, the ruthless repression of the anarchists and POUM? At most, he sometimes appeared to have willed himself to believe what, at some level, he must have known was not true, such as the ludicrous cover story of Nin's kidnapping. But whatever his private reservations (and disgust?), he explicitly supported Stalinist methods and presence in Spain. Given the shaky Loyalist military position by the time he arrived in March 1937, he believed then and later that Soviet leadership and "discipline," brutal as they were, provided the best means of overriding the factionalism and unprofessionalism of the Left and of winning the war. If some, like José Robles, fell afoul of this authoritarian presence, that was a regrettable but inconsequential result of wartime exigencies—collateral damage. Thus, when "friends" like Dos Passos complained about Stalinist methods in Spain, Hemingway dismissed their "liberal" hand-wringing, but in a manner so excessive that, like his earlier public disclaimers of political involvement, it appeared to conceal a contrasting view—and a bad conscience. His brutal responses to Dos Passos and others hint that their protests hit a nerve—that, on some level, he *was* bothered by the disappearances, the tortures, the political executions, the "mistakes."

Hemingway's coverage of the war as journalist, commentator, and author (up to 1940) was markedly uneven and often second-rate. Essentially, he considered his journalism and magazine articles as propaganda for the Loyalist side, though he did try to get his facts right about specific battles he covered and bring to bear his military expertise. As he stated much later, "I would not write anything in the war which could hurt the Republic which I believed in and tried to serve as well as I could" (*Selected Letters*, 789). Strict censorship of the dispatches abetted this aim, of course. That meant emphasizing every Loyalist victory, playing down Franco's steady progress, especially in 1938, and predicting an improving fate for the Loyalists despite mounting evidence to the contrary. His NANA articles presented excellent close-up descriptions of various battles and made astute assessments of military strategy, but they avoided all other aspects of the war and were unreliable in their long-range forecasts. His magazine articles were more self-indulgent cannon shots on various topics, particularly the folly of the U.S. State Department in following the British lead of non-intervention. Topics that might be damaging to the Loyalist cause in America were scrupulously avoided.

It was only in his creative writing—his play and stories—that Hemingway allowed himself to begin to address *one* of these taboo subjects, repressive counterespionage actions of the Loyalist government, which included torture and execution of fifth columnists, but also of many who were innocent, and the prevailing climate of fear and denunciation in Madrid. Hemingway's fictional treatment of these subjects is ambivalent. Like himself only more so, his protagonists are insiders: they're on a first-name basis with the chief executioner of Madrid; they secretly work for the head of counterintelligence; they can provide the essential phone number to enable or prevent an arrest. But as willing participants in this atmosphere of arrest and torture, fear and suspicion, his protagonists are also troubled by guilt ("The Denunciation") and burned out by the tortures and executions they've been party to (*The Fifth Column*).

Beyond this limited recognition of counterespionage brutality and fear, his wartime stories and drama refused to venture. They don't mention the earlier Republican atrocities committed against the clergy, landowners, and profascists though Hemingway's letters show that he was aware of them. And, although Hemingway hobnobbed with Soviet big shots at the Gaylord Hotel, the only references to them in his play and stories are intended solely to debunk the notion of a Soviet presence in Spain. For Hemingway to address these subjects more truthfully, it would take a bigger effort, written with greater detachment and objectivity *after* the war was lost, when ugly truths could no longer hurt the Republic—a big book that purported to tell the full, complicated truth about the war.

Synthesis

Three Pulls to the Left

CONSIDERED TOGETHER, WHAT do the leftward odysseys of these three writers reveal about the pull of politics on their lives and work? What patterns emerge linking the three; what contrasts distinguish them?

At first glance, Steinbeck and Hemingway have much more in common with each other than either does with Wright. Until the mid-1930s, the two were largely apolitical and certainly showed no interest in joining the Left. Before 1936, Steinbeck was caught up in his phalanx theory—his desire to study group behavior from a neutral distance. In the early thirties, Hemingway declared often and loudly his independence from politics and leftist writing in particular, though by late 1935 that façade had begun to crumble. Wright, by contrast, was drawn headlong towards radical politics with his first meeting of the John Reed Club in late 1933. His support of communism followed naturally from the warm welcome he received there—a welcome that sparked his literary ambitions— and from the hope the Communist Party offered his race. The ideological poems that followed were a natural expression of this dual discovery, this fusion of politics and career. Not only did Wright's pull to the Left predate those of the other two writers (though he was considerably younger), it lasted longer, continuing into the early 1940s. The primary index of this commitment was his membership in the CP-USA, which he joined early in 1934.

Joining or becoming associated with the Communist Party, as one measure of leftism, positions the three writers along a continuum rather than as a contrast. Wright is at one pole; Steinbeck, the seeming loner, is at the other. Hemingway falls between these extremes, beginning as a loner, but orbiting around Soviet power-brokers in Spain. They became his friends, tutors, and enablers, and he adhered to their deceptive and self-serving Party line in his journalism. Yet he was far removed from a communist ideology or identity. Different as their attitudes were towards joining the Party, all three writers joined the communist-organized League of American Writers (Wright in 1935, Steinbeck and Hemingway in 1937), and all three either worked for or donated money to such international leftist causes as the Spanish Republic.

Organizational involvement, however, should not be equated with the intensity of their commitment to the Left or to leftist causes. Wright's relationship with the Party was notoriously rocky: after his beloved John Reed Club was closed, his Party membership in Chicago caused him intense frustration, even abuse and harassment, and ultimately resulted in complete separation. His autobiographical writings to the contrary, however, his Party affiliation continued—and for a time improved—with his move to New York, not least because the New York branch found him a much-needed job in the Harlem office of the *Daily Worker*. But even before Wright's literary career caught fire with *Uncle Tom's Children*, he once again felt that conflict he had experienced in Chicago between carrying out onerous Party assignments, here journalistic, and needing time for his creative writing. When his transfer to the New York City branch of the Federal Writers' Project became valid and provided a better balance between subsistence income and time for his fiction writing, he quickly left the *Daily Worker*. In contrast to Wright, Steinbeck's commitment to *his* leftist cause—the plight of the California migrants—though thoroughly individual, even quixotic, was intense and took time and energy away from his creative writing. Hemingway's commitment to the Spanish Republic was also genuine and pushed him much further left; even more than Steinbeck's involvement, it usurped vast chunks of time and effort at the expense of his creative writing, which suffered in these years.

None of the writers' commitments to the Left was purely altruistic, however. Self-interest also played a part. For two of the three—Wright and Hemingway—this motive was obvious. Wright's emergence as a writer—indeed, his discovery of himself as a writer—was inextricably linked to his discovery of radical leftism. The Chicago John Reed Club encouraged him to write, provided intelligent criticism, and most important, opportunities for immediate publication. When that same encouragement to develop as a writer was not forthcoming from the communist cell he joined, conflict ensued. In New York, the same conflict simmered during Wright's tenure at the *Daily Worker*. Precious time and energy were the issues: Wright resented devoting them to what he correctly considered "ephemeral" writing. When his career began to soar in New York, he clearly needed the Party less than it needed him. In all contexts, then, his burgeoning career came first. Ideologically, however, he had no trouble supporting Party doctrine so long as it remained actively committed to fighting for his race.

Hemingway's overtures to the Left, beginning with his *New Masses* article "Who Murdered the Vets?" in 1935, occurred well before his commitment to Republican Spain and stemmed from his desire to restore his fallen standing with critics. His adoption of leftist themes in *To Have and Have Not*, albeit from an idiosyncratic perspective, had the same motive, though he cleverly concealed it by making most of the novel's leftists as reprehensible as the rich. When the Spanish Civil War broke out while he was writing that novel, it provided the perfect opportunity for getting involved in a leftist cause without seeming to cave to leftist pressure, since his love of Spain was well known and long-established. What he perhaps did not expect was how much further left his involvement in Spain would push him. In any case, his immediate motives for going left were fulfilled by 1937: he had once again become a hero and a brother-in-arms of leftist critics. Moreover, his involvement in another war provided just the subject he needed for his next novel. War had always been his specialty, but *this* war added devotion to a viable cause to war's essential issues of life and death, courage and cowardice. Exploring the many aspects of this political devotion would mark a new dimension in his war writing and differ significantly from the war themes in his earlier fiction, which had focused on being wounded in a meaningless war.

Steinbeck appears the exception to having self-interested motives for leftist involvement. Indeed, his support of the migrants in 1936 to 1938—requiring considerable outlays of time, energy, and money, and offering in return intense physical discomfort and frustration—was essentially altruistic. He obviously could have stayed home and devoted his time and energy to his professional career. But just as Hemingway's involvement in Spain provided the subject and some of the material for his next novel, so too did Steinbeck's personal dealings with and commitment to the migrants. He had known since his journalistic coverage of the migrants in 1936, well before he went to Visalia in 1938 that his next novel would be a big one and would address in some way the issue of the migrants flooding into California and the brutal repression and exploitation they experienced there. Thus, even though professional benefits were not in the forefront of his mind when he went to Visalia, every day he spent with migrants, and every report he received from Tom Collins about their behavior in the government camps, provided vivid material he would soon use in his new novel. Wright, too, was able to draw on experiences he had and people he met in the Party for *his* big novel, but this political source material was secondary to his larger themes. Though communism affects Bigger Thomas's life in several crucial ways, it never becomes central to his identity. Wright's experience with leftism benefitted him more at the beginning of his career in getting him started, inspiring him to write, and providing an ideological vision for his poetry.

If these writers' involvement in leftist causes provided the central subject (or at least some material) for the big novels they worked on in 1938 and 1939, in each case their commitment to these causes had ironically passed its peak by the time they were writing the novels themselves. Steinbeck poured his greatest rage against the big growers' power conglomerate into his aborted novel, "L'Affaire Lettuceberg." By the time he settled into writing *The Grapes of Wrath*, he had achieved a measure of detachment that enabled him to envision the story in a broader, though no less partisan, context. Wright's strongest commitment to the Party came in his first rush of discovery and enthusiasm in Chicago. By the time he wrote his stories in 1935 to 1936, he had already found his subject: a black man's experience in white racist America, whether in the South (*Uncle Tom's Children*) or, later, in the North (his new novel). By 1938, he had gained enough self-confidence and self-realization to realize that Party dictates about abandoning negro nationalism would not stop him, any more than would the anguish of black and white readers, who were bound to be appalled by the kind of protagonist he was creating in *Native Son*. Hemingway, too, by the time he started writing *For Whom the Bell Tolls*, no longer felt he had to maintain the Party line about the Soviets in Spain, or to ignore such infelicities in the Loyalist cause as atrocities committed in its name. Now that the war was over, he could stop being a propagandist and go back to the complex realism that had always guided his best writing. And he could tell a few truths that his journalism had either ignored or intentionally misrepresented.

Significantly, all three writers expected their new novels to shock at least some types of readers. Steinbeck and Wright were explicit about intending to shock. As he told his editor and publisher, Steinbeck knew he was writing a *J'Accuse!* and looked forward eagerly to the distress his "outrageous" novel (*Life in Letters*, 172) would cause not only the power brokers of California farming but ordinary readers. Wright explained his intent in the famous passage of "How 'Bigger' Was Born" that he aimed to make this novel "so hard and deep" that it would profoundly disturb liberal readers, who might otherwise comfort themselves with their mild distress about racism. Less sympathetic readers, too, would encounter a protagonist who was a sociopath of their own racist creation. When he wrote that his readers "would have to face it" in his novel, he assumed precisely the attitude of a dog's owner pushing the dog's face into the mess it had just made. Wright also knew that the Communist Party's literary overseers were sure to dislike the novel's racial perspective; and if he had already envisioned its conclusion, he knew that those guardians were certain to be discomfited by the novel's treatment of communists. Hemingway was less explicit about shocking his readers, less intent on doing so. Still, he knew that, in challenging the shibboleths of the Loyalist cause—in referring to Soviet brutalities, depicting Loyalist massacres, and debunking Loyalist legends—he was bound to offend the defenders of Loyalist virtue and Russian benevolence, such as his friends in the International Brigades.

In Wright's intent to shock and Hemingway's willingness to do so, some of the targets, significantly, were on the left. For Wright, the targets were liberal sympathizers and, indirectly, the literary overseers of the Party itself (at least their dictates about negro nationalism). For Hemingway, the Communist Party, particularly its acolytes in the International Brigade, was also the target in its mythology about the Spanish republic. These targets point towards the authors' ambivalence about communist doctrine and about their own leftist allegiance—ambivalence that would permeate the very fabric of these novels as a conscious authorial strategy. Steinbeck's case is quite different from the other two writers: his cause is more personal, the ideology he expresses is his own, his adherence to it more absolute, and his targets for shock-effect are the "baddies," not those supposedly on his side. Hence, the ambivalence in his novel, while certainly present, is more unconscious, more a question of inconsistency and fissures than of thematic intent.

Although further linkages among the three writers could be adduced, such as the role journalism played in forming their leftist attitudes, this seems an appropriate place to stop talking *around* their novels—the three major novels of 1939 and 1940—and to begin discussing the novels themselves.

PART 2

The Grapes of Wrath

Passionate Contradictions

I am completely partisan. Every effort I can bring to bear is and has been [at] the call of the common working people . . .

—Steinbeck to John Barry, 30 June 1938[1]

ONE REASON *The Grapes of Wrath* towers over so many other 1930s novels about tough times and embattled workers and families is that Steinbeck was determined to give his novel an epic breadth, which involved telling a story on multiple levels beyond simply the Joad family's struggle for self-preservation. Steinbeck referred to five such "layers" in the novel, without specifically identifying them.[2] However one construes these levels, arguably one of the most important beyond the Joads' story comprises the "general chapters" that present the migrants' experience collectively: from being "tractored off" their small farms in the Plains states to encountering various hardships and camaraderie on the road to suffering destitution and abuse from the power conglomerate in California. A few of these general chapters, however, sketch the history of the big farms in California and their current state held by "the great owners." These chapters not only present the land-owners' mentality but also prophesize their future. As such, these landowner chapters counterpoint the general chapters about the migrants, and together they present a macrocosm of the same conflicts the Joads experience on the individual level. Steinbeck's voice in these general chapters differs markedly from the brilliant realism of the Joads chapters. In presenting the migrants and especially the landowners as a whole, the narrative voice acquires the rolling cadences of the King James Bible, a quality Steinbeck himself noted:[3]

> The owners of the land came onto the land . . .
>
> And it came about that owners no longer worked on their farms. They farmed on paper; and they forgot the land, the smell, the feel of it, and remembered only that they owned it . . . (31, 232)

Appropriately, the voice is frequently prophetic in these general chapters and strives for a biblical sense of inevitability:

> And some day—the armies of bitterness will all be going the same way. And they'll all walk together, and there'll be a dead terror from it. (88)

Note, for example, how neatly "pharaoh" can be substituted for "great owners" in chapter 19. Both have "hardened their hearts," have closed their eyes and ears to warnings, and thus must lose their property:

> And the great owners, who must lose their land in an upheaval, the great owners with access to history, with eyes to read history and to know the great fact: when property accumulates in too few hands it is taken away. . . . The great owners ignored the three cries of history. The land fell into fewer hands, the number of the dispossessed increased, and every effort of the great owners was directed at repression. (238)[4]

> But Pharaoh shall not hearken unto you, that I may lay my hand upon Egypt, and bring forth mine armies, and my people the children of Israel, out of the land of Egypt by great judgments. . . . And the Lord hardened the heart of Pharaoh, and he hearkened not unto them; as the Lord had spoken unto Moses. (Exod. 7:4, 9:12, KJV)

Although some critics have found this biblical tone off-putting,[5] for many readers it is magisterial and perfectly matches the epic breadth of the general chapters. As well, the scope and gravity of the general chapters suggest the novel's mythic dimension by implying parallels to other collective journeys toward a better life: the land-hungry American pioneers heading West; the Israelites heading to the promised land; the American slaves struggling towards freedom. Steinbeck himself felt that the poetic rhythms and symbols of these chapters would expressively "open" the reader to the novel's "intellectual" themes.[6]

But if these general chapters give the novel its breadth, some of its tone, and its mythic resonance, they also enable Steinbeck to express his social theories and the radical political views he had developed before writing the novel. While these views are certainly implied—and sometimes stated—in the Joads' struggles and conflicts, they are explicit and prevalent in the general chapters, particularly in Steinbeck's prophecies. By the same token, however, the general chapters also reveal contradictions and ambivalence in Steinbeck's political and social views, as well as some historical distortions and occasions when his crystal ball was clouded. In this chapter, I wish to concentrate on Steinbeck's political and social themes, and particularly on their contradictions; therefore, I will focus on the general chapters and address the Joads' story as it develops these political themes.

Any first-time reader of this novel can easily identify the story's central conflict between, on one hand, the tenant farmers represented by the Joads, who are tractored off their small farms in the Plains states and migrate to California in search of a better life, and, on the other, the power complex that forced them off their land and that harasses and exploits them in California. The latter include the big landowners (often the banks); the Associated Farmers, which represents the big owners; the farm managers, the contact point of exploitation; the deputies and vigilantes that the owners hire to intimidate and harass the migrants to keep them moving and prevent them from organizing; and the townspeople and newspapers the Associated Farmers influence in its campaign to arouse fear and hatred of the migrants. The impoverished migrants, Steinbeck tells us, want two things, which are really one thing: food and land. Essentially—and hopelessly—they want to continue the kind of lives they left behind: farming a small plot of land, raising their own crops, feeding their families. They discover in California that all land—even the fallow land they eye hungrily—is owned; that

they are pitifully underpaid as laborers when they do find work;
and that they are forced to live in subhuman conditions in squalid
roadside camps or one-room cabins for crop pickers. In fact, their
wages are so low, their working conditions so miserable that they
and their families are starving amidst the abundance of crops. As
the one exception to the miserable conditions they must endure,
the few government-run sanitary camps treat them decently but
cannot provide work for them. The big owners lured the migrants
from the Plains with fliers falsely promising jobs so that the large
numbers these fliers would attract and the migrants' desperate need
would combine to drive wages below the subsistence level. Now,
however, the big growers are afraid of the migrants' huge numbers,
of their growing anger, and most of all of their capacity to organize.
Thus, the constant harassment.

This was the essential conflict Steinbeck discovered in his research beginning with "The Harvest Gypsies" in 1936, and this was
the human outrage he determined to dramatize in his novel. Explicitly in his newspaper articles and only a little less so in his novel,
he predicted that if the migrants' conditions weren't significantly
improved—specifically, in increasing the number of government
camps and through collective bargaining—and if the "fascistic"
abuses of the big growers were not curbed, the growing conflict
would inevitably explode (*Blood*, 30, 33). The novel does not quite
state that the explosion *will* happen, but that events are moving
powerfully and ineluctably in that direction. The novel's title po-
etically suggests that "the grapes of wrath are filling and growing
heavy, growing heavy for the vintage" (*Grapes*, 349). But the prophecy hinges on "if": "if they ever move under a leader—the end. . . .
[I]f they ever know themselves, the land will be theirs . . ." (238).

After two misfires, Steinbeck wrote the novel in a passionate heat, near the height of his identification with the migrants'
cause. The novel culminated over two years of research and political involvement, which included observing the migrants' living
conditions, both at squalid roadside Hoovervilles and at the model government camps; acquiring statistics about the scope of the
problem from the Resettlement Administration (RA) and about
the government camps from camp manager Tom Collins; financially aiding and feeding hungry families with food Steinbeck had

purchased and transported to the roadside camps in a van; helping move them and their meager belongings to higher ground—"in mud for three days and nights"—during the floods at Visalia; and calling attention to their plight—and to the hateful efforts of the Associated Farmers to block assistance to them—in newspaper articles and in a reprint of "The Harvest Gypsies." Over these two and a half years, the migrants had become far more than a problem to understand with detached observation; they became a cause to which Steinbeck was wholly devoted—and wholly partisan, as the epigraph shows. Thus, he made no effort to conceal his sympathy for the migrants and his intense hatred of the big growers and their power nexus. He intended his novel as an indictment and a prophecy of a forthcoming political explosion if the situation were not remedied quickly, and of a more sweeping political and economic transformation in future. But the very passion that fires the book also mars it. For although he took enough time and trouble to make the book more than the diatribe which had crippled "L'Affaire Lettuceberg" and to fashion it into a complex work of art, the novel nevertheless contains a number of contradictions and unintentional ambiguities, which suggests that the author had not thought through these issues as clearly as he might have, and had not resolved ambivalence and contradictions in his own political and social philosophy regarding these issues. The novel also suffers from Steinbeck's romantic mysticism, or sentimentality, regarding farming and machinery, as well as plot and character manipulations that too obviously further his themes at the expense of the reader's credence.

Let's begin with the Joads as representatives of the migrants. Who are they? What is their claim to the land they farm? And what drives them from this land? Steinbeck identifies them as "tenant farmers," correcting his earlier journalistic depictions of the migrants as small landowners ("Harvest Gypsies," 22) and sharecroppers (*Blood*, 32). Landowners, after all, could not be evicted by the banks unless the land was mortgaged, which in most cases it was. Tenants had even less claim, although this issue—"what constitutes ownership?"—is a central one and will be discussed presently. (What Steinbeck ignored about the actual migrations, perhaps because the facts did not cohere with his themes about farming and land, is that more migrants came from towns and cities than from farms; these laborers and shopkeepers migrated to California's cities in search of similar work.[7] How the Joads came to operate their farm is left somewhat vague. We know they have lived on it and worked it for a generation, since Grampa refers to his days on the land. But Steinbeck melds the Joads' history into the generic migrant history with such repeated statements in the general chapters as "Grampa took up the land, and he had to kill the Indians and drive them away" (*Grapes*, 33).[8] Two points are noteworthy here. First, "took up" is a pleasant euphemism for "stole"—or at best "squatted on"—and killing the former "owners" does not burnish the image of pioneering white settlers like Grampa. Steinbeck makes this point explicitly when he describes the same pattern in the history of California's big landowners:

> Once California belonged to Mexico and its land to Mexicans; and a horde of tattered feverish Americans poured in. And such was their hunger for land that they *took* the land—*stole* Sutter's land. . . . and they guarded with guns that land they had *stolen*. They put up houses and barns, they turned the earth and planted crops. And these things were possession, and possession was ownership. (231, emphasis added)

Tellingly, though Steinbeck softens Grampa's "taking up" the land, he does not mince words in describing the California theft, perhaps because that land soon belonged to rich men. Now, as their white landowning descendants—the big landowners—have become soft and detached from the land, they cannot deal with a repetition of the cycle in the land-hungry Plains migrants, who (in the general chapters) contemplate "taking" fallow land to feed their hungry families. In his seminal chapter 19 prophesying the breakup of the big farms "in an upheaval," Steinbeck predicts this "taking" will be widespread, an inevitable process he depicts as a historical "fact": "when property accumulates in too few hands it is taken away. And that companion fact: when a majority of the people are hungry and cold they will take by force what they need" (238). Because the "hunger" in these cycles of "taking" or stealing is not just physical hunger but also land hunger, the morality of the taking is left ambiguous, and Steinbeck, reverting back to his earlier, pseudo-scientific detachment as observer of historical processes, is content simply to describe—with evident satisfaction—that the same amoral taking will come around to plague the big landowners. From the Joads' perspective, however, this original theft—and murder—somewhat clouds their status as victims.[9]

The second point leads to the novel's central contradiction: that the Joads' experience is a microcosm of the migrants as a whole, in which an *individual* family that once farmed its own plot of land now cannot do so. What, then, is this family's aim—its dream—as it journeys to California (and by extension, the aims of thousands of like families)? One would have to conclude that these aims are to achieve the same kind of life on better land: an individual family farming its plot, raising its crops, feeding its members. The perfect symbol of this dream is the Edenic image that the Joad family, Ma particularly, envisions: "little white houses in among the orange trees. I wonder—that is, if we all get jobs an' all work—maybe we can get one of them little white houses. An' the little fellas go out an' pick oranges right off the tree" (91). Pa, too, expresses the small-farm dream: "we'll work an' we'll get a piece of growin' land with water" (188). Quite apart from the near impossibility of their achieving this aim under the conditions of California land ownership, this individual dream and the rugged individualism of the pioneering farmers do not cohere well with Steinbeck's major theme of privileging *collective* action both as a means to achieve the migrants' aims and as a mode of living preferable to the divisive selfishness of individual self-interest.

Significantly, Steinbeck is never definite about whether the Joads ever legally owned their farm, though in the generic history of Grampa taking the land from the Indians, his squatting would eventually give him title, just as Steinbeck explains happened to the California owners. "Owning," of course, is a controversial and important concept in the novel. Who owns the land: the bank that holds title—"a piece of paper"—or the farmer who works it?

> Sure, cried the tenant man, but it's our land. We measured it and broke it up. We were born on it, and we got killed and died on it. . . . That's what makes it ours—being born on it, working it, dying on it. That makes ownership, not a paper with numbers on it. (33)

Even in the big-farm milieu of California, the power nexus recognizes and thus tries to prevent the same process, that ownership results from working the land: "A crop raised—why, that makes ownership. Land hoed and the carrots eaten—a man might fight for the land he's taken food from. Get him off quick! He'll think he owns it. He might die fighting for the little plot among the Jimson weeds" (236).

By this standard—Steinbeck's obviously—the Joads own their land by having worked it for at least a generation; it is part of Steinbeck's mystic vision of how one belongs to the land, and vice versa, in working it by hand. Yet, when asked about it, Pa is ambiguous:

> "Till we got tractored off, we was people with a farm." . . . .
>> "Croppin'?" . . .
>> "Sure we was sharecroppin'. Use' ta own the place." (188)

Does he mean that they owned the place *before* they became share-croppers, or that in sharecropping they achieved the kind of squatting ownership described above? Either way, the bank eventually holds title—legal ownership.[10] Later in the novel Ma echoes Pa ("We was farm people") but then adds ambiguously, "till the debt" (307). Does she mean that they tried to buy the land, but couldn't pay off the mortgage debt? Or that they mortgaged the farm later to secure a bank loan, with the same result? The latter scenario raises the question of why, as small landholders, they went into debt. A season or a string of poor harvests? Continuous droughts? In the general chapter about being tractored off the land, the "squatting men" recount, "Then a bad year came and [Pa] had to borrow a little money. . . . The bank owned the land then, but we stayed and we got a little bit of what we raised" (33).

But there was another pervasive cause of debt for small Plains farmers like the Joads—a cause which Steinbeck conspicuously ignores. Encouraged by the banks, many small farmers in the late 1910s and early 1920s went into debt to buy farm machinery, notably tractors, to increase production when crop prices were high in the late teens. When those prices fell in the 1920s, these same farmers often could not pay off their debt, and many subsequently lost their farms.[11] There is no mention of the Joads owning such machinery—indeed, as poor tenants when the story begins, the likelihood they once did is remote. What is significant here is that, in making the Joads a family that plows by mule and harvests by hand, Steinbeck not only ignores the historical importance of machinery to these small farmers, but fashions a highly romantic (and highly distorted) myth of their *anti*-mechanistic values and pre-industrial status:

> There in the Middle and Southwest had lived a simple agrarian folk who had not changed with industry, who had not farmed with machines or known the power and danger of machines in private hands. They had not grown up in the paradoxes of industry. Their senses were still sharp to the ridiculousness of the industrial life.
>
> And then suddenly the machines pushed them out . . . (282)

This fanciful depiction of anachronistic farmers plays into Steinbeck's mystical conception of the pre-industrial farmers' oneness with land that they must break up, plant, and harvest by hand. By contrast, machines separate the farmer from the land, destroy that mystical oneness:

> And when a horse stops work and goes into the barn there is a life and a vitality left . . . . But when the motor of a tractor stops, it is as dead as the ore it came from. . . . [Tractoring the land] is easy and efficient. So easy that the wonder goes out of work, so efficient that the wonder goes out of land and the working of it, and with the wonder the deep understanding and the relation. And in the tractor man there grows the contempt that comes only to a stranger who has little understanding and no relation. . . . That [hand-farming] man . . . walking on the earth, turning his plow point for a stone . . . kneeling in the earth to eat his lunch; that man who is more than his elements knows the land that is more than its analysis. But the machine man, driving a dead tractor on land he does not know and love, understands only chemistry; and he is contemptuous of the land and of himself. . . . his home is not the land. (115–16)

Even the land, in Steinbeck's mythos, responds differently to the machine than to hand-farming because with the former, the organic link and mystic bond have been broken:

> And when that crop grew, and was harvested [by tractor], no man had crumbled a hot clod in his fingers or let the earth sift past his fingertips. No man had touched the seed, or lusted for the growth. Men ate what they had not raised, had no connection with the bread. That land bore under iron, and under iron gradually died; for it was not loved or hated, it had no prayers or curses. (36)

Although the hyper-romanticism of these passages might make actual farmers smile—if they did not own tractors, it was not from a romantic preference to till the soil with a hand plow—the passages square with Steinbeck's hostility to the machine as the means of both pushing the migrants off their land in the Plains and of indirectly helping to exploit them in California by enabling the cultivation of mega-farms.[12] But he was careful in *Grapes* not to overstress the migrants' unpreparedness for this large-scale mechanized farming (a point he had made in "The Harvest Gypsies") because the problem of two profoundly differing cultures encountering each other might seem insoluble, whereas the problems he wanted to underscore in *Grapes* had political solutions. Accordingly, he makes the younger Joad men—Tom and especially Al—comfortable handling machines; and in the harvesting scenes in California, the tractor is not dramatized as an adversary.

From the quotations and discussion above, it is clear that what drives the Joads—and the migrant families they represent—from their land and forces them to leave the only life they know for the bewildering one of exile and migration are the tractors and those who run them. The Joads are "tractored out" not merely by the "robotic" driver, desperate for his three dollars a day, but by the bank-landowners that send out the tractors literally to push the small farmers off their land and consolidate the small plots into large farms (à la California but without the fertility), from which the owners hope to squeeze a profit.

But what about the pervasive drought and dust storms, which in popular culture are still seen as *the* cause of the massive migration?[13]

As chapter 1 discusses, Steinbeck's weighing of these two causes—drought and tractors—changed over the span of his involvement with the migration, a change that reveals much about his political views when he wrote the novel. His 1936 "Harvest Gypsies" articles blame the migration solely on the drought (*Harvest Gypsies*, 21–22), while two years later the epilogue to *The Blood Is Strong* presents *both* the dust and "the tractors" as "displacing the sharecroppers" (32). Precisely as in *Grapes*, the epilogue of *Their Blood Is Strong* explains, "the land was in the hands of the banks and the finance companies and . . . these owners found that one man with a tractor could do the work of ten sharecropper families" (32). Significantly, the families are "dispossessed" of their land—a term that does not fit the action of a drought.

The novel continues this duality, but shifts its emphasis even more towards the banks and tractors as the culprit. Chapter 1 evocatively describes the drought and resulting dust pervading every inch and aspect of life in rural Oklahoma; chapter 5 *dramatizes* a family being "tractored out," featuring a generic farmer's dialogue with the owners or their representatives, and later with the tractor driver. Because of its later place in the narrative and more dramatic nature, chapter 5 takes precedence over chapter 1. More important, chapter 5 represents the Joads' experience. The drought does not break the small farmers; they remain "thinking—figuring" (4). But their farmhouses are broken by the tractor (39), forcing their residents to become migrants.[14] As the novel progresses, mention of the drought virtually disappears as a cause of the migration, while being "tractored out" is referred to several times. Without question, in shifting the cause to the banks and tractors, Steinbeck expresses his current political view that this tragic migration was man-made, caused by greed for profits.

Chapter 5 is the novel's first identification of the migrants' enemy: specifically, the land-owning banks, but in a broader sense a system that places profits before humane concerns.[15] Although the system is never precisely named, it is clearly capitalism. Steinbeck's characterization of it in this chapter is both interesting and implausible, even contradictory. As the owner's spokesman attempts to exculpate himself for evicting the farm family, he depicts the bank as an inhuman monster: "[T]hose creatures don't breathe air, don't eat side-meat. They breathe profits; they eat the interest on money. If they don't get it, they die. . . . The bank—the monster has to have profits all the time. It can't wait. . . . When the monster stops growing, it dies. It can't stay one size" (32). The passage is pleasing in the way that the adversary is so imaginatively described by its own servant, but it is also implausible. (At most, such a representative would likely mumble, "It's not my fault—I'm just following orders.") The "monster" depiction is one of many examples in which Steinbeck inserts his own views or voice at the expense of a scene's credibility. And if the monster is the profit system, or capitalism, Steinbeck has taken a leaf from Karl Marx, who argues in *Das Kapital* that capitalism, which thrives on surplus value (i.e., profits), must continuously grow and expand. It is not the only instance in which Steinbeck borrows Marxist ideology, even though he denied, by implication, that the novel had a "communist angle" (letter to Pascal Covici, 1 Jan. 1939, *Life in Letters*, 174).

The monster is also described as "sick," out of control: "Men made it, but they can't control it" (33). Although vivid, this depiction is of little comfort to the farmer, who wants to take revenge on a tangible culprit. The tractor driver tells him, "Maybe there's nobody to shoot. Maybe the thing isn't men at all" (38). "The thing" is thus as amorphous as "capitalism" itself, and the driver's implication is clear: you can't fight such a system. But the tenant farmer crucially draws the opposite conclusion and, given the novel's themes, the correct one: "We got a bad thing made by men, and by God that's something we can change" (38). Here is why the novel plays down the drought and emphasizes the tractor as proximate cause. The farmer realizes, "It's not like lightning or earthquakes" (28)—or drought. One can't change natural disasters in the short term;[16] one *can* change a bad man-made system. The question then becomes, how? That question becomes more compelling and insistent as the migrants discover that they have left one profit-corrupted system only to arrive, in California, at another, far more comprehensive one: the agribusiness that systematically exploits, harasses, and terrorizes them.

When "I" Becomes "We"

Steinbeck addresses the question of how to effect political change and correct social evils by returning to one of his favorite subjects—the phalanx or group—but he now treats it in a manner entirely different from his unsympathetic observations of the strikers in *In Dubious Battle*. There, the group itself was a kind of monster, thriving on blood, requiring a leader to guide it, think for it. In *Grapes*, it becomes the center of Steinbeck's political vision, battling the "I" of selfishness and separation. In fact, the conversion from "'I" to "we"—discussed explicitly in chapter 14—is arguably the linchpin of social change and connects the other themes in the novel. With one important exception discussed below, the novel consistently privileges the collective ("we") and either denigrates or shows the ineffectuality of the egocentric "I" of self-interest. The collective "we" is not only more humane (in people helping out other people) than the divisive and selfish "I," it is potentially far more powerful if and when it organizes itself.

Steinbeck examines the way the collective operates at several levels: the interfamilial, the impromptu mini-collective of the migrants' nightly roadside camp en route to California, the large collective of the sanitary camps of the RA, and the potential collectives of united political action in the farmworkers' organizing and striking for better wages, conditions, and treatment. Besides dramatizing its chief benefits—humane values and political power—Steinbeck considers the role of a leader, and how the collective's adversaries, the big growers, view it. Finally, he shapes the development and behavior of the Joad family members according to this central theme.

In the smallest scale, the family would seem the perfect model of the collective, particularly because, in the Joads, it occupies so much of the plot. Susan Shillinglaw, for example, writes, "In *The Grapes of Wrath*, the family unit is the measure of our humanity."[17] Yet, the "we" at this level can paradoxically support both selfishness *and* cooperation and often mixtures of both. Members vary sharply in their devotion to the family: Ma is consistently altruistic, Rosasharn and Al think mainly of themselves until the conclusion, and the kids—Ruthie and Winfield—act like kids. Not until the family has settled into a routine on the road does it really begin to function as a unit: "each member of the family grew into his proper place, grew into his duties; so that each member, old and young, had his place in the car; . . . when the cars pulled into the camping places, each member had his duty and went to it without instruction . . . . without command" (195). This division of labor also applied to farm life before the migration. But that life often elevated the family *as opposed to* other such families, as the family typically looks out only or primarily for itself. Tom's humorous stories about Pa stealing half an abandoned house and how neighbors mistakenly ransacked someone's house lightly illustrate this family-first mentality. A more serious example is the tractor driver who makes fifteen or twenty families homeless in order to feed his own family: "Can't think of that [the newly homeless]. Got to think of my own kids" (37). Ma, of course, is a shining exception to familial selfishness: she will never turn away a hungry stranger. But when the Joads first enter the squalid roadside Hooverville in California, even Ma worries about cooking a stew for the family with hungry outsider children eyeing her kettle: "I dunno what to do. I got to feed a fambly. What'm I gonna do with these here?" (257). By now, however, she has experienced many instances of kindness and sharing with other families; so, after futilely shooing away the children, she lets them scrape the remains. These instances of interfamily kindness are crucial to the story and even begin to break down the family's traditional integrity: "The families, which had been units of which the boundaries were a house at night, a farm by day, changed their boundaries [on the road]. In the long hot light, they were silent in the cars moving slowly westward, but at night [at roadside camps] they integrated with any group they found" (195–96). On the road, the Joads bond with the Wilsons when Grampa dies in the Wilsons' tent and receives the altruistic ministrations of Mrs. Wilson, who is seriously ill herself. In return, the Joad brothers fix the Wilsons' car, and the two families decide to travel together. Steinbeck's point could not be clearer. Apart, each family is overburdened; together, in sharing their burdens, they make better progress—they help each other out and give to each other all-important kindness. The same interfamily bonding occurs when the Joads and the Wainwrights share a boxcar: together, they midwife Rosasharn's delivery; they may even become kin.

This sharing can occur between individuals, of course. Early in the novel, Muley shares his rabbits with the hungry Tom and Casy. His explanation is eloquent in its simplicity: "if a fella's got somepin to eat an' another fella's hungry—why, the first fella ain't got no choice" (49). Al works on Floyd Knowles's car in the roadside Hooverville, and Timothy helps Tom find work when the Joads are living in the government camp. More often, however, the individual apart from the group—or insufficiently tied to the group—displays selfishness. As Casy says, he "bust the holiness" of "all workin' together" (81). Steinbeck ties this selfishness to property ownership: "If you who own the things people must have could understand this [process of "I" becoming "we"], you might preserve yourself. . . . But that you cannot know. For the quality of owning freezes you forever into 'I,' cuts you off forever from the 'we'" (152). Even the expectation of ownership can be enough to make one selfishly break off from the collective, as when Connie abandons Rosasharn (possibly for a tractor-driver's job), and when Al plans to leave the family to become a mechanic and spend his earnings on himself. In a sense, even Rosasharn's impending baby is a kind of future ownership, completely occupying her concern until the very end of the novel. Casy's first grace with the Joads presents this opposition between collective unity and selfish separatism on a spiritual level, as he blesses the former as "holy":

> I got thinkin' how we was holy when we was one thing, an' mankin' was holy when it was one thing. An' it on'y got unholy when one mis'able little fella got the bit in his teeth an' run off his own way, kickin' an' draggin' an' fightin'. Fella like that bust the holiness. But when they're all workin' together, not one fella for another fella, but one fella kind of harnessed to the whole shebang—that's right, that's holy. (81)

Though "the whole shebang" raises problems that will be discussed below, here one cannot help wondering if Steinbeck was thinking about Hitler as that "mis'able little fella." When the novel was being written in 1938, the "mis'able little fella" had indeed "got the bit in his teeth and run off his own way."

Beyond the interfamily level, the novel studies two forms of collective consciousness and behavior: the temporary roadside camps that formed and re-formed each night along Route 66 and the more permanent sanitary camps in California. In both of these contexts, the novel presents a democratic collective operating with remarkable efficiency to benefit its members. Steinbeck thought the roadside camp important enough to devote all of chapter 17 to describing its formation and functioning: "In the evening a strange thing happened: the twenty families became one family, the children were the children of all. . . . Every night a world created . . . relationships that make a world, established" (193–94). In calling these actions "building worlds," Steinbeck implies the collectivizing process can occur at all levels, and, like a sociologist, he identifies stages in the process:

> Then leaders emerged, then laws were made, then codes came into being. . . The families learned what rights must be observed . . . . what rights are monstrous . . . . [R]ules became laws, although no one told the families. . . . In the worlds, social conduct became fixed and rigid . . . . There grew up government in the worlds, with leaders, with elders. (194–95)

The central ethic in this world-building is sharing, just as it was at the individual level between Muley, Tom, and Casy: "they huddled together; they talked together; they shared their lives, their food, and the things they hoped for in the new country" (193). Conversely, selfishness is the cardinal sin: "it is unlawful in any way to foul the drinking water; it is unlawful to eat good rich food near one who is hungry, unless he is asked to share. . . . A man with food fed a hungry man, and thus insured himself against hunger" (194–95).

Although leaders for these collectives are briefly mentioned twice, they play no *dramatic* role in either laying down or enforcing these rules. This absence, so different from the leaders' dominant role in *In Dubious Battle*, points to Steinbeck's central belief that these communities could be self-governing as well as self-operating in emphasizing sharing and repressing selfishness. Here again,

Steinbeck directly echoes Marxist (technically, Engels') theory that in a socialist society ultimately the coercive state would "wither away." Was Steinbeck here presenting his vision of a better future to replace the selfishness of individual ownership? If so, his novel was perhaps more radical than he realized because this vision could certainly be called idealistic collectivism. And like other utopias, it seems quite implausible, or at best, exaggerated in the definiteness of its unwritten rules. Did Steinbeck actually witness these nighttime camps? That he followed and stayed with the migrants on their journey west from the Plains is, of course, a popular myth. In fact, he and Tom Collins followed the last part of the typical migrant journey in reverse, moving from the southern end of the Central Valley east toward the California border.[18] But I've come across no evidence that suggests Steinbeck spent any nights in these temporary highway camps en route to California, though he may well have gathered reports about them from migrants he did talk to in California. The conclusion then seems inescapable that he largely invented their perfectly cooperative nature to further his larger themes about the necessity of the collective "we" and its ethic of sharing. If so, the idealization parallels his romantic depictions of farming the land by hand discussed above.

One collective that Steinbeck definitely did not invent was the RA's sanitary camps for migrants, which he observed extensively and gathered data on, both thanks to camp manager Tom Collins.[19] Here, the camp's self-regulatory and self-governing nature does not derive merely from the migrants' intuitive understanding and consent to unwritten roadside rules of behavior. The procedures are explicit and even more democratic than the roadside camps. As Jim Rawley, the camp manager modeled directly on Collins, explains to Tom, the camp is run by committees comprised of the migrants themselves: "Central Committee keeps order an' makes rules. . . . Folks here elect their own cops" (287, 286). Tom's incredulous reaction explains how rare this phenomenon seems: "You mean to say the fellas that runs the camp is jus' fellas—campin' here?" The camp also features the luxury of hot water for bathing and laundry, which enables the migrants to regain their self-respect. Note how Steinbeck dramatizes the Joads' delight (Ma's especially)—"This here's the time the fambly got to get decent. Comin' acrost they wasn't no chance" (303)—as if to directly rebut the frequent charge that the migrants were dirty by choice. With hot water and flush toilets for sanitation, social groups and activities, and collective entertainment (music and dances), the camp does indeed seem like a heaven on earth, not only to the Joads, dirty and bedraggled from the journey and continuously harassed by deputies, but to readers who have identified with the Joads. Tom's response is thus shared by the reader, as Steinbeck intended: "Why ain't they more places like this?" Of the many reforms that the novel urges thematically, building more government sanitary camps is the most concrete and obvious; yet this self-evident good was, as Steinbeck well knew, intensely opposed by the Associated Farmers, for the logical reason that migrants coming from these camps, having regained their self-respect, would be harder to exploit and demean. As a fellow camper tells Tom, "Those folks in the camp are getting used to being treated like humans. When they go back to the squatters' camps, they'll be hard to handle" (297).[20]

As in the communal roadside camp, the importance of a leader (as authority figure and manipulator) here is minimal. There are no Macs and Jims from *In Dubious Battle*. When Ma asks Rawley if he's the "boss," he complains humorously, "'No. These people here worked me out of a job. They keep the camp clean, they keep order, they do everything. I never saw such people'" (304). Accordingly, his administrative presence is slight; and when the camp faces a planned disruption caused by outsiders in order to bring in the police, it is the committee members, not Rawley, who plan and successfully execute countermeasures. Once again, the state has nearly withered away in the collective's self-regulation.

The big growers' fear and attempted repression of these camps speak directly to Steinbeck's most important political theme: if the migrants can organize themselves to run this camp successfully, they can organize themselves as workers to strike for higher wages and better working conditions, and to resist police intimidation. Tom's friend Timothy sums it up:

"They're scairt we'll organize, I guess. An' maybe they're right. This here camp is an organization. People there look out for themselves. . . . I guess the big farmers is scairt of that. Can't throw us in jail—why it scares 'em. Figger maybe if we gov'n ourselves, maybe we'll do other things." (297)

Another camp member observes,

"Why don' them depities get in here an' raise hell like ever' place else? . . . I'll tell ya. It's cause we're all a-workin' together. Depity can't pick on one fella in this camp. He's pickin' on the whole darn camp. An' he don't dare. All we got to do is give a yell an' they's two hundred men out. Fella organizin' for the union . . . says we could do that any place. Jus' stick together." (357)

At this point Steinbeck could have had his characters break into "Solidarity Forever!" And in his "prophetic" mode, he continually raises the specter that this political solidarity is coming ever closer as "I" turns to "we":

And they'll all walk together, and there'll be a dead terror from it. (88)

If they ever get together there ain't nothin' that'll stop 'em. (236)

And always [the great owners] were in fear of a principal—three hundred thousand—if they ever move under a leader—the end. . . . [I]f they ever know themselves, the land will be theirs and all the gas, all the rifles in the world won't stop them. (238)

The one major exception to the novel's valuation of collective action is when it is used for ill, specifically by the Associated Farmers. The banks and big farmers have also organized to control the wages and conditions of the farm workers, to force small farmers to follow suit, to intimidate the migrants and prevent them organizing (via "deputies" and vigilantes), and to control the local newspapers and town councils to maintain the drumbeat against the migrants. But Steinbeck seems to devalue the long-term potential of this set of collective actions, not simply because they are evil in his view, but because they originate not in the unifying power of collective sharing and helping but in individual selfishness, in this case the selfishness of land capitalism run wild.

This same selfishness also applies to small businesses that would cheat the migrants and take advantage of their desperation. Chapter 7, told from the point of view of a used car salesman (already a stereotype of dishonesty in Steinbeck's time), is still a tour de force in its realistic speech and frenetic single-mindedness of rooking vulnerable customers. In another general chapter, Steinbeck imagines a highway garage owner trying to sell a migrant a defective tire, and the migrants later discussing the "son-of-a-bitch":

What do ya think a guy in business is? Like he says, he ain't in it for his health. That's what business is. . . . Fella in business got to lie an' cheat, but he calls it somepin else. That's what's important. You go steal that tire an' you're a thief, but he tried to steal your four dollars for a busted tire. They call that sound business. (121)

The passage recalls Woody Guthrie's maxim, "Some folks rob you with a gun; others use a fountain pen."

Steinbeck's animus against businessmen, big and small, at times seems excessive, as in the restaurant chapter:

little pot-bellied men . . . . In their lapels the insignia of lodges and service clubs, places where they can go and, by a weight of numbers of little worried men, reassure themselves that business is noble and not the curious ritualized thievery they know it is; that business men are intelligent in spite of the records of their stupidity; that they are kind and charitable in spite of the principles of sound business; that their lives are rich instead of the thin tiresome routines they know; . . . (155)

As the migrants' chief adversaries, the big growers receive the same prophetic mode as the migrants, but in reverse: exactly in proportion as the migrants come to realize their power, the big growers will lose theirs. If the big growers' identities are obscure,[21] their fate is clear: the growers' repressive actions will inevitably backfire and cause their demise. In fact, Steinbeck is at his most prophetic here, his voice a biblical Jeremiah in prophesying their inevitable doom: "And the great owners . . . ran to their destruction, and used every means that in the long run would destroy them" (238). This inevitability also sounds very much like the Marxian dictum that capitalism contains the seeds of its own destruction.

Of the owners' many sins, the most heinous in Steinbeck's eyes— to destroy crops to keep the price up—also has a Marxian ring:

> Men who can graft the trees and make the seed fertile and big can find no way to let the hungry people eat their produce. Men who have created new fruits in the world cannot create a system whereby their fruits may be eaten. And the failure hangs over the State like a great sorrow . . .
>
> [Crops] must be destroyed to keep up the price, and this is the saddest, bitterest thing of all. Carloads of oranges dumped on the ground. . . . A million people hungry, needing the fruit—and kerosene sprayed over the golden mountains . . .
>
> There is a crime here that goes beyond denunciation. There is a sorrow here that weeping cannot symbolize. There is a failure here that topples all our success. The fertile earth . . . and the ripe fruit. And children dying of pellagra must die because a profit cannot be taken from an orange. And coroners must fill in the certificates— died of malnutrition—because food must rot, must be forced to rot. (340–42)

Along with preventing migrants from working fallow land—"a sin . . . a crime against the thin children" (234)—the growers' destruction of the food that could prevent migrants from starving receives Steinbeck's most eloquent denunciation (note the cumulative power of the repetitive "There is" constructions). Here is the locus classicus of capitalism's failure, in which "self-interest and greed have trumped compassion . . . ."[22] But the critique was hardly new in 1938: American communists had pointed out as early as 1930 the paradox of starvation and deprivation in America amidst plenty.[23] Steinbeck's frequent references to and descriptions of starving children, however, turn a generalization into vivid documentation, and like the communists, he identifies the problem as a failed "system": the same profit system that has robbed the migrants of their farms.

The only thing the government camp cannot provide is the one material thing the Joads most need: work. Reluctantly, they leave this heaven and again submit themselves to the systematic hell of the big growers' exploitation. Soon they are used to unwittingly help break a strike, and from this point on their material well-being steadily declines as the family begins to break up. Realistically, as well as dramatically, this descent is necessary to the novel. To end the novel in the government camp would provide too comforting a solution and would not address the migrants' poverty or what a tiny percentage of migrants the camps could accommodate. It would also swallow up the Joads' separate stories—their individuality—into the collective. And in charting their descent into misery and abject poverty, Steinbeck works in his eyewitness experience at Visalia, where he worked to help desperate migrants cope with a flood. On one level, as the family's fortunes decline inexorably, Ma's worst fears seem to be happening: the family is breaking up. Connie and Noah are already gone; Al is talking of leaving; Pa and Uncle John, the nominal patriarchs, are too disheartened or guilt-ridden to be effectual; Rosasharn has a still-birth; and Ma's beloved Tom is forced to leave permanently.

But the message of the collective "we" has altered the Joads and Jim Casy profoundly, even to the point of damaging the novel's credibility. The most meaningful of these changes occur appropriately in the three most important characters—Casy, Tom, and Ma—and could be called conversion experiences. Casy, having already had a religious vision of "the whole shebang" and each person's relation to it, discovers his own purpose regarding it. He evolves from serving as sympathetic observer, ministering to the migrants' needs, à la Doc in *In Dubious Battle*, to becoming an activist in their struggle against their oppressors. He knocks out a deputy to keep him from firing into a crowd and enables Tom to escape by allowing himself to be arrested. But these spontaneous and altruistic acts blossom into full-blown radicalism as Casy becomes a strike organizer when we next encounter him. Here is the novel's only significant instance of the collective "we" realizing itself in political action. Tellingly, it is small scale, short-lived, and futile. Vigilantes make a martyr of Casy—Steinbeck's Christ symbolism was never more heavy-handed—and no evidence suggests that the strike succeeds.

Tom is clearly the beneficiary of Casy's martyrdom. If his death redeems Tom, it is from his loner mentality into political action: not in the revenge killing of Casy's murderer, but in the Casy-inspired revelation Tom has during his own sojourn into the wilderness while hiding from the law. In describing it to Ma, Tom significantly refers to Casy's philosophy of the "great big soul"—the "whole shebang"—and that an individual's soul is only a piece of this larger spiritual collective. Tom's conclusion—"a fella ain't no good alone"—is virtually identical to Hemingway's Harry Morgan's dying words in *To Have and Have Not*: "No matter how, a man alone ain't got no bloody fucking chance." Tom has also inherited the "we" philosophy of the government camp: "I been a-wonderin why we can't do that all over. . . . All work together for our own thing" (419). The credibility of Tom's conversion experience—his decision to carry on Casy's work of organizing—is problematic in its own right, but Steinbeck does not help matters by giving it an ersatz mysticism that is borrowed directly from "The Ballad of Joe Hill." In the song, Joe, an executed IWW organizer, comes back to announce that he's never truly died and will always be present "where workingmen defend their rights." Tom, too, will always be "all aroun' in the dark. I'll be ever'where—wherever you look. Wherever they's a fight so hungry people can eat, I'll be there. . . . An' when our folks eat the stuff they raise an' live in the houses they build—why, I'll be there" (419). At the very least, Steinbeck should have credited the Alfred Hayes lyrics with a footnote.

Appropriately, Ma's conversion is family-oriented, just as her life-long focus has been. Only now—after having gone through so much to try to hold together the Joad family and having experienced vital assistance from other migrant families—she realizes that her original vision was too narrow: "Use' ta be the fambly was fust. It ain't so now. It's anybody" (445). This is clearly Ma's version of "the whole shebang" and her family's relation to it. Typically, she puts her new vision into practice when she has Rosasharn nurse a starving man—a stranger—with the breast milk that would have gone to her baby. In this supremely altruistic act, Rosasharn, too, changes from the completely self-involved girl she had been throughout the novel. As Horst Groene concludes, "From their bitter experiences [the Joads] have learned that the solidarity of all oppressed people is more important than loyalty to the family . . ."[24]

In Rosasharn's abrupt transformation, however, the reader begins to smell a rat: the author too insistently pushes his theme of the necessary conversion from "I" to "we," from selfishness to helping each other out. Given her previous self-absorption, Rosasharn might realistically have protested Ma's silent urging before submitting to it. Instead, we get another dose of mystical union: "And the two women looked deep into each other. The girl's breath came short and gasping. She said 'Yes.'" Even worse, as Rosasharn nurses the man, she "smiled mysteriously" (454–55). This too-neat transformation applies to all the other adult Joads, no matter how weak the preparation for it. During the flood, Pa shakes off his lethargy and organizes(!) twenty men to try to dam up the raging river. Al suddenly abandons his selfish desire to leave the family and in fact protects them by standing up to the migrants angry at the failure of Pa's plan. He also abandons his alley-catting and assumes personal responsibility by planning to marry the Wainwright girl. Even Uncle John, paralyzed by guilt throughout the novel, rallies himself to dispose of Rosasharn's stillborn child in a heavy-handed scene that ironically plays off the story of Moses in the bulrushes and the African-American spiritual about Moses and Pharaoh, "Let My People Go"—only here death has replaced survival, and the Israelites' exodus from slavery becomes the Joads' exodus to nowhere. In pushing his conversion theme so insistently, Steinbeck sacrifices character credibility for thematic neatness. Indeed, these character transformations prevent the novel from ending in utter despair—the Joads, after all, seem at the end of their rope in now being homeless as well as broke, with disease and starvation lurking in the unrelenting rain. But all of these altruistic acts for the larger collective powerfully enforce what Ma, with her customary vision (and Steinbeck's intrusive theme) tells Tom: "we're the people that live. They ain't gonna wipe us out. Why, we're the people—we go on" (280). And clearly, it is their collective actions—helping out others—that enable them to go on. In intentionally eschewing a neat closure for the novel, Steinbeck signals that the Joads—and the migrants they represent—will "go on," no matter how much destitution and oppression they must overcome.

The Problem of the Collective "We"

As these problems of character development suggest, *The Grapes of Wrath* is not a flawless novel. Steinbeck's mystical passages can be off-putting and sometimes run counter to fact. His prophetic mode is so pervasive that his characters act as proxy prophets, even those from whom one does not expect prophecy:

> Casy: "They's gonna come somepin outa all these folks goin' wes'— outa all their farms lef' lonely. They's comin' a thing that's gonna change the whole country." (174)

> Ma: "A different time's comin." (280)

> Pa: "They's change a-comin'. . . . Maybe we won't live to see her. But she's a-comin.'" (345)

But overriding these problems, in my view, is the issue of how the novel's central theme of "I" becoming "we"—the collective mentality the migrants move toward to effect political change— coheres with the migrants' past and future. As I've attempted to demonstrate above, "I" becoming "we" is central to Steinbeck's political vision and to the novel's thematic evolution and prophecy: "three hundred thousand . . . if they ever know themselves, the land will be theirs and all the gas, all the rifles in the world won't stop them" (238). "We" is the condition that Casy dies for in organizing, that Tom plans to fight for. But this collective mentality and behavior align with neither the migrants' origins, nor with the personal qualities that Steinbeck most admires in them as farmers, nor with their ambitions and dreams for their life in California—all of which are individualistic (with the family as an extension of the individual).

As noted above, the migrant families, dating back to their origins on the Plains farms, were *individual*: the pioneering Grampa, who takes the land from the Indians and farms it, does so for himself and his immediate family and their descendants. Indeed, this rugged and ruthless individualism is something Steinbeck admires as he contrasts the migrants' hardy self-reliance and intimacy with the earth to the soft lives of the bankers and big growers, who have either forgotten or never experienced the feel of the land. When the banks push the small farmers off their land, they are tractoring off *individual* families like the Joads. Until the novel's climax, Tom, in particular, represents this tough individualism in his hatred of bullying and of being pushed around and exploited. In fact, his individualistic toughness nicely counterpoints Ma's familial strength as the twin supports of the family. Not until these farm families hit the road as *migrants* and encounter their likenesses at the nightly camping spots do they begin to acquire collective consciousness and behavior.

The dreams of these migrants, although vaguely expressed, are also individual, symbolized by the small white house amid the orange trees. Several things suggest that this image is only a mirage: the way the Joads, Ma in particular, cling to it even as the family's situation steadily worsens, each repetition becoming more ironic. It even appears slyly as the Joads are en route to becoming inadvertent strike-breakers: among the rich crops, "[w]hite houses stood in the greenery, roses growing over them" (366). But even imagined more prosaically, the migrants' vision is still based on the individual family, as when Pa predicts hopefully, "[W]e'll get work an' we'll get a piece of growin' land with water" (188) and when Ma declares, "I want a little house" (305). The plots of fallow California land that the migrant farmers eye so hungrily are just that—plots to be worked, often secretly, by one farmer, one family: "There's thirty thousan' acres, out west of here. Layin' there. Jesus what I could do with that, with five acres of that! Why, hell, I'd have everything to eat" (234–35). Critics as far back as Chester Eisenger have linked the migrants' dream of the self-sufficient small farm or plot to the Jeffersonian ideal. More recently, Charles Wollenberg writes regarding the actual migrants' failure to organize politically, "The dust bowl migrants still considered themselves independent farmers and found it difficult to give up their traditional rural individualism."[25]

When Steinbeck describes the migrants' dreams *collectively*, he is vague: "[T]he new barbarians wanted only two things—land and food; and to them the two were one" (233). Similarly, when Tom expresses to Ma his collective vision, it too is vague: "All work together for our own thing—all farm our own lan'" (419). But does "our own" mean collective or family ownership? And just how would the migrants "work together"? Another example of Steinbeck's vagueness regarding collective aspirations appears in a passage that seems to hedge on his Luddite hatred of machines, particularly tractors:

> Is a tractor bad? Is the power that turns the long furrows wrong? If this tractor were ours it would be good—not mine but ours. If our tractor turned the long furrows of our land, it would be good. Not my land, but ours. But this tractor does two things—it turns the land and turns us off the land. (151)

By tying the tractor here to his all-important collective theme—"not mine but ours"—Steinbeck reclaims the possibility of the tractor being a useful tool, rather than a means of human displacement. But what does "ours" mean in this context? Does the tractor belong to a family or to a collective? Once again, Steinbeck is hazy.

Both the past experience of the migrants with their small farms on the Plains and their halting expression of their dreams in California suggest that what they want are individual small farms, the kind they had worked before they migrated. When he was writing the first version of the novel in 1938, Steinbeck stated this ambition clearly: "The Oklahoman knows just exactly what he wants. He wants a piece of land. And he goes after it and gets it."[26] Thus, a paradox emerges in Steinbeck's vision: tough individualists, who once worked their own farms, must now work together as migrants in order to work separately on their own plots of land.[27] And if individualism prevails in their new dream, does it lead to the selfishness that Steinbeck so often associates with individualism?

One might question whether this sequence is indeed a paradox by pointing out the example of the labor union. Workers join the union for the mutual benefits they derive from its collective strength, then leave their jobs each night to return to their individual homes and families. But land ownership complicates the theme of collectivism since not merely the labor, but the land ownership itself would have to be shared for true collectivism to prevail. Does the novel promote Soviet-style collective farms or the smaller collectives of the Israeli kibbutz—both of which existed when Steinbeck was writing? Nothing in the text affirms these possibilities; hence, the paradox remains and results, I believe, from Steinbeck's failure to think through the inconsistencies and contradictions of his novel's collective vision. If he was aware of the paradox, it may explain why his generalized statements about the migrants' aims are so vague.

A parallel contradiction appears on a philosophical level in Casy's vision of the "whole shebang," which he explains to Tom:

> I figured about the Holy Sperit & the Jesus road. I figgered, "Why do we hang it on God or Jesus? Maybe," I figgered, "maybe it's all men an' all women we love, maybe that's the Holy Sperit—the human sperit—the whole shebang. Maybe all men got one big soul ever'body's a part of." . . . all of a sudden—I knew it. I knew it so deep down that it was true . . . (24)

As critics have observed, the "one big soul" that everyone is part of, "is not only *like* the vision of Emerson, but is straight *out of* Emerson['s concept] of the over-soul."[28] But the author of "Self-Reliance" was hardly a collectivist, and the unity he envisions is transcendental.[29] For Casy, that spirit or soul itself resides in the collective ("mankind") when it was a monad ("one thing," 81). But when was mankind ever so united and indivisible? Through Casy, Steinbeck posits a humanistic philosophy, but in his striving to assert the collective as a spiritual concept, he imagines its origins in a nonexistent perfection that parallels the mystic unity he sees in the unmechanized farmer and his land.

Once Casy's philosophy turns to activism, the unity that he finds holy devolves to the unity of the oppressed only and pointedly excludes the oppressors. Though just before his death, he assumes a Christlike forgiveness of his attackers ("You fellas don' know what you're doing," 386), he did not hesitate earlier to attack a deputy himself, and the very act for which he is martyred (leading a strike) is obviously divisive in opposing strikers and landowners. To complicate matters further, Casy mixes his quasi-Emersonism with Whitman's mystic sense of perceiving collective America (e.g., "I Hear America Singing"):

> I'm gonna work in the fiel's . . . an' I'm gonna be near to folks. . . . I'm
> gonna try to learn. . . . gonna hear 'em talk, gonna hear 'em sing. . . .
> the poetry of folks talkin'. All that's holy . . . (94)

> Listen to people a-talkin', an' purty soon I hear the way folks are
> feelin'. (250)

And for good measure, Casy throws in a little Libertarianism, when
he tells Uncle John, "On'y one thing in this wol' I'm sure of, an'
that's I'm sure nobody got a right to mess with a fella's life. He
got to do it all hisself. Help him, maybe, but not tell him what to
do" (224). Would this hands-off philosophy apply to the ego-driven
"little fella" who would "bust the holiness" (81)? The contradictions here, like those of collectivism and individualism, point to an
author who, in his passionate presentation of his newly developed
political vision, has overlooked some essential problems.

That passion was never more evident than in Steinbeck's prophecies of doom for the big growers and of a coming political and social
reckoning in the migrants' growing anger and in the looming possibility of their coming together politically. Although he is careful
to qualify this coming together—it remains the novel's big "if"—
hanging over these prophecies is a sense of historical inevitability.
And Steinbeck, like Marx before him, becomes merely the close observer of these historical processes, pointing out a pattern that anyone "with access to history, with eyes to read history" (238) could
discern. Thus, what happens to the California farmland—once tak-
en by the land-hungry, then consolidated, then retaken by the newly disinherited—is an inevitable cycle. The prophecies of chapter
19 that spell out the big owners' doom are presented as historical
"facts," and Steinbeck assumes the persona not just of seer but of
detached observer of history and sociology, the same persona that
accompanied his phalanx theory. His earlier treatment of the phalanx in *In Dubious Battle* was from a disinterested perspective—he
had no particular sympathy for the mob of strikers and described
them in unflattering animal terms. In *Grapes*, however, his intense
partisanship skews the pseudo-historical detachment of his prophecies: they are not simply what *will* happen, but what he wants to
see happen.

And in any case, his prophecies were mostly wrong: Steinbeck's crystal ball was cloudy and thoroughly unreliable. The big farms were never broken up—they grew even bigger. And the inevitable explosion of migrant wrath never occurred. Despite the huge success of his novel, public concern with the migrant problem sharply diminished with the coming of a new world war.[30] As will be discussed in chapter 8, neither the committee to aid the migrants to which Steinbeck lent his name, nor the congressional committee investigating labor-management relations in California farming (the La Follette Committee) significantly improved the plight of the migrants. What ultimately rescued the migrants was something Steinbeck could not have foreseen in 1938—not legislative reforms preventing their abuse and exploitation, not even a proliferation of sanitary camps to treat them decently, but (beginning in late 1940 and exploding in 1941) massive federal defense spending in California that provided jobs—scores of thousands of jobs—with wages beyond the Joads' wildest dreams. Thus the farming Joads become the industrial Joads. It is as if Al's dream of becoming a mechanic became the family's real future—a richly ironic outcome, given Steinbeck's mystic reverence for small farming and his deep distrust of machines. And if the Joads finally did buy their white cottage, it would probably have been in a big city, near an aircraft plant or shipyard.

Conclusion

Critics concur that Steinbeck was never more politically radical than when he wrote *The Grapes of Wrath*. Robert DeMott concludes about this period that "John Steinbeck never became what dyed-in-the-wool activists would consider fully radicalized, but by putting his pen to the service of a political cause, he was stepping as close to being a firebrand as he ever would." Susan Shillinglaw agrees that Steinbeck was "never a communist, even though he edged close to the cause in the mid- to late 1930s." Moreover, "[r]evolution simmers just below the surface of this novel about searing injustice." And Rick Wartzman writes, "If Steinbeck wasn't calling for open revolt, he was surely tiptoeing close to that edge."[31] All three of these critics stop short of saying that Steinbeck *was* fomenting revolution in this novel or was "fully radicalized." Steinbeck himself, however, was less cautious in skirting this revolutionary label. In the novel's collectivistic theme, in its Marxian parallels noted above and in opinions the author expressed in his letters, the question lingers about the extremity of his radical beliefs and intent in *Grapes*. Was Steinbeck, as his bitterest critics charged, a communist attempting to foment a revolution through his novel? And even without communist ideology, wasn't he attempting to upend a corrupt, selfish system—capitalism—and replace it with something more humane?

One point is indisputable: Steinbeck did not consider himself a communist or an advocate of Soviet-style communism. He disliked the rigid categorical thinking of the communists: "All the terms are phony—proletarian—bourgeois . . . it's all just people. Write about people not classes," he advised George Albee.[32] He assumed, correctly, that his enemies would tar his novel as communist, but in denying this "angle" to his publisher, Pat Covici, he does call his book "revolutionary": "The fascist crowd will try to sabotage this book because it is revolutionary. They [will] try to give it the communist angle. However, The Battle Hymn of the Republic [which Steinbeck had included in its entirety] is American and intensely so" (1 Jan. 1939, *Life in Letters*, 174). Strange logic, here—that if a book is "American," it cannot be communistic. Members of the CP-USA may have thought otherwise.

But if Steinbeck wasn't a communist, he nonetheless makes clear in his letters and in the novel itself that it is the capitalist *system* that must be—and will be—radically changed if not replaced, not merely individual abuses within that system. "There is little question in my mind," he predicted, "that the principle of private ownership as a means of production is not long with us. This is not in terms of what I think is right or wrong or good or bad, but . . . what is inevitable."[33] He writes to George Hedley that because the migrants are "coming from an agrarian pattern and being suddenly confronted with our capitalist industrialism, the paradoxes and ridiculous thinking of that system is [*sic*] doubly apparent [to them] . . . these migrant people with their clear thrust are destined to be a large determining factor in the imminent social change. And I love them for it."[34] That "imminent social change" would result in a new "system," as he predicted in written answers to questions for a radio program in 1939: "I believe that out of these qualities [of the migrants] will grow a new system and a new life which will be better than the one we have" (52).[35] In the novel's philippic against the intentional destruction of crops, the narrator asserts, "Men who have created new fruits in the world cannot create a system whereby their fruits may be eaten" (348). This "system" is not merely one of redistribution within capitalism; it is a system that replaces the profit motive with humane values, first and foremost of which is to feed starving children. The "monster" that sends the tractors to "disinherit" the migrants "breathes profits": it is bigger, even, than "the bank"—it is capitalism. Still, if it was "made by men," it can be changed by men—this is what the tenant farmer concludes, and it is Steinbeck's conclusion too.

Then there are those Marxian paraphrases that pepper the novel. Capitalism thrives on profits; it must continue to grow or die (32). In its ruthless exploitation of the worker, it contains the seeds of its own destruction (chap. 19). Under a collectivistic system, authoritarian government will wither away (chap. 17 and p. 287). Intentional waste amidst hunger is the ultimate failure of capitalism (348–49). The migrants want land and food (231; the Bolsheviks promised the Russian people peace, land, and bread). Finally, the demise of capitalism is an historical inevitability (238). These allusions do not, of course, prove that Steinbeck was a communist, but at this point in his life he shared their hatred of capitalism. As he stated in the letter quoted in the epigraph to this chapter, "I am actively opposed to any man or group who, through financial or political control of means of production and distribution, is able to control and dominate the lives of workers." And he agreed with the communists that an economic system so ruthless, so fascistic in its methods, was doomed.[36]

What would replace it? Here, Steinbeck grows vague, revealing contradictions in his thinking and vision, as discussed above. The "we" that the novel enshrines appears to make him a collectivist. But both in the migrants' individualistic history and dreams for the future and in the novel's remarkably slender evidence that a political "we" will change the system, or at least correct its abuses, Steinbeck reveals uncertainty, conflictedness. He is wise enough to avoid the upbeat ending demanded of social realism. No mass strike breaks the big growers' stranglehold on farm labor. Casy's clandestine strike meeting is broken up; Casy's head is broken; the tiny strike itself will be broken. And outside of the government camps, no other collective action occurs in the novel, except some anecdotal stories and the futile effort by the migrants to resist the flood.[37] The collective "we"—so boldly proclaimed in the general chapters, so perfectly realized in the government camp—seems to shrivel to the familial "we" of the Joads in the final chapters. At most, the novel follows the social realist pattern of showing a significant change in the consciousness of the key characters: Casy and the Joads have adopted the transfamilial "we" and abandoned the selfish "I." Probably, Tom, like the spirit of Joe Hill, "went on to organize." And because of this changed consciousness, the Joads—and the migrants—will go on. But where, how, and to what end are left out intentionally. And wisely.[38]

Does this weakness of collective action suggest doubts in Steinbeck's outlook? His statements outside the novel and his prophecies within it are all to the contrary, of course. A "new system," a better one, *will* grow out of the migrants' toughness and resistance to their exploitation—he was certain of that—but he could not quite bring his novel around to show it happening. To do so might take the edge off the novel's anger and Steinbeck's aim to arouse the reader to action. But just as the novel's contradictions reflect an author blinded by his passionate partisanship, its failure to show the "we" coalescing politically hints at a submerged doubt Steinbeck did not wish to face: a doubt in the efficacy of the "we."

Native Son

Who Is Bigger Thomas?

FIRST-TIME READERS OF *Native Son* almost invariably discover a novel they can't put down—at least until book 3. But the headlong plot, which accelerates to breakneck speed until Bigger Thomas is captured at the end of book 2, was not Richard Wright's chief concern. Characterization was. As Wright explained in "How 'Bigger' Was Born," an invaluable essay drawn from lectures shortly after the novel was published, "always, from start to finish, it was Bigger's story, Bigger's fear, Bigger's flight, and Bigger's fate that I tried to depict. I wrote with the conviction in mind . . . that the main burden of all serious fiction consists almost wholly of character-destiny . . ." Accordingly, "I restricted the novel to what Bigger saw and felt, to the limits of his feelings and thoughts, even when I was conveying *more* than that to the reader. . . . I gave no more reality to the other characters than that which Bigger himself saw."[1] Not surprisingly, then, Wright devoted virtually all of this lengthy essay to explicating the central character, tracing his sources in Wright's experience, discussing his psychological makeup, his potential links to political groups, his development, and the psychological hurdles Wright had to overcome in creating him. Thus, comprehending the novel means understanding Bigger Thomas—and the political consequences Wright faced in creating him. The former task would seem easy since Wright explains so much about Bigger's feelings in the narrative and in his appended essay. Yet, Bigger changes over the course of the novel; there are several Biggers in *Native Son*, and, correspondingly, several kinds of narratives for the reader to untangle. How well these personas and narratives cohere, then, becomes a central issue in evaluating the novel. Intrinsically tied to these issues of multiplicity and coherence are the novel's political themes, Bigger's relations to them, and what these relations suggest about Wright's political identity at the end of the decade.

Who, then, is Bigger Thomas? Let's begin with his name. Oddly, for having a name that denotes comparatively large size, Bigger is not tall—he's described as "five feet, nine inches" in a hostile *Chicago Tribune* story (279). The story also states, "His shoulders are huge, muscular," but this feature may be exaggerated to strengthen an apelike resemblance the article wants to convey. Along with Bigger's "hunched" shoulders ("as if about to spring upon you at any moment") are long arms dangling to his knees, and a protruding lower jaw "reminding one of a jungle beast" (279).[2] No doubt, Bigger *is* powerful, but it is because he uses that strength so brutally, whenever his fear turns to rage and violence (as when he attacks Gus), that he seems so menacing. In that sense only, he appears "bigger" than others.[3] I would suggest that there's another, more disturbing meaning to his name In "How 'Bigger' Was Born," Wright hints at it in describing the real-life "Biggers" on whom he modeled Bigger Thomas (434–37). They all share one quality: rebellion against white domination. They were "the only Negroes I know of who consistently violated Jim Crow laws and got away with it, at least for a brief spell. Eventually, the whites who restricted their lives made them pay a terrible price" (437). Twice, Wright uses the word "bad" in describing these Biggers and the fear they instilled in blacks *and* whites. He says of "Bigger No. 1," "we were afraid [to ask him to return our playthings], and Bigger was bad. We had seen him clout boys when he was angry and we did not want to run that risk" (434). "Bad" is elaborated for Bigger No. 3, "whom the white folks called 'a bad nigger.' He carried his life in his hands in a literal fashion" (435). Wright uses almost the same words to describe Bigger Thomas "taking his life into his hands . . ." (461). "Bigger," therefore, compresses "B" (from "bad") and "nigger."[4] He is the bad nigger of the novel, feared by his friends, feared and hated by nearly all whites.[5] Wright has thus created a name—and a character—that combines the marginalized and nightmarish Other, the object of the whites' greatest contempt and deepest fear: the dangerous nigger. In listing the "mental censors" he had to over-come in creating this character, Wright makes the same association in imagining the response of white readers to Bigger: "What will white people think if I draw the picture of such a Negro boy? Will they not at once say: 'See, didn't we tell you all along that niggers are like that?'" (448).

This construction of the Other as protagonist is all the more dar-ing considering the limitations Wright gives him. In "How 'Bigger' Was Born," Wright describes Bigger as "resentful toward whites, sullen, angry, ignorant, emotionally unstable, depressed and unac-countably elated at times and unable even, because of his own lack of inner organization which American oppression has fostered in him, to unite with members of his own race" (448). Several times in this essay, Wright refers to Bigger's inarticulateness regarding "[h]is emotional and intellectual life": "The most I could say for Bigger was that he felt the *need* for a whole life and *acted* out of that need; that was all." His feelings towards other blacks are "*snarled* and *confused*"; towards whites, "his intense hatred . . . had placed him like a wild animal at bay" (451, Wright's emphasis). Wright even suggests that this "dark and brutal" young man (450) is the em-bodiment of the Jungian shadow archetype: "There seems to hover somewhere in that dark part of all our lives, . . . an objectless, time-less, spaceless element of primal fear and dread, . . . an impelling influence upon our lives all out of proportion to its obscurity" (452).

In making his protagonist not only "brutal" and violent, but in-articulate, emotionally limited and intellectually stunted, Wright intentionally created an unsympathetic antihero, a protagonist far more to be dreaded, especially by white readers, than sympa-thized with. Again, this was his intent. As he famously stated in "How 'Bigger' Was Born," he would make his novel "so hard and deep"—and his protagonist so repellent—that "bankers' daughters . . . would have to face it without the consolation of tears" (454). His confrontational attitude towards readers here recalls Stein-beck's aim in making *The Grapes of Wrath* intentionally offensive, but Wright goes much further, making Bigger not merely unsym-pathetic in his limited mentality, but genuinely fearsome in his capacity for rage and violence, as if to say to white America, "This is what you've created. How do you like it?" Arnold Rampersad said of the "brutalized and limited" Bigger, "it is hard to think of a central character in all of literature who is less likable than Bigger Thomas."[6] How remarkable then that this novel, which features a repellent black man suffocating a young white woman, decapitating her, burning her body, and crushing the head of a helpless black woman, was selected by Book-of-the-Month Club, that epitome of white middlebrow taste, as one of its two main selections for March 1940—the club's first offering by an African-American author!

"Powerful impulses in a world he feared"

Native Son has often been called a deterministic novel, but despite its final book being titled "Fate," determinism applies only to book 1 (and not all of that book). As soon as Bigger inadvertently kills Mary Dalton, he stops being driven by his fear, stops simply *reacting* to forces that he cannot control. Before that momentous act, he is indeed a barely controlled bundle of "undisciplined and unchannelized impulses," as Wright describes him ("How 'Bigger' Was Born," 445). After it, he is a different person altogether. He is reborn.

The brilliantly conceived opening scene acts as a kind of *précis* for the entire novel in its dual meaning: Bigger, in a life-threatening situation, skillfully traps and kills a rat. Desperation, courage, and resourcefulness triumph over fear. But Bigger is also the black rat, cornered, baring his fangs, ultimately doomed. Finally, Bigger's taunting his frightened sister with the dead rat brings out his cruelty and complete detachment from his family. As he does so often, Wright explains the complex sensibility forcing this detachment in terms Bigger could never have articulated for himself:

> He hated his family because he knew they were suffering and that he was powerless to help them. He knew that the moment he allowed himself to feel to its fullness how they lived, the shame and misery of their lives, he would be swept out of himself with fear and despair. So he held toward them an attitude of iron reserve; . . . And toward himself he was even more exacting. He knew that the moment he allowed what his life meant to enter fully into his consciousness, he would either kill himself or someone else. So he denied himself and acted tough. (10)

"Fear and despair"; hatred and violence ("kill himself or someone else")—these are the electric currents alternating through Bigger's brain. And they are directly linked: fear, the aptly chosen title for book 1, invariably snaps over into rage and a desire for violence: to "blot out" or crush the source of his fearful anxiety. The pattern recurs and intensifies several times in book 1, always when the clarifying line separating whites and blacks threatens to be erased. Robbing the white-owned delicatessen "would be a violation of ultimate taboo; it would be a trespassing into territory where the full wrath of an alien white world would be turned loose upon them; . . . a symbolic challenge of the white world's rule over them; a challenge which they yearned to make, but were afraid to" (17). Here, Wright distinguishes Bigger's aberrant personality from his friends' normal fear: *Bigger*'s fear results not merely in intimidation, but violence: his two attacks on Gus ineptly conceal his fear, but relieve his anxiety about having to carry through his plan. The distinction is important: Bigger is the only one of the group to act this way.

When he doesn't fear or act out of that fear with violence, real or imagined, Bigger broods. Wright is at his best here in dramatizing his character's continuous and barely stifled rage against the profound unfairness of a world that lets white boys become pilots, but prevents a young black man from doing more than looking on enviously. Here, Wright inserts two lines that make Bigger's fate appear determined: "'Sometimes I feel like something awful's going to happen to me,' Bigger spoke with a tinge of bitter pride in his voice. . . . 'It's like I was going to do something I can't help . . .'" (20, 22). Again, however, one cannot ascribe this premonition simply to race. Gus too quietly rages against racist restriction, but as in the pool hall, he is not the one who explodes. There is something particular to Bigger's psychological makeup that makes violence the only relief from the fear and rage that he, as a poor black man, must continuously suffer: "Confidence could only come again through action so violent that it would make him forget. These were the rhythms of his life: indifference and violence" (29).

And escape. Wright is sufficiently astute as a psychologist to realize that no one could maintain Bigger's tensions without either imploding or seeking periodic relief. Thus, the importance of the movie that Bigger attends with Jack—and a major reason why

Wright's agreement to cut controversial sections of this scene (at the Book-of-the-Month Club's insistence) damaged the narrative (fortunately repaired in the restored edition). That Bigger and Jack masturbate in the darkened theater is more than just shock-the-bourgeoisie realism. The masturbation combines with the sexually teasing images of Mary Dalton on the screen and the prurient voice-over ("Ha! He's after her! There! He's got her! Oh, boy, don't you wish you were down here in Florida?")[7] to anticipate the novel's highly charged sexual complex: Bigger's and Mary's desire for each other (versus the racist stereotype of the oversexed black man and the vulnerable white woman, which Wright was all too familiar with from living in the Deep South). Note how the tribal images of the featured film, *Trader Horn*, reinforce this stereotype—"He . . . saw pictures of naked black men and women whirling in wild dances and heard drums beating . . ."—then morph into a symbolic foreshadowing of black and white intermingling: "the African scene changed and was replaced by images in his own mind of white men and women dressed in black and white clothes, laughing, talking, drinking and dancing" (33). These movie-house images of sexual arousal and stereotype point toward Bigger's transgression of the ultimate racial taboo, a black man in a white woman's bedroom (compared to which robbing a white delicatessen is minor), and toward the prosecution's unchallenged, matter-of-fact assumption that Bigger raped Mary Dalton.

Throughout the novel, white is the realistic and symbolic color that most arouses Bigger's fear-hate-violence syndrome. Often, it is juxtaposed to the novel's two other symbolic colors: black and red. Outside the Daltons' home in an all-white neighborhood, Bigger sees the white snow surrounded by "a high, black, iron picket fence" and feels "fear and emptiness . . . . This was not his world; . . . he wanted to strike something with his fist" (44). The "white home," the deep white rug, the "white-haired" Mr. Dalton, the white cat, and finally Mrs. Dalton's "ghost"-like appearance: "Her face and hair were completely white"—Wright piles on these images insistently (and, one feels, excessively) to hammer home the simple, but profound fact of Bigger's intense self-consciousness as a black man in a white world, a poor man in a rich world. That the Daltons' whiteness abstracts them—Bigger's first perception of each Dalton is "a white girl," "a tall, thin white woman," etc.— ironically reverses the same racist abstraction applied to blacks ("They all look alike") and becomes crucial in the climactic scene in which Mrs. Dalton comes into Mary's bedroom. Bigger repeatedly sees Mrs. Dalton there as "a white blur"—the hovering ghost of the white world. Wright later explains, "To Bigger and his kind, white people were not really crazy people; they were a sort of great natural force, like a stormy sky looming overhead. . . . As long as he and his black folks did not go beyond certain limits, there was no need to fear that white force" (114). But, of course, for a black man to be caught in a white girl's bedroom goes far beyond those limits; hence the fear that Mrs. Dalton's ghostly blur arouses.

Even before that scene, however, Wright dramatizes several transgressions of racial boundaries that set off the fear-rage-violence sequence in Bigger's mind, only now it is the whites—Mary and her communist boyfriend, Jan—who transgress. Virtually all of their actions with Bigger in their one scene together—actions which stem from a well-meaning egalitarianism that is both painfully naïve and unintentionally condescending—violate the boundaries Bigger is familiar with: their insistence on riding in the front seat with him, on going to a black restaurant Bigger knows (and where he is recognized to his extreme embarrassment), on eating and drinking with him. Finally, there is Mary's appalling speech: "Never in my life have I been inside of a Negro home. Yet they *must* live like we live. They're *human*." (70). Bigger's response, by now, has become predictable:

> Bigger knew that they were thinking of his life and the life of his people. Suddenly he wanted to seize some heavy object in his hand and grip it with all the strength of his body and in some strange way rise up and stand in naked space above the speeding car and with one final blow blot it out—with himself and them in it. (70)

Much later, he recounts to Max, "She acted and talked in a way that made me hate her. She made me feel like a dog. I was so mad I wanted to cry" (350). He wants not just to kill them, but to become the same inevitable *force* that is insurmountable and apocalyptic: the white force. Considering that Jan is a communist and Mary a sympathizer, their condescending treatment of Bigger does not reflect well on their politics, or at least on their political sophistication, as one communist reviewer complained.[8] But it does reveal an important fact about Wright's relative weighting of psychological and political themes in this novel. As he stated in "How 'Bigger' Was Born," his intent, first and last, was to stay true to Bigger's consciousness. For Bigger to respond positively to Mary and Jan's egalitarian actions would violate his characterization. Psychological reality takes precedence over any desire to make the Communist Party look good in this scene.

One final aspect of Bigger's construction in book 1 must be considered: the mingling of his desire for Mary with his hatred of her and generalized fear. As in the movie theater scene, the restored cuts from the 1940 edition reveal several details of Bigger's encounter with Mary after Jan leaves that shade the scene differently from how it appeared originally. In the 1940 edition, Mary's actions result primarily from her drunken obliviousness. At most, she drunkenly expresses her desire when, as Bigger carries her, "she swayed against him," and on the bed, he feels "her move against him" (1940 ed., 84). In the restored text, Mary is far more aggressive, not merely responding to, but initiating moves toward intercourse:

> He tightened his arms as his lips pressed tightly against her and he felt her body moving strongly. The thought that Jan had had her a lot flashed through his mind. He kissed her again and felt the sharp bones of her hips move in a hard and veritable grind. Her mouth was open and her breath came slow and deep. (84)

It is clear that in the restored version, Mary is coming on to Bigger even more than he is to her, arousing him even more than he was already aroused by her drunken approachability. But because their intercourse is so much more imminent than in the 1940 edition, so is the danger of the situation (the ultimate transgression) and, with it, Bigger's hatred of Mary and his generalized fear:

[Outside the house] He watched her with a mingled feeling of help-lessness, admiration, and hate. (82)

[In the kitchen] He . . . whispered in excitement and fear . . . (83)

[At the back stairs] His fingers felt the soft curves of her body and he was still, looking at her, enveloped in a sense of physical elation. This little bitch! he thought. (84)

When Mrs. Dalton—the "white blur"—appears, his desire, fear, and hatred fuse into "hysterical terror" and "frenzy" to escape detection in this epitome of racial transgression (85). His stifling of Mary's moans, then, results not merely from hatred, and certainly not from a conscious intent to kill her, but from his overwhelming fear of the "white blur moving toward him"—fear that characteristically translates itself into the desperate strength Bigger had shown with—and as—the cornered rat.

Caedo, ergo sum

Given the fear-driven personality so well dramatized in book 1, one might have expected Bigger to panic after killing Mary: to run as far and as fast as he possibly can. Instead, he begins immediately "to construct a case for 'them'" (88)—a plan that deflects the attention of whites away from himself, cleverly implicates Jan, and requires—in an act of incomparable boldness—that he decapitate and burn Mary's body in the Dalton furnace. Bigger now thinks ratiocinatively: he plans; he plots; he gets beyond his imprisoning self-consciousness to imagine and anticipate what *other* people— white people—might think and conclude. Who *is* this Bigger Thomas? Surely not the character we knew in book 1!

Such drastic character transformation typically fails in fiction if it is insufficiently justified, hence incredible. But Bigger's change is thoroughly credible—and all the more disturbing for its believability—because the psychological complex that has previously stunted him—racist-bred fear and despair becoming self-defeating violence—has been removed, as if surgically, by a single act: killing a white woman in her bedroom. Though he did not plan to do so, Bigger has violated the supreme racial taboo for a black man. Wright is explicit, not once but several times, about the transformative effect of this act on Bigger's mentality:

> [His family] did not know that he had murdered a white girl and cut her head off and burnt her body. The thought of what he had done, the awful horror of it, the daring associated with such actions, formed for him *for the first time in his life* a barrier of protection between him and a world he feared. *He had murdered and had created a new life for himself.* It was something that was all his own, and it was the first time in his life he had anything that others could not take from him. (105, emphasis added)[9]

> Though he had killed by accident, not once did he feel the need to tell himself that it had been an accident. . . . The hidden meaning of his life . . . had spilled out. No; it was no accident, and he would never say that it was. There was in him a kind of terrified *pride* in feeling and thinking that some day he would be able to say publicly that he had done it. (106, emphasis added)

To murder and create "a new life for himself," to think of it as an intentional act, hence an intentional defiance of the supreme racial taboo, and to feel, for the first time, pride—these constructions of Bigger's panicked act indicate the magnitude of his transformation. Through the act of killing—and killing not just anyone, but a rich, young white woman—he has been reborn and has achieved a fully functioning consciousness, where before "iron reserve"— repression—prevailed. "Caedo, ergo sum"—Wright one-ups Descartes, and this insight into what is necessary to achieve full realization of *self* is at once brilliant and terrifying. (Though the concept was still unusual in 1940, leaving aside Dostoevsky, it has become all too familiar in nightly news stories describing nonentities of all ilks with access to automatic weapons and crowds.)

Book 2 ("Flight") resolves into Bigger leading the law on a merry chase, showing what he's capable of imagining once the mind-forged manacles have snapped open. Wright's themes here are transparent and hugely ironic. Bigger's inarticulateness and violent physicality did not mean that he was stupid; given the chance, he shows he can outsmart the white lawmen. Hence, the deliciously ironic headline during the chase: "[Police] feel that the plan of the murder and kidnapping was too elaborate to be the work of a Negro mind" (245). But if Bigger is too smart for the white lawmen, he must still master himself and repress remnants of the old, fearful Bigger—and this he fails to do. In revising the manuscript for Book-of-the-Month Club, Wright added two passages to the original text explaining why Bigger didn't empty the ashes in the Dalton furnace—a negligence that leads to the discovery of Mary's remains and destroys Bigger's schemes. In both instances, Bigger's fear and guilt paralyze him:

> At the moment he stooped to grasp the protruding handle of the lower bin to shake it to and fro, a vivid image of Mary's face as he had seen it upon the bed . . . gleamed at him from the smoldering embers and he rose abruptly, giddy and hysterical with guilt and fear. . . . [H]e could not shake the ashes now. (1940 ed., 113–14)

> He stood a moment looking through the cracks into the humming fire, blindingly red now. But how long would it keep that way, if he did not shake the ashes down? He remembered the last time he had tried and how hysterical he had felt. He must do better than this. He stooped and touched the handle of the ash bin . . . keeping his eyes averted as he did so. He imagined that if he shook it he would see pieces of bone falling into the bin and he knew that he would not be able to endure it. He jerked upright and, lashed by fiery whips of fear and guilt, backed hurriedly to the door. For the life of him, he could not bring himself to shake those ashes. (1940 ed., 161)

Doubtless, Wright felt these passages were essential to explaining what would otherwise become Bigger's foolish oversight, but they also show that Bigger is still capable of feeling guilt and fear when he approaches the scene of his crime and the possible remains of Mary's body. What is more interesting is that, in *lacking* these explanations, the pre-book club text shows that Bigger's transformation has been so thorough that he feels no guilt. This guiltlessness squares with another passage:

> He did not feel sorry for Mary; she was not real to him, not a human being; he had not known her long or well enough for that. He felt that

his murder of her was more than amply justified by the fear and shame she had made him feel. . . . Mary had served to set off his emotions, emotions conditioned by many Marys. And now that he had killed Mary he felt a lessening of tension in his muscles; he had shed an invisible burden he had long carried. (114)[10]

The sociopathic implications of this absence of guilt in the pre-book club version are fully realized when Bigger brutally murders Bessie—an act that alters the meaning of his transformation. Unlike his killing of Mary, this killing is a murder. It is intentional and calculated. It is not an automatic response to overwhelming fear. But is it necessary? If Bessie had become a liability, surely Bigger could have abandoned her and been no worse off, since she would not know his next move when the police apprehended her. Instead, Bigger "coldly" determines to kill her, and Wright reverts to the deterministic mentality of book 1 to explain—or rather, exculpate—Bigger's thinking: "as if the decision were being handed down to him by some logic not his own, over which he had no control, but which he had to obey" (229). The inconsistency here with the calculating, self-commanding Bigger is glaring.

Like his post-facto justification of killing Mary, Bigger blames the victim: "it was her own fault. She had bothered him so much that he had had to tell her" (234). Again, Wright suggests fear-driven determinism by retrieving the earlier image of Bigger's fear, the "white blur," but now quite out of context. Again, he attempts to make the murder an affirmative act by having Bigger think "Yes!" as he crushes Bessie's skull with a brick. And, like the "guilt" passages he added in the revision, Wright includes a brief mention of Bigger's hypothetical guilt after the murder, when he contemplates going after the money on Bessie's body: "He did not want to see her again. He felt that if he should ever see her face again he would be overcome with a sense of guilt so deep as to be unbearable" (239).

The entire scene is sordid in the extreme, not least because Bigger rapes Bessie before murdering her. If a white man had done these acts to Bessie, he would rightly be condemned as a sick racist, brutalizing a weak, pathetic black woman. Conversely, if

Bigger's accomplice had been a white woman, would he have felt so free to do these acts? In acquiring a near-guiltless morality, he has unwittingly adopted the mentality of his—and Wright's— most hated adversary: the Southern white racist who feels free to commit any outrage against what he considers a black inferior.

The Nietzschean superman morality—or rather, a perversion of it—that Bigger unwittingly adopts, as well as Wright's unconvincing attempts to justify Bessie's murder through determinism, point to another significant fact about the new Bigger in book 2. In describing the new life Bigger has created by killing Mary, the novel has essentially shifted its genre from deterministic (Bigger driven by fear) to existential: Bigger experiencing selfhood and freedom by determining and living by his own moral code. When Bigger returns to the Daltons the morning after killing Mary, "[i]t was a kind of eagerness he felt, a confidence, a fullness, a *freedom*; his whole life was caught up in a supreme and meaningful act" (116, emphasis added). He feels enabled: "Now that the ice was broken, could he not do other things? What was there to stop him? . . . Things were becoming clear . . ." (106).

This existential sensibility did not derive from Wright's familiarity with the French existentialists. As Michel Fabre points out, Wright had not yet met Camus and Sartre, nor read their work at the time: "Resemblances [between the writing of Camus and Wright] are coincidental, more a result of convergence."[11] Nonetheless, Bigger's sensibility displays existential authenticity. He rejects all extant moral codes, especially religious, in guiding his actions, which he alone determines:

> [A] new feeling had been born in him, a feeling that all but blotted out the fear of death. . . . As long as he could take his life into his own hands and dispose of it as he pleased, as long as he could decide just when and where he would run to, he need not be afraid. He felt that he had his destiny in his grasp. He was more alive than he could ever remember having been. (149)

This self-determination becomes even stronger after Bigger's murder of Bessie. No sooner has Bigger *imagined* how guilty he would feel if he should again see Bessie's mutilated face than the narrator states,

> [O]ut of it all, over and above all that had happened, impalpable but real, there remained to him a queer sense of power. *He* had done this. *He* had brought all this about. In all of his life these two murders were the most meaningful things that had ever happened to him. He was living, truly and deeply . . . . Never had he had the chance to live out the consequences of his actions; never had his will been so free as in this night and day of fear and murder and flight. (239, author's emphasis)

In his jail-cell discussion with Max, Bigger has shed any twinges of guilt he might have felt about the two killings. When Max asks Bigger if he's sorry for killing Mary, Bigger's response is coldly pragmatic: "What's the use of being sorry? That won't help me none" (348). Regarding Bessie's murder, he states, "after killing that white woman, it wasn't hard to kill somebody else. I didn't have to think much about killing Bessie" (352). He concludes, "I ain't worried none about them women I killed. For a little while I was free. . . . It was wrong, but I was feeling all right" (354).

Bigger's existential morality may well be sociopathic in showing no remorse over these killings,[12] but it is an indelible and chillingly memorable feature of his new personality. Thus, Wright's effort to reintroduce determinism to explain Bigger's murder of Bessie is not only inconsistent with Bigger's existential code, it violates the novel's larger plan, realized in book 3.

Red Herring

Readers who find the first two books of *Native Son* compelling are typically let down by book 3, with its static and lengthy scenes in Bigger's jail cell, in court, and especially in Max's interminably long defense speech.[13] About the speech—which runs twenty-three pages in the restored edition—sympathetic readers of the manuscript (Jane Newton, who read the pages as soon as Wright had typed them, and his editor, Edward Aswell) urged drastic cuts. But Wright steadfastly refused. The speech—and book 3 generally—were too central to his own views to tamper with. As Fabre observes, "Wright admitted that he had planned this section in order to express certain ideas which the [limited] nature of his main character made impossible to set forth earlier. . . . [T]his last section was to serve as a repository for his ideological views, as articulated by Bigger's lawyer" (*Unfinished Quest*, 173).

Though Wright was never explicit about the ideas he wished to convey in book 3, they were undoubtedly political, an attempt to weave his view of racism and his collectivistic ideology into the thematic fabric of the novel and, specifically, into Bigger's identity and awareness. That ideology conceives Bigger's condition and fate as part of a larger, proletarian struggle—a recognition that could profoundly change Bigger's consciousness. The plot situation is now propitious to develop what Wright awkwardly called "the impliedly political . . . level of reality in Bigger's life" ("How 'Bigger' Was Born," 452). Caught in the implacable grip of the law, Bigger is no longer free to act on his own, hence to determine himself ruthlessly. Now, he *receives* contrasting appeals, e.g., the reverend's, and can only react. Political themes previously implicit or crudely instrumental now come to the fore. Where before, Bigger had simply used communism as a red herring to distract the law, and the communists, Jan and Mary, had come off badly, now the communists are sincere and central to Bigger's evolving consciousness. Jan is given a long, self-humbling speech in Bigger's cell that wipes away his earlier condescension and offers sincere friendship. More important, Boris Max, Bigger's communist lawyer and sole defender, appointed by the Party's legal arm, becomes his empathetic interlocutor, even his friend and would-be mentor.[14] The logical—and simplistic—political outcome of Jan and Max's interventions would be a jailhouse conversion: Bigger, though Max's guidance, realizing that he was never alone in his oppression, that what seemed racial oppression was really class-based, enabling Bigger to depart the world with a vision of solidarity with the oppressed of all races and nationalities. Wright describes this same awakening in his first encounter with the John Reed Club literature; in relating the condition of oppressed blacks to the revolutionary struggle of workers worldwide, it showed him that "Negro experience could find a home, a functioning value and role" ("I Tried," pt. 1, 62). Doubtless, the temptation to have Bigger undergo this same, empowering discovery must have been strong, and it would have had the added benefit of winning the approval of the Party's literary critics, who typically credited such newly gained collectivistic consciousness as an upbeat proletarian conclusion. Such a conclusion would also resolve any potential doubts the Party might have harbored about Wright's ideological priorities (recall that his colleagues at the *Daily Worker* had plenty of doubts about him), and, more important, might seem to resolve—at least in fiction—Wright's own doubts about his role in the Party. Fabre writes, "He could feel the critical eyes of certain members of the Party--people whom he considered his friends and whose judgment he respected and even depended on—fixed on him" (*Unfinished Quest*, 174).

But although book 3 approaches Bigger's political discovery of his place among the oppressed, it ultimately takes a different path, which makes the collectivistic theme seem far more ambiguous and raises questions about Wright's own relationship to the Communist Party vis-à-vis his commitment to his literary vision. Even his preference (in "How 'Bigger' Was Born") for such phrases as "collectivistic," "proletarian ideal," and "labor movement and its ideology" (449, 441), rather than "communist" or "communistic," in describing his political sympathies suggests that, whether consciously or not, Wright was putting some space between his beliefs and conventional communist ideology. Similarly, he describes Bigger's relationship with other oppressed peoples as "abstract linkages," while his racial consciousness is "the concrete picture" (442).

In the novel, these tensions are more obvious. There is no doubt that both Jan and Max profoundly affect Bigger's self-concept, just as his killings had done in the first two books. Following Jan's speech expressing his desire to forgive Bigger and "to help that guy if he lets me" (288), Wright describes its impact: "Jan had spoken a declaration of friendship . . . . For the first time in his life, a white man became a human being to him; . . . He saw Jan as though someone had performed an operation upon his eyes, or as though someone had snatched a deforming mask from Jan's face" (288–89). Bigger's discovery, however, is profoundly racial, not political: a *white* man "became a human being," not a white blur; a white man

had penetrated the psychological barrier ("flung aside the curtain")
Bigger had erected in self-defense.

Max's effort to discover precisely what motivated Bigger in his
two killings affects Bigger even more profoundly. Wright likens it
to the transformative self-discovery Bigger experiences after killing
Mary: "in Max's asking of those questions he felt a recognition of
his life, of his feelings, of his person that he had never encountered
before" (360). He even feels the same physical sense of release:

> [N]ow that he had killed Mary he felt a lessening of tension in his
> muscles; he had shed an invisible burden he had long carried. (114)

> He could not remember when he had felt as relaxed as this before. . . .
> [H]e discovered that he had spoken to Max as he had never spoken to
> anyone in his life; not even to himself. And his talking had eased from
> his shoulders a heavy burden. (359)[15]

What had taken a killing to achieve before—a transgression of the
white barrier—is now realized through sympathetic conversation,
and the barrier itself falls. But Wright pushes the implications of
Bigger's discovery much further:

> He wondered if it were possible that after all everybody in the world
> felt alike. Did those who hated him have in them the same thing Max
> had seen in him[?] . . . For the first time in his life he had gained a
> pinnacle of feeling upon which he could stand and see vague relations
> that he had never dreamed of. If that white looming mountain of hate
> were not a mountain at all, but people, people like himself, and like
> Jan—then he was faced with a high hope, the like of which he had
> never thought could be, and a despair the full depths of which he
> knew he could not stand to feel . . .
>
> He stood in the middle of the cell floor and tried to see himself in
> relation to other men, a thing he had always feared to try to do, so
> deeply stained was his own mind with the hate of others for him. . . .
> For the first time in his life he felt ground beneath his feet, and he
> wanted to stay there. (360–61)

This is as close as Bigger comes in the novel to feeling solidarity with the oppressed (really, with all humankind)—a feeling Wright describes with eloquence:

> If he reached out with his hands, and his hands were electric wires . . . if he reached out with his hands and touched other people . . . would there be a reply, a shock? Not that he wanted those hearts to turn their warmth to him; . . . But just to know that they were there and warm! . . . . And in that touch, response of recognition, there would be union, identity; there would be a supporting oneness, a wholeness which had been denied him all his life. (362)

This intimation of solidarity offers Bigger the same freedom from fear that his killings had provided earlier. Against his anticipation of death, he has a complementary "vision [of] life, an image of himself standing amid throngs of men, lost in the welter of their lives with the hope of emerging again, different, unafraid" (364). But no sooner has Wright articulated this vision than it fades into the contrasting vision of death and despair: "But so far only the certainty of death was his; only the unabating hate of the white faces could be seen; only the same dark cell, the long lonely hours, only the cold bars remained" (364). This vision of political solidarity, promising a second transformation of Bigger's consciousness and identity to supersede his first rebirth as existential superman, lingers teasingly until the novel's final pages. But its failure to be realized ironically derives from the one man who could have helped Bigger achieve it: his communist lawyer, Max.

Max's long speech on Bigger's behalf has been much debated by reviewers and scholars, most finding it "ill-related to the book itself" and overly ideological.[16] That Wright used the speech to present his own ideological views of the racism that twisted Bigger, as Fabre asserts (*Unfinished Quest*, 173), is no doubt true, but that fact alone should not prevent us from critiquing the speech or from speculating on Wright's authorial distance from Max's approach to Bigger's case. Max's strategy—plead guilty to all charges, avoid trial by an inevitably biased jury, and appeal to the judge's sense of fairness through an impassioned speech—is controversial to say the least. He makes no effort to challenge the State's unproven charges: that Bigger raped Mary and that he "murdered" her intentionally.[17]

In fact, Max intentionally ignores the specifics of the case: "Let us not concern ourselves with the part of Bigger Thomas's confession that says he murdered accidentally, that he did not rape the girl. It really does not matter" (403). (Does not matter? One can imagine innumerable defense attorneys falling off their chairs reading this last sentence.) Instead, Max follows a strategy that Communist Party lawyers used often: make the defendant a symbolic martyr for the abuses (here, racism) of the capitalist system. Bigger is merely "a tiny social symbol in relation to our whole sick social organism" (383). Max then launches into a rambling argument that Bigger's acts are the inevitable result of centuries-old systematic racism, which has created "a separate nation, stunted, stripped, and held captive *within* this nation, devoid of political, social, economic, and property rights" (397, Wright's emphasis). Bigger's violence becomes the expression of "a new form of life" (391) within this separate nation, and Max darkly warns of riots and "another civil war" (403–4) if the country does not change course. At times, he cannot resist inserting boilerplate Marxist rhetoric:

> [I]f the misunderstanding of what this boy's life means is an indication of how men of wealth and property are misreading the consciousness of the submerged millions today, [another civil war] may truly come. (403)

> When the men of wealth urge the use and show of force, quick death, swift revenge, then it is to protect a little spot of private security against the resentful millions from whom they have filched it . . . (405)

Wright may well have supported all of these arguments, and at times Max virtually quotes the narrator, as when he states that Bigger "murdered many times [before], but there are no corpses" (400, cf. 106). But Max makes more extreme claims as well: "Multiply Bigger Thomas twelve million times, . . . and you have the psychology of the Negro people" (397). This may come as news to the Guses of the black community (not to mention Reverend Hammond, Bigger's mother, et al.) who are able to sublimate their anger. Who, then, is the norm? Another example of Max's extreme claims: "The actions that resulted in the death of those two women were as instinctive and inevitable as breathing or blinking one's eyes. It was an act of *creation*!" (400, author's emphasis). From his conversations with Bigger, Max may well have discerned how Mary's killing created a new life for Bigger, but how would a judge be expected to react to such a statement, which appears, on its surface, so grotesquely absurd? Or again, in describing the benefits for Bigger of a life term in prison (404), Max does not anticipate the inevitable rebuttal: Why should this murderer be rewarded?

Then, there are the errors: "He was impelled toward murder [of Mary] as much through the thirst for excitement, exultation, and elation as he was through fear!" (401). Here, Max confuses cause and effect. Similarly, "He sought another life and accidentally found one, found it at the expense of all we cherish and hold dear" (398). Max digresses several times, for example his discussion of "the kind of happiness we are seeking" (398–99) and the questions of whether Bigger loved Bessie and love's relation to sex (401–2). It is worth recalling that Max is an old man—he describes himself that way to Bigger (423). Perhaps what Wright is really showing us in this speech is the well-intentioned, but often erratic ramblings of an old-line Marxist for whom Bigger Thomas is essentially just a symbol of an exploited and repressed class. Perhaps for that very reason, Bigger "had not understood the speech, but he had felt the meaning of some of it from the tone of Max's voice" (406).

The strongest evidence that Wright's view and Max's are not identical is the wedge Wright drives between Bigger and Max in the novel's final pages. When Max visits Bigger's cell after the death sentence, Bigger is hungry for more of their intimate conversation, which had given Bigger his first sense of connection to the larger world. But Max does not comprehend this need; twice Bigger thinks, "Max did not even *know*!" The narrator adds, he was "devoid of the deeper awareness that Bigger sought so hungrily" (423). When Max does attempt to provide Bigger some comfort—though comfort is not what Bigger wants at this crucial moment—he presents his own Marxist perspective: "Bigger . . . in the work I'm doing, I look at the world in a way that shows no whites and no blacks, no civilized and no savages. . . . When men are trying to change human life on earth, those little things don't matter" (424). Those "little things" have been Bigger's whole life. And Bigger is not concerned with chang- ing the world at this point; he wants, desperately, to understand his place in it, his connection to everyone else: "Mr. Max, I know the folks who sent me here to die hated me; I know that. B-b-but you reckon th-they was like m-me, trying to g-get something like I was, and when I'm dead and gone they'll be saying like I'm saying now that they didn't mean to hurt nobody . . . th-that they was t-trying to get something, too . . . ?" (425). The remarkable thing about this intimation is that it unites Bigger with *all* people, op- pressor and oppressed alike, and might therefore give him his birth- right, his place within humankind, rather than outside of it. Thus, his visionary question transcends Max's philosophy of unity only within the working class. When Max hesitates to respond, Bigger demands an answer, so desperate is he for this final revelation. But Max's reluctance—"You're asking me to say things I don't want to say"—reveals the profound chasm between their world views. Max is a communist: class opposition between the rich and poor, own- ers and everyone else, is intrinsic to his beliefs. Bigger's question implies a *universal* brotherhood, where even the whites who hate him (and hate, by extension, all blacks) ultimately have the same human needs and desires. This universality of the human condition is what Max cannot acknowledge. Instead, he tries to give Bigger a dramatic view of the world outside his cell window—a view which *could* provide the climactic revelation that Bigger so desperately needs before his execution.

But Max's construction of that view is purely Marxist. He says of the distant building in the Loop, "What you felt, what you want- ed, is what keeps those buildings standing there. When millions of men are desiring and longing, those buildings grow and unfold. But, Bigger, those buildings aren't growing any more. A few men are squeezing those buildings tightly in their hands" (427). Just as in his final summation, Max describes the owners as afraid: "They want to keep what they own, even if it makes others suffer. In order to keep it, they push men down in the mud and tell them that they are beasts." And Max's vision, like Steinbeck's depiction of the ex- ploitive landowners, predictably, entails class conflict—"men like you get angry and fight to reenter those buildings, to live again" (427).

Essentially, Max tries to get Bigger to transcend his racial identity and see his relationship to all of the oppressed: "You're black, but that's only part of it. . . . But, Bigger, they [the owners] say that *all* people who work are inferior. And the rich people don't want to change things; they'll lose too much" (428, author's emphasis). This is the straight Communist Party line: class supersedes race. Bigger is first and foremost a member of the oppressed proletariat.

But this Marxist conception makes no impact on Bigger. He has tried—and failed—to go beyond its rigid confines in his unanswered question; now he construes Max's dramatic lesson in a wholly personal way: "Sounds funny, Mr. Max, but when I think about what you say I kind of feel what I wanted. It makes me feel I was kind of right." Bigger thus reverts to the existential self-discovery triggered by his killing: "[W]hen I think of why all the killing was, I begin to feel what I wanted, what I am. . . . I didn't want to kill! . . . But what I killed for, I *am*! It must've been pretty deep in me to make me kill! . . . I didn't know I was really alive in this world until I felt things hard enough to kill for 'em" (429, Wright's emphasis).

Now, it's Bigger who can see—"he felt he had to make Max understand how he saw things now"—and Max who is blind: "Max groped for his hat like a blind man . . ." (429).[18] Gone is Bigger's intimation of unity with "other men"; his final sense of selfhood is his first one: *Caedo, ergo sum*. Max's response to Bigger's declaration is telling: he backs away; he pleads "despairingly": "No; no; no . . . Bigger, not that." Could there be a more complete repudiation of the Marxist view that Max represents, after which Max staggers out of Bigger's cell vanquished and despairing, while Bigger smiles "a faint, wry, *bitter* smile" (429–30, emphasis added)?[19] Wright states in "How 'Bigger' Was Born" that Max's role in the last scene was to "register the moral—or what *I* felt was the moral—horror of Negro life in the United States." But that depiction of horror is constricted by his Marxist philosophy, hence his weakness at the end. Conversely, Wright describes Bigger's final self-realization in glowing terms of strength and confidence: "I ended it . . . showing Bigger living dangerously, taking his life into his own hands, accepting what life had made him" (461). Keneth Kinnamon writes of this final scene, "The difficulty seems to be that Wright superimposed a consciously held intellectual conviction on a story that otherwise engaged his imagination and experience on the deepest emotional levels. . . . Though Wright thinks that he agrees with Max's rebuttal in the final scene, his heart is really with Bigger's statement."[20]

Conclusion

Wright's emphasis in this novel has been, first and last, on Bigger; and it is Bigger's *self*-discovery, not the philosophy that others attempt to impose on him, that finally matters. But how much of this fictional resolution applies to Wright himself? Was this ending a personal statement that, just as his literary devotion to "true" characterization takes precedence over ideological correctness, so his sense of himself as an artist expressing negro nationalism supersedes his identity as Party *apparachnik*? Wright candidly reveals his priorities in "How 'Bigger' Was Born," when he describes, as one of the "mental censors" inhibiting his writing, the Party's potential reaction to his focus on Bigger's psychology. The passage deserves to be quoted at length:

> What would my own white and black comrades in the Communist party say? . . .
>
> How could I create such complex and wide schemes of associational thought and feeling . . . without being mistaken for a "smuggler of reaction," "an ideological confusionist," or "an individualistic and dangerous element"? Though my heart is with the collectivist and proletarian ideal, I solved this problem by assuring myself that honest politics and honest feeling in imaginative representation ought to be able to meet on common healthy ground without fear, suspicion, and quarreling. Further, and more importantly, I steeled myself by coming to the conclusion that whether politicians accepted or rejected Bigger did not really matter; my task . . . was to free myself of this burden of impressions and feelings, recast them into the image of Bigger and make him *true*. Lastly, I felt that a right more immediately deeper than that of politics or race was at stake; that is, a *human* right, the right of a man to think and feel honestly. And especially did this personal and human right bear hard upon me, for temperamentally I am inclined to satisfy the claims of my own ideals rather than the expectations of others. . . . I was but fulfilling what I felt to be the laws of my own growth. (448–49, Wright's emphasis)

In short, Wright's needs to express himself and to grow as an artist—his "human right . . . to think and feel honestly"—took clear precedence over his political conformity and the Party's political acceptance. In the same passage, he describes the goals of "politics"—read "Party critics"—as "rigid and simply drawn." And, according to Fabre, he didn't expect their praise for this novel (*Unfinished Quest*, 374). It is no coincidence that the slurs he imagines his comrades hurling at him—"smuggler of reaction," etc.—were echoes of those that the communists of his Chicago cell had already slandered him with, according to "I Tried to Be a Communist" (pt. 2, 48).

As noted in chapter 2, the Communist Party at the time was attempting to discourage negro nationalism (i.e., a specific focus on blacks as a race) in favor of locating racial issues within the larger struggles of the proletariat and the Popular Front—precisely Max's point of view in the concluding scene. Wright agreed with this weighting in principle (in his 1937 "Blueprint for Negro Writing," for example), but did not follow it in practice. All but one of the stories in *Uncle Tom's Children* focused on the specific conflicts blacks faced in the Jim Crow South. And *Native Son*, as Wright freely acknowledged, concentrates on Bigger's racial consciousness to the exclusion of all other characters, white and black. Moreover, in "How 'Bigger' Was Born," Wright specifically calls Bigger "a Negro nationalist" because "he was not allowed to live as an American. Such was his way of life *and mine;* neither Bigger nor I resided fully in either camp. Of this dual aspect of Bigger's social consciousness, I placed the nationalistic side first, . . . In other words his nationalistic complex was for me a concept through which I could grasp more of the total meaning of his life than I could in any other way" (451, emphasis added). Bigger's "nationalistic complex" was "the concrete picture"; his "linkages" to other oppressed people were merely theoretical, "abstract" (442).[21]

This defiance of communist priorities, disregard for what the comrades might say about his novel, and assertion of his artistic needs show that Wright's self-concept as an artist—an increasingly prominent artist—now took precedence over any obligations he felt to the Party. Is it coincidental, then, that a similar conflict in *Native Son* between Party ideology (Max's "window" speech in

Bigger's cell) and Bigger's self-assertive rebuttal resolves itself with the triumphant assertion of this black man's identity, while the spokesman for Marxist ideology backs out of Bigger's cell blindly? Or that Bigger's intimation of universal brotherhood makes Max's insistent assertion of class conflict seem stunted? Wright may have *intended* in book 3 to link Bigger's experience to a nascent Marxist consciousness, but that's not the way the narrative worked out.

Finally, if Wright was fully conscious of his diminution of Marxist ideology in favor of negro nationalism in his fiction—as "How 'Bigger' Was Born" indicates—was he using the fiction to begin his own disengagement from the Party—and at least to signal that beginning? Or was he trying to have it both ways, as Kinneman suggests—and deceiving himself that such was possible? Though either side of this question is arguable, I lean toward the latter view. The passage quoted above—"I solved this problem by assuring myself that honest politics and honest feeling in imaginative representation ought to be able to meet on common healthy ground without fear, suspicion, and quarreling"—is wishful thinking; it hinges on "ought," the ideal. But Wright had also noted the "rigid and simple" thinking of Party critics, qualities not likely to enable them to meet the author "on common healthy ground." He had already experienced this rigidity with the Chicago communists, resulting in his complete break from that cell and exit from that city. And he did not expect Party critics to like the novel.

In the years he was writing and revising *Native Son*, 1938 and 1939, Wright was still grateful to the Communist Party for supporting him in New York, albeit through time-consuming journalism, and for getting him started as a writer through the John Reed Club of Chicago. He stated in the *Daily Worker* when *Uncle Tom's Children* was published that he owed his literary development to the Party.[22] But this generous, perhaps exaggerated acknowledgment, as well as his party-line "Blueprint for Negro Writing," were prosaic statements for leftist newspapers and magazines. In those media, as in his numerous lectures, he seemed quite willing to follow the Party line and conduct himself as a faithful Party member. When it came to his artistic work, however, nobody could dictate how he should write. This was not simply a case of "practice what you preach," which would make Wright seem a hypocrite. Rather, at this point in his ideological and creative development, Wright *wanted* to believe that his two lives, creative and political, were reconcilable, that his artistic vision was inextricable from his Marxist ideology. It would require more painful experiences with the Party—in its responses to his novel, the ideological acrobatics it expected him to perform, and its abandonment of the cause Wright most cherished—before he was able to resolve this issue of personal identity and ideology with certainty.

For Whom the Bell Tolls

Robert Jordan's (and Ernest Hemingway's) "True Book"

SEVERAL TIMES IN Hemingway's *For Whom the Bell Tolls*, the protagonist Robert Jordan thinks about the "true" book he will write after the Spanish Civil War ends. For example, "And what are you going to do afterwards? I am going back [to the University of Montana] and earn my living teaching Spanish as before, and I am going to write a true book" (178). He adds sardonically, "I'll bet that will be easy." He cannot write the book in the fictional present, of course, fighting as a *partizan* behind enemy lines for the Spanish Loyalists. But after the war ends, when Jordan is presumably free to write whatever he wants, and when his revelations will not affect the war's outcome (or, more precisely, not damage the Loyalist cause), *then* Jordan can write his book.

Of course, Jordan never lives to see that day, and in this sense his unrealized intentions are a kind of tease. But the subjects he plans to write about are revealing of both his own and his author's political-moral dilemmas and thus worth examining in both contexts. For Jordan is a projection of the author, and the "true" book Jordan *intends* to write is, self-reflexively, part of the book that his creator, Ernest Hemingway, *does* write. Describing Jordan's unrealized intentions, therefore, becomes a means of evaluating Hemingway's achievement.

What kind of a book would Jordan have written? Though he is never specific about its nature, several of its features can be deduced from contextual references and from related issues in the novel. He may have envisioned a full-scale history of the war, but

Jordan's academic training is in language, not history. More likely, he intends a memoir of his firsthand experiences and observations fighting for the Loyalists: "He would write a book when he got through with this. But only about the things he knew, truly, and about what he knew. But I will have to be a much better writer than I am now to handle them, he thought. The things he had come to know in this war were not so simple" (264). In both of the passages quoted above, two qualities of this future book recur: first, it must be "true"; second, getting at that truth will not be easy: the war's "truths"—as Jordan had already discovered—"were not so simple." Why this emphasis on "true," with its implications of setting the record straight and rebutting lies, misrepresentations, and myths? The immediate answers are textual and can be found in Jordan's experiences as a *partizan* and in what he's learned about the war in his close dealings with the Soviets, who were covertly running it and who strongly influenced the Republican government, as described in chapter 3. Contextually, however, "true" also refers to the author's knowledge and opinions about the war and its participants, views that he previously repressed or distorted in his propagandistic journalism and only hinted at in his Spanish Civil War fiction and drama. In this sense, Hemingway's novel aims to correct misrepresentations and replace myths about the war and the Loyalists with disillusioning truths. It also aims at another kind of truth: the moral ambiguity complicating military action.

"True," of course, is a loaded word and, paradoxically equivocal: *Whose* truth? "True" from what perspective? But increasingly in Hemingway's 1930s writing and thereafter, the word appears as an absolute—as if there were *one* truth, one quality that writing either embodies or does not. As Hemingway uses it, the word is also an honorific.[1] For example, when Jordan's friend and mentor, the Russian journalist Karkov, explains why he "bothers" with Jordan, that is, tries to "educate" him in the truths behind the official propaganda and lies, he praises Jordan's veracity in his one book on Spain: "I think you write absolutely truly and that is very rare" (264). Although Karkov's compliment sheds no light on "true" and "truly," one might conclude from Karkov's own job of manipulating "truths" that the word means for both himself and Jordan an awareness of multiple sides of issues and personalities that have been previously distorted as being one-sided: good and bad, black and white.

Why will writing this true book be so difficult for Jordan? What are these complicated "things" he had learned in this war? And how did these things affect his outlook on the war and, equally important, his view of himself as participant? Two areas of Jordan's experience must be examined: his relationship with the Russians, Karkov in particular, and with Pilar's guerrilla band. Both situations force him to re-examine his views about his political and moral values and about the war generally. What had once seemed a clear-cut, idealistic purpose and self-concept in a political conflict of right (Loyalists) and wrong (the fascists) evolves into ambiguous aims and loyalties, a conflicted self-concept, and a war that is no longer black and white.

The Russians: "a very corrupting business"

Very early in the novel, the Soviet presence in Spain is apparent. Jordan smokes Russian cigarettes; he receives his mission from General Golz, who describes himself as a *"Général Sovietique"* and refers to Jordan as a *partizan* using "the Russian term" (16).[2] Moreover, the previous *partizan* who worked with Pilar's group was named Kashkin, another Russian. Later in the novel, Hemingway devotes most of chapter 18 to describing Jordan's relationship with Karkov at Gaylord's Hotel and what Jordan learns there about the war, such as how many Loyalist generals, even those with Spanish surnames, speak Russian and were trained in Russia.[3]

Why should the Russian presence matter, especially since Jordan seems to take it for granted? Soviet support of the Loyalist side in sending arms was common knowledge. Less well known, because the Soviets strove to keep it secret, was the *extent* of Soviet military leadership beyond "advisers," the Soviets' manipulation of the Republican government, their purges of anti-Stalinist parties on the left and their persecution and murder of party leaders (see chapter 3). Moreover, Jordan works for the Russians. The papers and a special stamp he carries show that he works for the S.I.M., the Military Intelligence Service. Although organized by a Spaniard, the Republican Minister of Defense Indalecio Prieto, the S.I.M. quickly became controlled by the Soviets and run by the Soviet head of the NKVD in Spain, the notorious Alexandr Orlov, who also supervised guerrilla warfare operations behind fascist lines.[4] Thus, Orlov (never mentioned in the novel) would theoretically have been Robert Jordan's boss. The significance of the Russian presence in the novel is thus twofold: as a major factor in Robert Jordan's complex characterization, and as a truth about the war that Hemingway can finally reveal after years of denial. The two meanings meet in a brief anecdote the narrator recounts about Karkov. Early in the war, the journalist was responsible for concealing the national origin of three wounded Russians, even if it meant killing them, "since, at the time, it was of the greatest importance that there should be no evidence of any Russian intervention to justify an open intervention by the fascists . . ." (254). Although Hemingway was wrong about the reason for the concealment—Nazi Germany had already intervened in the war within weeks of its outbreak, not after the first Soviet "advisers" arrived—he was correct about the concealment itself, particularly in the Russian origins or Russian training of Loyalist generals.[5] Thus, in recalling his education at Gaylord's, Jordan remembers,

> Gaylord's was the place where you met famous peasant and worker Spanish commanders who had sprung to arms from the people at the start of the war without any previous military training and found that many of them spoke Russian. That had been the first big disillusion to him a few months back and he had started to be cynical to himself about it. (245)[6]

Although he justifies to himself the necessity of these generals gaining their military education in Russia, Jordan must not only "accept the necessity for all the deception" (247), but participate in the lying and cover-up. He seems to affirm Karkov's rationalization: "If a thing was right fundamentally the lying was not supposed to matter. There was a lot of lying though. He did not care for the lying at first. He hated it. Then later he had come to like it. It was part of being an insider but it was a very corrupting business" (245–46). Hemingway, too, felt he had to lie. As shown in chapter 3, during the years he covered the war as a journalist for NANA and various magazines, and wrote stories and a play about the war, he steadfastly denied the Soviet presence in Spain. Those who asserted it in his articles and stories are made to look ridiculous, or are ironical, as in the case of Max's assertion about his and Philip Rawlings' "Russian" identity in *The Fifth Column*. Hemingway even carried the denial into his private life, lecturing Dos Passos in a letter of late March 1938 (*Selected Letters*, 463–64) that the generals Dos Passos had supposedly written about in an article on Spain were *not* Russian (see chapter 3). It must have come as a relief to Hemingway that he could now write freely about the extensive Russian presence in Spain at the time of the novel's action, the end of May 1937.[7]

Jordan's feelings about the education he receives at Gaylord's and from Karkov are profoundly ambivalent: he likes being an insider (as Hemingway did) and "to know how it really was; not how it was supposed to be" (247). But he "corrupted very easily" (245, 255), and the disillusioning view of the war he gains from the Russians bothers him more than he admits. Part of this corruption is in taking advantage of the good food and drink available at the hotel: "Gaylord's itself had seemed indecently luxurious and corrupt. . . . [T]he food was too good for a besieged city . . ." (247, 245). Jordan "had at first been repelled by the whole business and then had accepted it and enjoyed it" (248).

Besides eating well at Gaylord's, Jordan admires his chief contact there: "Karkov was the most intelligent man he had ever met. . . . [H]e had more brains and more inner dignity and outer insolence and humor than any man that he had ever known" (247). As described in chapter 3, Karkov was modeled directly on Mikhail Koltsov, a central figure of the Soviet presence in Spain as correspondent for *Pravda* and chief propagandist who put a Stalinist spin on the deadly leftist rivalries in Republican Spain. Like Koltsov, Karkov is centrally positioned to know the inside stories behind the propaganda he himself helped create. As Koltsov shared many of these stories with Hemingway, so Karkov does with Robert Jordan. Finally, through Koltsov, Hemingway met several Loyalist generals who regularly frequented Gaylord's. Presumably, this is where Jordan first met General Golz.

But Karkov's influence on Robert Jordan—like Koltsov's on Hemingway—goes beyond sharing insider information and arranging contacts. Karkov gives Jordan an intentionally distorted view of Soviet political operations in Spain, such as its purge of the anti-Stalinist POUM party in the late spring of 1937. Karkov recounts his public denunciation of POUM for *Pravda*, replete with hyperbolic exaggerations: "I have sent a cable describing the wickedness of that infamous organization of Trotskyite murders and their fascist machinations all beneath contempt . . ." (263). Privately, however, he confides to Jordan, "[B]etween us, it is not very serious, the P.O.U.M." and he calls them "very silly people." Karkov mentions casually that the POUM had plotted to kill him (Karkov), Generals Walter and Modesto, and Defense Minister Prieto—not exactly unserious actions, if true—and that the POUM received "a little fascist money." When Jordan asks about the POUM "putsch"[8] and if many were killed in it, Karkov blithely answers, "Not so many as were shot afterwards or will be shot." In fact, nearly a thousand POUM supporters were arrested in Catalonia in the Soviet purge.[9] The charges that Koltsov casually made against POUM—planning assassinations, being in the pay of the fascists—were Soviet propaganda (probably invented and spread by Koltsov) to justify its purge, but Hemingway repeated these charges uncritically in his articles condemning the POUM (see chapter 8).

About the POUM's leader, Andrés Nin, Karkov is even more duplicitous. He tells Jordan, "We had him but he escaped from our hands" (263). To Jordan's question about Nin's present whereabouts, Karkov answers, "In Paris. We say he is in Paris." In fact, the "escape to Paris" story was spread by the Soviets (and likewise the story that Nin had been kidnapped by the Anarchists) to cover up the NKVD's arrest, torture, and assassination of Nin (on Stalin's direct orders) in mid-June, 1937.[10] Note how Karkov hints that the Paris story is a lie ("We *say* he is in Paris"), but Jordan does not pursue that lead. Neither did Hemingway, who, ten months after the novel's action, March 1938, was still insisting to Dos Passos that Nin was alive. Karkov, like Koltsov, is indeed "intelligent"—and far too devious for a Robert Jordan to follow along the Byzantine twists of Soviet lies and political manipulations. Carlos Baker claims that Jordan "is in no way 'sucked in'" by communist lies,[11] but Jordan's acceptance at face value of Karkov's lie shows otherwise.

Even more corrosive than the corrupting influence of good food, inside stories, and Karkov's lies at Gaylord's is Jordan's exposure to the Russians' cynicism and brutal repression of rivals: "You could remember the men you knew who died in the fighting around Pozoblanco; but it was a joke at Gaylord's" (255). It is no joke to Jordan, however. Fighting and possibly dying for one's beliefs is something he obviously believes in as a *partizan*. For the power behind the throne to snicker at such risk and sacrifice and to distort it as propaganda—"'Our glorious troops continue to advance without losing a foot of ground,' Karkov repeated in English. 'It is in the communiqué'" (255)—must have been profoundly disillusioning for Jordan.

So must political assassination, though Jordan reacts ambivalently when Karkov reveals—a shocking admission—that it "is practiced very extensively, . . . very, very extensively" (261). This is precisely what Hemingway had denied in his journalism though he knew it was practiced regularly in Madrid against suspected fifth columnists. In his Spanish Civil War stories and play, he had approached the subject, but never acknowledged that Russians were involved. Jordan's reaction to Karkov's revelation is murky. Responding to Karkov's tepid admission that he himself did not "like" the shootings, Jordan says, "I don't mind them, . . . I do not like them but I do not mind them any more" (261). What does he mean by "do not mind them"? That he can accept them as politically necessary? That they do not offend his moral sensibility? Following his first confrontation with Pablo in the cave, Jordan rejects the gypsy's suggestion to shoot Pablo without provocation: "That is to assassinate. . . . It is repugnant to me and it is not how one should act for the cause" (70). Much later in the novel, he recalls shooting two fascist prisoners "[b]ecause I had to . . ." (321). (Why did he have to?) He thinks to himself with the same puzzling contradiction that he expresses to Karkov, "And you did not mind that [killing them]? No. Nor did you like it? No. I decided never to do it again. . . . I have avoided killing those who are unarmed" (321). Is Jordan then a hypocrite, willing to accept political assassination so long as others pull the trigger? The contradiction between morally disapproving of an act enough to avoid it in future and not "minding" it remains unresolved. Jordan cautions himself, "if you are not absolutely straight in your head you have no right to do the things you do for all of them are crimes . . ." (321). But he admits to Karkov, "My mind is in suspension until we win the war" (261). Presumably, this is one of those moral issues he will sort out when he writes his "true" book. But in the meantime, how is he to reconcile this ambivalence about political murder with his knowledge of the Soviets' actions and with his personal mission to fight for the Republic in a war that the Soviets are largely running?

In the face of these lies, cynicism, and brutality, Jordan is unsure of his values. He knows that he has lost much of his earlier idealism in fighting for the Loyalists: "You are a long way from how you felt in the Sierra and at Carabanchel and at Usera, he thought." Yet, he wonders, "[W]as it merely that you lost the naïveté that you started with?" (255). Just as Gaylord's Hotel is a metonym for Jordan's disillusionment, so a different address, 63 Velasquez, headquarters for the International Brigades in Madrid, symbolizes his earlier idealism. Appropriately, the volunteers' idealistic communism is described in religious terms: "puritanical," "crusade," "the feeling you expected to have and did not have when you made your first communion." It is noteworthy that neither Jordan nor Hemingway as narrator belittles this idealism; in fact, the narrator's description of it is moving:

> It gave you a part in something that you could believe in wholly and completely and in which you felt an absolute brotherhood with the others who were engaged in it. It was something that you had never known before but that you had experienced now and you gave such importance to it and the reasons for it that your own death seemed of complete unimportance; . . . But the best thing was that there was something you could do about this feeling and this necessity too. You could fight. (251)

Although Jordan quickly dismisses this "feeling"—"And in the fighting soon there was no purity of feeling for those who survived . . . Not after the first six months" (251–52)—it has obviously lingered in his own sense of purpose in the war. In this respect, Hemingway's decision to make Jordan, initially, a loner working independently behind the lines, instead of, say, a volunteer in the Abraham Lincoln Brigade, enables Jordan to maintain his *non*-communist idealism by fusing it with his professional pride as a skillful operative, an independent contractor, so to speak, who can, to some extent, separate himself from the corrupt larger context.[12] Thus, when Jordan has had enough of Karkov's cynicism, he says, "I like it better at the front, . . . The closer to the front the better the people" (264).

In one important respect, Jordan does not simply compartmentalize his mind and actions to protect them from Russian cynicism and corruption. He accepts and supports Soviet control of the war. This support is important because Hemingway goes to considerable lengths to show that Jordan is *not* a communist, both in his conversation with Pilar (75)[13] and several times in his thoughts:

You're not a real Marxist and you know it. (322)

And what about a planned society and the rest of it? That was for the others to do. . . . What were his politics then? He had none now, he told himself. (178)

If anything, Jordan's politics are closer to libertarian—just as Hemingway's were in the early 1930s: "[A]ll people should be left alone and you should interfere with no one" (178). Elsewhere, Jordan's beliefs are clichés to illustrate that he has no politics: "You believe in Liberty, Equality and Fraternity. You believe in Life, Liberty and the Pursuit of Happiness" (322). "Liberty" is the common denominator. Why should a non-communist, who believes, vaguely, in "liberty" for all, support Russian authoritarian control, risk his life repeatedly to carry out Soviet orders, and work for a Soviet-run secret police agency that freely practices political assassinations? Hemingway provides a clear explanation—so clear that it matches the author's explanation of his own allegiance:

He was under Communist discipline for the duration of the war. Here in Spain the Communists offered the best discipline and the soundest and sanest for the prosecution of the war. He accepted their discipline for the duration of the war because, in the conduct of the war, they were the only party whose discipline he could respect. (178)[14]

Significantly, "discipline" appears four times in three sentences. Its meaning, however, is slippery, shaded by political context. Leftist Spain in 1936 and 1937 was fractured into numerous parties (each with its initials that foreigners found confusing): communists, anti-Stalinist Marxists, socialists, workers' parties, anarcho-syndicalists, etc. Many of these parties levied armed militias early in the war; and as these squabbling militias fought alongside each other, the inevitable result was disunity, chaotic planning, miscommunication, poor internal security, and botched efforts. Once in positions of power, the Soviets abolished these militias, sometimes purged the parties themselves (as with the POUM and the anarchists) and, most important, unified the command structure by putting their own people in charge. "Discipline" in this respect means authoritarian control imposed from the top down. But the word is also a euphemism for summary execution of deserters, stragglers, and slackers. Jordan thinks at one point, "They [the Russian-trained generals] were Communists and they were disciplinarians. The discipline they would enforce would make good troops. Lister was murderous in discipline. He was a true fanatic and he had the complete Spanish lack of respect for life" (250). It is worth recalling that in Hemingway's Spanish Civil War story "Under the Ridge," two men in leather coats—battle police—track down a French deserter "like hunting dogs" and shoot him. Jordan, clearly speaking for Hemingway, obviously approves of this ruthless discipline because it makes good soldiers.[15] (The irony of fighting fascist ideology with fascist tactics does not seem to have impressed itself on either Jordan or his author.) For Jordan, then, desirable ends (winning the war, which would enable people to live freely) justify ruthless, authoritarian means that repress freedom. He frames the desired ends both negatively—"If the Republic lost it would be impossible for those who believed in it to live in Spain" (178)—and positively in the repression of fascism: "[A]s long as we can hold them here [in Spain] we keep the fascists tied up. They can't attack any other country until they finish with us . . ." (454).[16] Probably, he could justify the Soviets' political assassinations under the same blanket rationale: necessary for the war effort.

Nonetheless, once Jordan leaves the corrupting milieu of Madrid and Gaylord's to operate behind enemy lines, he maintains a political persona much closer to his formerly idealistic one at 63 Velazquez. Consider the narrative's description of his purpose: "He fought now in this war because it had started in a country that he loved and he believed in the Republic and that if it were destroyed life would be unbearable for all those people who believed in it" (178). "Believed in the Republic" sounds like a part of a catechism, though elsewhere he is less certain about his faith (103). Pilar, a true believer herself, recognizes his belief and teases him when he refuses the facetious title of "Don": "Thou are very religious about thy politics" (75). He is not only a loner, free of the internal politics of other groups, but also maintains a puritanical life, which, until he meets Maria, allows no time for women. (Presumably, they are reserved for the corrupting milieu of Madrid and Gaylord's.) His purpose is that of a devoted soldier and technician—to carry out his orders skillfully and efficiently, with no regard for his survival: "He was serving in a war and he gave absolute loyalty and as complete a performance as he could give while he was serving" (150). When Pilar asks him what he believes in, giving the word a religious connotation, he replies simply "In my work" (42). He is a "bridge-blower" (25), merely an instrument "to do your duty" (52). Obviously lonely, he admires the "round, cool *companionship* of the trigger guard" of his pistol (65, emphasis added).

The novel never resolves this major contradiction—disjunction, really—in Jordan's beliefs and character between his "behind the lines" idealism and his participation in the cynical corruption of Gaylord's. At most, it simply shows him thinking ironically about how different the two worlds are, how he could never take Maria to Gaylord's (245). Presumably, this disconnection is one of those problems he will work out later when he writes his "true" book. Instead, however, Hemingway largely shifts the terms of the conflict by having this loner become involved with Pilar's group.

Jordan's Evolving Identity: Working with Pilar's Band

Hemingway's strategy of requiring Jordan to work with this guerrilla band is probably the most important change in Jordan's war history—and, arguably, the most intriguing thematic development in Hemingway's oeuvre since the 1920s. Taking the latter first, the typical Hemingway hero—Nick Adams, Jake Barnes, Frederic

Henry (in books 1 and 3 of *A Farewell to Arms*), Colonel Cantwell, Santiago—is a loner, as Robert Jordan was previously; even those with family attachments, such as Harry Morgan and Thomas Hudson, typically work alone. Jordan, however, does not just work with Pilar's band, he gradually comes to regard them as a surrogate family. And of course, with Maria, he discovers love. This is as close as Hemingway ever gets to a collectivistic theme in his fiction—to developing Harry Morgan's dying realization that one man alone cannot get by in this world—and it enables Hemingway to write about Spanish people in this Spanish war, not merely about Western foreigners in Madrid, which his stories and play had depicted. Though he has been criticized with some justification for resorting to stereotypes—the gypsy especially and Pilar as earth mother—he also deserves credit for creating vivid, memorable characters among Pilar's band, each with a distinct personality, some, like Pablo's, quite complex. Who can forget the brilliant sketch of the minor character Fernando, with his fussy, officious, ponderous but ultimately sympathetic nature?

In having Jordan work with Pilar's group, however, Hemingway not only complicates the plot, but also poses several more ethical dilemmas for Jordan beyond the idealism-cynical corruption complex of his relationship with Karkov and Gaylord's. Consider, for example, Jordan's typical hit-and-run method of executing his guerrilla operations. He himself acknowledges that a single operative's clean getaway leaves the locals who helped him to face fascist retribution:

> Because of our mobility and because we did not have to stay afterwards to take the punishment we never knew how anything really ended, he thought. . . . You did your job and cleared out. The next time you came that way you heard that they [the peasants who had helped you] had been shot . . .
>
> But you were always gone when it happened. The *partizans* did their damage and pulled out. The peasants stayed and took the punishment. (149)

Hypothetically, if the *partizan* barely knows these locals, he can perhaps repress his concern for them as he moves on to new assignments. But what if he gets to know them well, as Jordan does Pilar's band? Jordan fully realizes how risky his bridge-blowing mission is, how unlikely it is that he and his assistants will survive: "So now he was compelled to use these people whom he liked as you should use troops toward whom you have no feeling at all if you were to be successful" (177). Again, ends and means. But the moral issue and its attendant guilt haunt Jordan: "[W]as it not a betrayal of them all to get them to do this? Perhaps it was" (178). His rationalization—that even if he left Pilar's band alone, fascist cavalry would still "hunt them out of these hills in a week"—is weak, since the band has survived in this hideout for a long time. As Jordan gets to know Pilar's group better in working with them—and as Hemingway transforms them from abstract "group" to distinct, often complex individuals—Jordan undergoes a remarkable change from loner, concerned only about his mission, to family man concerned for *both* the success of his mission and the safety of his adopted family.

The transformation is most dramatic, of course, in his love affair with Maria. For Jordan, this love is couched as a discovery, "the most important thing that can happen to a human being" (322) because of its existential meaning in defying *nada*: "He knew he himself was nothing, and he knew death was nothing. . . . In the last few days he had learned that he himself, with another person, could be everything" (416). Precisely as in *A Farewell to Arms* (but not elsewhere in Hemingway), one against the world becomes two against the world. But this expansion of caring extends to Pilar's group as a whole, a bonding accelerated by the intensity of their few days together. Initially, his declaration of this new relationship sounds perfunctory. When Pilar and Maria try to comfort Joaquín, who has recounted the fascists' murder of his family, Jordan can only echo Maria's declaration that "We are all thy family" and generalizes Pilar's familial statement "He's your brother" to "We are all brothers" (154). On the night before the attack, however, he fully realizes his new identity:

I have been all my life in these hills since I have been here. Anselmo is my oldest friend. I know him better than I know Charles, than I know Chub, than I know Guy, than I know Mike, and I know them well. Agustín, with his vile mouth, is my brother, and I never had a brother. Maria is my true love and my wife. . . . She is also my sister, and I never had a sister, and my daughter, and I never will have a daughter. (402)[17]

Claiming not to care about his own fate, Jordan comes to care very much about his new family's survival. Note the change in the outcome he hopes for:

What if they were killed tomorrow? What did it matter as long as they did the bridge properly? (375)

That I blow it well and that she gets out all right. . . . That is all I want now. (456)

But not just "she"—"they." This focused altruism clarifies the hazy idealism of his purpose in Spain: from fighting for "the people" to fighting for *these* people. Ultimately, his sense of belonging to this family convinces Jordan to sacrifice himself to enable the group's escape and potential survival. Hemingway thus resolves Jordan's "ends and means" dilemma of exploiting the group by having Jordan himself, not just other group members, pay the ultimate price. Thus, he too is an exploited means to a proximate end, the value of which appears increasingly doubtful in its contribution to an attack that is nearly certain to fail.

Before that outcome, however, Jordan is faced with another moral dilemma of ends and means. To ensure the group's successful escape he must deal with the murderous Pablo, who can procure more horses and guide the group out of the territory. Jordan knows that Pablo has committed civilian murders far beyond any war-based justification—in fact, much of Pablo's drunkenness and passivity throughout the novel derives from his guilt in organizing and conducting the massacre that Pilar so vividly recounts. But Jordan needs Pablo's assistance in planning the escape. Thus, when Pablo returns to the group after destroying Jordan's detonators and exploder, instead of shooting him on sight, Jordan thinks, "But I'm glad to see you, you son of a bitch" and says as much (411).

The practical problem here—having to work with a "son of a bitch"—is hardly remarkable; everyone has experienced it. But

Hemingway quickly turns it into a moral problem, as Jordan senses how Pablo will procure the extra horses needed for the group's escape: "I wonder what the bastard is planning now, Robert Jordan said. But I am pretty sure I know. Well, that is his, not mine. Thank God I do not know these new men" (426). Jordan's compartmentalizing, ends-and-means logic is in full gear: he simply refuses to assume any moral responsibility for Pablo's likely murder of the new recruits for their horses. As if to seal their understanding and Jordan's acquiescence, they shake hands, giving Jordan "the strangest feeling he had felt that morning." If this is tantamount to shaking hands with the devil, Jordan fully accepts it: "We must be allies now" (426).

When Pablo confirms Jordan's suspicion, it is Agustín, not Jordan, who is morally outraged and bluntly asks Pablo, "Did you shoot them all?" Jordan, meanwhile, is silent and morally evasive:

> Robert Jordan was thinking, keep your mouth shut. It is none of your business now. . . . This is an inter-tribal matter. Don't make moral judgments. What do you expect from a murderer? You're working with a murderer. Keep your mouth shut. You knew enough about him before. This is nothing new. But you dirty bastard, he thought. You dirty, rotten bastard. (479)

The ineffectuality of these unspoken slurs attests to Jordan's moral equivocation here. The good end requires dirty means. Jordan may or may not attempt to sort out these ironies in his true book, but Hemingway makes clear in *his* book that the morality of actions in the real world, and especially in war, is seldom clear-cut. A "rotten bastard" may fight on the "right" side. And a decent soldier, like the fascist Lieutenant Berrendo, can fight on the wrong side and still be personally disgusted by barbarous acts he is forced to order, such as the beheading of Sordo's men. By having Jordan shoot Berrendo at the end of the novel to forestall the pursuing fascists, Hemingway presents a final ironic twist on the ambiguity of good and evil in wartime: flawed good kills flawed good.

If Jordan can turn a blind eye toward Pablo's killing, what about his own? Arguably, this issue becomes the most important moral quandary that he must ponder. Again, his contact with Pilar's group—with Anselmo specifically—limns this issue in sharp relief and forces Jordan to think about it. In their early conversation, Anselmo states unequivocally that he considers killing a man, even a fascist, a sin, for which he must atone later. Jordan's first response to Anselmo's declaration is to agree: "Nobody [likes to kill] except those who are disturbed in the head" (48). Killing is only justifiable "when it is necessary. When it is for the cause." Both of these justifications beg the question, Who decides what is "necessary" or "for the cause" and by what criteria? When does "killing" become murder or assassination?

Later, however, when Jordan revisits the issue in his thoughts, he is far less glib about his own behavior and motives regarding killing. Demolition, for example, is a practical problem, "[b]ut there was plenty that was not so good that went with it . . ." (181). Jordan here alludes to killing people—the guards at bridges, for example, or soldiers on sabotaged trains—but, significantly, instead of "killing," he uses the word "assassination" with its repugnant connotations and in a curiously inflated and stilted sentence: "There was the constant attempt to approximate the conditions of successful assassination that accompanied the demolition."[18] Jordan has told Karkov that he doesn't "like" assassination. He refuses to assassinate Pablo and has resolved never again to kill disarmed prisoners (321). But when he thinks about "assassination" accompanying demolition, he makes a remarkable admission to himself: "God knows you took it easily enough. . . . You took to it a little too readily if you ask me" (181). Later, he extends this admission of "taking to" killing:

> And you, he thought, you have never been corrupted by it? You never had it in the Sierra? Nor at Usera? Nor through all the time in Estremadura? Not at any time? *Qué va*, he told himself. At every train.
> . . . [A]dmit that you have liked to kill as all who are soldiers by choice have enjoyed it at some time whether they lie about it or not. . . . Do not lie to yourself, he thought. . . . You have been tainted with it for a long time now. (304)

This admission of enjoying killing clearly contradicts his agreement with Anselmo that only the mentally sick enjoy killing. But if

Jordan is honest enough at times to break through correct poses and confront something ugly in himself, he still grapples with the issue, for he cannot truly accept the image of himself as one who enjoys killing, who has been "corrupted" by it. When thinking about the sensitive subject of how many people he's killed, he engages in a mental dialogue on the morality of killing:

> Do you think you have a right to kill any one? No. But I have to. . . . Don't you know it is wrong to kill? Yes. But you do it? Yes. And you still believe absolutely that your cause is right? Yes.
>
> It is right, he told himself, not reassuringly, but proudly. I believe in the people and their right to govern themselves as they wish. But you mustn't believe in killing, he told himself. You must do it as a necessity but you must not believe in it. If you believe in it the whole thing is wrong. (321)

Here, he sounds like Anselmo: killing is an ugly necessity, not something to "take to" or "believe in." But since this dialogue follows Jordan's admission to himself that at times he *has* enjoyed killing, his mind seems confused, struggling with conflicting urges to be brutally candid and still feel morally justified. Once again, it is not an issue Jordan can resolve in the middle of an action in which he knows he will kill more people. To be torn by the moral dilemmas arising from these killings might well paralyze him when he needs, above all, to act with certainty and resolve. Hence, his continuous postponement of sorting out these issues: "[I]f he was going to form judgments he would form them afterwards" (150). *Then*, when he writes about it in his true book, "you will get rid of all that [the moral problem of killing and the resulting guilt] by writing about it . . . Once you write it down it is all gone. It will be a good book if you can write it" (181). Given the revelations about PTSD that have emerged in the past half century, it would appear that Jordan's expectation of getting rid of the problem by writing about it is optimistic.

Detonating Myths

The "true book" Robert Jordan envisions would doubtless have addressed controversial issues beyond his personal dilemmas, as his observations of the Russians in Spain have already shown. The novel treats two other such issues: the massacre of civilians and the character of two revered and legendary Loyalists. Jordan never personally encounters the legendary figures, but his author was determined to set the record straight on both topics, or at least provide counterbalancing views—his "truths"—just as the official Loyalist version of these issues was becoming enshrined as myths. In no small way, Hemingway was compensating—perhaps overcompensating—for his own contribution to some of these myths—that there were no Russians, no Loyalist terror, no Loyalist massacres—in his propagandistic journalism. Hence his urge, now that the war was over, to blow them sky-high just as his hero blows the bridge—regardless of the collateral damage his reputation would sustain among those who still cherished the myths, such as his friends in the Abraham Lincoln Brigade.

The official Loyalist view of civilian massacres acknowledges that they were committed by both sides but with a significant difference. The persecutions of priests, large landowners, and pro-fascists, often occurring before the war began, were seen as spontaneous outbreaks by "uncontrollables," which the government halted early in the war as it imposed police authority. Fascist atrocities, by contrast, were planned, systematic, far more widespread—committed against entire towns that had supported the Loyalists—and continuous to the war's end and beyond. Robert Jordan repeats this comparison: "I know we did dreadful things to them too. But it was because we were uneducated and knew no better. But they [the fascists] did that on purpose and deliberately" (374). Historians have largely confirmed this view—it is not, therefore, technically a myth.[19] One might have expected, therefore, that Hemingway would have reinforced it by dramatizing—not merely mentioning—a fascist atrocity against civilians, as Picasso did in his painting of the German bombing of Guernica. Hemingway's Spanish Civil War journalism, in fact, presents a distorted version of this new total war. It states frequently how Franco's shelling and bombing of Madrid intended to kill and did kill many civilians. It never once mentions atrocities committed by Loyalists, just as it ignores the terror and repression fostered by the Russian and Republican police. The novel, however, would be different. Hemingway had known of Loyalist atrocities even before he came to Spain for the first time, as his letter to Harry Sylvester acknowledges (5 Feb. 1937, *Selected Letters*, 456). Robert Jordan also knew about these early massacres: "I've always known about the [Loyalist atrocities], he thought. What we did to them at the start. I've always known it and hated it . . ." (149). But neither Jordan nor pro-Loyalist readers expected to encounter a Loyalist atrocity as Pilar dramatizes it in her account of a massacre in her hometown.

In its content, Pilar's story does not significantly challenge the official view that early Loyalist massacres were largely spontaneous and committed by "uncontrollables." Though Pablo does help organize this one, it goes far beyond anything he could have envisioned. But it's the way that Pilar/Hemingway present the story that is so disturbing. Instead of simply having Pilar *refer* to the massacre (as Pablo does in a telling passage expressing his guilt), or recollect it in a page or two, Hemingway devotes thirty-two pages (in the Scribner Classics edition), with only brief interruptions, to her vividly dramatized *recreation* of the massacre. Neither Maria's recollection of her family's execution by the fascists, nor her account of being gang-raped by the Moors, nor Joaquín's brief narrative of how the fascists murdered his family—nor all three combined—comes anywhere close to the length of Pilar's narrative. But far more important than length is Pilar's (and Hemingway's) dramatic art in recreating the massacre using fictional techniques. Jordan thinks,

> You only heard the statement of the loss. You did not see the father fall as Pilar made him see the fascists die in that story she had told by the stream. . . . You did not see the mother shot, nor the sister, nor the brother. You heard about it; . . . Pilar had made him see it in that town. (148–49)

Somewhat helplessly, Jordan wrestles with having to acknowledge "What we did. Not what the others did to us." Pilar's story will go into his "true book": "He would try to write it and if he had luck and could remember it perhaps he could get it down as she told it" (149). The self-reflexiveness of this passage is a little dizzying, since Hemingway *has* gotten it down by creating a character to tell it through the fictional techniques he himself practiced. Pilar's story, then, becomes a testament to the power of fiction to make events more real than historical narrative can.

Why would Hemingway choose to dramatize at such length this Loyalist massacre instead of a fascist one from the many that occurred in the same towns? Maria's account of the fascists' execution of her parents is moving, indeed affects Jordan, but does not come close to the emotive power of Pilar's story. Hemingway surely realized that, even with the war lost in 1940, his narrative would be sharply criticized by Loyalist survivors, his (former) friends of the Abraham Lincoln Brigade in particular, and leftist critics in general, for besmirching the memory of the Loyalist cause and complicating the myth of a righteous war between good and evil. Yet, his desire to "tell all" and balance the record in *his* true book took precedence over this predictable critical battering. Like the revelation of the Russians' presence in Spain and their repressive acts, it seems that this acknowledgment of Loyalist massacres must have come as a kind of relief, releasing repressed knowledge that he had bottled up for years.

If counterbalancing the official Loyalist view of atrocities was challenging for Hemingway, debunking two Republican "stars"— André Marty (the French commissar who created and was attached to the International Brigades) and the inspirational Dolores Ibárruri (popularly called La Pasionaria)—seems to have come easily. He had always enjoyed ridiculing VIPs and self-important blowhards, after all,[20] and the Spanish Civil War had its share of humbugs. While in Spain, he had encountered both Marty and Ibárruri and apparently disliked them both on sight. Numerous observers have testified to Marty's paranoidal instability, which drove him to execute hundreds of members of the International Brigade as spies.[21] In the novel, he is described as "crazy as a bedbug. . . . [a man who] has a mania for shooting people" (441) and depicted as a paranoid who suspects everyone (including General Golz) of disloyalty and collusion with the fascists. He is ultimately responsible for blocking Andrés's mission to deliver Jordan's all-important message to General Golz to call off what would surely be a futile attack. But Hemingway's description of Marty seems self-indulgently excessive: "His face looked as though it were modelled from the waste material you find under the claws of a very old lion" (439). He is an easy target, and by limiting the problem of political executions to a madman, Hemingway sidesteps the larger issue of supposedly rational men like Karkov (Koltsov) ordering these executions dispassionately for political purposes.

La Pasionaria, whom Hemingway and company had filmed in *The Spanish Earth* making a rousing speech, also comes in for ridicule, albeit small-scale. Hemingway had no use for her impassioned style or her Joan-of-Arc saintly aura: "Dolores always made me vomit always," he wrote a friend.[22] But unlike Marty, she was a symbol of Loyalist idealism; thus, any tampering with her legend would certainly bring down on Hemingway the wrath of the myth-protectors. The novel depicts her as a hypocrite and an ill-informed rumormonger. One of El Sordo's men complains about her sending her own son safely out of the country to Russia, while she exhorts Spanish women to give their sons to the war effort (326).[23] On the eve of the big Loyalist offensive, she brings "wonderful news" that the fascists are fighting among themselves in Segovia. The journalist announcing this gushes, "She was . . . in such a state of radiant exultation as I have never seen. The truth of the news shone from her face . . . with a light that was not of this world. . . . Goodness and truth shine from her as from a true saint of the people. Not for nothing is she called La Pasionaria." (378). The skeptical Karkov advises the journalist to write it up immediately for *Izvestia*—that official repository of lies. A more reliable source, an officer in uniform, is also skeptical of La Pasionaria's news: "Beautiful if true." Of course, it was not true, and La Pasionaria and her minions are made to look like fools.

Conclusion

Robert Jordan dies long before he can write his true book. Thus, he never reconciles the contradictions or resolves the moral quandaries he faces—and postpones—during his time in Spain. The problems of his political affiliations—having no politics, yet supporting and fighting under Russian command and "discipline"; his idealistic commitment to duty behind the lines versus "corrupting" too easily at Gaylord's; his democratic belief in "the Republic" and the Spanish people, particularly the people of Pilar's band; and his knowledge of (and participation in) the cynical, ruthlessly authoritarian Soviet control of the war—all remain unresolved. Likewise, his moral quandaries—his disgust with assassination despite his participation in it and acceptance of its practice by the Soviets; his willingness to work with people like Pablo and ignore their murders; his knowledge of atrocities committed by the Loyalists, as well as by the fascists; and the contradiction between his not wanting to "believe in" killing and his having enjoyed it at times—are all left hanging, as Jordan heroically sacrifices himself to hold off the pursuing fascists.

As I've observed, however, Jordan's hypothetical "true book" is really Hemingway's actual attempt at one, at least in bringing out these issues which complicate the meaning of the Spanish Civil War and remove it from the simplistic realm of good (Loyalists) versus evil (fascists) and right versus wrong. In this novel, Hemingway acknowledges historical realities about the war that he had previously either denied or intentionally ignored in his Spanish Civil War journalism, stories, and play—realities that he believed could not be discussed while the war was still being fought without harming the Loyalist cause.

Some of these "truths" were relatively uncomplicated, albeit shocking, such as the Loyalist atrocity that Pilar describes so vividly. Hemingway's point was simply to show "what we did," as well as what was done to "us" by the fascists. Though they conducted their bloody work far more extensively and systematically, the fascists did not hold a monopoly on atrocities; the Loyalists also had blood on their hands. Similarly, puncturing the myth of La Pasionaria and displaying the murderous paranoia of André Marty do not seem especially revelatory, though both depictions enraged the myth-protectors of the Abraham Lincoln Brigade. Hemingway probably enjoyed deflating the quasi-religious adulation surrounding the former and dramatizing the mental aberrations of the latter.

Describing the Russians' presence and their sinister actions in Spain (in the metonym of "Gaylord's"), however, was a far more complicated business because of Hemingway's own entangled relations with the Russians' covert political leadership, primarily Mikhail Koltsov. Like Robert Jordan, Hemingway enjoyed being an insider at Gaylord's and learning some of the truths behind the manufactured lies. And like Jordan, he "corrupted easily," enjoying his access to the good food and drink provided by the Russians. (Unlike Jordan, he also liked being courted for his fame by Soviet operatives and receiving privileges that other journalists lacked.) He also shared Jordan's admiration of Karkov's (Koltsov's) intellect and wit. But at the same time, he made Karkov an enigmatic, slippery figure, at once candid and cynical, mentoring Jordan as a kind of political neophyte, but also misleading him, as in their conversation about Andrés Nin. Hemingway, too, was misled—otherwise, he would not have maintained so vehemently to Dos Passos and others in 1938 the Soviet lie that Nin was still alive. The interesting question here is when—or even whether—Hemingway, at the time of writing the novel (1939–40), realized he had been deceived. Jordan never does, which would certainly undermine *his* efforts to write "truly" about Karkov and the secret regime. Was Hemingway then reflecting his own ignorance or realistically characterizing a somewhat naïve American, who, in May 1937, would not have discerned the lie? The many sides to Jordan's character—idealist, pragmatist, romantic, and cynic; corrupted and selflessly devoted to a cause; puritan and lover—do not cohere, and neither does his status as an apolitical operative who works for a ruthless regime, simply because the author's views also did not cohere. Hemingway does have Karkov acknowledge political assassinations (a major achievement!) and refer to the purge of rival leftist parties like POUM. But Jordan responds ambiguously to the former, and the latter purges are presented, uncritically, from the official Soviet perspective, just as Hemingway presented them in his journalism.

Concerning the more immediate moral issues that arise in Robert Jordan's actions as *partizan*, Hemingway was on surer ground for several reasons. It is the realm of physical action conducted on a small scale, which has always been the author's *métier*. Jordan has considerable control over the parameters of his assignment—he is not merely the passive and sometimes misinformed witness and recipient of complex meanings that he is at Gaylord's. Behind the lines, he is the one to decide how and whether to recognize moral issues. Moreover, these issues pull against Jordan's pragmatism as an operative, against the amoral demands of *necessity* in fulfilling his mission. And in each case, Jordan yields to that necessity, placing the fulfillment of his mission above all other considerations. Thus, though he is morally troubled by having to exploit and endanger Pilar's group, he does not hesitate for a moment to do so. Though he pretty much knows that Pablo will murder his recruits for their horses, he says nothing to prevent the murders or to criticize him afterwards. And though he would like to share Anselmo's humanistic hatred of killing, he admits to himself that he has enjoyed it at times and has thus been corrupted by it. In all these quandaries, pragmatism prevails: the bridge must be blown, guards killed, and the group—what's left of it—escape. What Hemingway achieves in portraying these unresolved issues is the recognition of how even the most straightforward actions and objectives, especially in war, can entail moral complications.

Repeatedly, in evaluating Hemingway's handling of these political and moral issues, I have used words like "recognizes," "brings out," "acknowledges." Even to do this much (or little) regarding these issues, Hemingway deserves credit. He has recanted his one-sided, propagandistic journalism and has gone far beyond his earlier Spanish Civil War stories and drama in daring to challenge rapidly hardening myths and to recognize repellent truths about the Loyalist cause. His novel shatters the largest myth: that the Spanish Civil War represented a simplistic opposition of good (Loyalist) and evil (fascist). Just to have made the fascist Lieutenant Berrendo a sympathetic character muddies these distinctions. In Hemingway's novel, the war has become a much more complicated affair, as his protagonist realizes (264). And Hemingway has achieved all this knowing he would incur the wrath of the myth-protectors.

What he has not done is to have his protagonist resolve any of these issues, but rather postpone them for a book that will never be written. This lack of resolution may seem an evasion on Hemingway's part—a cop-out. But perhaps the novel's larger point is that in the muddle and exigencies of civil war, power politics, and military action, there is no resolution for these issues, particularly for a soldier—a *partizan*—who must *act*, who makes the fulfillment of his mission, regardless of moral qualms and compromises, his highest priority. Even when one can still distinguish the larger end (and Robert Jordan is never in doubt about the ultimate end of winning the war), there are still the dirty means. In a world of lies, deceit, and brutality on all sides, idealism can scarcely survive and moral certainty easily becomes self-deception. Clear distinctions between right and wrong, rectitude and corruption, must yield to pervasive ambiguity. Yet, even in such a moral fog, one must still decide and act. These are the equivocal truths that Robert Jordan must learn for his true book and that Ernest Hemingway presents in his.

PART 3

Falling Away

SHORTLY AFTER THE publication of their major novels in 1939 and 1940, Steinbeck, Hemingway, and Wright all moved away from the Left. For Hemingway and Steinbeck, the least political of the trio, this separation was immediate and relatively easy; for Wright, more formally tied by Communist Party membership, disaffiliation was difficult and took a few years. What led to these political separations will be the central topic of this chapter, but before examining the writers' histories individually, it would be useful to note similarities and differences in their lives and political experiences.

Though all three writers achieved huge popular and critical success with their novels, that acclaim was not unanimous. All three novels—and their authors—were politically attacked: Hemingway and, to a lesser degree, Wright were criticized from the left, specifically the CP-USA. Steinbeck was ferociously attacked from the right by the Associated Farmers and its cohorts, enraged by his accusations in *The Grapes of Wrath*, and by some reviewers and self-appointed guardians of public morals. Those attacks undermined, again in varying degrees, what otherwise might have been the reaping of rewards following the intensive effort each writer expended on his novel. Steinbeck was devastated by the uproar *Grapes* caused; Hemingway, always thin-skinned about negative criticism, was furious at the far Left's repeated charges against *For Whom the Bell Tolls*; Wright's response was less intense, but he was clearly disturbed by the CP-USA's mixed response to *Native Son* and attempted to rebut the criticisms.

Partly to escape the turmoil aroused by their novels and simply just to get away from fiction-writing and the literary world for a while, all three writers took major trips outside the United States following the publication of their novels: Wright and his wife of seven months, Dhimah Rose Meidman, went to Mexico for eleven weeks in March 1940. At exactly the same time, Steinbeck, with his close friend and mentor Ed Ricketts, hired a boat and crew and undertook a seven-week biological research trip along the Gulf of California. In January 1941, Hemingway and his new spouse, Martha Gellhorn, both on journalistic assignments, undertook a five-month fact-finding tour of China and the Far East. For both Hemingway and Steinbeck, the trips involved close observation and fact-gathering, though the contexts were sharply different: political and military for Hemingway, biological for Steinbeck. Again, the importance of these trips varied with the writer: for Wright, it was primarily a vacation; for Hemingway, a change of scene and a way to keep close to his peripatetic wife, Marty; for Steinbeck, however, this trip was truly an escape and represented the very real possibility of a new career in science.

As the travelling companions of Wright and Hemingway indicate, these writers had also made significant changes in their marital status shortly following publication of their novels: in November 1940 Hemingway divorced Pauline, his second wife of thirteen years, and married Martha Gellhorn; Wright, who had impulsively married in May 1939, just as impulsively separated from his wife after their Mexican trip (a trip which included her children, mother, and dancing coach). Though Steinbeck didn't formally divorce Carol Steinbeck for a few more years, their marriage was in serious trouble by 1940 and he had already taken up with the woman who would become his second wife, Gwyn Conger.

Curiously, all three writers experimented in these years with visual documentaries, as if to test the waters for an expansion of—or a diversion from—their callings as novelists. Two helped make documentary films: Hemingway participated significantly in making *The Spanish Earth* in 1937; Steinbeck, having previously worked with the filmmaker Pare Lorentz on the documentary *The Fight for Life*, collaborated with Herbert Kline in 1940 on a blend of documentary and fictional narrative, *The Forgotten Village*, about a

Mexican town's resistance to modern medicine. While in Mexico, he met Richard Wright, who had come up to see the filming. A year later, Wright himself collaborated with photographer Ed Rosskam on a documentary photo-history of African-Americans, *12 Million Black Voices*. Again, these documentaries had differing impacts for the writers: for Hemingway, the film was simply a propagandistic means to help the Spanish Republic. Steinbeck, searching for a calling with a more lasting impact on the human condition, went to Mexico immediately after returning from his biological research trip, but was disenchanted by the filmmaking experience. Wright's collaboration on *12 Million Black Voices*—he wrote the text and took one photograph—continued to broaden his study of the black experience in America from a loosely Marxist perspective.

Finally, and most important for this study, the political attitudes of at least two of the three writers, Hemingway and Steinbeck, not only moved away from the Left in 1939/40, but, surprisingly, *toward* the federal government in the authors wanting to be of service as America's entry into World War II seemed increasingly certain. Deep down, both writers had never really abandoned their belief that people should be left alone to determine their own lives and politics without external coercion. Compare these comments:

Steinbeck: I believe profoundly in democratic processes and the right of people to live in freedom and govern themselves.

Hemingway (via Robert Jordan): [A]ll people should be left alone and you should interfere with no one.[1]

Accordingly, both writers were disgusted by the Soviet Union's invasion of Finland in November 1939 (and, presumably, by its pact with Nazi Germany three months earlier).[2] Steinbeck, always a supporter of the underdog, donated money to Finland, knowing it would make him *persona non grata* in leftist circles. Hemingway, soon to be vilified by the Party for his new novel, had a more personal concern about Finland: Martha Gellhorn was there covering the Russian invasion. While in Spain, Hemingway had excoriated what he considered the fascist-infiltrated State Department for not aiding Loyalist Spain, but in 1941 he quietly offered to provide U.S.

Naval Intelligence with his observations about Japanese intentions, Chinese resistance, and American vulnerabilities in the Pacific, gathered from his journalistic fact-finding trip. When the Hemingways returned in May 1941, they were debriefed in Washington. Steinbeck, too, expressed a desire to help his country. After film making in Mexico, he felt that Nazi propaganda there was effective. In June 1940, he managed to arrange an audience with President Roosevelt to urge that America create its own agency to disseminate information-propaganda in the Americas to counter the Nazis. He would soon be working for such a group. Of course, these moves away from international leftism and towards a new appreciation of America at the end of the 1930s were not particular to these writers. As early as 1937, John Dos Passos presciently saw America as the last best hope for democracy among the growing totalitarianism of Europe.[3] For Hemingway and Steinbeck these efforts betokened a turning away from international leftism's condemnation of capitalist America and toward a more patriotic stance, which Pearl Harbor greatly intensified. Early in World War II both writers used their craft to further the war effort: Steinbeck by writing *The Moon Is Down*, a propagandistic novella and play depicting an occupied country's heroic resistance to the Nazis; Hemingway by compiling an anthology of war writing, *Men at War*. Both writers eventually covered the war as journalists.

Only Wright in the years before Pearl Harbor grimly adhered to the Communist Party's fluctuating positions, first demanding American neutrality, then, after the Nazi invasion of the Soviet Union, calling for aid to Russia and England. But Wright's own disenchantment with the Party was quietly growing and finally came to a head in 1941/42. Significantly, in shedding their links to leftism, all three writers moved—or returned—to a belief in individualism.

I. Steinbeck: 1939–42
Sturm und Drang

Steinbeck had expected an uproar over *The Grapes of Wrath* but profoundly underestimated its intensity and duration—and overestimated his capacity to endure it. He was like a boy who intentionally stirs a hornet's nest expecting perhaps one sting and receiving twenty. And he was in no physical condition to withstand the tumult.

Writing the novel had exhausted him and, as Benson notes, he now suffered a number of long-lasting physical ailments, chief of which was severe neuritis in his legs (*Steinbeck, Writer*, 391). It wasn't just the personal attacks and abuse the novel aroused, though they were bad enough. Even the fame and celebrity were torture for this shy and private writer. Requests poured in ceaselessly for endorsements, for participation in good (and crackpot) causes, for money. As he complained to his agent, Elizabeth Otis, just weeks after the novel appeared, "The telegrams and telephones—all day long—speak . . . speak . . . speak, like hungry birds. Why the hell do people insist on speaking? The telephone is a thing of horror. And the demands for money—scholarships, memorial prizes . . ." (18 April 1939, *Life in Letters*, 183). Two months later, the flood of requests had risen: "The whole thing is getting me down and I don't know what to do about it. The telephone never stops ringing, telegrams all the time, fifty to seventy-five letters a day all wanting something. . . . I don't know what to do" (letter to Elizabeth Otis, 22 June 1939, *Life*, 185). One thing he *could* have done was to hire a personal secretary—or a staff of them—to screen these requests, instead of unfairly relying on Carol to handle them, a task that wore her out; but Steinbeck refused to even consider hiring an assistant.

He was particularly wary of well-meaning groups seeking to enlist him in various causes; as he complained to his uncle Joe Hamilton, "Every liberal organization in the country is living my life for me, plotting my work for me, telling me how to think, how to work, what to do; telling me who my enemies are and my friends, defining my politics and my sympathies, typing me, and making a symbol of me . . ."[4] Then there were the negative reviews and abuse aimed not just at the novel but at Steinbeck personally. Leading the charge—predictably, since the group was Steinbeck's chief target in *Grapes*—was the Associated Farmers, which orchestrated a campaign of editorials and speakers nationwide to attack the book as a farrago of lies and distortions and to accuse Steinbeck of communist subversion and promoting class warfare.[5] Innumerable articles and letters to the editor condemning the novel appeared all over the nation but especially in California. Several writers wrote rebuttals to the novel, attempting to show how well-treated the migrants were; books, pamphlets, even films appeared with such comforting titles as *Of Human Kindness*, *Plums of Plenty*, *Grapes of Gladness*, as well as the inevitable *The Truth about John Steinbeck and the Migrants*.[6] None of these efforts is today considered a credible rebuttal, but they all added fuel to the controversy. The novel even made it to Congress. Representative Lyle Boren from Oklahoma, feeling somehow that his entire state was maligned, spoke against the novel, calling it "a black, infernal creation of a twisted, distorted mind" (Benson, *Steinbeck, Writer*, 418–19). Not to be outdone, the *Oklahoma Democrat* added, "[T]his book exposes nothing but the total depravity, vulgarity and degraded mentality of the author."[7]

As these Oklahomans' choice adjectives suggest, some readers considered the book obscene and immoral. Members of the clergy (including Archbishop Spellman of New York) and editorial writers condemned in particular the final scene in which Rosasharn nurses the starving stranger. Westbrook Pegler, in his syndicated column, wrote that the novel "contains the dirtiest language I have ever seen on paper."[8] Libraries and municipalities across the country— Kern County (Bakersfield), California; Kansas City; Buffalo; East St. Louis, Illinois—banned it.[9] Taking a leaf from Nazi Germany, a few towns, such as Bakersfield and East St. Louis, burned it publicly. Threats against Steinbeck's life were made, and Steinbeck took them seriously enough to start carrying a gun and to send to the FBI data about the migrant problem that he wanted to survive him, even though he realized that the FBI was already investigating him and that J. Edgar Hoover "considered me the most dangerously subversive influence in the West" (letter of 4 March 1939, quoted in Benson, *Steinbeck, Writer*, 394). Fearing a scheme to entrap him in a scandal, Steinbeck even avoided hotels for meetings and traveled under a pseudonym.

The fact that the novel was a huge popular success and that by far the majority of the reviews were enthusiastic; that many critics considered it as the best thing he had ever written;[10] that it won the National Book Award and the Pulitzer Prize; that most of the letters that came in attested to how deeply moved the correspondents were; that it was praised by Eleanor Roosevelt in her syndicated newspaper column "My Day" and later lauded by the president in a radio address;[11] that Hollywood was anxious to make a quality film of the novel and not only to pay handsomely for the rights, but also to give Steinbeck considerable control in the choice of director, actors, and script—none of these facts, singly or combined, outweighed in Steinbeck's eyes the horror of the controversy, negative attacks, and incessant, pestering requests that his novel had aroused. In the letter of 22 June 1939 to Elizabeth Otis quoted above, the author added a dark prediction: "Something has to be worked out or I am finished writing. . . . There is one possibility and that is that I go out of the country. I thought this thing would die down but it is only worse day by day" (*Life in Letters*, 185).

Escape and "A New Start"

Steinbeck was serious about getting out of the country, but he was not thinking about merely geographical escape. Something much greater was at stake: his career as a novelist. As he wrote his friend Dook Sheffield in November 1939 during the uproar over *Grapes*, "I must make a new start. I've worked the novel—I know it as far as I can take it . . . a clumsy vehicle at best. And I don't know the form of the new but I know there is a new which will be adequate and shaped by the new thinking" (*Life in Letters*, 194). The new start Steinbeck refers to here is biology; the "new thinking" is scientific: both empirical—close observation of an aspect of nature, from which reliable inferences can be drawn, and ecological—understanding the relation of a living organism to its environment. Both interests were inspired by Steinbeck's close friend and mentor, Ed Ricketts.

When Steinbeck expressed these ambitions to his friend, World War II was only six weeks old. A major factor in his new turn towards science was his disgust at international politics and what it said about human nature. Science offered not only a different realm and mode of *objective* investigation (compare his passionate subjectivism in taking up the migrants' cause) but potentially a more lasting type of understanding and worldview, transcending the shifting alliances and feuds of the political "isms." In the letter to Dook Sheffield quoted above, he wrote:

The world is sick now. There are things in the tide pools easier to understand than Stalinist, Hiterlite, Democrat, capitalist confusion, and voodoo. So I'm going to those things which are relatively more lasting to find a new basic picture. I have too a conviction that a new world is growing under the old, the way a new finger nail grows under a bruised one. I think all the economists and sociologists will be surprised some day to find that they did not forsee [sic] nor understand it. . . . Communist, Fascist, Democrat may find that the real origin of the future lies on the microscope plates of obscure young men, who, puzzled with order and disorder in quantum and neutron, build gradually a picture which will seep down until it is the fibre of the future. (*Life in Letters*, 193–94)

The turmoil that the war promised was a macrocosmic expression of the turmoil in his own life: both realms were driven by conflicting and often benighted passions. His striving for justice for the migrants was met by counterpassions in the defenders of the status quo. His marital life was also in turmoil. Scientific observation promised a realm of detachment, calm, and results that in the long run seemed more profound than the fate of nations.

Before embarking on this new calling, however, Steinbeck dabbled with another: documentary filmmaking. While writing *Grapes*, his friendship with the documentarist Pare Lorentz had undoubtedly influenced the scope of the novel's general chapters, particularly Steinbeck's hostility to mechanization, which was the theme of Lorentz's radio play at the time, *Ecce Homo!* In Hollywood, they had discussed collaborating on a film, and in April 1939, Lorentz invited Steinbeck to Chicago to help make a new film, *The Fight for Life*, about the need for good public health care at the Chicago Maternity Center. Steinbeck eagerly responded, not least to get away from the mounting furor over his novel. Like Hemingway in Spain two years earlier, he did grunt work, carrying equipment, scouting locations, interviewing hospital staff. Though he did not especially enjoy the work—"I've never worked such long hours in my life" he complained to his publisher, Pat Covici (Benson, *Steinbeck, Writer*, 401)—he continued to help Lorentz that summer, when the film crew moved to Hollywood. Ultimately, this interest in making documentary films on social themes led to Steinbeck's co-directing and writing the narrative for a film made in Mexico the following year, *The Forgotten Village*.

In the meantime, however, he pursued his more compelling interest in biology for what he seriously thought of as a new career. Ed Ricketts had been Steinbeck's close friend and mentor before Steinbeck became involved in the migrant issue; now, he returned to Ricketts, as tutor as well as mentor. Again, he began spending long hours in Ricketts' laboratory-home on the Monterey coast, but now it was not just for good conversation, music, and drink. Under Ricketts' tutelage, Steinbeck laid out a crash course for himself in biology. "I have to go back and start over," he explained to Dook Sheffield. "I bought half the stock in Ed's lab, which gives me equipment, a teacher, a library to work in" (13 Nov. 1939, *Life in Letters*, 193). And work he did, throwing himself into it with the enthusiasm of a convert to a new religion, reading intensively, working in Ricketts' laboratory, and going out on collecting trips with him. Most important, Steinbeck planned to co-author with Ricketts two books: first, a high school-level textbook (Steinbeck referred to it in letters as a "handbook") about sea life along the shore of the San Francisco Bay area, a book for which Steinbeck would be educating himself in the subject in order to write about it. The second, more important book would result from a research trip the two would conduct in the Gulf of California, in which they would collect, examine, categorize, and compare specimens of sea life at various points along the shore. They hoped their findings would make "an important contribution to basic scientific knowledge" (Benson, *Steinbeck, Writer*, 427).

As he eagerly undertook the enormous planning and preparing required for this research trip, which included hiring a boat and crew, provisioning it with supplies for several weeks, buying a good microscope, and getting the necessary permissions from Mexico, Steinbeck had found a way out of his beleaguered authorship of *Grapes*: "I can't tell you what all this means to me, in happiness and energy," he wrote to Elizabeth Otis in December 1939. "I was washed up and now I'm alive again, with work to be done and worth doing" (*Life in Letters*, 196). He might well have been singing "Amazing Grace."

And What About the Migrants?

Conspicuously absent in Steinbeck's roller-coaster moods and plans was a continuing concern for California's migrant farmers—a concern which had increasingly obsessed him since he had written the "Harvest Gypsies" articles in 1936. It is true that, while rejecting the torrent of requests for his participation in good causes, he *did* lend his name and efforts to "The John Steinbeck Committee," organized by Helen Gahagan Douglas and others in Hollywood to raise money for migrant relief. He attended several fund-raising dinners and personally autographed special editions of *Grapes*, which were auctioned off at a banquet (Benson, *Steinbeck, Writer*, 424). Moreover, his novel aroused interest in Washington about the migrants' condition. Eleanor Roosevelt made a tour of migrant camps in 1940. And even earlier, his novel and Carey McWilliams's *Factories in the Field* helped spur a U.S. Senate investigation of migrant conditions and growers' activities in California. The La Follette Committee held twenty-eight days of hearings in late 1939 and early 1940, calling over four hundred witnesses, and produced over 2,500 pages of testimony.[12] The committee's conclusions, particularly regarding the Associated Farmers, thoroughly validated Steinbeck's depiction of them. As Dick Meister and Anne Loftis summarize and quote from the report,

> [I]t detailed the "shocking degree of human misery" among the farm workers and thoroughly exposed the violent tactics used by the Associated Farmers in carrying out the organization's openly admitted policy of taking the law into its own hands.
>
> The committee charged the Associated Farmers with "the most flagrant and violent infringement of civil liberties," through use of espionage, blacklisting, strikebreaking, brutality and "sheer vigilanteeism."

These actions, the report concluded, "repeatedly and flagrantly violated . . . [t]he civil rights of strikers, unions . . . and many of the agricultural laborers in California . . ."[13]

Although the La Follette Report recommended that farm workers' rights be protected under the National Labor Relations Act (which would obviously prohibit the Associated Farmers' bullying tactics), unaccountably the report was not issued until October 1942—more than two and a half years after the hearings ended (Benson, *Steinbeck, Writer*, 423) and long after the burgeoning war industries of

California had mooted the whole problem of the migrants' treatment by luring them to high-paying factory jobs. Thus, in the period under consideration here, 1939 to 1940, Steinbeck could only *hope* that the Senate committee would break the Associated Farmers' hold on migrant farm labor. In fact, it did not. As Susan Shillinglaw observes, "Neither the publication of *The Grapes of Wrath*, nor the formation of the John Steinbeck Committee, nor the findings of the La Follette Committee changed wages substantially, or caused more government camps to be built, or eased labor/management tensions."[14]

Essentially, then, Steinbeck turned his back on the whole issue to which he had passionately committed himself. Biographers' explanations for his abandonment of the migrants' cause cover most of what has been discussed above. Jay Parini writes, "The drift back to Pacific Grove [Ricketts's lab] was, in part, a response to the madness of his new life . . . It involved an instinct for self-preservation as well . . ."[15] The controversy over the novel "wore him out," Jackson Benson asserts. Steinbeck worried "that he would be dragged into a political thicket against his will. He hated to be branded or categorized, and above all, he feared being labeled forever as a social-political writer. He was particularly wary of attempts by the Marxists to adopt and use him." For support, Benson quotes Helen Hosmer (editor of *Their Blood Is Strong*), who, on visiting Steinbeck with a "Marxist-radical" friend and finding him "jittery" about meeting them, concluded that "the one thing in the world he didn't want to be identified with was the Reds" (*Steinbeck, Writer,* 424–25).

These explanations are valid, but don't quite get at the key question of Steinbeck's erratic behavior. Yes, he was exhausted and beleaguered, but when he eventually recovered his strength, renewed leftist political commitment did not follow. And fear of being linked to the communists or categorized as a sociopolitical writer never hindered him in the least from writing *Grapes*, when he *knew* he would face these charges and stereotypes. Then, he had entered the "political thicket" eagerly. What had changed in his thinking to account for this post-publication timidity, or, worse, indifference?

I would suggest two explanations: psychological and political-philosophical. Parini quotes Steinbeck's third wife, Elaine, that

Steinbeck '"had a strong tendency to depression. He wasn't a classic manic-depressive, but he was borderline. When he was writing, he could be immensely cheerful. When he wasn't, he could become impossibly glum.'"[16] Parini notes that Steinbeck's "overuse of alcohol to counteract mood swings" supports Elaine Steinbeck's analysis of borderline bipolarity.[17] So did his behavior in these years. Consider the almost manic enthusiasm and determination with which he threw himself into the migrants' cause and, again, into his planned career change to biology (Parini even calls the latter commitment "a sudden mania").[18] Intervening was the deep chasm brought on by the assaults from critics of *Grapes* and the pestering from the general public. Steinbeck's language in his letters to Elizabeth Otis reveals precisely these psychological peaks and valleys, particularly how his new venture in biological research had rescued him (*Life in Letters*, 196). Earlier in this letter he describes with boyish enthusiasm an even larger microscope he hopes to purchase to replace the good one he has just ordered: "My dream for some time in the future is a research scope with an oil immersion lens, but that costs about 600 dollars and I'm not getting it right now. The SKW will be fine for the trip. But that research model. Oh boy! Oh boy! Sometime I'll have one" (*Life*, 196). The migrant issue, then, was inexorably linked to all the horrors Steinbeck was now trying to escape: the controversy aroused by the novel, the huge disruption of his private life. Steinbeck did not so much abandon the migrants—though his subsequent letters scarcely mention them outside of references to the La Follette Committee—as avoid the source of his depression. If, as Parini asserts, his turn to biology reflected "an instinct for self-preservation," so did his turn away from the migrant issue.

The political explanation of this turn does not stem from any fear on Steinbeck's part of being associated with or used by the communists. He was prepared for the "communist" smear campaign well before the book was published, and his letters don't show that these accusations intimidated him. Rather, the political context refers to his profound disgust, at the outbreak of World War II, with *all* of the "isms"—or, as he repeated in several letters, "Stalinist, Hiterlite, Democrat, capitalist"—which had colluded to unleash another round of mass killing on a global scale. In its betrayal of the Popular Front against fascism, communist Russia was no different—and certainly no better—than the other isms. Its invasion of Finland in November 1939 moved Steinbeck to contribute money to the Finns not, as Benson surmises, "to combat the constant editorial charge that he was a 'tool of Moscow'" (*Steinbeck, Writer*, 434), but because he sympathized with the little guy when menaced by a bully—just as he had with the migrant farmers overwhelmed by the big growers and the Associated Farmers. He explained in an unpublished statement,

> The Russian invasion of Finland, horrible as it is offers a possibility for clarification of the position of such nonpolitical liberals as I, who believes [*sic*] profoundly in democratic processes and the rights of peoples to live in freedom and to govern themselves. Such liberals have been too long kicked around among the ideologies. When the Spanish people were overwhelmed by a selfish native minority, backed by foreign war money and arms, I contributed to and believed in their cause. When China was invaded by a Japanese army of conquest, I believed in and contributed to the cause of the people of China. In the first two cases I was called a communist. Now that Finland is invaded my position has not changed. I believe in and shall contribute to the cause of the Finnish people. It is amusing that I will be called a reactionary for this.[19]

His hatred of bullying and aggressive coercion—at all levels—never diminished. As he stated in 1962, "The thing that arouses me to fury more than anything else is the imposition of force by a stronger on a weaker for reasons of self-interest or greed. . . . It's the one unforgivable thing I can think of."[20] It was this political attitude of "A plague on both your houses!" that drove him to seek refuge in scientific investigation. In a letter to Wilbur Needham, 29 September 1940, he wrote,

> [I]t has recently seemed to me silly to try to solve the equation [of "the formulae of the present"]. So I went back to biology where the factors are at least observable if one has the eyes. That work has been of some solace. The world of men is fit now mainly for satire but a ghastly satire for the insanc . . . The voices spoken by all sides—left-right, center, fascist-communist, Willkie are nonsense words having

no relation to an obvious change and movement of the species. (Benson, *Steinbeck, Writer,* 467)

Sounding remarkably like Robinson Jeffers in his seminal poem "May–June, 1940," Steinbeck felt that political ideology had poisoned people's minds. His turn towards biology, echoing his earlier sociological study of the phalanx, was a turn towards what he considered sanity, towards a kind of ascertainable knowledge and understanding that he felt transcended and outlasted the bloody vicissitudes of politics: "a world picture not dominated by Hitler and Moscow but something more vital and surviving than either" (letter to Elizabeth Otis, 26 March 1940, *Life in Letters,* 201). Not the migrant issue specifically, but his political passion for it became part of the political worldview he now rejected.

The Log from "The Sea of Cortez," The Forgotten Village, and The Moon Is Down

In turning to science, Steinbeck also renewed his longstanding quasi-scientific fascination with non-teleological thinking and the behavior of people in groups (the phalanx) versus their capacity to act and think for themselves—interests he had absorbed a decade earlier from Ed Ricketts. His next three projects—*The Log from "The Sea of Cortez,"* his collaboration on the film *The Forgotten Village,* and the novella and play *The Moon Is Down*—all reflect one or both of these interests and, when linked to *In Dubious Battle,* form a kind of continuity—fluctuating to be sure—in Steinbeck's worldview.

The *Log,* when it was finally published in 1941, is a strange amalgam of travel narrative interspersed with Steinbeck's—and Ricketts'—philosophical musings.[21] Richard Astro, in his introduction to the Penguin edition, calls the book "a celebration of the holistic vision the authors shared, and . . . this is depicted in terms more mystical and intuitive than scientific. . . . [The book is] an exercise in speculative metaphysics, grounded in the factual record of the trip itself."[22] The core of this holistic vision appears in the lengthy entry "March 24 Easter Sunday." The timing is intentionally ironic since Steinbeck and Ricketts use this Christian holy day celebrating Christ's resurrection to denigrate teleological thinking, or "the evaluating of causes and effects, the [assertion of the] purposiveness of events. . . . what 'should be' in terms of an end pattern (which is often a subjective or an anthropomorphic projection) . . . [and which] presumes the bettering of conditions . . ." (112).

Pushed far enough, teleological thinking leads to narrow belief and dogma:

[T]he greatest fallacy in, or rather the greatest objection to, teleological thinking is in connection with the emotional content, the belief. People get to believing and even to professing the apparent answers thus arrived at, suffering mental constrictions by emotionally closing their minds to any of the further and possibly opposite "answers" which might otherwise be unearthed by honest effort—answers which, if faced realistically, would give rise to a struggle and to a possible rebirth which might place the whole problem in a new and more significant light. (118)

Opposing this causal, end-oriented thinking, the authors proffer non-teleological or "'is' thinking" (112). Such thinking

consider[s] events as outgrowths and expressions rather than as results; conscious acceptance as a desideratum, and certainly as an all-important prerequisite. Non-teleological thinking concerns itself primarily not with what should be, or could be, or might be, but rather with what actually "is"—attempting at most to answer the already sufficiently difficult questions *what* or *how*, instead of *why*. (112, Steinbeck's emphasis)

Instead of searching for narrow causality, "*is* thinking" emphasizes acceptance (in a manner the authors link to "the Oriental concept of *being*" [125]) and "relational thinking": "Everything impinges on everything else, often into radically different systems, although in such cases faintly. We doubt very much if there are any truly 'closed systems'" (118). "Relational thinking," which Ricketts had been espousing since the early 1930s, was a prototype of ecology, the relation of each living organism to all others and to its environment. He and his new disciple Steinbeck were ahead of their time in espousing this kind of biological understanding, but scientists would likely have difficulty accepting the authors' bias against causal thinking. This bias would also pose problems for Steinbeck's next project, a film.

The Forgotten Village, a quasi-documentary film[23] that Steinbeck worked on with Herbert Kline in Mexico, immediately followed Steinbeck's research trip along the Gulf of California. (That he turned so abruptly to this entirely different medium and never returned to biological investigation once he had finished writing the *Log* speaks strongly to Steinbeck's impulsive, if not bipolar mental state at the time.) It is worth noting that Kline originally proposed that the film depict a poor Mexican family amidst a political revolution, but Steinbeck rejected the revolutionary angle—no more politics, thank you—in favor of a theme melding his new obsession with science and his renewed interest in group behavior as opposed to individualist thought (Benson, *Steinbeck, Writer*, 452–53). The story line presents a village suffering from a cholera-infected water supply and facing a choice: continue as it always has, accepting the resulting illnesses and deaths and relying on the ineffectual village healer, or turn towards modern medicine's vaccinations to treat those infected. The young protagonist, Juan Diego, is all for modern medicine, but the healer, demanding the town stick to its traditions, accuses the outsider doctors of "evil urban witchcraft" and using horses' blood in the injections. When the boy rescues his sick sister with a vaccination, he is ostracized from his family and the town and eventually journeys to the city with the aim of becoming a doctor.[24] In this conflict between tradition and modernity, Steinbeck's clear bias towards medical science derived partly from his earlier work on Pare Lorentz's documentary, *The Fight for Life*, which urged decent health care for the poor of Chicago. But the villagers' collective resistance also reflects Steinbeck's notion of the phalanx of group thinking and behavior—in this case to support superstition and ignorance—while Juan's resistance represents independent thinking. Interestingly, Steinbeck does not here support the "'is' thinking" he lauded in *Log* (which was written after the film). The doctors clearly apply causal teleology to trace the villagers' sickness back to its causes in infected water and to promulgate the benefit of an effective antidote.[25]

The negative depiction of the phalanx in *Village* versus the positive one of independent thinking figures strongly in Steinbeck's next work, the short play and novella *The Moon Is Down*. Steinbeck wrote it while volunteering his time in New York for the Foreign Information Service (FIS), a government propaganda agency which had been created partly through his earlier suggestion to President Roosevelt that the United States needed to counter Nazi propaganda in Latin and South America. The United States was now in the war, and Steinbeck's patriotism, already evidenced in the concern he expressed to Roosevelt, had risen to the fore. As part of his assignment, he interviewed many recent refugees from Nazi-occupied countries, and from their reports he began to develop dramatic themes about occupation and resistance. As he recalled, "if I could write the experiences of the occupied . . . such an account might even be a blueprint, setting forth what might be expected and what could be done about it" (Benson, *Steinbeck, Writer*, 488). Originally, he set the story in America as a wake-up call, but objections from his FIS superiors that it might demoralize American readers led him to change the setting to an occupied country in Europe, unnamed but clearly resembling Norway and Denmark.

The essential conflict in *The Moon Is Down* is not subtle: the characters themselves are made to spell it out. It is not only between the anonymous occupiers (based obviously on the Nazis) and the occupied townspeople, but also between the occupiers' "herd mentality"—a phrase the heroic mayor of the town explicitly uses—and the thinking of "free men." Though the herd mentality—a Nietzschean synonym for the phalanx—enables its holders to act as an efficient, smoothly functioning, militarily powerful machine by stifling independent thought and dissent, the individualistic, freethinking people of the occupied country ultimately prevail. As Mayor Orden conveniently summarizes, "Free men cannot start a war, but once it is started, they can fight on in defeat. Herd men, followers of a leader, cannot do that, and so it is always the herd men who win battles and the free men who win wars" (268–69). The play depicts the steadily growing resistance of the occupied: from their initial dismay and disorganization during the invasion, to sullen passive resistance, to active rebellion aided by dynamite air-dropped by the Allies. Meanwhile the occupiers, beginning with their atypically conflicted leader, Colonel Lanser,[26] develop an increasing malaise in having to live with the hatred and passive resistance of the townspeople, a malaise that undermines their ability to deal with active rebellion. Predictably, Mayor Orden goes to a hero's death, but the occupied "free" people will clearly prevail.

Besides the propagandistic sentimentality of the plot and (except for Colonel Lanser) the two-dimensional characterization, the story gets several things wrong. A commanding officer of the Nazi-like herd is unlikely to admit to his enemy, "one of the tendencies of the military mind is an inability to learn, an inability to see beyond the killing which is its job" (236). Similarly, the colonel's underling (Captain Loft) is unlikely to have openly challenged his superior's "defeatist talk" (260), unless he is looking to face a firing squad for rank insubordination. The good mayor's predictions are also, sadly, wrong: following Stalingrad, the Nazis fought tenaciously for two and a half years while facing ever more certain defeat.

But *Moon*'s biggest weakness is conceptual and shows a contradiction similar to the one in *The Grapes of Wrath* discussed in chapter 5. Repeatedly, the mayor and his friend Dr. Winter (playing the familiar Steinbeckian role of the wise observer) describe the townspeople as freethinking and independent:

Mayor: "My people don't like to have others think for them. Maybe they are different from your people." (221)

Dr. Winter: "[W]e are a free people; we have as many heads as we have people, and in a time of need, leaders pop up among us like mushrooms." (265)

Dramatically, we see this independence enacted repeatedly in the way that not only the mayor but ordinary townspeople defy the occupiers, one citizen declaring repeatedly, "I am a free man" (238). But to resist the occupiers, the freethinking townspeople must *organize* themselves, must indeed begin to take on herd-like qualities that temporarily stifle freethinking in order to act efficiently and effectively. Hemingway realized this—perhaps too well—in supporting brutal Soviet discipline. Steinbeck does not. His mayor mentions to Colonel Lanser at one point the townspeople's ability to make decisions collectively and to act with unanimity on their own instead of following his (the mayor's) orders:

> Orden: "When the town makes up its mind what it wants to do, I'll probably do that."
> Lanser: "But you are the authority." . . .
> Orden: "[A]uthority is in the town. . . . This means we cannot act as quickly as you can, but when *a direction is set* we all act together." (221, emphasis added)

Passive voice obscures a key question. Who sets this direction? One leader? Many? Or does the town act without a leader as a self-regulating collective, as the migrants of *The Grapes of Wrath* did in the government camp? In that novel, Steinbeck praised the rugged independence of the migrant farmers, while at the same time showing the contradictory need for "I" to become "we." In *The Moon Is Down*, he does not focus on the paradox of good people acquiring phalanx-like unanimity by following a leader because it would destroy his more important opposition of free individuals prevailing over the herd-like occupiers.[27]

The trend of Steinbeck's thinking over the seven tumultuous years from 1936 to 1942 is clearly towards independent thought and against the herd mentality of the phalanx. *The Grapes of Wrath* stands as a partial exception to this trend because in that novel Steinbeck gave the *potential* coming together of the migrant farmers ("when I becomes we") a decidedly positive meaning. But the phalanx of collectivism never quite materializes in *Grapes*; and, as I argue in chapter 5, the concept conflicts with Steinbeck's praise of the migrant farmers' rugged individualism and individual aims. Not coincidentally, Steinbeck himself was nearly at the apex of his political engagement when he wrote the novel—a white-hot commitment to the migrants and hatred of the big growers and the Associated Farmers, an involvement he was never again to duplicate. Though none of his subsequent books achieved the narrative detachment of *In Dubious Battle*, neither do they reflect their author's intensity of political engagement and belief in political solutions seen in *Grapes*. Steinbeck's subsequent detachment from political leftism,[28] furthered by his emotional fragility, his attraction to science, his reaction to world politics, and his longer fascination with the workings of the phalanx, led inexorably to his belief in individualistic thought. As Robert DeMott observes, "After 1940 much of his important writing centered on explorations of a new topic—the dimensions of individual choice and imaginative consciousness."[29] If he had failed to dramatize convincingly his belief in individual free thought in *The Moon Is Down*, he stated it eloquently in this passage from *East of Eden*:

> And this I believe: that the free, exploring mind of the individual human is the most valuable thing in the world. And this I would fight for: the freedom of the mind to take any direction it wishes, undirected. And this I must fight against: any idea, religion, or government which limits or destroys the individual. This is what I am and what I am about. (131)

II. Hemingway: 1939–42
"The Ideology Boys"

Well before *For Whom the Bell Tolls* was published (October 1940), Hemingway's brief romance with the Left was turning sour. The pivotal year appears to have been 1939 in two respects. First, by the beginning of the year, the Spanish Republic was in its death throes, its fall to fascism now a certainty. And, as described in chapter 7, Hemingway, in writing his novel, no longer felt obliged to maintain the Party line or to promulgate hopeful fantasies of Loyalist survival as he had in his journalism. Beyond Spain, the world picture had radically changed in late 1939. Germany's invasion of Poland, bringing on World War II, was not shocking, given the Nazis' history of broken promises and aggressive expansion, but the Soviet Union had committed two acts that shook not only Hemingway's lingering sympathy for the communists (if he still harbored any), but that of thousands of other leftist sympathizers and fellow travelers: signing a Non-Aggression Pact with Hitler on 23 August and invading neighboring Finland on 30 November. The Pact enabled two other Soviet expansions: taking the eastern half of Poland a few weeks after the Nazis invaded from the west, and occupying the Baltic countries: Lithuania, Latvia, and Estonia. Combined, these actions presented a duplicitous, expansive Russia that had abruptly reversed its self-proclaimed role as the bulwark against fascism and had indeed begun to resemble Nazi Germany in its bullying aggression against weaker neighbors.

Unlike many other prominent leftists, Hemingway does not appear to have commented in writing about the Nazi-Soviet Pact.[30] But he had a personal reason for caring about Finland—Martha Gellhorn was there, covering the crisis for *Collier's*. On 8 December 1939, Hemingway wrote his editor, Max Perkins, "Marty Gellhorn has been in Helsinki and at Finnish front since it started. I imagine it did not take her long to realize that those bi-motored Katuskas were no longer our planes" (*Selected Letters*, 498). Having once helped defend a beleaguered democracy in Spain, Soviet bombers were now attacking a smaller neighbor; they were no longer "our planes." In the same letter, Hemingway criticized American communists whose ideological conformity to the Party line now required them to support Russia's actions—communists such as his critics, present and anticipated, from the Abraham Lincoln Brigade. He noted sarcastically that Alvah Bessie, a writer and veteran of the Brigade, hadn't liked the ideology of his Spanish Civil War story "Under the Ridge"[31] and continued,

> What do those guys use for Ideology nowadays? . . . Those poor unfortunate bastards need all the ideology they can get and I would not want to deprive anyone of [it] anymore than would make cracks about religion to a nun. But Max *it is a foul business and it was a foul business plenty of times in Spain too.*
>
> . . . [W]hat was wrong with [Bessie's] outfit was too much ideology and not enough military training, discipline or materiel.

He goes on to describe Loyalist battles lost by "the ideology boys." (*Selected Letters*, 498, emphasis added).

This letter shows how detached Hemingway felt from the communists worldwide, and it squares completely with the anti-ideological position that Robert Jordan, in *For Whom the Bell Tolls*, secretly held: "And what about a planned society and the rest of it? That was for the others to do. . . . What were his politics then? He had none now, he told himself. But don't tell any one else that, he thought" (178). Echoing his protagonist's caution, Hemingway did not want "the ideology boys" to know the political themes running through the novel before it was published. A few months earlier, he wrote Perkins that "his story contained what people with Communist party obligations could never write, what most of them could never know or—if they knew—allow themselves to believe.[32] He anticipated—accurately—that Pilar's lengthy recounting of a Loyalist massacre would infuriate the comrades, and he cautioned Perkins not to show them this chapter. Soon enough they would have their chance to howl about the "truths" of his novel that challenged their "illusions."[33] But to have to maintain those illusions of Loyalist purity in Spain and Russian benignity and decency everywhere against blatant evidence to the contrary, not only because the comrades were required to, but because they could not even allow themselves to believe otherwise was indeed "a foul business." And he would have none of it. Now that the Spanish war was over, he had reverted to being a writer, he told Perkins, "not a Catholic writer or a Party writer or even an American writer, but only a writer trying to tell the truth as he had personally learned it."[34]

"Tourist" or Truth-Teller? Leftist Responses to *For Whom the Bell Tolls* and Its Author

Hemingway was correct in anticipating that the comrades would not like his novel, but like Steinbeck, who had also underestimated the storm of protest against *Grapes*, he was taken aback by the intensity of this small uproar. The popular and critical success of *For Whom the Bell Tolls* effectively put him back on top among American novelists—and filled his coffers with royalties and Hollywood contracts. All the more disconcerting, then, were the shrill attacks from the far Left—and Hemingway was never one to brook negative criticism.

The novel divided the Left: liberal leftists like Edmund Wilson and Malcolm Cowley admired it; communists like Mike Gold and Alvah Bessie despised it, as did other members of the Abraham Lincoln Brigade. But not all Spanish Civil War veterans hated it: a few significant figures who fought for the Loyalists praised it.[35] Ironically, both pro- and anti-Stalinist leftists criticized it for opposing reasons. The pro-Stalinists felt the negative depiction of the

Russians distorted the truth. The anti-Stalinist *Partisan Review* felt Hemingway hadn't gone far enough in dramatizing their evil. Lionel Trilling complained about Robert Jordan's ambivalence: "He can 'experience' all the [Russians'] badness, but he cannot deal with it, dare not judge it."[36] Edmund Wilson, on the other hand, praised the novel for this same refusal to be more partisan: "[I]n approaching the role of the Communists in Spain, Hemingway's judgments are not made to fit into the categories of a political line . . ." Wilson was astute enough to notice how this new position contrasted with Hemingway's "Stalinist melodrama of the days of 1937, a way of thinking certainly alien to his artistic nature . . ."[37] He concluded, "The whole picture of the Russians and their followers in Spain— which will put *The New Masses* to the trouble of immediately denouncing a former favorite . . .—looks absolutely authentic."[38]

As Hemingway expected and Wilson predicted, the "ideology boys"—Stalinists of the *New Masses* and the Lincoln Brigade— attacked the novel for three specific elements: Pilar's narrative of the Loyalist massacre (with no correspondingly dramatic narrative of a fascist massacre); Hemingway's brutal portrait of André Marty and satirical treatment of Dolores Ibárruri; and his depiction of the Russians. Repeatedly, in reviews and letters, they called Hemingway a journalistic "tourist" in Spain, who understood neither the Spanish people nor what the war was really about. Though their criticisms were obviously slanted by their politics and perspective, some complaints had validity. For readers familiar with the atrocities routinely carried out by the fascists, Pilar's dramatized narrative does assume disproportionate weight. La Pasionaria was certainly not alone in sheltering her son in a foreign country, and he was not old enough for combat anyway. André Marty had organized the International Brigades, hence the Brigaders' intense loyalty to him. And surely not all the Russians in Spain were as cynical as Karkov, their chief representative in the novel.

Mike Gold, editor of *New Masses* and columnist in the *Daily Worker*, devoted one of his "Change the World" columns to the novel, writing in his typically vituperative, *ad hominem* style. Because Hemingway has always lived "the limited life of a rich rentier, of a sportsman and tourist," Gold asserts, his great talent is "limited, narrow and mutilated by class egotism" and by "the poverty of his mind." For Hemingway, the Spanish Civil War was merely an adventure, "a thrill": "and the man who has no real principles, who does not understand democracy or Communism, or have the slightest wish to understand, may join in the Spanish Civil War for various personal reasons and be loyal for a few years. When the cause seems lost, however, when the democracy seems defeated, he will desert, leaving a trail of alibis, whines and slanders."[39]

What especially angered Gold was Robert Jordan's self-confessed lack of a Marxist ideology: "[C]an the man who has no politics and hence no loyalty to democracy or the people write a true book about the Spanish Civil War, which was a political war made by the people in defense of democracy and their right to bread?" Echoing the other Marxist critics, Gold notes the supposedly one-sided dramatization of Loyalist atrocities (Pilar's story), the "slander" of "Russian technicians and officers" and of La Pasionaria and André Marty. He concludes that "'For Whom the Bell Tolls' is only the story of Hemingway in Spain. It is a minor story."[40] Gold's review overlooks Jordan's strong empathy for Pilar's group (surely an embodiment of "the people"); it assumes that a belief in "democracy" must be leftist rather than Jordan's vague libertarianism, and it maintains the Party fiction that the Russians in Spain were "technicians." But Gold does hit on one vulnerability with partial accuracy: the "personal reasons" that pushed Hemingway to become involved in Spain (see chapter 3).

With less invective and more reflection, Alvah Bessie expressed similar disapproval:

> [D]epth of understanding [in the novel] there is none; breadth of conception is heartbreakingly lacking; there is no searching, no probing, no grappling with the truths of human life that is more than superficial. . . . [T]he cause of Spain does not, in any *essential* way, figure as a motivating power. . . . In the widest sense, that cause is actually *irrelevant* to the narrative.[41]

Dismissing the novel as a *"Cosmopolitan [magazine]* love story against a background of the Spanish Civil War,"* Bessie railed against the novel's depictions of the Soviets in Spain, who were made to look "sinister and reprehensible," when they, in fact, "command the entire respect and adherence of the Spanish people . . ." Like many other Brigade veterans, Bessie resented the novel's depiction of André Marty, "the man who was the organizational genius and spirit of the Brigades" and "a revolutionary figure of the first magnitude," who is here portrayed as "a criminal imbecile." Hemingway's distorted views of the war, Bessie concludes, gave aid and comfort to "our universal enemy": fascism, the Martin Dies Committee (House Committee on Un-American Activities), the Hearst press, etc. Ignoring the passage in the novel praising the idealism of the International Brigades, Bessie predicted that "every living and dead representative of the Abraham Lincoln Battalion [will be] attacked and slandered because of the great authority that attaches to Hemingway's name and his known connection with Spain." Though explicated without Gold's viciousness, Bessie's criticisms are straight party-line: the claim that the Russians "command the entire respect and adherence of the Spanish people" was especially ludicrous in 1940, since by late 1938 they had essentially pulled out of the war, withdrawing their military "advisers" and sharply cutting material aid, when it was clear that the Loyalists would lose. Anti-Stalinist leftists like Edmund Wilson and Dwight Macdonald even charged the Soviets with acting "as a police force to avert the real social revolution."[42]

When paired with the anti-Stalinist reviews in *Partisan Review*, Bessie and Gold's reviews show that Hemingway's novel had become a pawn in the intensifying battle between pro- and anti-Stalinists on the Left. Interestingly, except for Wilson, they agreed on the shallowness of the novel's—and author's—political sophistication. Another revealing feature of the Gold and Bessie reviews— and of the Lincoln Brigade's "Open Letter" to Hemingway and aspects of Milton Wolff's personal letter—is the lockstep agreement on the novel's greatest sins and the repetition of key words, such as "mutilate," "slander," and "malign," even the insulting appellation "tourist" applied to Hemingway.[43] Given the "discipline" the Comintern enforced on its votaries (which, ironically, Hemingway admired), it seems at least arguable that these documents (excluding Wolff's letter) had a common author, urtext, or summary of key arguments originating in the Soviet Union.

Hemingway and the Abraham Lincoln Brigade: 1939–47

Bessie's criticisms of *For Whom the Bell Tolls* reflect one stage in Hemingway's difficult relationship with the Veterans of the Abraham Lincoln Brigade (VALB) beginning in 1939 and lasting well past the next decade. Delineating all its rises and falls goes beyond the boundaries of this study, but a few landmarks suggest Hemingway's contradictory feelings of irritation and personal sympathy towards the group and indifference, if not hostility, to their communist ideology. In 1939, when both he and the Brigade had detached themselves from the war, his relations with the veterans were friendly. He had written a complimentary portrait of the Brigade's last commander, Milton Wolff, for an exhibition catalog of Jo Davidson's Spanish Civil War sculptures,[44] and in March wrote a foreword to Joe North's pamphlet, *Men in the Ranks: The Story of 12 Americans in Spain*, which was published by the VALB.[45] North, in turn, asked Hemingway to contribute a piece to a *New Masses* commemorative issue honoring the VALB (published 14 Feb. 1939).[46]

The piece became "On the American Dead in Spain," a brief but highly poetic elegy to the Brigade veterans who had fallen at the Battle of Jarama in 1937. Echoing a line from the Ecclesiastes passage he had used as an epigraph to *The Sun Also Rises* ("the earth abideth forever"), Hemingway describes how "our dead are a part of the earth of Spain now and the earth of Spain can never die. . . . Our dead will live with it forever." By linking the earth's endurance to the perennial struggle for freedom, the elegy's message is clear: "Just as the earth can never die, neither will those who have ever been free return to slavery. . . . [N]o system of tyranny ever will prevail in Spain. . . . [T]he earth can never be conquered. For the earth endureth forever" (*New Masses Anthology*, 307). The tone is all the more moving in its underlying melancholy about the now-certain fascist victory; thus, the elegy must look to liberty's inevitable triumph in the future, which will finally justify the deaths of these veterans. North later noted that the elegy "has [since] been translated into almost all major languages of the world" (308). That Hemingway published it in the CP-USA's literary journal does not, however, imply that he "honored" its Stalinist politics, as Cary Nelson argues.[47] What Hemingway admired about these veterans was not their politics but their courage and willingness to back up their beliefs with arms at the risk of their lives. "I like communists when they're soldiers," Hemingway told Joe North in 1938, "but when they're priests, I hate them."[48] But if the elegy's venue, *New Masses*, did not signal Hemingway's ideological sympathy, it nonetheless rounded out his brief affair with the far Left that had begun with his publication in *New Masses* of "Who Murdered the Vets?" in 1935.

From this high point of mutual admiration, Hemingway's relations with the VALB steadily deteriorated once his novel appeared in October 1940. In public and private, many (but not all) Brigade veterans, especially those in the New York chapter, attacked the novel. Besides the Bessie review, the VALB published a lengthy "Open Letter" in the 22 November issue of the *Daily Worker*, stating that "we deeply resent and condemn the picture of the [Loyalist] cause . . . portrayed in your novel."[49] Though the letter is co-signed by three officers of the VALB, it was drafted by Alvah Bessie and thus repeats the same criticisms of his *New Masses* review.[50] According to the "Open Letter," the novel presents a picture of the war "so drastically mutilated and distorted . . . as to slander the cause for which we fought." The specific examples of this mutilation are the same ones mentioned by Bessie and Gold. Worst of all, the authors conclude, the novel does not apply "the most basic lessons of Spain" to "the world today," namely that, except for the Soviet Union, "all of the other [powerful states]—Germany, Italy, England, France, and the United States—united to crush the Spanish Republic . . ." This conclusion, lumping the neutral states with those actively involved in fighting against the Republic, praising the Soviet Union as "a great bulwark of peace, democracy and freedom," and depicting the new world war as a "bloody and reactionary imperialist butchery," was straight party-line and absurd in expecting Hemingway to deal with "the world today" in his novel.

The New York branch of the VALB still wasn't finished with Hemingway. It organized a number of public symposia to rebut the novel. For 11 January 1941, the topic was "An Answer to Ernest Hemingway by the Men Who Fought in Spain." Speakers included Bessie and Wolff. Two months later, another symposium on the novel was entitled "Masterpiece or Potboiler."[51] Either at the January symposium or separately, Hemingway even met with VALB members to rebut the charges of Bessie's review and the "Open Letter." Bessie recalls,

> At the meeting Hemingway vigorously defended his novel, stating that it was . . . "a true book," an accurate reflection of the crucial war in which we had all been involved. He also said that, like Robert Jordan, he "had no politics," that he had "tried to read the books [including *Das Kapital*]" but that "they hurt my head."[52]

Unwilling to leave it at public denunciations, Milton Wolff wrote Hemingway a long personal letter, criticizing the Pilar massacre story, the depictions of Marty and especially of La Pasionaria. Wolff later recalled, "the business about Dolores, La Pasionaria, sent me through the roof. For me, and I imagine for all of the International Brigaders, Pasionaria was the heart of our fight against fascism. . . . [H]er impassioned speeches . . . were the banners we carried into battle."[53] Like Bessie, Wolff assumed that the novel would play into the hands of Franco sympathizers. Like Gold, he got personal: "I called him a tourist in Spain, . . . that he could not know his ass from his elbow as to what the war was about . . ." Hemingway's response was predictable; as Wolff recounts, "he called me a prick. . . . [and concluded] 'We are no longer friends.'"[54] But also predictable was Hemingway's partial retraction (of the "prick" epithet) once he had blown off steam. More important, when Wolff approached him seven years later, Hemingway's reception was quite different.

One sentence in Hemingway's letter to Wolff reveals how Hemingway thought of these VALB attacks: "you'll keep on denouncing me every time you are ordered to . . ."[55] For Hemingway, the veterans were obediently following the Party line—they were, after all, the "ideology boys"—and, as E. E. Cummings put it, "moscow pipes good kumrads dance."[56] All the more reason not to take the carping of Bessie, Wolff, et al. too seriously—except that Hemingway was always thin-skinned about negative criticism, and the attacks bothered him.

By 1947, the bad feeling between Hemingway and the VALB seemed largely gone. To commemorate the tenth anniversary of the Lincoln Brigade's involvement in Spain, Wolff (summoning up his courage) invited Hemingway to come from Cuba to New York to read "On the American Dead in Spain." Though he declined, Hemingway made a recording of the elegy, along with a humorous introduction, and sent them in his stead. Nelson argues, somewhat ambiguously, that this gesture, in the intensifying anti-communist milieu of 1947, showed that Hemingway stood "with the Vets."[57] It would be more accurate to say that the gesture showed no hard feelings, not any ideological agreement.

No sooner was *For Whom the Bell Tolls* published than Hemingway, like Steinbeck after *Grapes*, turned to other, non-leftist matters. He divorced his second wife, Pauline, and married Martha Gellhorn in November 1940. And since Gellhorn had already accepted a *Collier's* assignment to cover the Sino-Japanese war, Hemingway accompanied her, obtaining his own journalistic assignment from the liberal newspaper *PM* to write several dispatches, giving his impressions of such Chinese luminaries as Chiang Kai-shek and Madame Chiang, and of the Chinese army's condition and capacity to resist the Japanese. A covert purpose for the five-month trip was intelligence-gathering for the U.S. government. The leftist sympathies Hemingway had shown in Spain, in varying degrees, were now behind him.[58] The war that he had predicted if fascism weren't stopped in Spain had truly arrived all over the globe, and even the barely neutral United States would soon be pulled in, arousing his patriotism. After Pearl Harbor, Hemingway's attentions were entirely taken up by America's role in this war. His next writing project was to edit an anthology of war pieces, *Men at War*, and he was already making plans for his own intelligence-gathering by using his yacht to search for Cuban shoreline hiding places for German submarines and a wilder scheme to turn the yacht into a kind of Q-ship for attacking those submarines.

To say, then, that Hemingway *abandoned* his leftism after Spain is imprecise. With the death of the Spanish Republic, it simply fell away from him as if it had never existed. The Stalinists' sharply critical reviews of *For Whom the Bell Tolls* cannot fully account for this evaporation, for those reviews were a narrow exception to the overwhelming praise the novel received even from Spanish Civil War veterans, and Hemingway could construe the vitriol of the Stalinists as mindless devotion to a myth and obedience to ideological orders—an ideology he did not share and an obedience that his independent nature despised.

Given how easily Hemingway shed his leftism, would it be fair to conclude that it never really existed in the first place? That he had—as Mike Gold et al. charged—merely adopted it as a pose for personal reasons? Some evidence supports this view. Before Spain, his overtures to the Left (notably his accusatory article "Who Murdered the Vets?" in *New Masses*) were arguably intended to win back liberal and leftist critics who had excoriated not only his early 1930s books but also his detachment from contemporary politics. *To Have and Have Not* furthered these overtures to the Left with Harry Morgan's dying words, but Hemingway cleverly avoided the appearance of caving in to leftist critics by keeping Morgan an iconoclast and by slamming the professional leftists in the story. Even the author's initial decision to become involved with the Spanish Civil War was partly motivated by this desire to continue ingratiating himself with the Left.

But the Spanish war did something to his apolitical sensibilities. His initial motives for moving left had been achieved: the standing ovation he received at the American Writers' Congress in 1937 proved that. In Spain, he became genuinely committed to the Loyalist cause, admired the idealists who had come there to fight for it, and determined to use his journalism propagandistically to further that cause. If Hemingway's political aim as a journalist had been to support a democratic, anti-fascist Spain (as Robert Jordan's was), it would have jibed with his previous support of democratic, anti-authoritarian governments (for example, in Italy and Cuba). But why did he become such a strong supporter of the Soviet presence in Spain? And why did he affirm with such ferocity in his journalism and letters all aspects of the Communist Party line in Spain, such as denying the presence of Soviet-trained generals, denying that Loyalist terror prevailed in Madrid, and uncritically repeating Soviet accusations against competing leftist parties such as the POUM?

The reasons for this Stalinism, as Edmund Wilson correctly identified it, were many. As described in chapter 3, the communists in Spain worked on Hemingway, seeing his recruitment to their cause as a major coup. But to consider him merely a dupe of the

Soviets would be a distortion. Though clearly influenced by this Soviet courtship and by Mikhail Koltsov's confidences in particular, Hemingway arrived at his own conclusion: that the Loyalist cause was so fractured by rival leftist parties that only authoritarian control from above—Soviet control—could forcibly unify these factions into an effective fighting force. Such unification required harsh "discipline" enforced politically (repressing rival parties), civilly (maintaining a climate of fear and denunciation against rampant spying, torturing and executing suspected fifth columnists), and militarily (summarily shooting deserters and slackers). In his fiction and letters, Hemingway expressed exactly the same view: that only this Russian discipline—what others would call Stalinist terror—offered any hope of a Loyalist victory. "The first thing was to win the war," Robert Jordan thinks. "If we did not win the war everything was lost" (150). And that all-important end justified unsavory means, even if those means became increasingly indistinguishable from fascist tactics. In one of his dispatches from the Far East, Hemingway later expressed what he had learned in Spain: "No country which is at war remains a democracy for long. War always brings on a temporary dictatorship."[59]

Note that the aims and issues in Hemingway's Stalinism were essentially practical and military: victory and what was required to achieve it. Hemingway's interest in theoretical Marxism—"a planned society and the rest of it," as Jordan glibly puts it—simply did not exist. Yet, to claim that Hemingway "at his best was always an antipolitical writer" and that his anti-fascism "never made him a communist sympathizer," as Allen Josephs asserts,[60] oversimplifies his complex attitudes and ignores his pragmatic Stalinism in 1937 and 1938. When the aim of that pragmatism died in the Loyalists' defeat, his pro-Soviet leftism did also. That the Soviets had subsequently acted so despicably in treating with the Nazis and invading Finland only reinforced his political separation, as did the Party's attacks on his novel.

In Hemingway's various kinds of writing about the war, "truth" was a highly variable component. In his newspaper dispatches he limits it to analyses and descriptions of particular battles. His overly optimistic long-range predictions and intentional omission of uglier realities on the Loyalist side show his intent to use the medium as propaganda to further the cause. The question remains, however, how clearly in 1937 and 1938 he could distinguish Soviet propaganda and lies, such as those about Andrés Nin and José Robles, from the truth. What he knowingly repressed in his journalism, however, began to leak into the short fiction and drama, media too close to his heart to fully demean as propaganda. But the process was halting and gradual: the play and stories acknowledge some unpleasantries about the Loyalists—torture and execution of suspected fifth columnists, the climate of fear in civilian Madrid, the inadequacies of Loyalist attacks—but still repress others, such as the Russian presence. Written during the war with little authorial distance, the stories and play reflect two sides of Hemingway—artistic realist and propagandistic advocate—competing for dominance.

For Whom the Bell Tolls goes much further in recognizing serious dissonances in the Loyalist cause partly because revealing them could no longer affect the Republic's fate. But the author may have been driven by a more personal motive. Was the novel's determination to be a "true book"—to reveal "extensive" Soviet assassinations, cynicism, and corruption, as well as Loyalist massacres, and prominent Loyalist crazies and phonies—a kind of expiation for the intentional omissions and lies in the earlier work? Was it a reassertion of Hemingway the artist? He knew these revelations would infuriate the self-appointed protectors of the Loyalist myth—the party-line adherents in the VALB—but he went ahead anyway. The truth of art was what mattered now.

III. Wright: 1939–44

Richard Wright had much to be proud of in considering the impact *Native Son* made on the reading public. It had sold very well as a Book-of-the-Month Club selection and received widespread praise from literary critics and book reviewers.[61] Moreover, it confirmed and expanded the acclaim he had received from *Uncle Tom's Children*. He was now not only the leading black author of his time, but also had broken into the previously all-white echelon of major novelists. But like Steinbeck with the Associated Farmers and Hemingway with the Lincoln Brigade, Wright was vexed by unenthusiastic and sometimes hostile reviews from one political faction: his own Communist Party.

Mike Gold, virtually the official communist spokesperson, pirouetted like a weathervane over the novel. In his first review, published in the *Sunday Worker* almost a month after the novel appeared, he was enthusiastic:

> It is a rare and special thing that Wright has done, as no American writer before him. He has written a story on the racial theme without sentimentalizing it. . . . The story of *Native Son* . . . will burn itself on the imagination of this country, I believe, as has no other novel about Negroes since *Uncle Tom's Cabin*.[62]

True to form, Gold credits Wright's "Communist training" for giving him the "moral courage to reveal without fear every ugly secret of a democracy that is based on the blood and suffering of an oppressed nation within the nation." He even attributes Wright's "communist honesty" to his beneficial experience writing for the *Daily Worker*, when in fact Wright resented how that job stole valuable time from his fiction-writing. But Gold also recognized Wright's daring "to take the worst that is charged against his folk, and to throw it back as a challenge in the face of the oppressor."

Black communists, however, judged the novel more harshly. James W. Ford (the CP-USA's candidate for vice president of the United States in 1932, 1936, and 1940) raised the Party's longstanding criticism of Wright for his emphasis on race over class.[63] Benjamin Davis Jr. offered a lengthy mixed review of the novel in the *Sunday Worker*. Calling it "the most powerful and important novel of 1940," Davis praised the novel's "terrific indictment of capitalist America" which "burns . . . the responsibility [for the racism that the Negro people experience every day] deep into the conscience of the American people." But Davis faulted Wright for having "exaggerated [Bigger] into a symbol of the whole Negro people," when "[t]he average unemployed Negro youth does not become a rapist and a murderer." Worse, the novel did not show the "hundreds of thousands of Negroes swelling progressive ranks . . ." Finally, Davis criticizes as unrepresentative the novel's depictions of communists. Mary and Jan are "dilettante types" with "patronizing attitudes." Max's legal defense of Bigger is incompetent; the real International Labor Defense would have "chuck[ed] him out of the case." The novel never shows a communist "in action . . . fighting for better conditions for Bigger families . . ."[64]

Gold responded to this last criticism by defending the novel in a second review.[65] Praising Wright's daring to focus his "fictional spotlight" so relentlessly on "a Negro slum boy," he writes, "The critics believe that Wright should have included Negro Communists, militant and intellectual Negroes. But that is a completely other story, big enough for another book. It might have drawn attention away from . . . the story of the Biggers." Black communists compose only a tiny minority of blacks, Gold continued; to focus on this unrepresentative sliver would amount to "Communist escapism."

Still later, however, Gold moved closer to Davis's critique. Responding to a lecture by Wright in which he supposedly depicted Bigger Thomas as "a symbol of the Negro people," Gold strongly disagreed, dismissing Bigger as one of the "lumpen proletariat": "He is only a small and hopeless fragment" and not at all representative of "the whole Negro people."[66] Even Wright's sometime Party friend Ted Ward expressed doubts about the novel's political skepticism: "[Y]our trouble was you had not studied the Theory of the Proletarian Revolution." He warned Wright that members of the Harlem branch of the CP-USA "were all for setting up a bureau to which writers like you would have to submit their materials before publishing them"—for vetting and censorship, in short.[67]

Stung by these responses, Wright defended himself to Mike Gold in a lengthy, revealing letter probably written after Gold's defense of the novel but before his reversal.[68] The letter is a collection of Wright's grievances in fending off Party pressures and criticisms. Its tone, however, is less angry than resigned—as if Wright had already decided that the movement he had committed himself to had little understanding of, or relevance to, his aims as a black author. He tells Gold, "To be quite frank until you spoke up in its defense, I'd all but given up hope that our movement could look deeper into the book, that we could doff our set of stock-reactions and think creatively about it." Specific examples of these "stock-reactions" follow: that fiction should be used solely for agitprop ("Party officials . . . . have a tendency to sneer at more imaginative attempts"); that "all party comrades should be represented in fiction as white knights charging heroically into the enemy"; that Party authors should view characters "through the lens of . . . political theory" and avoid "the dark hidden places of the human personality." If he had followed these pro forma expectations, Wright concludes, he would have had to abandon the Bigger Thomases. As he had written in "How 'Bigger' Was Born," Wright saw in Bigger's frustration the possibilities of fascist allegiance, a potential among disaffected blacks that the Communists simply didn't understand. He writes Gold, "I do not agree with Ben Davis when he implies that the majority of the Negroes are with the labor movement. . . . Despite all the heroic struggles the Party has put forward to win the Negro, it is still possible for a wave of nationalism to sweep the Negro people today." Essentially, Wright had not changed his view of the Party's obtuseness about blacks from what he felt—or later *claimed* that he felt—as a new Party member in Chicago: "The Communists, I felt, had oversimplified the experience of those whom they sought to lead. In their efforts to recruit masses, they had missed the meaning of the lives of the masses, had conceived of people in too abstract a manner" ("I Tried," pt. 1, 63).

Wright's objections about the party's literary shallowness and dogmatic rigidity parallel his descriptions in "I Tried" about the Chicago cell's hostility to his budding creative efforts then. His complaints to Gold show clearly that the problem, as Wright now conceived it, was not particular to a few intolerant individuals, but was intrinsic to Party ideology. He had already ignored that ideology by focusing on racial, not class-oriented, psychology and by portraying the communists as out of touch with how Bigger finally comes to see himself. Having succeeded brilliantly in doing so, he was not about to become a Party hack. Fabre writes that the letter to Gold "contain[s] the germs of dissent, hidden but growing, which eventually caused his rupture with the Party" (*Unfinished Quest*, 186). But there is nothing hidden about Wright's dissent: the cracks in his allegiance are already visible.

But they were not yet fatal. In political matters outside of his creative writing, Wright was quite willing to express the Party line in his speeches and articles and let the Party use his name on petitions from its front groups. Ignoring the widespread disillusionment of his leftist friends, he supported the Soviets' pact with the Nazis as "a great step toward peace"—even though it enabled Hitler to begin World War II a week later. In fostering "peaceful relations between Germany and the Soviet Union," the Pact "struck a blow against the imperialist war intrigues of Chamberlain on the continent," he told Angelo Herndon. Without mentioning the expansionism of Germany and Russia, he identified England and France as the imperialist powers that "oppress more Negroes and colonial peoples than all the Empires of the world combined."[69]

He also adopted the Party position on the Soviet invasion of Finland. In the interview quoted above he declared, "The Finnish situation is being used by the big imperialist powers as a smoke screen for involving the whole world in war." Liberals who supported aid to Finland were "dupes and suckers."[70] Given the oppressive imperialism of the Allies, Wright concluded that "the Negro has no stake in this war" and should instead be encouraged by negro intellectuals to unite with "white workers and genuine progressives in the fight against war."

The phrasing of Wright's statements is so hackneyed in its Party-line conformity that one wonders how someone who made his living by shaping language could use it. There seems little doubt that he did believe these positions, but in expressing them, he seems to have put his mind on autopilot and let Party rhetoric do the talking. More revealing of his own thinking was his idiosyncratic belief—expressed in an unpublished article—that in defying expectations of the Western powers, the Soviets' behavior "extends the area of human feeling . . . illuminates new possibilities for human life . . . and creates incalculable surprises." Thus, "[t]he rightness or wrongness of a given set of tactical actions by the Communist Party does not strike me as being of any great ultimate importance."[71]

It was relatively easy for Wright to support the Party's position (from September 1939 to June 1941) on America's non-intervention in the European war, since he felt that blacks would only be supporting Western imperialism and Jim Crow by fighting in a segregated American military. He was elected to the board of the American Peace Mobilization (a Party-sponsored group) in the summer of 1940 and supported the Party's nominees, Earl Browder and James W. Ford, in the national election that fall: "That Ford should be a candidate for Vice President of the United States is an achievement for the Negro people, an achievement recognized and supported only by the Communist Party."[72] More difficult for Wright was fulfilling the time-consuming expectations imposed on prominent Party members, when his mind was on his next writing projects and on the stage version of *Native Son* that he was co-writing with Paul Green. This conflict of responsibilities had plagued him in Chicago and in his humdrum duties in the Harlem office of the *Daily Worker*. Only now, his proven literary achievement made it especially tiresome to fulfill such Party expectations as sending congratulations to *New Masses* on its thirtieth anniversary. He had to be reminded three times, twice by telegram (Fabre, *Unfinished Quest*, 220).

What really upset Wright, however, was in having the Communist Party abruptly reverse—and even censor—his fervent declaration that the best possible course for black people was to oppose America's involvement in the imperialist war in Europe. He expressed this position in speeches—such as the one he gave at a meeting of the League of American Writers in spring 1941—and articles, the most famous of which was "Not My People's War," a written version of the League speech. In this article, Wright describes the attitude of American blacks toward the war and such noble-sounding rhetoric as Roosevelt's "Four Freedoms" as "chronic distrust" and skepticism due to the government's failure to improve their second-class status after they fought in the last war, as well as its current failures to desegregate the military, pass an anti-lynching bill, etc. Equating American, British, and German imperialism, Wright declares,

> The cry of the Negro people today is for peace. The cry of America today is for peace. The cry of the common people of the world today is for peace.
>
> The Soviet Union and its leaders stand today as living testimony of the profound hatred of war and to the sincere love of peace . . .[73]

New Masses printed Wright's article on 17 June 1941—five days before Germany invaded the Soviet Union. Immediately, the Communist Party line reversed itself from advocating "peace" to urging involvement in "the anti-fascist struggle." It was embarrassing enough for Wright to see his pacifist article in *New Masses* followed three weeks later by a collective article in the same magazine, "Why This Is Our War,"[74] and to witness the American Peace Mobilization renamed "American People's Mobilization"—mobilized to give war aid to the Soviet Union, of course. But Wright experienced a more personal and humiliating reversal shortly after, when he was to accept the prestigious Spingarn Medal in August at the NAACP's annual meeting in Houston. As Fabre recounts,

> Wright's acceptance speech had been given to the press a few days in advance. Its tenor was so close to "Not My People's War" that the Party leaders forced him to change it at the last minute into an appeal for Blacks to volunteer to defend democracy. He had so many reservations about the conditions of black participation in the war that he submitted very unwillingly; this episode marked the beginning of both his ultimate split with the Communists and the hatred of authoritarianism that inspired so much of *The Outsider*. (*Unfinished Quest*, 226)

It was more than "the beginning" of his separation, however, since he had already been experiencing significant tensions with the Party, from hostile reviews and threats of censorship to burdensome demands on his time, described above. The Houston debacle was one of two upheavals that destroyed his allegiance to the Party. The *coup de grâce*, however, had already occurred.

In that same summer of 1941, A. Philip Randolph, president of the Brotherhood of Sleeping Car Porters union, called for a massive march on Washington to protest segregation in the military and racial discrimination in the newly burgeoning defense industries. Wright fully expected the Party to support the march, which promised to attract as many as one hundred thousand people. The Party, however, in its new pro-war position, wanted nothing—certainly not a racial issue—to interfere with the U.S. government's arms mobilization (read, Lend Lease for Russia) and movement towards war with Germany. It therefore opposed the march on Washington, as well as legal challenges to discrimination (Fabre, *Unfinished Quest*, 229). More specifically, through James W. Ford and Benjamin Davis Jr., it informed Wright in no uncertain terms to stay out of the controversy.[75] At the eleventh hour, Roosevelt prevented the march by creating the Fair Employment Practices Committee to prevent discriminatory hiring (while ignoring the problem of a segregated military), but this was not the central issue for Wright. Here was the first instance of a massive black demonstration, a march guaranteed to dramatize racial discrimination and military segregation to the general public and the press as no public event ever had since the Civil War. Here was a coming together and *collective action* of black people—ordinary working-class people—which Wright had long dreamed of and dramatized in his story "Fire and Cloud." And the CP-USA, which had always proclaimed itself the champion of black people in America, refused to support the march. For Wright, it amounted to blatant hypocrisy and the destruction of his chief reason for being a communist. As Fabre puts it succinctly, "Wright viewed communism as only a means for black liberation" (*Unfinished Quest*, 184). Everything else—communist theory regarding capitalism, the proletariat, class warfare, imperialism, etc.—was important only as it impinged on the central issue for Wright of improving the status of blacks in America. Now that the Party had revealed its true colors nationally and had demonstrated ruthless authoritarianism against Wright personally in telling him what he could and could not speak and write about or support politically, he had no further reason to belong to the Party and abide its hypocrisies, deceits, and interference in his personal life. Although he later identified 1942 as the year that he quietly broke from the Communist Party, the triggering events occurred the previous year.

America was soon at war, and Wright had to rethink his previous antiwar position. Though he never slid into a patriotic stance with the ease of Steinbeck and Hemingway—he refused to write on behalf of a war bond drive, for example (Fabre, *Unfinished Quest*, 227)—he quickly arrived at a viable position "to rally the Negro people to stand shoulder to shoulder with the administration in a solid national front to wage war until victory is won."[76] Without for a moment ignoring American racism, he urged blacks, first, to realize that they had more to lose if the fascist powers prevailed and hence to join the fight to defeat them, and second, to "fight to preserve the kind of America where the struggle for *the extension of democracy* can be taken up with renewed vigor when our enemies are crushed."[77] Here was the "double victory" theme that enabled black writers such as Langston Hughes and black newspapers to support the war effort: victory over fascism abroad, victory over racism and Jim Crow at home. In placing the fight for the second victory *after* the first, Wright was not advocating postponing the struggle against racism. More likely, its placement in following World War II reflected Wright's determination that returning black GIs not experience the dismal fate of black soldiers returning from World War I. Like Steinbeck and Hemingway, he tried to find his own way to help the war effort, volunteering (like Steinbeck) for anti-fascist propaganda work, though aimed, as always, at a black population. Once again, he saw himself as a liaison between that group and the larger white one, only this time the larger group would be the U.S. government, not the Communist Party. But his Party membership worked against him, and his proposals and efforts to volunteer were ignored.

Ironically, the Party allegiance that had blocked this acceptance was now a thing of the past. As he recalled much later in a letter to his editor, Edward Aswell, "I broke with the Communist Party in 1942; I left under my own steam" (Fabre, *Unfinished Quest*, 230). And quietly: no public declarations, no recriminations—yet. He simply refused requests for his time and participation in Party events.[78] By 1943, however, he was already working on his autobiography, then titled *American Hunger*, which included the story of his Chicago years with his hopeful involvement in the John Reed Club and his disillusionment with the Chicago cell of the Communist Party. Although the Chicago section was subsequently cut from the autobiography, Wright surely knew that, if published, it would bring down on him the Party's full wrath, reserved specially for apostates. Yet he was determined to make this story public, and after it was cut from *Black Boy*, as the autobiography was now titled, he sent it to several prominent national magazines, which would have given it wide exposure. The *Atlantic Monthly* accepted the Chicago section, but limited it to Wright's experiences with the local John Reed Club and the Party cell, publishing it in two installments under the confessional title "I Tried to Be a Communist."[79]

Wright's narrative of his experiences with the John Reed Club and the Chicago cell of the Party describes a familiar, even clichéd arc of discovery, hope and enthusiasm, shock and disillusionment, and finally separation. His experiences with the club are uniformly encouraging (though there are several disillusioning hints that his progress there was at least partly due to his race). As a member of the Communist Party cell, however, his hopes collapse, as the narrative recounts the cell's increasingly callous treatment of Wright, culminating in his physical expulsion from a May Day protest march. Where his fellow club members had encouraged his creative writing, the communist leadership of the Chicago cell inhibited it, allowing him no free time to write and showing little understanding or sympathy and intense suspicion of his literary ambitions and his intellectualism. He also observed at a Party meeting how viciously its members could attack one of their own—in this case, a one-sided trial of an outcast, Ross, whom Wright had naively attempted to write about. Years later, he would portray this brutality in *The Outsider*. He himself experienced this venom in the over-the-top epithets—"bastard intellectual," "petty bourgeois degenerate"— Party leaders hurled at him for wanting to write about blacks (thus furthering negro nationalism) and for challenging the Party's decisions. He witnessed the demands for rigid conformity to the Party line—"Members of the party do not violate the party's decision"— and how other cell members fearfully abandoned him when he challenged the decision to close the John Reed Clubs. He felt the Party's paranoid distrust and suspicion as it spied on his activities and discussed him behind his back once his relations with the Party began to curdle. And as it reached out to harass him in his other occupations—instigating rebellion, he believed, against his projects in the Federal Negro Theatre of Chicago—he had more than a taste of the Party's vindictiveness. When he had had enough and tried to withdraw from the Party, he was informed, "No one can resign from the Communist Party": one could only be expelled— excommunicated, really—enabling the Party to save face while it humiliated and humbled the "traitor." Reduced to adjectives, the Party in these *Atlantic Monthly* articles appears as rigid, narrow-minded, authoritarian, maniacally conformist, fearful of independent thought, cold, and cruel, even sadistic.

To be sure, Wright's perspective in "I Tried" is biased, distorted by his later disillusionment with the Party retroactively applied to the years from 1934 to 1937. The narrative is also strangely truncated, omitting his entire history with the Party, some of which was encouraging, after he moved to New York in 1937, and on up until the present. The abridged narrative thus emphasizes Wright's naïveté and disillusionment—he learned his lesson, by God!—and excludes his strong, continuing ideological commitment to the Party. But the very lack of complexity in these articles—there is not one sympathetic or even nuanced characterization of a Party member in the entire story—makes Wright's portrait of the Chicago communists scarily powerful. It's a kind of monster movie—a clutch of automatons that the naïve protagonist has stumbled into—and its unstated but obvious message is "Beware!" Little wonder, then, that "I Tried to be a Communist" was included in the 1949 collection of disillusionment narratives of ex-communists, *The God That Failed*, as anti-communism was reaching its apex in America.

For Wright, the finality of announcing his split from the Party was simultaneously a source of relief and unease. As he wrote Ralph Ellison on 1 September 1944, "Now it is over, I feel a great sense of freedom. I'm greatly relieved. Believe me."[80] Yet, as Fabre observes, this new sense of freedom cost him the former security he had enjoyed as a Party member: "Not only was Wright without allies in his fight against racial attacks, he had now to protect himself against his former friends" (*Unfinished Quest*, 256).

Once Wright's attack on the Communist Party went public with the *Atlantic* articles, the Party's response was predictable. James W. Ford spoke for the Party in the *Daily Worker* when he charged that the articles were not only "a conglomeration of anti-Communism and anti-Semitism," but were "disgusting and damaging to [Negroes'] dignity." Wright's self-centered aloofness, Ford continues, prevented him from understanding how the Party "afforded him a broad platform to reach masses of people" by involving him in their everyday problems (as his *Daily Worker* assignments had done). Samuel Sillen, writing in *New Masses*, charged Wright with embracing "defeatism," exalting "blindness," and abandoning not merely the communists but "the larger progressive movements . . ."[81] When *Black Boy* appeared in 1945, even though the narrative stops before Wright's involvement with the Left, Party critics continued to attack him, signaling their future responses to his work. Isador Schneider, while praising Wright's insight into the "neurotic behavior patterns" produced by racism, criticized the book as a distorted "picture of the Negro people" and "an almost unbroken record of hostility, cruelty, alienation, guilt sense, and violence." These qualities, Schneider continues, particularly Wright's sense of isolation, inform "the squalid close" of his relations with the Communist Party, which Wright published elsewhere, "as it renders his own self-justifications [in those articles] more specious and contradictory than was apparent at the time."[82]

In other reviews, the standard clichés the Party reserved for the excommunicated recurred: "counter-revolutionary perspective of a renegade," "intense confusionism" (Fabre, *Unfinished Quest*, 279). When, in a 1946 article in *New Masses*, Albert Maltz dared to praise Wright's artistry in *Black Boy* and refused to predict his future decline, *New Masses* ran several stinging rebuttals by such prominent comrades as Howard Fast, Joe North, Alvah Bessie, and John Howard Lawson to set Maltz straight. Maltz was forced to admit that his article was "one-sided [and] non-dialectical" and thence relegated Wright to the "pervert[ed]" talents and "tools and agents of reaction," a circle of hell he shared with Steinbeck, Dos Passos, James T. Farrell, and Kenneth Fearing.[83]

By now, however, the baying of the Party's critics must have seemed to Wright the way Hemingway described hearing his own leftist critics crying like coyotes in the mid-1930s (though without Hemingway's self-satisfied smugness).Wright was moving on, geographically and creatively. He and his spouse, Ellen, having spent half a year in France in 1946 and receiving a warm welcome from French writers and intellectuals, permanently moved there in 1947. Philosophically and in his fiction, he had already gravitated towards a kind of asocial, existential perspective, visible as early as Bigger Thomas's self-creation and more sharply delineated in his unfinished novel "The Man Who Lived Underground." Upon meeting Sartre, Camus, and others, Wright's existential predisposition solidified into a carefully thought out philosophy, which thoroughly informed his next major novel, *The Outsider* (1953). At the same time, however, although he wanted nothing further to do with the Communist Party, he did not abandon his political efforts for racial advancement, only now he broadened his focus beyond America to include the Third World. To explore these new themes and political perspectives goes beyond the confines of this study. But in examining Wright's tortuous relationship with the Communist Party, one last literary encounter must be considered: how he depicts Party members in *The Outsider*.

One Last Shot

Having shed his former identity in Chicago, Cross Damon, the protagonist of *The Outsider*, must now determine an entirely new one in New York. Wright makes clear that Damon's quest is existential ("his decisive life struggle was a personal fight for the realization of himself") and not even affected by his being black ("emotionally he was not of them" [195]). But Damon does consider communism as a possible belief system: "his attitude [toward it] was ambivalent; he found as much in it to hate as to admire. He knew the imperialistic wars of the Western World far too well to be snared into believing that Stalin was the historical essence of the Satanic" (196–97). Communist ideology was still useful in interpreting "the processes of modern industrial society" and in showing that "one form of social consciousness, designated as bourgeois, had been outlived . . ." But its crippling weaknesses for Damon were decisive:

> [H]e emphatically spurned the slavish class consciousness with which the Communists sought to replace [bourgeois social consciousness]. Above all he loathed the Communist attempt to destroy human subjectivity; for him, his subjectivity was the essence of his life, and for him to deny it was as impossible as it would have been for him to deny himself the right to live. (197)

If Damon speaks for Wright in this passage—and I think that he unquestionably does—several aspects of it are revealing. First, "imperialistic wars" shows that even as Wright rejected communism, he had not fully abandoned either its rhetoric or analysis of the capitalistic West. Yet, the Party's insistence on "slavish" conformity of thought and its denial of "human subjectivity" were the overriding factors for Wright/Damon. Although this passage prepares us for Damon's dramatic encounters with the communist characters, Gil Blount and Jack Hilton, soon to follow, its abrupt appearance here with no preparation makes it seem that adherence to or rejection of communism was still an issue Wright felt he had to explain.

The scenes with Blount and Hilton dramatize precisely the shortcomings of communism discussed in the quotation above and add a few more. Words describing Blount repeatedly emphasize his coldness, rigidity, arrogance, and complete lack of pity for the suffering of an underling, Bob, and later for Blount's wife, Eva. Blount boasts to Damon, "We Communists do not admit any subjectivity in human life," a statement Damon describes as "horrible" (235–37). The characterization of Hilton is, if anything, a more extreme example of the same inhumanity, adding the asceticism and strained intensity of an El Grecoesque fanatic: "The face was emaciated . . . hands . . . clasped tightly in front of him, as though his strained nerves had to have something to hold onto . . ." (246). When Bob, the naïve recent convert, protests the Party's edict that he cease organizing his union, Hilton's replies are virtual clichés of Party doctrine:

> You don't discuss decisions of the Party. You *obey* them.
>
> The Party is not obliged to justify its decisions to you or anybody.
>
> You are an instrument of the Party. You exist to execute the Party's will.
>
> [B]eing a communist . . . means negating yourself, blotting out your personal life and listening only to the voice of the Party. The Party wants you to *obey*! (245–48, author's emphasis)

Still defiant, Bob threatens to continue organizing, impelling Hilton to preview his grim future: "You can be expelled. . . . And the Party will blacklist you throughout the labor movement. The Party will kill you. You can't *fight* the Party. *Understand* that?" (247, author's emphasis).

The entire scene, which Damon is implausibly permitted to witness, recalls the scene Wright was required to witness in "I Tried": the one-sided trial and formal expulsion of Ross. But where Wright's persona in the articles was closer to Bob's in the novel—the naïve recent convert having trouble with the Party—Damon's response to Bob's takedown places him closer to Blount and Hilton: "This man [Blount] thinks he is cold; well I'm just as cold as he is . . . Maybe more . . . He is trying to use me, but I'll make *use* of his trying to use me" (242). And in fact, Damon's only reason for associating with the Communists is to gain temporary cover while he "reforge[s] himself anew" (254). Damon's coldness regarding the communists, however, is not limited to expediency. When he is first repelled by Gil Blount's manner, he thinks, "How easily he could kill Gil with no regret" (240). Later, after Damon reads in Eva's diary of how Blount has made her suffer, Damon is ready to act on his murderous desire.

The scene in which Damon murders both Herndon, the racist and fascist, and Blount clearly symbolizes Wright's rejection of both fascism and communism as equally totalitarian, equally repressive, equally destructive of the human spirit. Ironically, however, Damon is imbued with this same inhumanity in murdering these oppressors without qualm or hesitation, just as he earlier murdered Joe to remain anonymous. Killing Hilton next becomes easy and inevitable. The dual motives—Damon learning that the communists drove Bob to his death by betraying his illegal immigrant status, and Hilton's discovery of Damon's link to the double murder—are convenient. But the more compelling reason is "Hilton's assumption that he could have made a slave of him [Damon]" (409). Significantly, before he is shot, Hilton reveals his secret nihilism: "You're groping for some overall concept with which to tie all life together. There is none . . ." (401). Power and control, not ideology, are the common denominators driving human behavior.

In depicting the novel's most important communist characters as inhuman automatons and in giving the reader the queasy satisfaction of seeing them murdered, Wright leaves little doubt about his feelings about the Party nine years after he publicly separated from it. In retrospect, the separation resembles a bad divorce with bitter recriminations on all sides. What stands out especially, however, is that so long after that divorce, Wright still felt the need to take one last shot at the Party—as if, for all his declarations in *The Outsider* about the self-created individual, he couldn't quite shake the hold his involvement with the Communist Party exerted on his mind.

Conclusion

ONE TRUISM THAT emerges from the journeys of these three writers toward and away from the Left is the tenuousness of a political allegiance created by a single issue or a few such issues, rather than by a compelling ideological belief, in this case in communist theory and doctrine. Should these binding issues become moot for some reason, the resulting political commitment itself is undermined and may easily dissolve. Such was the case with the three authors of this study. For Hemingway, the issue that drew him to the far left was defeating the fascists in the Spanish Civil War. Wright's allegiance to the CP-USA was many-sided, but essentially it depended on the party's ideological and practical support of African-American causes and opposition to racism. When these ties were severed—the Spanish War lost, discrimination against American blacks ignored by the party in 1941/42—each writer was cut adrift from his previous political commitment. Hemingway no longer needed to defend Stalinist methods in Spain or to ignore repugnant truths about the Loyalist cause. Wright no longer had to tolerate the mounting aggravations the party caused him. Steinbeck's case is somewhat different in that the single issue that had politicized him intensively, the plight of the migrants, had not gone away in 1939/40. But Steinbeck had, physically and psychologically. After the hullabaloo over *The Grapes of Wrath*, he was simply no longer able to commit himself to any political issue for many months.

Of course, as shown in chapter 8, the factors affecting these leftist commitments and disaffiliations were more complex than a single

309

issue for each author. Hemingway and Wright once had careerist motives for moving left, but both authors had achieved those aims by the late 1930s. Hemingway was the Left's fair-haired boy by the summer of 1937 and had largely won over leftist critics. Wright had achieved artistic success in 1938 and no longer needed the Party's literary venues and encouragement. Each might have abandoned the Left then had not more compelling issues—Spain for Hemingway and the plight of African-Americans for Wright—continued their political involvement.

Analogously, the authors also had other reasons for separating from the Left. Hemingway and Wright both felt increasingly harassed by the Communist Party as the 1940s began. Hemingway resented the Party's ideological attacks on his novel and his presence in Spain. As a Party member, Wright had to abide a host of irritants: the Party's mostly negative criticism of *Native Son*; its rigid insistence on conformity to its literary priorities, such as avoiding negro nationalism; and its demands on his time. He resented even more the Party's blithe assumption that he would reverse his political position whenever it ordered him to, regardless of the embarrassment it caused him. Steinbeck, too, felt harassed, not by the Party but by the attacks of conservative critics and the incessant demands for his time, money, and support of good and not-so-good causes.

Finally, the Soviet Union's treacherous actions in 1939—signing the Non-Aggression Pact with Nazi Germany that facilitated the German invasion of Poland, occupying the eastern half of Poland and the Baltic countries, and especially invading Finland—alienated Hemingway and particularly Steinbeck from any further sympathy with the Communist Party. Wright, the good soldier, obeyed and supported the Party line from August 1939 through June 1941, which viewed World War II as a capitalist war, regarding which progressives and non-belligerents like the United States should remain neutral. It was only when the Party reversed this political position after the Nazi invasion of Russia and humiliated Wright by forcing him to pull his antiwar speech at the last minute that helped decide him against any further obedience.

This last alienating factor of Russia's behavior at the end of the 1930s, as well as the Party's abrupt reversals of doctrine to justify this behavior, situate the responses of these three authors within the larger leftist milieu. The Nazi-Soviet Non-Aggression Pact, for example, abruptly reversed five years of Popular Front ideology, in which Russia proclaimed itself the bulwark against rising fascism. In the mid-1930s, in response to Soviet appeals for a Popular Front, increasing numbers of writers, artists, and intellectuals, deeply concerned about the rise and expansion of Nazism and fascism, had gravitated toward the Communist Party, some joining, many others becoming fellow travelers. This was the "single issue" appeal of the Left writ large, and it continued through the latter half of the 1930s. It motivated many, like Hemingway, to see the Civil War in Spain as the practical test of the Popular Front's will to fight fascism and to serve the Loyalist cause however supporters could: carrying a rifle, driving an ambulance, reporting on the Loyalist side, donating money. Given the idealism imbuing this anti-fascist cause, it is hardly surprising that the newer adherents to the Left would view the Soviet Union's pact with Hitler as not merely a reversal, but a betrayal of everything Russia had pretended to be previously. As Richard Pells observes, the Pact "destroyed the remaining moral and ideological foundations of their world . . . [and] would stand as a mockery to the fragile hopes and assumptions of the 1930s."[1] The Party's lame arguments supporting the Pact only added insult to injury. As Alfred Kazin recalled, "Day after day I followed the *Daily Worker* with savage joy at its confusion as [it] . . . now tried to explain the secret contribution that the noble Stalin, the great Stalin, the all-wise and farseeing Stalin, had made to the cause of world peace."[2] Further disillusions—the Soviet occupation of eastern Poland and the Baltic countries and its war against Finland—followed in short order.

As the single issue linking thousands to the Party was undermined, so disaffiliations followed. Many leftists turned in their membership cards to the CP-USA, literally and figuratively, at the turn of the decade. Among the prominent writers who declared their separation from either the CP-USA or the League of American Writers after the Nazi-Soviet Pact were Granville Hicks, Kenneth Fearing, Malcolm Cowley, Thomas Mann, Van Wyck Brooks, Archibald MacLeish, Lewis Mumford, Heywood Broun, Lewis Gannett, Max Lerner, and Matthew Josephson.[3]

To be sure, disaffection from the CP-USA and the Soviets was a more complex process than presented here. Some, like Edmund Wilson, began to disaffiliate as a result of the Moscow Trials in the mid-1930s. *Partisan Review* re-emerged at this time as a prominent anti-Stalinist leftist magazine. The Stalinists' repressive manipulation of the Spanish Republic alienated others, like John Dos Passos and George Orwell. For many Soviet supporters, however, these earlier disillusionments acted more as dissonance that sorely tried but did not destroy their faith. It took the Nazi-Soviet Pact and Russia's subsequent treacheries to do that.

Dissonance, unresolved tensions, and especially contradictions—the consequences of a fraught single-issue belief in Leftism—also permeate the major novels examined in this study. But each novel expresses these contradictions, and the author's sense of them, differently. In *The Grapes of Wrath*, Steinbeck seemed largely unaware of the contradiction between the individualism that marked the migrants' history and future aims—individualism that Steinbeck deeply admired—and the collectivism he felt was necessary for them to overcome the power of the big landowners' conglomerate. *Native Son* presented the two sides of its contradiction—existential self-realization through killing and ideological self-realization through communism—as a kind of competition for Bigger Thomas's soul. Obviously, this competition was partly autobiographical, reflecting Wright's creative need to express an extreme example of his people's suffering under racism and his (Wright's) belief in communism's potential to alleviate that suffering. In the novel, particularly in book 3, he seems to want it both ways. But despite his best intentions of sympathetically presenting the novel's communists, particularly Bigger's attorney Boris Max, it is existential self-creation that finally wins and which, it could be argued, represented the more profound value for Wright in the last years of the decade. Of the three authors, Hemingway was the most fully aware of the contradictions he wrote into *For Whom the Bell Tolls*, for he makes them an authorial strategy, using Robert Jordan as an alter ego who experiences, without resolving, the same tensions Hemingway did. Only now, Hemingway can reveal them, where before, in his journalism, and partially in his play and short fiction, he repressed and denied them.

Certainly, the single-issue tie to the Left did not apply to those holding a strong ideological belief in Marxism, a faith which typically predated the Popular Front. For these true believers, separation from the Left, if it occurred at all, was not nearly so abrupt and dramatic as described above, since deep convictions in the rightness of a doctrine can survive particular disillusionments. And for some believers, like Richard Wright, the Party's explanations of the Nazi-Soviet Pact and Russia's pose as the new champion of peace and anti-imperialism were sufficient justifications to remain in the fold—for the time being. Several prominent writers stayed in or close to the Communist Party following the Pact, such as Dashiell Hammett, Theodore Dreiser, Ben Hecht, Lillian Hellman, Dalton Trumbo, and, of course, Mike Gold.

The three authors examined in this study, however, had all cut their ties to the Left by 1941 or 1942 at the latest. Hemingway, Steinbeck, and eventually Wright experienced the same disillusionment described above with the Communist Party's policies and actions; only its specific sources varied with each author. For Hemingway, it was primarily the murderous repression and lies of the Russian controllers and counterintelligence in Spain, which he described to his editor as early as 1938 as "a carnival of treachery and rotten-ness" (*Selected Letters*, 474). For Steinbeck, the new world war created by Germany's invasion of Poland (and by French and British appeasement) and followed shortly by Russia's invasion of Finland seemed to undermine the efficacy of working for any particular cause. In this worldwide pathology, only the studies of scientists removed from the melee (for a time, even Steinbeck himself) seemed meaningful in the long term. And for Wright, the Party that had once given him his start as a writer through its Chicago John Reed Club and offered hope for his people now lost both of these appeals by 1941. He had achieved literary success on his own, and the Party seemed to turn its back on the welfare of African-Americans when it refused to support the black-organized march on Washington planned for July 1941 and further refused to fight discrimination in the war industries and segregation in the U.S. military. Once the Party decided that these actions would interfere with its new goal of encouraging total mobilization of the U.S. arms industries so as to aid the Soviet Union and Britain, a disillusioned Wright quietly cut his ties to the Party.

Like so many others who became politically involved in the thirties, Steinbeck, Wright, and Hemingway had to move on in the 1940s without the comforts—and complications—of a leftist political cause or organization.

Notes

Introduction

1. No Pulitzer or National Book Award for fiction was awarded in 1941, despite the importance of *Native Son* and *For Whom the Bell Tolls*. Two of the films made from these novels—*The Grapes of Wrath* (1940) and *For Whom the Bell Tolls* (1942)—received excellent big-budget productions and won several Academy Awards. The stage version of *Native Son*, scripted by Wright and Paul Green and directed by Orson Welles, opened in 1941; the novel wasn't filmed until 1951 in Argentina, and was dubbed into English.

2. As applied to the 1930s, the terms "leftist," "leftism" and "the Left," though nebulous, refer to ideologies beyond liberalism, residing at the far end of the political continuum. These positions range from belief in (or sympathy for) communism and a concomitant desire for the abolition of capitalism to a desire for radical political and economic reform within the existing system, such as redistribution of wealth, collectivism, empowerment of the working class, and strong anti-fascism.

3. Hemingway's political encounters while a foreign correspondent in the early 1920s did not affect his fundamentally apolitical attitudes in the later 1920s and early 1930s, except to encourage a preference for democracy over fascism.

4. The John Reed Clubs were created by the CP-USA in late 1929 for young writers and artists to meet and discuss their work in a Marxist milieu. The clubs published their own leftist magazines, which gave fledgling writers like Richard Wright the chance to see their work in print. Chapter 2 discusses the clubs and their successors, the American Writers' Congress and the League of American Writers, in more detail.

5. Folsom, *Days of Anger, Days of Hope*, passim.

6. See Cowley, *Dream of the Golden Mountains*, chaps. 2–5.

7. In the United States, 418 writers responded to a survey about the Spanish Civil War sent by the League of American Writers. Of those, 410 supported the Loyalists; seven were neutral; one supported the fascists (Folsom, *Days of Anger, Days of Hope*, 30–31). The league published selected responses in a pamphlet entitled *Writers Take Sides: Letters about the War in Spain from 418 American Authors.*

8. Steinbeck, "The Harvest Gypsies," *San Francisco News* (Oct. 1936); *Writers Take Sides*, quoted in DeMott, Introduction to *Working Days*, liv n12.

9. Wright, "How 'Bigger' Was Born" (supplement to *Native Son*, restored text), 446–47.

10. See, for example, the petition battle of 1939 between "The Committee for Cultural Freedom" and "The League for Cultural Freedom and Socialism" and "The Committee of 400" and how this welter of committees and petitions befuddled the poet William Carlos Williams (Cohen, *Beleaguered Poets and Leftist Critics*, 221–23).

11. In Auden's poem "September 1, 1939."

Chapter 1

1. Wald, "Steinbeck and the Proletarian Novel," 673, 683n. Wald claims that Steinbeck "moved far leftward after 1932"—though much evidence contradicts this early date (Review of *A Political Companion*, 1–4).

2. Benson, "Through a Political Glass Darkly" (hereafter "Political Glass"), 48; Benson, *Steinbeck, Writer*, 371.

3. Shillinglaw, *On Reading* The Grapes of Wrath, 103.

4. Formed in 1934, the Associated Farmers, Inc. operated in forty-two counties in California and controlled "more than half of California's agricultural output" (Helen Hosmer, quoted in Shillinglaw, *On Reading* The Grapes of Wrath, 85). The group included bankers (especially from Bank of America, a huge landowner) and corporation executives, and it "controlled Chambers of Commerce across the state."

5. Journalist Anna Louise Strong was a strong supporter of unions and the Soviet Union. Mike Gold, founding editor of the influential *New Masses* (the CP-USA's literary magazine) since 1926, was probably the most outspoken and best-known American exponent of communism in these years.

6. Shillinglaw, *On Reading* The Grapes of Wrath, 103.

7. Compare the view of another Steinbeck biographer, Jay Parini, that "Steinbeck became more and more involved with the situation of laborers and migrant workers in the Monterey areas now, conscience-stricken by the injustice that was everywhere apparent" (*Steinbeck*, 151).

8. Carol soon grew skeptical of Ricketts's influence. Parini notes that "[s]he often complained that her husband had fallen 'too much under the sway of Ed Ricketts' and his friends; indeed, she felt he was 'too

impressionable in general . . .'" (*Steinbeck*, 171). This alleged impressionability, however, does not square with Steinbeck's apparent detachment from Lincoln Steffens and the young leftists around him.

9. Steinbeck, "About Ed Ricketts," 256.

10. *Steinbeck: A Life in Letters*, 75, emphasis added.

11. Benson, "Through a Political Glass Darkly," 48.

12. Steinbeck linked the unresolved ending to his interest in the larger rhythms of human action: "There is a cycle in the life of a man but there is no ending in the life of Man. I tried to show this by stopping on a high point, leaving out any conclusion" (*Life in Letters*, 99).

13. Parini, *Steinbeck*, 151. Parini's view (166–67) that "[t]he reader's sympathies inevitably lie with the poor strikers, the apple pickers, who are ruthlessly mistreated by everyone" is also questionable. They are mistreated, yes, but Steinbeck's many animalistic depictions of them make them less than sympathetic. Alan Wald, too, assumes that Steinbeck's socio-biological philosophy "prepared [him] for sympathy with the struggle of agrarian workers" ("Steinbeck and the Proletarian Novel," 673).

14. Parini, *Steinbeck*, 163; Marsh, "*In Dubious Battle* and Other Recent Works of Fiction."

15. Parini, *Steinbeck*, 154.

16. McCarthy, "Minority Report," 326–27. Cf., Wald's claim that [t]he reviews [of *In Dubious Battle*] take for granted that Steinbeck is in complete sympathy with the cause of the landless migrants [*sic*]" ("Steinbeck and the Proletarian Novel," 678).

17. Windschuttle, "Steinbeck's Myth of the Okies."

18. Letter to Mavis McIntosh, 2 April 1935, quoted in Parini, *Steinbeck*, 153–54.

19. Though Steinbeck has been accused of inflating the number of migrants coming to California (Windschuttle, "Steinbeck's Myth of the Okies"), historians generally estimate the total number in the hundreds of thousands (Gregory, *American Exodus*, 12). Parini writes, "In 1936 alone almost ninety thousand Okies crossed the California border . . ." (*Steinbeck*, 175).

20. Gregory, *American Exodus*, 15.

21. According to Carey McWilliams, one of the first to analyze the change in farm labor, by 1937 "the bulk of the state's migratory workers were white Americans" (*Factories in the Field*, 305). Regarding the racist implications of Steinbeck's interest in white migrants, see the "Harvest Gypsies" section, p. 34.

22. Parini (*Steinbeck*, 174) offers a different explanation: novelty ("Steinbeck always liked moving on to another project, especially one that would offer him a new kind of experience." Steinbeck's erratic actions after publishing *The Grapes of Wrath* (discussed in chapter 8) lend credence to this view.

23. At the time of Steinbeck's research in 1936, the Resettlement Administration had constructed two "sanitary camps" at Marysville and Arvin ("Weedpatch"). The Arvin camp originally accommodated ninety-six families but was doubled in size (Loftis, "Steinbeck and the Federal Migrant Camps," 79, 86). In "The Harvest Gypsies," Steinbeck claimed it held two hundred families. By October 1938, when *Grapes* was finished, nine camps were operating, housing about two hundred families each (Shillinglaw, *On Reading* The Grapes of Wrath, 172). By 1940, fifteen camps were completed or under construction (Benson, "'To Tom,'" 163).

24. As Walter J. Stein observes, however, the "early spurt of participatory democracy [in these camps] was more apparent than real" and tended to fade in a few years (*California and the Dust Bowl Migration*, 176).

25. Shillinglaw, *On Reading* The Grapes of Wrath, 124.

26. Parini, *Steinbeck*, 174–75.

27. Note the plural "trips." Steinbeck returned to the valley in late September, revisited Weedpatch, and returned through Salinas to observe developments of the lettuce strike there (Benson, *Steinbeck, Writer*, 348).

28. Benson notes that Steinbeck enclosed a small check for the migrants at Collins's camp and promised to raise money from charitable organizations for books for the migrant children at the camp (Benson, *Steinbeck, Writer*, 347).

29. *San Francisco News*, 5–12 Oct. 1936; a few of these articles (the second, third, fourth, and fifth) were titled "California's Harvest Gypsies." They were reprinted as *The Harvest Gypsies: On the Road to The Grapes of Wrath*; quotations below refer to this edition. The articles were also reprinted with an epilogue (published separately as "Starvation Under the Orange Trees") in 1938 by the Simon J. Lubin Society of California under the title *Their Blood Is Strong*. Steinbeck also wrote a shorter, more general article—"Dubious Battle in California"—for *The Nation*, 12 Sept. 1936, 302–4.

30. Parini writes, "Like so many writers of this era, he considered it part of a writer's responsibility to bear witness, to address a social crisis with the hope of effecting some kind of change" (*Steinbeck*, 177). That hope often led writers to abandon a strictly neutral, or objective, stance. As William Stott points out, documentary reportage, although it employs facts, statistics, and often first-person reporting, is far more exhortative than objective (ibid., 25–26). In reporting on "conditions" around the country, documentary reportage counteracted the tendency of newspapers to suppress bad news during the Depression. Steinbeck, too, felt that the major California papers weren't sufficiently covering the migrant problem.

31. Benson, "To Tom," 181. Parini similarly describes Steinbeck's approach as "judicious and balanced, though a polemical tone underlies it. Steinbeck's compassion was obvious throughout and he made no bones about demanding justice" (*Steinbeck*, 181).

32. In asserting Steinbeck's factual errors about the migrants in *The Grapes of Wrath*, Windschuttle states that "California . . . had a much more generous unemployment relief system: $40 a month for a family of four, . . . [compared to $10 to $12 a month average in the southwest.] . . . . [This relief] allowed [agricultural workers] to drop their nomad status and settle with their children in one place . . ." Apparently, Windschuttle doesn't credit what Steinbeck saw with his own eyes—and what was confirmed in numerous other first-person observations by Collins and others—that the farmer-migrants were not allowed to "settle," were intentionally kept moving, so as to be ineligible for unemployment benefits, relief, medical assistance, and education for their children.

33. Wollenberg, Introduction to *Harvest Gypsies*, xi–xii; Godfrey, "'They Ain't Human,'" 107–34; Hearle, "These Are American People," 243–54.

34. The photo of Thompson with two of her children, however, was not the version that *Life* magazine would make iconic. Lange's photos accompanied all but the last of the articles and were often grouped as contrasts. For articles four and five (the former discussing the government camps), Lange contrasted squalid roadside camps with neat, orderly structures of the government camps. The caption to the photos for article four reads, "The old and the new—how California's migratory farm workers lived and still live and how the Federal Government has reclaimed some for civilization with its two camps."

35. Quoted in Wartzman, *Obscene*, 98–99, 91.

36. Parini, *Steinbeck*, 181.

37. Ibid., 178. Letter ca. August 1936.

38. October 1936, quoted in Benson, "To Tom," 180. In another undated letter to Otis, Steinbeck described the impending explosion as a "civil war" in the making (quoted in Shillinglaw, *On Reading* The Grapes of Wrath, 100).

39. *Writers Take Sides*, quoted in DeMott, Introduction to *Working Days*, liv n12.

40. According to Shillinglaw (*On Reading* The Grapes of Wrath, 51), "Carol Steinbeck said later that her husband fell in love with the Okies and that it was love, and not a burning social conscience, that propelled him through three years of research and composition." While writing *Grapes*, Steinbeck wrote in his *Journal* (entry # 28): "To love and admire the people who are so much stronger and purer and braver than I am."

41. Parini, *Steinbeck*, 171.

42. This dream strikingly anticipates the Joads' dream in *The Grapes of Wrath* of owning the little white cottage amid the fruit orchards.

43. French, "First Theatrical Production of Steinbeck's *Of Mice and Men*."

44. Parini, *Steinbeck*, 188.

45. Shillinglaw, *On Reading* The Grapes of Wrath, 105; Wald, Review of *A Political Companion*, 1; Parini, *Steinbeck*, 190, 191.

46. Quoted in DeMott, Introduction to *Working Days*, xxxvi.

47. Quoted and paraphrased in Walther, "Oklahomans Steinbeck's Theme."

48. DeMott, Introduction to *Working Days*, liv, n11.

49. Steinbeck was not exaggerating. In the larger San Joaquin Valley, according to McWilliams, "over 50,000 workers [were] destitute and starving" (*Factories in the Field*, 315).

50. Shillinglaw, *On Reading* The Grapes of Wrath, 60.

51. *Life* never printed the article because Steinbeck refused to soften his angry prose and withdrew the article. It did print the Visalia photos taken by Horace Bristol later, when *The Grapes of Wrath* became a best-seller, and again when the film version of the novel came out in 1940 (Benson, *Steinbeck, Writer*, 371; Benson, "To Tom," 185).

52. Unpublished autobiographical novel, quoted in Benson, *Steinbeck, Writer*, 369–70.

53. Letter to John Barry, 30 June 1938. Steinbeck refused to participate in this forum and ridiculed its façade of non-partisanship (*Working Days*, 151–52, entry #36 n).

54. "Starvation Under the Orange Trees," reprinted as "Epilogue: Spring 1938," in *Their Blood Is Strong*, 33.

55. Benson, *Steinbeck, Writer*, 372. About this time, Steinbeck enlisted a new ally, Pare Lorentz, the creator of the powerful documentary *The Plow That Broke the Plains*. According to Parini, Lorentz "wrote to several editors whom he knew about [the Visalia articles'] value. But the articles were turned down everywhere; the material was just too threatening" (*Steinbeck*, 201).

56. Shillinglaw, *On Reading* The Grapes of Wrath, 61.

57. Actually, both designations—landowner and sharecropper—were atypical. As Gregory notes, in the Plains states, tenant farming was far more common than sharecropping. In *The Grapes of Wrath*, Steinbeck changed "sharecropper" to the more accurate "tenant farmers."

58. Scholars disagree on precisely when Steinbeck began "L'Affaire Lettuceberg." Benson states that it was in late fall, 1936 (*Steinbeck, Writer*, 348). Parini (*Steinbeck*, 201) and DeMott (*Working Days*, xxxvii) place it in the spring of 1938, just before Steinbeck started writing *The Grapes of Wrath*. His letter about it to Annie Laurie Williams (May 1938) shows he was working on it then; but he may have begun this satire of Salinas residents after he returned from Salinas in 1936 and then put it aside. Early in 1937, Steinbeck refers to his "new book" having struck a snag, but he doesn't identify the book (letter to Elizabeth Otis, *Life in Letters*, 134).

59. Letter to Annie Laurie Williams, May 1938, quoted in DeMott, Introduction to *Working Days*, xxxix.

60. Letter Elizabeth Otis, ca. mid-May 1938, quoted in ibid., lv n14.

61. Shillinglaw, *On Reading* The Grapes of Wrath, 61.

62. Steinbeck cautioned Tom Collins likewise: "My old feud with the ass[ociated] farmers is stirring again and I don't want my movements traced" (Benson, *Steinbeck, Writer*, 369). Benson writes, "He was particularly worried about a conspiracy designed [by the Associated Farmers] to discredit him."

63. Steinbeck writes Elizabeth Otis, "I like it because it is a march and this book is a kind of march—because it is in our own revolutionary tradition and because in reference to this book it has a larger meaning" (10 Sept. 1938, *Life in Letters*, 171).

Chapter 2

1. Originally, Wright's account of his experiences with the CP-USA was to be part of the Chicago section ("The Horror and the Glory") of his autobiography titled *American Hunger*. Wright deleted this section from the published autobiography, *Black Boy* (see note 3 below), but published the parts of it dealing with the Communist Party in two consecutive issues of *Atlantic Monthly*, August and September 1944, under the rather sensational title, "I Tried to Be a Communist." These articles were republished in the 1949 book, *The God that Failed* (edited by Richard H. Crossman), a collection of disillusioned narratives of former Communists. Arnold Rampersad ("Notes," *Richard Wright: Later Works*, 869) notes two other articles containing material from the Chicago section: "American Hunger," *Mademoiselle* (Sept. 1945) and "Early Days in Chicago," *Cross Section* (1944).

2. Wright recalls being told, when he proposed resigning, "No one can resign from the Communist Party" ("I Tried," pt. 2, 51). In his novel *The Outsider* (1953), he includes a similar scene.

3. An interesting question is why he originally stopped his biography and experience with the CP-USA with the Chicago years. According to Michel Fabre (*Unfinished Quest*, 254), Wright's editor at Harper's, Edward Aswell, in advising that the Chicago section be deleted from the autobiography, felt it should be published as a separate volume of autobiography which included the New York years. Wright's response to Aswell's suggestion is not known.

4. Fabre, while noting that Wright "often combined several episodes into one for effect," nevertheless feels that Wright "was faithful to the psychological truth of what happened" (*Unfinished Quest*, 137).

5. For a complete list of Wright's published Chicago poems, see Fabre, *Unfinished Quest*, 625–26. Appendix B of Fabre, *World of Richard Wright* reprints the poems. My count excludes an untitled, unpublished poem from the period (see Webb, 357).

6. Wright, "I Tried" pt. 1, 62, 63. Wright, in fact, refers to his poetry as "crude" three times in two pages (once quoting *Left Front*'s editor); Kinnamon, "Wright: Proletarian Poet," 243.

7. Kinnamon, "Wright: Proletarian Poet," 246.

8. Kinnamon, *Emergence*, 53.

9. Wright later recognized political motives for his election, namely the feuding between the club's artists and writers, each side feeling it benefitted from Wright's election ("I Tried," pt. 1, 63). But considering the ambitious program he instituted once he was elected, the members probably sensed and wanted his vitality to rejuvenate the club in addition to pursuing their partisan motives.

10. Wright's recollection here is suspect. He appears to make his joining the CP-USA conditional on the Party accepting *his* policy—a highly unlikely occurrence from the Party's perspective. More likely, he stated his policy when asked to be executive secretary of the John Reed Club. Possibly, however, the two invitations occurred simultaneously.

11. Wright refers to other writers of the local club resisting the closing of *Left Front* ("I Tried," pt. 1, 63). Indeed, the New York City chapter of the John Reed Club refused to shut down its magazine, *Partisan Review*. The magazine continued publishing and eventually became an anti-Stalinist bastion and rival to the party-line *New Masses*.

12. Ellen Wright's recollection, quoted in Fabre, *Unfinished Quest*, 551n16. Fabre feels this discouragement did not take place until the early 1940s; but it was in the mid-1930s that Wright was trying to find a publisher for the novel.

13. In fairness to this unnamed director, Orson Welles practiced the same kind of conversion quite successfully for the Harlem branch of the FTP in his "Voodoo *Macbeth*" by setting Shakespeare's play in Haiti.

14. *Daily Worker*, 8 June 1937, in Wright, *Byline*, 237. Wright ignores earlier artistic and discussion groups, such as those occurring during the Harlem Renaissance or including W. E. B. Du Bois.

15. Wright later used parts of *Lawd Today!* in the first section of *The Outsider* (1953). The whole novel was published posthumously in 1963. From "Tarbaby's Dawn," which was based on Wright's life in the South, he drew a short story, "Almos' a Man," which later became the much-anthologized "The Man Who Was Almost a Man."

16. Wright, letter to his editor, 6 October 1959, quoted in Fabre, *Unfinished Quest*, 138.

17. Note the similarity of this optimistic belief—that political understanding by the oppressed inevitably dooms the oppressive society—to Steinbeck's famous passage in *The Grapes of Wrath*: "And always [the great owners] were in fear of a principal—three hundred thousand—. . . if they ever know themselves, the land will be theirs and all the gas, all the rifles in the world won't stop them" (238).

18. "Negro nationalism" was the Party's label for literature about blacks that was typically realistic but without any revolutionary implications. That is, it viewed them as a distinct group rather than as part of the oppressed working class.

19. See Burnshaw, "Wallace Stevens and the Statue," 24, 26. Hurston never forgave Wright for his blast and took revenge in her reviews of his books.

20. Richard Yarborough asserts that the *Story* award "marked a real turning point in Wright's career," Introduction to *Uncle Tom's Children*, xviii. Harper's first edition included "Big Boy Leaves Home," "Down By the Riverside," "Long Black Song," and "Fire and Cloud." The second edition added "Bright and Morning Star" and introduced the stories with "The Ethics of Living Jim Crow."

21. Yarborough, Introduction to *Uncle Tom's Children*, xxiii.

22. "My Day," *New York World-Telegram*, 1 April 1938, 25, quoted in Rowley, *Wright: Life and Times*, 142.

23. In *Black Boy*, Wright describes his early reading focusing on Dreiser, Crane, and Norris, in addition to Mencken, of course. His first novel, *Lawd Today!* is also written in a naturalistic style.

24. Interestingly, "Bright and Morning Star" was Wright's first published story in *New Masses* (10 May 1938), which hailed it "as the latest triumph of a great writer" (Fabre, *Unfinished Quest*, 164).

25. Even in "Fire and Cloud," the most ideological of the stories, race plays a major role, for not only is the protagonist black, but the savage beating he suffers from whites, which decides him on political action, results from racism. He is called "nigger," not "red" or "trouble-maker."

26. Yarborough, Introduction to *Uncle Tom's Children*, x.

27. Ibid.

28. *Book Union Bulletin*, April 1938, 2, quoted in Kinnamon, *Emergence*, 109.

29. "Hope, Despair, and Terror," *New York Harold Tribune Books*, 8 May 1838, 3, quoted in ibid., 111.

30. "Richard Wright's Prize Novellas," *New Masses*, 29 March 1938, 23, quoted in ibid., 110.

31. "Lynch Patterns," *Partisan Review* 4 (May 1938): 58, quoted in ibid., 111.

32. Cowley, "Long Black Song," *New Republic*, 6 Apr. 1938, 280; Poore, "Books of the Times," *New York Times*, 2 Apr. 1938, 13; Van Gelder, "Four Tragic Tales," *New York Times Book Review*, 3 Apr. 1938, 7, 16; Locke, "The Negro: 'New' or Newer—a Retrospective Review of the Literature of the Negro for 1938," *Opportunity* 17 (Jan. 1939): 8. All of these reviews are quoted in Kinnamon, *Emergence*, 111, 109–10. "A Garbage Can Book," *Jackson (MS) Daily News*, 26 Apr. 1938, 6.

33. Although Wright's position with the Harlem branch of the *Daily Worker* is frequently identified as "editor," it was essentially "staff reporter" (confirmed by Bryant, email to author).

34. Bryant, Introduction to Wright, *Byline*, ix; Rowley, *Wright: Life and Times*, 128.

35. "A.L.P. Assemblyman Urges State Control of Price of Milk," in Wright, *Byline*, 33–34.

36. "Bates Tells of Spain's Fight for Strong Republican Army," in ibid., 112–15.

37. "less than interested": letter of Herbert Caro to Wright, 16 Aug. 1937; "asked to produce": letter of Abe Aaron to Wright, 25 Aug. 1937. Both letters are quoted in ibid., xii.

38. Bryant, Introduction to Wright, *Byline*, x, xiii.

39. "High Tide in Harlem: Joe Louis as a Symbol of Freedom," in Wright, *Byline*, 157.

40. Rowley, *Wright: Life and Times*, 128.

41. Letter written 2 Nov. 1937, in ibid., 129.

42. Ibid., 128–29. Rowley also cites Wright's irreverent depiction of the *Daily Worker* as "Stalin's newspaper" (129, 540n10). But Wright made this remark "jokingly" in a newspaper interview in March 1940, when, with his novel *Native Son* just published, he felt far more independent of the Party.

43. *International Literature*, 7 (1938): 104, reprinted in Kinnamon, *Emergence*, 117n83. The Moscow Trials (1936–38) divided American leftists into pro- and anti-Stalinist factions. Such prominent writers as Nelson Algren, Jack Conroy, Dashiell Hammett, Lillian Hellman, Langston Hughes, Dorothy Parker, and Irwin Shaw also signed this pro-Stalinist statement, to their later embarrassment.

44. Davis, "Story of a Winner." Wright pours it on a bit thick here: he certainly did not need the Party to provide his "first full-bodied vision of Negro life in America."

45. Ellison, "Remembering Richard Wright," 666–67. When Ellison refers to the "Communist rank and file," one wonders if his focus has expanded (or blurred) somewhat from Wright's newspaper colleagues.

46. Rowley, *Wright: Life and Times*, 138.

47. Ibid., 158.

48. Ibid., 160.

Chapter 3

1. Hemingway did publish one book of short stories in this period— *Winner Take Nothing* (1933)—but, as noted below, the collection was not considered his strongest.

2. Letter to Max Perkins, 19 April 1936, in Hemingway and Perkins, *Only Thing That Counts*, 242–43.

3. Donaldson, "Last Great Cause" (hereafter "Cause"), 372.

4. Encountering migrants: letter to Mike Strater, 14 July 1932, paraphrased in Baker, *Ernest Hemingway: Life Story* (hereafter *Life Story*), 230. "Now they are all broke": letter to Guy Hickok, 14 October 1932, in Hemingway, *Selected Letters*, 373. Baker (*Life Story*, 230) notes that Hemingway "had already begun to construct a little myth about the extremity of his poverty during the early days in Paris."

5. Josephson, *Infidel in the Temple*, 428.

6. Unpublished letter, 19 April 1936, quoted in Reynolds, *Hemingway: The 1930s*, 225.

7. Kinnamon, "Hemingway and Politics," 159.

8. Hemingway may well have exaggerated his "disillusionmcnt" with post-World War I politics; the tone of many of his journalistic dispatches from Europe then was satiric rather than bitter or angry.

9. See Cohen, *Beleaguered Poets and Leftist Critics*, chap. 1.

10. "Brutality" and "sudden death": Fadiman, "Letter to Mr. Hemingway"; "isolatoes": letter from Charles Strauss, Sept. 1935, quoted in Baker, *Life Story*, 277; "lost generation": letters to Paul Romaine, 6 and 9 July 1932, in Hemingway, *Selected Letters*, 363–64, 365–66; "strike": Hicks, "Small Game Hunting."

11. Letter, 5 Feb. 1937, quoted and paraphrased in Shi, *Matthew Josephson*, 178.

12. Unpublished letter to Arnold Gingrich, 19 Apr. 1936, quoted and paraphrased in Reynolds, *Hemingway: 1930s*, 225.

13. Quoted and paraphrased in Baker, *Life Story*, 247. For Eastman's review, see below.

14. Quoted and paraphrased in ibid., 280.

15. Hicks, "Bulls and Bottles"; Cowley, "A Farewell to Spain."

16. Baker, *Life Story*, 234; Eastman, "Bull in the Afternoon." The review brought published protests from Archibald MacLeish and Hemingway himself, who later physically tussled with Eastman in Max Perkins's office.

17. Baker summarizes the reviews negatively: "[T]he new collection was otherwise held to be the poorest and least interesting that he had yet placed on view" (Baker, *Life Story*, 246).

18. Chamberlain, "Books of the Times."

19. Wilson, "Letter to the Russians about Hemingway," *New Republic*, 11 Dec. 1935, 135. Wilson also swipes at Hemingway's "rubbishy" articles in "the men's wear magazine, Esquire."

20. Hicks, "Small Game Hunting."

21. For example, because of the Popular Front against fascism, membership in the CP-USA reached a peak in 1935, and many writers and intellectuals who didn't join the party became sympathetic "fellow travelers."

22. Shi, *Matthew Josephson*, 178.

23. See Kennedy, *Dreams in the Mirror*, 360–61.

24. Dos Passos's two recent novels, *The 42nd Parallel* (1930) and *1919* (1932), made him the Left's premier writer in these years.

25. Hemingway, "Who Murdered the Vets?" *New Masses*, 17 Sept. 1935, 9–10, reprinted in *New Masses Anthology*, 181–87.

26. Donaldson, "Last Great Cause," 375.

27. Quoted in Solow, "Substitution, at Left Tackle," 62.

28. Schneider, "Fetish of Simplicity," 184–86.

29. Forsythe, "In This Corner, Mr. Hemingway," 26. Forsythe's snideness was a response to Hemingway's slams at leftist critics in his December 1935 *Esquire* article, "Old Newsman Writes" (quoted above).

30. Unpublished letter, 1927, quoted in Mellow, *Hemingway: A Life Without Consequences* (hereafter *A Life Without Consequences*), 474.

31. According to Baker, "He was quick to say privately that his willingness to write for the *New Masses* implied no change in his point of view towards those who ran it" (*Life Story*, 279).

32. Ibid., 615n.

33. Donaldson, "Last Great Cause," 376.

34. Hicks, "Small Game Hunting."

35. Mellow, *A Life Without Consequences*, 482. See also Donaldson's identical view ("Last Great Cause," 376). Mellow balances this claim by stating that "others were quick to condemn Hemingway for his tardy espousal of political causes" (482). But he does not document these condemnations.

36. Reynolds, *Hemingway: 1930s*, 211.

37. According to Ilya Ehrenburg (*Memoirs: 1921–1941*, 302), one of the organizers of the Congress.

38. Donaldson, "Last Great Cause," 378.

39. Unpublished letter quoted in Reynolds, *Hemingway: 1930s*, 225. In a letter to Max Perkins, 11 July 1936, Hemingway also refers to wanting to capture "the mechanics of revolution" (*Only Thing That Counts*, 243).

40. One exception is the short story "The Revolutionist" in *In Our Time*. But the story treats the title character as an ineffectual idealist who is continually arrested.

41. Morgan's justification for killing Sing—to prevent Sing from killing the other Chinese on board—is barely plausible. Among many other instances of Hemingway's obsession with violence in this novel is his presenting for the reader's delectation the sound of a machine-gun being fired against someone's head: "like hitting a pumpkin with a club" (172–73).

42. For Hemingway's vendetta against Harold Loeb, the model of Robert Cohen, see Baker, *Life Story*, 150–51, 154.

43. Cowley, "Hemingway: Work in Progress," 305–6; Kazin, "Hemingway's First Book on His Own People," 3, in *Critical Reception*, 179–80,

174–76; Rahv, "The Social Muse and the Great Kudu," 62, 63, 64. But Rahv also considers Harry's final realization "false and imposed" (63).

44. Baker, *Life Story*, 282.

45. Reynolds, *Hemingway: 1930s*, 269–70.

46. Although Hemingway claimed that he had "two chapters done on a novel" by late October 1938 (*Selected Letters*, 472), "he personally counted March 1, 1939 as [*For Whom the Bell Tolls'*] real beginning" (Baker, *Life Story*, 339)—after Barcelona had fallen to Franco.

47. Quoted in Vernon, *Hemingway's Second War*, 11.

48. According to Donaldson ("Last Great Cause," 380), he received $1,000 for each mailed article (up to 1,200 words) and $500 for each cabled dispatch, making him the highest paid war correspondent at the time.

49. Seldes's interpolation, quoted in Vernon, *Hemingway's Second War*, 13–14.

50. Ibid., 14; Herbst, *Starched Blue Sky*, 150.

51. Vernon, *Hemingway's Second War*, 13.

52. Ibid., 6.

53. Ibid., 10, 231n25.

54. Donaldson, "Last Great Cause," 379.

55. 5 Feb. 1937, Hemingway, *Selected Letters*, 456. Considering his future blowup with John Dos Passos, Hemingway's views here ironically anticipate Dos Passos's own in 1939: "[M]y sympathies . . . lie with the private in the front line against the brass hat; with the hodcarrier against the strawboss . . . ; with the laboratory worker against the stuffed shirt in a mortarboard; with the criminal against the cop" (Response to questionnaire, 27). Re: "shooting pigeons," see Hemingway's story "The Denunciation" (discussed below).

56. Wolfert, "Hemingway Off to Spain to Write About the War," 30, quoted in Watson, "Joris Ivens," 43.

57. Donaldson, "Last Great Cause," 380.

58. Hemingway's captions emphasize the brutality of modern war, which targeted civilians as well as soldiers. The captions also recognize Germany's and Italy's direct involvement in Spain (Watson, "Joris Ivens" 44).

59. Ibid., 42.

60. Shoots, *Living Dangerously*, 109. Though Ivens's wife characterized him as "a free-lance communist," Shoots states that "he remained absolutely faithful to the party, its organization and its political line."

61. Ibid., 110, 116.

62. Watson, "Joris Ivens," 40.

63. Koch, *Breaking Point*, 54–55, 61. Vernon, however, doubts that this courting of Hemingway was a Comintern scheme and sees it as "an opportunity seized rather than a job tasked" (*Hemingway's Second War*, 102).

64. Ivens, *The Camera and I*, 111.

65. Watson, "Joris Ivens," 44–45; Vernon, *Hemingway's Second War*, 107. Nevertheless, compared to Ivens's later memoirs and interviews with William Watson, *Camera* understates Ivens's efforts to cultivate Hemingway. For example, it omits the fact that the two met in Valencia (where Hemingway first arrived in Spain) and traveled together to Madrid.

66. Ivens, personal interview with William B. Watson, 26 June 1982, quoted in Watson, "Joris Ivens," 49.

67. Baker, *Life Story*, 307; Watson, "Joris Ivens," 39.

68. From Ivens's *Ou la mémoire*, quoted in Watson, "Joris Ivens," 50.

69. Moorehead, *Gellhorn*, 126.

70. Vernon, *Hemingway's Second War*, 26.

71. Letter to Bernard Berenson, 14 Oct. 1952, Hemingway, *Selected Letters*, 789.

72. Donaldson, "Last Great Cause," 393, 408, 393.

73. Koch, *Breaking Point*, 56.

74. Regler, *Owl of Minerva*, 292–93.

75. Koch, *Breaking Point*, 88–99.

76. Although Hemingway biographers tend to credit Sydney Franklin, Hemingway's factotum, with finding these scarce resources (for example driving a car loaded with food and liquor—and with Martha Gellhorn—from Valencia to Madrid), Franklin's scrounging was doubtless facilitated by the Republican government for the same reason they provided Hemingway with cars and gasoline unavailable to other correspondents.

77. Watson, "Joris Ivens," 52–53.

78. Ibid., 52.

79. Ivens, *The Camera and I*, 113; Watson, "Joris Ivens," 50.

80. Ibid., 49.

81. Ivens's letter to Hemingway, 26 Apr. 1937, paraphrased in Vernon, *Hemingway's Second War*, 97.

82. Romaine to Carlos Baker, unpublished letter, 4 Feb. 1963, quoted in Baker, *Life Story*, 314.

83. Donaldson, *Fitzgerald and Hemingway*, 211, 212.

84. McManus, "'The Spanish Earth' at the 55th St. Playhouse Is a Plea for Democracy"; McManus, "Realism Invades Gotham."

85. Watson, Introduction to "Hemingway's Spanish Civil War Dispatches" (hereafter "Dispatches"), 4. Quotations and paraphrases from the dispatches themselves will be cited as "Dispatches." Dates reflect composition, not publication.

86. White, Introduction to Hemingway, *By-Line*, 7.

87. Cowles, *Looking for Trouble*, 20.

88. Dispatch 8 (18–19 Apr. 1937, 30–33) is a rather touching description of Hemingway's visit to a wounded American volunteer in hospital.

89. Knightley, *First Casualty*, 212–14.

90. The literary quality of some dispatches also has direct links to past and future Hemingway fiction. He "borrows" directly from chapter 2 of *In Our Time* to describe the refugees fleeing Franco's forces: "Bedding, sewing machines, blankets, cooking utensils, mattresses wrapped in mats, and sacks of grain for the horses and mules were piled in the carts and goats and sheep were tethered to the tailboards. There was no panic. They were just plodding along." (Dispatch 19, 3 Apr. 1938, 69)

And he creates scenes he will recycle later in *For Whom the Bell Tolls*. El Sordo's hopeless stand against the fascist bombing planes in the novel has its origins in "a company of infantry making a last stand on the hillside and bare ridge" against forty-five minutes of "unmolested" bombing by "fifteen Heinkel light bombers" (Dispatch 24, 15 Apr. 1938, 80).

91. Watson, Introduction to "Dispatches," 7.

92. Watson argues plausibly that, given the "May Day" date of this dispatch, it may have been intended for a communist party publication, hence its more extreme tone ("Editorial note," 87).

93. Watson, Introduction to "Humanity," 115.

94. Donaldson, "Last Great Cause," 433, 434.

95. The exceptions are "My Pal, the Gorilla Gargantua" (28 July 1938) about the Joe Louis-Max Schmeling fight; "Program for U.S. Realism" (11 Aug. 1938), cynical advice on how America should cash in on the next European war; and the last article, "The Next Outbreak of Peace" (12 Jan. 1939), which predicts German and Italian political moves following the Munich Agreement of October 1938.

96. Though these articles probably did not have to pass Republican censorship, Hemingway still had to watch what he wrote to remain in the government's good graces (Alex Vernon's view, in correspondence with the author).

97. Watson, Introduction to "Humanity," 114–15.

98. Mellow, *A Life Without Consequences*, 513.

99. Donaldson, "Last Great Cause," 438.

100. Similarly, propaganda may have dictated Hemingway using the word "heroic" ("the present heroic resistance of the Valencia-Tereul road")—the kind of adjective that Frederic Henry had come to distrust in *A Farewell to Arms*.

101. *Pravda* ("Truth"), the article's venue, may have informed Hemingway's use of "truth" in this passage—an unintentionally ironic commentary. Hemingway liked the passage well enough to develop it in *For Whom the Bell Tolls*: the "absolute brotherhood" of the International Brigade volunteers "was something that you had never known before but . . . you gave such importance to it and the reasons for it that your own death seemed of complete unimportance" (251).

102. The general was Vladimir Gorev, former head of Soviet military intelligence and now military attaché in Spain (Mellow, *A Life Without*

Consequences, 506), whose presence in Spain "was to be kept secret" (Koch, *Breaking Point*, 55), part of the larger covert presence of Soviet personnel, whose aim, according to Koch, was to "assert Soviet interests in the war, and prepare for a Soviet takeover of the Spanish government" (ibid., 55). The "takeover" claim reflects Koch's unfortunate tendency to dramatic overstatement.

103. That Robles came from a monarchist family and that his brother, imprisoned by the Loyalists, supported the fascists, did not help his case. Among the many explanations for his execution—e.g., fascist spy, traitor, victim of the anarchists—Dos Passos's own hypothesis is the one most accepted by historians:

> Russian agents felt that Robles knew too much about the relations between the Spanish war ministry and the Kremlin and was not, from their very special point of view, politically reliable. As always in such cases, personal enmities and social feuds probably contributed ("The Death of José Robles," letter to *New Republic*, 625).

104. Ibid., 624. Others, besides, Dos Passos, have offered their own self-aggrandizing versions of who informed him of the death and when. Josie Herbst's version in *Starched Blue Sky* (150–51, 154–57), often repeated by biographers and critics (e.g., Koch, Baker, Donaldson), is contradicted by her diary notes (quoted in Vernon, *Hemingway's Second War*, 101–2). Hemingway's unreliable version is in "Treachery in the Aragon" (discussed below).

105. Letter to Scott Fitzgerald, 9 Oct. 1928, quoted in Morris, *Ambulance Drivers*, 191.

106. Shi, *Matthew Josephson*, 178.

107. Mellow, *A Life Without Consequences*, 509–10. Although loosely attached to the POUM, Orwell initially shared Hemingway's view that the Russian communists "had a definite practical policy . . . [and] were the only people who looked capable of winning the war" (*Homage to Catalonia*, 63). But in their instigation of the "May Days" and brutal repression of the POUM, Orwell came to see communist policy as anti-revolutionary (51–57).

108. Donaldson, "Last Great Cause," 400.

109. This article became "Farewell to Europe!" For Dos Passos, this political disillusionment had been a long time coming: as far back as 1932, his novel *1919* depicts a professional communist, Don Stevens, as arrogant and self-serving, concerned only with his own rise in Party ranks. *The Big Money* (1936) presents an even nastier picture of Stevens using idealistic communists for his purposes. And in 1934 Dos Passos, appalled at the American communists' breakup of a socialist rally at Madison Square Garden, signed an open letter condemning it.

110. White, letter to the editor, *Emporia Gazette* (Kansas), 30 Dec. 1970, quoted in Dos Passos, *Fourteenth Chronicle*, 496.

111. Virginia Spencer Carr, relying on Dos Passos's notes and fictionalized version of the encounter in his novel *Century's Ebb*, narrates a more dramatic variant: "'You do that,' [Hemingway] said, holding the fist right before Dos's eyes, 'and you will be finished, destroyed. The reviewers in New York will absolutely crucify you. These people . . . know how to turn you into a back number. I've seen them do it. What they did once they can do again'" (*Dos Passos: A Life*, 372).

112. Watson writes, "The typescript draft reads like the slurred speech of a drunk. Words are left out, phrases are jumbled, the logic of an argument gets reversed, and the usual discipline of Hemingway's style seems all but forgotten in the rambling chaos of so many sentences" ("Dispatches," 33).

113. Alex Vernon argues that technically "Hemingway's reportage was accurate: he had never known anyone 'disappeared.' The day after the dispatch, 22 [*sic* 21?] April, they both learned that Robles had indeed been executed . . ." (27). But even if the news of Robles' death came after the dispatch, Dos Passos had almost certainly already expressed his concern about the translator's disappearance. And Hemingway knew from Pepé Quintanilla, head of counter-intelligence in Madrid, that many in Madrid had been falsely arrested and executed.

114. Reprinted in Dos Passos, *Travel Books*, 618–22.

115. Knightley (*First Casualty*, 198) identifies the journalist in "Fresh Air" as Frederick Voigt, the Berlin representative of the *Manchester Guardian*.

116. Whether Hemingway was naïve in parroting the official line about terror and Robles is open to question. Several close associates of Hemingway refer to his naïve or childlike manner at times: Josie Herbst (*Starched Blue Sky*, 150–51), Herbert Matthews (*The Education of a Correspondent*, 95), Gustav Regler (*The Owl of Minerva*, 293), and Milton Wolff (quoted in Moorehead, *Gellhorn*, 118). But Regler also respected Hemingway's understanding of the political and military situations, entrusting him with confidential information (*Owl of Minerva*, 292–93). And Arturo Barea, who, as chief Loyalist censor in Madrid, met with Hemingway often, felt that his naïveté was a pose. Barea describes him as "questioning, skeptical and intelligent in his curiosity, skillfully stressing his political ignorance . . ." ("Not Spain," 211).

117. Hemingway, *Selected Letters*, 463–65. Like his dispatch denying disappearances (discussed above), the letter is rambling and incoherent. Without warning, it shifts into accusations about Dos Passos being "crooked about money," then complains about him not repaying debts to Hemingway, and finally, accuses Dos Passos of "knifing" Hemingway "in the back" for money while singing a fascist anthem (464). The letter's incoherence,

self-righteousness and self-pity suggest that Hemingway was drunk when he wrote it. But these emotions and his compulsion to correct Dos Passos's claims—even those the writer did not make—show the obvious strain Hemingway was under in maintaining Soviet myths about the war.

118. Dos Passos, "The Fiesta at the Fifteenth Brigade."

119. Koch. *Breaking Point*, 253; Payne, *The Spanish Civil War, the Soviet Union, and Communism*, 165.

120. Dos Passos, "The Villages Are the Heart of Spain."

121. In *For Whom the Bell Tolls* (263), Karkov gives Jordan the "escape" version of Nin's disappearance.

122. Payne, *Spanish Civil War*, passim.

123. Ibid., 162, 165, 211.

124. Ibid., 205.

125. Ibid., 213.

126. Ibid., 197. The POUM had the temerity to publicly oppose the second round of Moscow Trials, declare the victims innocent, and accuse Stalinists of betraying the revolution.

127. Ibid., 190.

128. Donaldson, "Last Great Cause," 416.

129. Cowles, *Looking for Trouble*, 29–30.

130. Ibid., 30.

131. Vernon, *Hemingway's Second War*, 26.

132. Payne, *Spanish Civil War*, 103.

133. Vernon, *Hemingway's Second War*, 26.

134. Ibid.

135. Cowles, *Looking for Trouble*, 30.

136. Herbst, *Starched Blue Sky*, 154.

137. Cowles, *Looking for Trouble*, 30.

138. Knightley, *First Casualty*, 213.

139. Wolff describes himself (in his novel *Another Hill*) as expressing doubts about the truth of the tortures referred to in *The Fifth Column*. Hemingway responded: "We're not playing games, *mi capitán*. They play dirty, we play dirty" (quoted in Vernon, *Hemingway's Second War*, 29).

140. Watson, "Joris Ivens," 53.

141. Knightley, *First Casualty*, 214.

142. Hemingway later told Bernard Berenson, "I tried to do that [give a true account of the war] when I wrote the book. But I did not start on the book until after the Republic had lost the war and it was over because I would not write anything in the war which could hurt the Republic which I believed in . . ." (14 Oct. 1952, Hemingway, *Selected Letters*, 789).

143. Letter to Max Perkins, 28 Oct. 1938, ibid., 474.

144. His one attempt at drama was a three-page scenario, "Today is Friday," presenting the reaction of a few Roman soldiers to Christ's crucifixion. Critics generally ignore this playlet when they don't denigrate it.

145. Compare Robert Jordan's response, when the journalist Karkov reveals that political assassinations are practiced "very, very extensively": "I don't mind them, . . . I do not like them but I do not mind them any more" (*For Whom the Bell Tolls*, 261).

146. During their raid, Philip answers Max with the Russian "Da," and Max sardonically explains to the prisoners: "You see. We are all Russians. Everybody is Russians in Madrid" (ibid., 74).

147. For example, Solow, "Clash of Certainties," 108–9.

148. Baker, *Life Story*, 338.

149. The story "Nobody Ever Dies," written in December, 1938, after Hemingway had returned to the States, has been called a Spanish Civil War story (Edgerton, "Nobody Ever Dies," 331–40). But it is set in Cuba, and its only link to the war is that the protagonist, Enrique, had fought and been wounded in the war on the Loyalist side.

150. Arturo Barea's criticism of *For Whom the Bell Tolls* is apposite here: "[H]e lived the somewhat unreal life of a war correspondent in the shell-pitted Hotel Florida, among foreign journalists, . . . but he never shared [Spaniards'] lives, neither in Madrid, nor in the Trenches" ("Not Spain," 212).

151. He is called throughout "Mr. Emmunds" by his Greek comrade, whose slightly broken and accented English may be slurring "Edmonds."

Chapter 5

1. Quoted in Steinbeck, *Working Days*, 151–52, Entry #36 n.

2. Steinbeck to Pascal Covici, 16 January 1939, *Life in Letters*, 138.

3. Shillinglaw, *On Reading* The Grapes of Wrath, 35.

4. Tom's final vision of his mystical presence "when our folks eat the stuff they raise and live in the houses they build" also has a biblical antecedent in *Isaiah* 65:21–22, as Peter Lisca identifies: "And they shall build houses and inhabit them, they shall not build and another inhabit; they shall not plant and another eat" (*Wide World of John Steinbeck*, 174).

5. Malcolm Cowley found the voice of these prophetic chapters shrill, hinting at Steinbeck's underlying uncertainty ("American Tragedy," 382–83); Edmund Wilson found the chapters preachy (*Boys in the Back Room*, 42); and Frederick Hoffman called Steinbeck's philosophizing intellectually shallow and "wretched violations of aesthetic taste . . ." (*Modern Novel*, 152–53). More recently, William Howarth described the general chapters as "simplistic editorials, haranguing the reader with dire prophecy, crude analysis, and cryptophilosophy . . ." ("Mother of Literature," 94).

6. Steinbeck to Herbert Sturz, 1953, quoted in Shillinglaw, *On Reading* The Grapes of Wrath, 36.

7. Gregory, *American Exodus*, 15.

8. Cf., "Grampa took his lan' from the Injuns" (*Grapes*, 237).

9. Many recent critics (e.g., Hearle, Denning, Godfrey) have sharply criticized Steinbeck for privileging the racial origins of the hungry migrants, as he had done in "The Harvest Gypsies" and *Their Blood Is Strong*.

10. Critics divide on how the Joads owned the land. Chester Eisinger assumes Pa's claim is a "freehold," i.e., a squatter's claim ("Jeffersonian Agrarianism," 153). Susan Shillinglaw, conversely, implies title ownership by asserting a downward spiral for the Joads: "from landowners, to croppers, to migrants . . ." (*On Reading* The Grapes of Wrath, 131, 109).

11. See Fitzgerald, "Accounting for Change," 190–91.

12. In ignoring the tractor's actual importance to Plains farmers, Steinbeck missed an excellent irony: the tractors that promised easier farming (and indirectly caused farmers to lose farm-ownership through debt) later turned on them and physically pushed them off of those farms.

13. Technically, the Joads' farm in Sallisaw County, Oklahoma, was east of the area where the worst dust storms prevailed: western Oklahoma, western Kansas, the Texas Panhandle, and southeastern Colorado (see Egan, *The Worst Hard Time*). But the farm was part of the much larger region that was seriously affected by a long-term drought from about 1930 to 1938. Still, in popular culture, such as Woody Guthrie's *Dust Bowl Ballads*, dust, far more than banks and tractors, is blamed for the migrants' leaving their farms. One artistic document that does refer to the tractor in precisely the same way Steinbeck does is Dorothea Lange's powerful photograph "Power farming displaces tenants, Texas panhandle, 1938," showing long furrows leading up to and surrounding an abandoned farmhouse.

14. In the journal he kept while working on the novel, Steinbeck writes that he hears in the tractors "the eviction sound and the tonal reason for the [Joads'] movement" (*Working Days*, 23).

15. In describing the "forces" that have turned against the Joads in Oklahoma, Robert Con Davis has described the banks as "mismanaged" (Introduction to *Twentieth Century Interpretations*, 5). I'd say the opposite: The banks are managed skillfully, if brutally, to extract the last measure of profit from the land at the expense of the tenants. One could, however, fault Steinbeck for not distinguishing between the large corporate banks, such as Bank of America ("Bank of the West" in the novel), which worked closely with the Associated Farmers, and small, individually owned banks that likely would have dealt with the Oklahoma Joads. These small banks do not comfortably fit the novel's depiction of them as an amorphous "monster."

16. The Roosevelt administration did try to address a major cause of the dust storms by having its agricultural agents teach soil-conserving terraced farming.

17. Shillinglaw, *On Reading* The Grapes of Wrath, 49.

18. This trip, which occurred in fall 1937, moved from Gridley (the locale of a government camp) to Stockton, Fresno, Arvin (another government

camp), Barstow, Needles, and Brawley (Parini, *Steinbeck*, 194). In returning from Europe with his wife, Carol, earlier that summer, Steinbeck did follow Route 66, but, according to Carol, "made no conscious effort to do any research for his book along the way" (Benson, *Steinbeck, Writer*, 360).

19. For the most thorough discussion of the Steinbeck-Collins friendship and collaboration, see Benson, "To Tom," 151–210.

20. The migrants' exploiters complain about precisely the same thing: When Tom asks at a farm-camp if there is any warm water, the guards are appalled at his temerity: "It's them gov'ment camps," [the second guard] said. . . . "We ain't gonna have no peace till we wipe them camps out" (378).

21. Perhaps fearing a lawsuit, Steinbeck changed Bank of America to "Bank of the West" (294). In "The Harvest Gypsies," he was more explicit.

22. Shillinglaw, *On Reading* The Grapes of Wrath, 147.

23. Malcolm Cowley (*Dream*, 32–33) recounts how the leader of the American Communist Party, William Z. Foster, declared at a congressional committee session in late 1930, "Millions of workers must go hungry because there is too much wheat. Millions of workers must go without clothes because the warehouses are full to overflowing with everything that is needed. Millions of workers must freeze because there is too much coal. This is the logic of the capitalist system."

24. Groene, "Agrarianism and Technology," 133.

25. Eisenger, "Jeffersonian Agrarianism," 149–54; Wollenberg, Introduction to *The Harvest Gypsies*, xii.

26. Steinbeck quoted DeMott, Introduction to *Working Days*, liv n11. He stated the same thing in "The Harvest Gypsies": "In [the migrants'] heads . . . there is one urge and one overwhelming need, to acquire a little land again, and to settle on it. . . ." (22).

27. I do not claim this paradox is an original discovery, only that it is the novel's central contradiction. As far back as 1939, in a review of the novel, Earle Birney writes, "There are overtones of mysticism and sentimental individualism which occasionally confuse the dominant social philosophy" ("A Must Book," 94). More recently, Stuart L. Burns writes that the Joads' "agrarian individualism" is incompatible with Steinbeck's "sympathy for communism" ("The Turtle or the Gopher," 103). (As I argue below, however, Steinbeck's central theme is collectivistic rather than communistic.) Some critics, conversely, don't find these elements contradictory, e.g., Eisinger: "The Okies are Steinbeck's protagonists in a kind of revolutionary social action . . . . The democratic way for Steinbeck is to achieve through collective action the individual security on the land that Jefferson prized so highly" (154).

28. Brooks, Lewis, and Warren, *American Literature: The Makers and the Making*, vol. D, 2454.

29. "[W]ithin man is the soul of the whole; the wise silence; the universal beauty, to which every part and particle is equally related, the eternal ONE. And this deep power in which we exist and whose beatitude is all accessible to us, is not only self-sufficing and perfect in every hour, but the act of seeing and the thing seen, the seer and the spectacle, the subject and the object, are one. We see the world piece by piece, as the sun, the moon, the animal, the tree; but the whole, of which these are shining parts, is the soul" (Emerson, "The Over-Soul," in *Selected Writings*, 262).

30. James Agee experienced even greater public indifference to sharecropper destitution two years later, when he finally published *Let Us Now Praise Famous Men* in 1941. By then, public attention was completely taken up by the war, especially once the United States became involved.

31. DeMott, Introduction to *Working Days*, xxxviii–xxxix; Shillinglaw, *On Reading* The Grapes of Wrath, 102, 86; Wartzman, "John Steinbeck in the 1930s: Living Under the Gun," 5.

32. Shillinglaw, *On Reading* The Grapes of Wrath, 47.

33. "Undated Q&A with JS, probably 1939," quoted in Wartzman, *Obscene*, 194–95.

34. Shillinglaw, *On Reading* The Grapes of Wrath, 185–86.

35. Ibid., 52.

36. Critics in the 1950s and early 1960s tended to downplay or dismiss altogether Steinbeck's politically radical aims in *Grapes*. See French, *John Steinbeck* (2nd ed.), chap. 6; and Lisca, *Wide World of John Steinbeck*, 150–51. These critics, publishing originally in 1961 and 1958, respectively, seem intent on shielding Steinbeck from the anti-communist zealots of the 1950s and from the anti-political attitudes of formalist criticism that prevailed then.

37. Nonetheless, at least one early reviewer felt that Steinbeck was projecting a political outcome of "revolution" (Birney, "A Must Book," 95). And of course, many hostile reviewers and public commentators accused Steinbeck of fomenting class warfare (see chapter 8).

38. The open ending of *Grapes*, with the Joads seemingly at the end of their rope, has not prevented some critics from extrapolating a happy ending, e.g., "the Joads' deep affinity with the natural world . . . in time . . . will subdue the adversity of the moment. . . . Thus, Steinbeck suggests repeatedly that . . . after a period of desperate wandering and confusion, at a time projected into the ideal 'future' the novel adumbrates, the wandering will end and the truly just community will exist" (Davis, Introduction to *Twentieth Century Interpretations*, 5).

Chapter 6

1. "How 'Bigger' Was Born," 459–60. Subsequent references to *Native Son* are to this "Restored Text" edition (1998) except as noted. Differences

between the 1940 edition and the restored text edition will be discussed below.

2. As Keneth Kinnamon has shown (*Emergence*, 120–21), Wright took this racist description directly from the Chicago *Tribune*'s description (27 May 1938) of Robert Nixon, a black man accused (and subsequently convicted) of killing a white woman.

3. Wright had used a similar name for his protagonist in the first of his *Uncle Tom's Children* stories, "Big Boy Leaves Home." Although Big Boy's size is not stated, he is big enough to jump on his three friends and fight off their attempt to overcome him.

4. I am reluctant to use this offensive word and apologize to those it offends; but none other will serve. The stereotype of the "bad nigger" connoted to many whites and blacks alike an image of menace: the black man with a razor or a knife in his pocket and an eagerness to use it; scars from previous fights; a hair-trigger temper; a jail record.

5. This reading of Bigger's name is certainly not original; in fact, *Time* magazine entitled its review of *Native Son* "Bad Nigger" (72). And Dan McCall entitles a chapter of *The Example of Richard Wright* "The Bad Nigger."

6. Rampersad, Introduction to *Native Son*, xix.

7. Without question, the newsreel showing the same Mary whom Bigger will meet a few hours later is one of those manipulated scenes that Wright argued were thematically necessary in "How 'Bigger' Was Born" even at the expense of "plausibility" (458).

8. Davis, "Richard Wright's 'Native Son,'" 4, 6.

9. The echo of a line in "The Love Song of J. Alfred Prufrock"—"time to murder and create"—was probably intentional, since Wright had read and admired Eliot's great poem.

10. Wright stated in "How 'Bigger' Was Born," "The entire guilt theme was woven in *after* the first draft was written" (461, Wright's emphasis). Fabre speculates that Wright added such passages as those quoted above as he was finishing the second draft (*Unfinished Quest*, 557n9). But a comparison of the two editions shows that he added them even later, as he revised the text to meet Book-of-the-Month Club's requirements.

11. Fabre, "Richard Wright, French Existentialism and *The Outsider*," 188.

12. We see this same lack of affect in the protagonist of *The Outsider*, Cross Damon, regarding the several murders he commits. Clearly, this was a theme that fascinated Wright.

13. The speech is so long that even one of Wright's most sympathetic critics, Keneth Kinnamon, describes it by quoting Samuel Johnson's quip about *Paradise Lost*: "none ever wished it longer than it was." Yet Kinnamon notes that it was five pages longer in galley proof! (Introduction, 15).

14. In "The Conclusion of Richard Wright's *Native Son*," Paul N. Siegel asserts, "The novel indicates that Max is not a Communist party member" (95). It seems highly unlikely, however, that the Party's legal arm, the International Labor Defense (called "Labor Defenders" in the novel), would employ a non-communist as a staff attorney. In any case—and far more important—Max employs a Marxist perspective loosely in his defense speech and distinctly in his final scene with Bigger.

15. Bigger's experience here recalls the Fisher King of the Grail legend, who was healed by the Grail knight's questions.

16. "Ill-related": Howe, "Black Boys and Native Sons," 104. Critical views of Max's speech and his final encounter with Bigger are summarized in Siegel, "The Conclusion," *passim.*

17. Max's use of "murder" throughout the speech and elsewhere is also highly questionable, as in "he murdered accidentally" (403). One essential characteristic in the legal definition of murder is "malice aforethought," which Bigger clearly did not possess in stifling Mary. He hated her, but had no intention of killing her in the bedroom scene. Thus, to "murder accidentally" is a contradiction in terms. Elsewhere, Max makes a lame effort to distinguish killing and murder: "But did Bigger Thomas really *murder*? . . . Looked at from the outside, maybe it was murder; yes. But to him it was *not* murder" (399, author's emphasis). Critics of *Native Son* often echo this sloppy use of "murder" in discussing Bigger's guilt, for example, "There is, moreover, no ambiguity about the nature and extent of Bigger's guilt in the murders he commits . . ." (Foley, "Politics of Poetics," 191).

18. Throughout the novel, blindness has functioned as a transparent symbol: Mrs. Dalton is literally blind; Mr. Dalton is blind to the irony of making millions as a slumlord while providing the Band-Aid of ping-pong tables for a boy's club; Bigger, *after* killing Mary, realizes how blind his family—and everyone else—still is (106–7).

19. Some critics (for example, Siegel, "The Conclusion," 102), in trying to rescue the novel's Marxist vision, emphasize Bigger's last request of Max: "Tell Jan hello . . ." But to consider this greeting as a sign of some sort of political solidarity with communist Jan strikes me as pretty thin gruel. What Bigger is responding to is Jan's friendship. Moreover, the failure of Max's appeal and Bigger's renascent existentialism rules out *Native Son* as a proletarian novel, as some critics have called it (e.g., Foley, "Politics of Poetics," 191).

20. Kinnamon, *Emergence*, 142. In a different frame of mind, Kinnamon writes in his "Introduction" (3), "Critics who read *Native Son* as a black nationalist repudiation of Marxism—Bigger's instinctive black triumph over Boris Max's arid white theorizing—would do well to ponder these words" (Wright's in "How 'Bigger' Was Born," 441), describing how his "contact with the labor movement and its ideology" helped him see Bigger's links

to whites. But besides describing his *own* Marxist revelation—a very different matter from characterizing Bigger's mentality—Wright here refers to his earliest experience with the John Reed Club after "I went to live in Chicago" (441). When he wrote *Native Son* his views about communism moderated from that initial enthusiasm.

21. In conceiving Bigger as a "negro nationalist," Wright may well have felt that he was offering readers a warning that aligned with Popular Front ideology: that Bigger's alienation and barely repressed rage made him a potential follower of fascism. In "How 'Bigger' was Born," Wright describes this possibility (446–47), but in the novel Bigger never considers fascism, expressing only a fantasy of bombing people from his plane (17). In sum, the racial emphasis in Bigger's characterization reflects a psychological realism that runs counter not only to Communist Party ideology, but to Wright's own theorizing.

22. Davis, "Story of a Winner," 7.

Chapter 7

1. In *Death in the Afternoon*, Hemingway urges writers who want to save the world to "see it clear and as a whole. Then any part you make will represent the whole if it's made truly" (278). The foreword to *Green Hills of Africa* states, "The writer has attempted to write an absolutely true book to see whether the shape of a country and the pattern of a month's action can, if truly presented, compete with a work of the imagination." Two years later, at the American Writers' Congress in 1937, he declared, "A writer's problem does not change. It is always how to write truly" (quoted in Baker, "Spanish Tragedy," 108). At times in his later writing, the word becomes inadvertent self-parody, as in "Just tell me true . . ." (*Across the River and into the Trees*, 225).

2. Golz was at least partially based on General Walter, "a pseudonym for General Karol Swierczewski, a Polish-born career Russian officer" (Vernon, *Hemingway's Second War*, 157).

3. Baker ("Spanish Tragedy," 118–19) aptly describes Gaylord's as representing the "cold, practical, hard-minded, cynical ruthlessness of the Comintern mind, completely unsentimental and in no way deceived by the propaganda which it daily originated and disseminated."

4. Hemingway's war chronology is a bit off regarding S.I.M. It was not created until 9 August 1937, more than two months after Jordan's mission (Beevor, *Battle for Spain*, 305). Although organized to combat Fascist intelligence-gathering, the S.I.M. applied NKVD tactics against rival leftist groups, which included illegal arrests, torture, and approximately one thousand executions, according to Gabriel Jackson (*Spanish Republic*, 553). For Orlov's role as NKVD intelligence chief, see Payne, *Spanish Civil War*, 134–35, 227–29.

5. Ibid., 165. The likeliest reason for the concealment was the realistic fear that other western powers would not intervene on behalf of the Republican government if they felt it was controlled by the Soviet Union.

6. Jordan mentions the Loyalist generals like El Campesino, Enrique Lister "from Galicia," and Juan Modesto from Andalucía, who all spoke Russian, the latter "a true party man" (246).

7. Critics disagree about the novel's place in Hemingway's separation from his earlier support of the Party line in Spain. Scott Donaldson feels the real turning point between Hemingway the propagandist and the artist was in his Spanish Civil War stories ("Last Great Cause," 441). Stephen Koch (*Breaking Point*, 276) is closer to my view that the novel marks the real break, though the stories and play partially recognized some ugly truths.

8. "Putsch" exaggerates the POUM's aim in these street battles (usually called the "May Days"), which was not to overthrow the Republican government. Historians generally concur that the Soviet NKVD provoked the battles by planting secret operatives in the various factions to justify purging their hated rivals, the POUM and the Anarcho-Syndicalists, which they proceeded to do in the months following.

9. Payne, *Spanish Civil War*, 227–29.

10. Hemingway's fictional chronology is a bit confused here. The Jordan narrative takes place in the last week of May 1937 (192), and his conversation with Karkov even earlier; but Nin's arrest did not occur until 16 June.

11. Baker, "Spanish Tragedy," 120.

12. Alex Vernon points out another advantage to Jordan's "loner" status: "A solo Robert Jordan, without a uniform, afforded Hemingway the liberty of a complex character unfettered by actual [Lincoln Brigade] history and politics" (*Hemingway's Second War*, 149)

13. In manuscript, the issue was more ambiguous. When Pilar asks Jordan if he is a communist, he answers affirmatively. Astonishingly, Hemingway changed his answer to "No I am an anti-fascist" at the request of Book-of-the-Month Club (ibid., 168), just as Richard Wright softened his text for the same group.

14. Hemingway expressed the same reason for having "accepted Communist discipline" in a letter to Max Perkins, ca. 13 January 1940, paraphrased in Baker, *Life Story*, 346.

15. In both his journalism and in the passage from *For Whom the Bell Tolls* quoted above, Hemingway does not qualify his affirmation of Soviet "discipline" in providing war leadership; hence, he does not appear "unenthusiastic" about it, as Alex Vernon claims (*Hemingway's Second War*, 164). Nor does he disapprove of the narrower meaning of discipline— military execution for cowardice and desertion, such as in "Under the Ridge"—as Charles Molesworth asserts ("Hemingway's Code," 87).

Regarding the execution in that story, the narrator declares, "In war, it is necessary to have discipline" (*Fifth Column*, 147).

16. Hemingway expressed the same view—that a Loyalist victory in Spain could retard the progress of the Axis powers—in his article "Dying Well or Badly" for *Ken* magazine in April 1938. Perhaps in 1937 this view was tenable, but by early 1938 it proved a false hope with the German *Anschluss* of Austria.

17. Perhaps Jordan's disrespect for his own family (excluding, of course, his heroic grandfather) accelerates this surrogate adoption. His father is a coward in Jordan's eyes not for killing himself, but for submitting to his wife's bullying. Curiously, the two most important members of his new family, Pilar and Pablo, are excluded from Jordan's rumination.

18. Jordan immediately criticizes this sentence in words anticipating the famous essay "Politics and the English Language" by George Orwell, another and even more disillusioned Spanish Civil War veteran. Jordan thinks, "Did big words make it [assassination] more palatable?" (181).

19. Helen Graham, for example, writes (*Spanish Republic at War*, 116) that unlike the spontaneous, uncontrolled atrocities committed by the Loyalists, "[a]trocities committed by the fascists . . . were systematic, sanctioned, conducted by the military, and sustained throughout the war."

20. Recall, for examples, his journalistic depiction of Mussolini pretending to read to read a book he held upside down ("Mussolini: The Biggest Bluff in Europe," reprinted in *By-Line*, 64); his slams against T. S. Eliot and, later, Gertrude Stein; and his portrayals of the incompetent doctors in *A Farewell to Arms* and the government administrator, Mr. Harrison, in *To Have and Have Not*.

21. Ilya Ehrenberg, for example, wrote that Marty "was always suspecting everyone of treason" and considered him "a mentally sick man" (*Memoirs*, 397). But not all agreed. Alvah Bessie was incensed that Hemingway had attacked this "man who was the organizational genius and spirit of the [International] Brigades" (see chapter 8). Marty allegedly boasted of having killed at least five hundred International Brigade members (Beevor, *Battle for Spain*, 161). Although Payne states that "no clear evidence" confirms the story of Marty's boast (*Spanish Civil War*, 351n40), Beevor notes that "Soviet documents . . . indicate that Marty's obsession with fifth column infiltrators and the execution of deserters and 'cowards' may well have contributed to the high rate of executions [1 percent of the International Brigade]" (*Battle for Spain*, 469n11).

22. Letter to Jay Allen, ca. 8 Apr. 1940, quoted in Baker, *Life Story*, 347.

23. Defenders of La Pasionaria, like Alvah Bessie and Milton Wolff, rebutted this charge of hypocrisy by pointing out that many other parents who could afford it sent their children out of the country to protect them and that La Pasionaria's son was too young to fight (see chapter 8).

Chapter 8

1. Steinbeck, unpublished statement, ca. Nov.–Dec. 1939, quoted in Benson, "Through a Political Glass Darkly," 52; Hemingway, *For Whom the Bell Tolls*, 178.

2. Though I have not found references from either Hemingway or Steinbeck to the Nazi-Soviet Pact, it seems likely that, like so many of their disillusioned colleagues on the left, they were shocked and disgusted by the Soviet Union's actions. Wright supported the Pact.

3. Dos Passos, "Farewell to Europe!" *Travel Books*, 618–22. See also Pells, *Radical Visions and American Dreams*, 310–19.

4. Shillinglaw, *On Reading* The Grapes of Wrath, 166.

5. For example, George Thomas Miron wrote in his pamphlet-length book *The Truth about John Steinbeck and the Migrants*, "I can think of no other novel which advances the idea of class war and the hatred of class against class . . . more than does *The Grapes of Wrath*" (quoted in Wartzman, *Obscene*, 192).

6. Wartzman, focusing primarily on Kern County's efforts to ban the novel, critiques the content of the titles listed here.

7. Ibid., 58.

8. Pegler quoted in ibid., 57, 56.

9. Shockley, "The Reception of *The Grapes of Wrath* in Oklahoma," 231.

10. Among the numerous enthusiastic reviews, two radical reviewers—Granville Hicks, writing for *New Masses* and Joseph Davis in the *Daily Worker*—both considered the book a superb example of the proletarian novel (Wald, "Steinbeck and the proletarian novel," 671).

11. For Eleanor Roosevelt ("My Day," 28 June 1939), reading the novel was "an unforgettable experience." In direct rebuttal to those who found Rosasharn's nursing of the stranger obscene, she found it proof that "[e]ven from life's sorrows some good must come." In his radio address of 19 Jan. 1940, FDR concluded, "There are 500,000 Americans that live in the covers of that book" (quoted in Wartzman, *Obscene*, 5–6).

12. Ibid., 228.

13. Meister and Loftis, *A Long Time Coming*, 46.

14. Shillinglaw, *On Reading* The Grapes of Wrath, 174.

15. Parini, *Steinbeck*, 235.

16. Ibid., 372.

17. Elaine Steinbeck's description of her husband applies perfectly to Ernest Hemingway (as well as innumerable other writers): happy while writing, especially when it was going well, and depressed when a novel was finished.

18. Parini, *Steinbeck*, 239.

19. Quoted in Benson, "Through a Political Glass Darkly," 51–52. Steinbeck did not conceal his support of Finland, and "Marxist acquaintances

were shocked or outraged" (ibid., 52). Cf. Alan Wald's dubious claim (Review of *A Political Companion*, 2–3) that "there exists no public condemnations [by Steinbeck] of the Stalin regime or its policies during that decade [of the 1930s]."

20. Shillinglaw, *On Reading* The Grapes of Wrath, 92–93.

21. Originally, *The Sea of Cortez* contained a narrative of the trip and "a phyletic catalog describing the animals collected." Viking Press subsequently published in 1951 the narrative separately as *The Log from "The Sea of Cortez"* (Astro, introduction to *The Log*, xvi). Though Steinbeck's name appears as the sole author of *The Log*, his and Ricketts' collaboration on the narrative, especially in the philosophical passages, was such that scholars today cannot agree on their individual contributions.

22. Ibid., xvii.

23. Marijane Osborn calls it a "pseudo-documentary" because of its obvious bias towards science ("Participatory Parables," 229).

24. Ibid., 231.

25. Ricketts sharply critiqued this bias towards modern science in the film, but his ideas (expressed in "Thesis and Materials for a Script on Mexico") seem to romanticize the villagers as having achieved an inner peace in their simple lives, despite their preventable suffering and deaths from disease (ibid., 231–32).

26. Colonel Lanser's humane side conflicts with his need to be ruthless as commander of the occupying forces (head of the herd). His complex characterization exemplifies Steinbeck's dilemma between creating a many-sided, even sympathetic character and recognizing the historical fact of Nazi brutality. The author was sharply criticized for making Lanser seem too humane, just as Hemingway was criticized for his sympathetic depiction of the fascist Lieutenant Berrendo in *For Whom the Bell Tolls*.

27. In *John Steinbeck and Edward F. Ricketts*, Astro asserts that two phalanxes operate in *The Moon Is Down*: the destructive (the occupiers) and the creative (the townspeople), the concept for the latter influenced by Ed Ricketts' ideas (156–57). But, as noted, Steinbeck is intentionally vague about the townspeople's supposed phalanx for reasons explained above, while his depiction of the destructive phalanx of the occupiers is vivid and definite.

28. But not from political liberalism: in later years he actively aided Adlai Stevenson's presidential campaigns and even wrote articles supporting President Johnson's escalation of the Vietnam War, a war he covered as a journalist. But these political involvements were the expressions of an outspoken individualist. He had long since abandoned his brief flirtation with collectivism.

29. DeMott, Introduction to *Working Days*, xlvi. To be sure, the short novel *Cannery Row* presents a sympathetic view of a small collective ("Mack and the boys"). But this group of individualists certainly does not

embody a phalanx. As John H. Timmerman (*John Steinbeck's Fiction*, 162–66) and others have plausibly argued, in the group's non-conforming, live-for-today *modus operandi*, the novel dramatizes the non-teleological thinking Steinbeck praised in the *Log*.

30. The forthcoming volume of Hemingway's complete letters covering this period may disprove this statement. But the co-editor of these volumes, Dr. Sandra Spanier, informs me that she does not recall seeing a Hemingway response to the Nazi-Soviet Pact in the unpublished letters.

31. Bessie criticized "Under the Ridge" for showing "the resentment of native Spaniards against the Russian battle police" (Baker, *Life Story*, 628n).

32. Letter from 27 Oct. 1939, paraphrased in ibid., 343.

33. Ibid., 346.

34. Letter, ca. 13 Jan. 1940, paraphrased in ibid., 346.

35. Poet Edwin Rolfe, Morris Maken (secretary of the Veterans of the International Brigade), and even Milton Wolff, the last commander of the Lincoln Brigade, later confirmed Hemingway's portrait of André Marty's irrationality. Arturo Barea and Maken found the novel's portrait of the Russians essentially accurate. And prominent Loyalist military leaders like Hans Kahle (former commander to 15th Brigade and 45th Division), Gustavo Duran, a lieutenant-colonel in the 69th Division, Mirko Markovich, commander of the George Washington Battalion, and Steve Nelson, the battalion's political commissar, all praised the novel (Nelson, *Remembering Spain*, 12, 25; Baker, *Life Story*, 356).

36. Trilling, quoted in Meyers, *Hemingway: The Critical Heritage*, 334.

37. Previously, Wilson had criticized Hemingway for uncritically adopting the communist line in Spain: "Soon the Stalinists had taken him in tow, and he was feverishly denouncing as Fascists other writers who criticized the Kremlin" ("Hemingway: Gauge of Morale," 308). Wilson was one such writer Hemingway had criticized (see Mellow, *Life Without Consequences*, 515).

38. Wilson, "Return of Ernest Hemingway," 591.

39. Gold, "Great Tradition," 5–6.

40. Ibid., 6.

41. Bessie, "Hemingway's 'For Whom the Bell Tolls,'" 25–29 (Bessie's emphasis).

42. Wilson, "Hemingway: Gauge of Morale," 308.

43. Still another CP review—Art Shields, "Hemingway's Travesty on Spain's Fight for Freedom" in the same issue of the *Sunday Worker* as Mike Gold's (8 Dec. 1940, 4)—uses "slanders" and "maligns" as it lists the same authorial transgressions.

44. Reprinted in "The Last Commander and the Unpublished Letters," *American Dialog* 1 (Oct.–Nov. 1964): 10.

45. Nelson, "Honor and Trauma," 21.

46. I assume the piece was commissioned because Hemingway accompanied the elegy with a note to North beginning "Here is the piece," and explaining how he had condensed it from three thousand words (*New Masses Anthology*, 308).

47. Nelson, "Honor and Trauma," 21.

48. Baker, *Life Story*, 330.

49. VALB, "Open Letter to Ernest Hemingway."

50. The signers were Milton Wolff, "National Commander," Fred P. Keller Jr., "New York Post Commander," and Irving Goff, "Acting Secretary-Treasurer." An identical typed version of the "Open Letter" in the Alvah Bessie papers bears the authorial notation: "AB in consultation with VALB board."

51. Nelson, "Honor and Trauma," 22, 24.

52. "A Postscript," April 1970, appended to a reprint of Bessie's *For Whom the Bell Tolls* review, in *The Merrill Studies*, 13. Bessie may have embroidered his recollection since it is hard to imagine Hemingway admitting that reading Marx (or anyone) "hurt his head."

53. Wolff, "Hemingway's 'On the American Dead in Spain,'" 12–13.

54. Ibid., 13, 14.

55. Baker, *Life Story*, 357.

56. "kumrads die because they're told)" in *E. E. Cummings: Complete Poems*, 440.

57. Nelson, "Honor and Trauma," 25.

58. Baker offers a revealing glimpse of Hemingway's political sensibilities in this period. En route to the Far East, he stopped in Hawaii and addressed a gathering of professors at the University of Hawaii, where "he spoke bitterly of the leftist attack on *For Whom the Bell Tolls*" (*Life Story*, 359).

59. Hemingway, "Ernest Hemingway Says Aid to China Gives U.S. Two-Ocean Navy Security For Price of One Battleship," 6.

60. Josephs, "Hemingway and the Spanish Civil War," 183, 180.

61. The best survey of contemporary reviews is in Samuel Sillen's article "The Response to 'Native Son,'" (25–27), the first of a two-part series Sillen published in *New Masses*. Sillen concludes, "Most readers and critics are agreed that *Native Son* is a novel of tremendous dramatic impact. On the social meaning of the novel there is a division of opinion" (26).

62. Gold, "Dick Wright Gives America a Significant Picture in *Native Son*," Sec. 2, 7.

63. Paraphrased in Fabre, *Unfinished Quest*, 184.

64. Davis, "Richard Wright's 'Native Son,'" 4, 6.

65. Gold, "Still More Reflections," 29 April 1940, 7.

66. Gold, "Open Letter," 29 Sept. 1940, 8.

67. Letter to Richard Wright, 23 May 1940, quoted in Rowley, *Wright: Life and Times*, 201.

68. Fabre dates the letter (in the Richard Wright papers) as early May 1940 (*Unfinished Quest*, 186).

69. Herndon, "Negroes Have No Stake in This War," interview with Richard Wright, 7.

70. Wright's position on Finland may not have been as absolute as these quotes suggest. According to Fabre, he "differed with [Theodore] Dreiser, who was a staunch defender of Russia's invasion of Finland" (*Unfinished Quest*, 192).

71. "There Are Still Men Left," unpublished article (summer 1939), quoted in Fabre, *Unfinished Quest*, 193.

72. "'Native Son' Author Backs Ford, Browder; Richard Wright's Statement," 1, 5.

73. Wright, "Not My People's War," 8–9, 12. Wright dismisses the peace-loving Soviets' invasion of Finland as "a brief spell of fighting" (12).

74. According to Franklin Folsom, executive secretary of the League of American Writers, Wright called him as soon as the German invasion was announced over the radio, asking, "What do we do now?" (*Days of Anger, Days of Hope*, 226). Wright himself signed a collective statement from the League, "Writers and War," dated 5 August, calling for "all immediate and necessary measures in support of Great Britain and the Soviet Union to insure the military defeat of the fascist aggressors."

75. According to Ellen Wright, Ben Davis "suggested that [Wright] go back to his novels and leave politics to the Party" (quoted in Fabre, *Unfinished Quest*, 229).

76. Undated and unaddressed telegram, quoted in *Unfinished Quest*, 227.

77. Wright, Introduction to *12 Million Black Voices* (condensed version) in *Coronet*, 78, emphasis added.

78. Rowley, *Wright: Life and Times*, 264.

79. *Atlantic Monthly*, pt. 1, Aug. 1944, 61–70; pt. 2, Sept. 1944, 48–56. Since I have quoted extensively from these important articles in chapter 2, I will limit my discussion here to a more general description.

80. Rowley, *Wright: Life and Times*, 294.

81. Ford, "A Disservice to the Negro People," 6; Sillen, "Richard Wright in Retreat," 25.

82. Schneider, "One Apart," 23–24.

83. Maltz, "What Shall We Ask of Writers?" 21; Maltz, "Moving Forward," 8–10.

Conclusion

1. Pells, *Radical Visions and American Dreams*, 347.

2. Kazin, *Starting Out in the Thirties*, 141.

3. For others who separated then, see Folsom, *Days of Anger, Days of Hope*, 178–79.

Works Cited

Historical Context

Aaron, Daniel, *Writers on the Left.* New York: Avon, 1965.

Cohen, Milton A. *Beleaguered Poets and Leftist Critics: Stevens, Frost, Cummings, and Williams in the 1930s.* Tuscaloosa: University of Alabama Press, 2009.

Cowley, Malcolm. *The Dream of the Golden Mountains: Remembering the 1930s.* New York: Penguin, 1981.

———. *Exile's Return: A Literary Odyssey of the 1920s.* Edited with introduction by Donald Faulkner. New York: Penguin, 1994.

Cummings, E. E. "kumrads die because they're told)." In *E. E. Cummings: Complete Poems 1904–1962*, edited by George J. Firmage. New York: Liveright, 1991.

Folsom, Franklin. *Days of Anger, Days of Hope: A Memoir of the League of American Writers 1937–1942.* Niwot: University of Colorado Press, 1994.

Josephson, Matthew. *Infidel in the Temple: A Memoir of the Nineteen-Thirties.* New York: Knopf, 1967.

Kazin, Alfred. *Starting Out in the Thirties.* Boston: Little Brown, 1965.

Kennedy, Richard N. *Dreams in the Mirror: A Biography of E. E. Cummings.* New York: Liveright, 1979.

League of American Writers. *Writers Take Sides: Letters about the War in Spain from 418 American Authors.* New York: League of American Writers, 1938.

Loftis, Anne. "Steinbeck and the Federal Migrant Camps." *San Jose Studies* 16, no. 1 (Winter 1990): 76-90.

Meister, Dick, and Anne Loftis. *A Long Time Coming: The Struggle to Unionize America's Farm Workers.* New York: Collier Macmillan, 1977.

New Masses: An Anthology of the Rebel Thirties. Edited with a prologue by Joseph North. New York: International Publishers, 1969.

Pells, Richard. *Radical Visions and American Dreams: Culture and Thought in the Depression Years.* New York: Harper & Row, 1973.

"Statement of American Intellectuals," *International Literature* 7 (1938): 104. Reprinted in Kinnamon, *Emergence of Richard Wright,* 117n83.

Stott, William. *Documentary Expression in Thirties America.* New York: Oxford University Press, 1973.

Steinbeck

Agee, James. *Let Us Now Praise Famous Men.* Boston: Houghton Mifflin, 1941.

Astro, Richard. Introduction to Steinbeck and Ricketts, *The Log from "The Sea of Cortez,"* vii–xxiii.

———. *John Steinbeck and Edward F. Ricketts: The Shaping of a Novelist.* Minneapolis: University of Minnesota Press, 1973.

Benson, Jackson J. *John Steinbeck, Writer A Biography.* New York: Penguin, 1984; 1990.

———. "Through a Political Glass Darkly: The Example of John Steinbeck." *American Fiction* 12, no. 1 (Spring 1984): 45–59.

———. "'To Tom Who Lived It': John Steinbeck and the Man from Weedpatch." *Journal of Modern Literature* 5, no. 2 (Apr. 1976): 151–210.

Brooks, Cleanth, R. W. B. Lewis, and Robert Penn Warren. *American Literature: The Makers and the Making.* Vol. D. New York: St. Martin's Press, 1975.

Burns, Stuart L. "The Turtle or the Gopher: Another Look at the Ending of *The Grapes of Wrath.*" In Davis, *Twentieth Century Interpretations of* The Grapes of Wrath, 100–104.

Collins, Tom. Unpublished autobiographical novel. Excerpted in *Journal of Modern Literature* 5 (Apr. 1976): 211–32.

Davis, Robert Con, ed. *Twentieth Century Interpretations of* The Grapes of Wrath. Englewood Cliffs, NJ: Spectrum, 1982.

DeMott, Robert. Introduction to *Working Days: The Journals of* The Grapes of Wrath, by John Steinbeck, xxi–lvii. New York: Penguin, 1990.

Denning, Michael. *The Cultural Front: The Laboring of American Culture in the Twentieth Century.* New York: Verso, 1997.

Egan, Timothy. *The Worst Hard Time: The Untold Story of Those Who Survived the Great American Dust Bowl.* New York: Mariner Books, 2006.

Eisinger, Chester. "Jeffersonian Agrarianism in *The Grapes of Wrath.*" *University of Kansas City Review* 14 (1947): 149–54.

Emerson, Ralph Waldo. "The Over-Soul." In *The Selected Writings of Ralph Waldo Emerson*, edited by Brooks Atkinson. New York: Modern Library, 1950.

Fitzgerald, Deborah. "Accounting for Change: Farmers and the Modernizing State." In *The Countryside in the Age of the Modern State: Political Histories of Rural America*, edited by Catherine McNichol Stock and Robert D. Johnston, 189–212. New York: Cornell University Press, 2001.

French, Warren. "The First Theatrical Production of Steinbeck's *Of Mice and Men*." *American Literature* 36 (Jan. 1965): 525–27.

———. *John Steinbeck*. 2nd ed. rev. Boston: Twayne Publishers, 1975.

Godfrey, Molly. "'They Ain't Human': John Steinbeck, Proletarian Fiction and the Racial Politics of 'The People.'" *Modern Fiction Studies* 59, no. 1 (Spring 2013): 107–34.

Gregory, James M. *American Exodus: The Dust Bowl Migration and Okie Culture in California*. New York: Oxford University Press, 1989.

Groene, Horst. "Agrarianism and Technology in Steinbeck's *The Grapes of Wrath*." In Davis, *Twentieth Century Interpretations of* The Grapes of Wrath, 128–33.

Guthrie, Woody. *Dust Bowl Ballads*. Rounder Records Corp., 1988.

Hearle, Kevin. "These Are American People: The Spectre of Eugenics in *Their Blood Is Strong* and *The Grapes of Wrath*." In *Beyond Boundaries: Rereading John Steinbeck*, edited by Susan Shillinglaw and Kevin Hearle, 243–54. Tuscaloosa: University of Alabama Press, 2002.

Hosmer, Helen, ed. "Who Are the Associated Farmers?" (pamphlet). Simon J. Lubin Society of California 1 (Sept.–Oct. 1938): 2–19.

Howarth, William. "The Mother of Literature: Journalism and *The Grapes of Wrath*." In Wyatt, *New Essays on* The Grapes of Wrath, 71–99.

Lisca, Peter. *The Wide World of John Steinbeck*. 1958. New York: Gordian Press, 1981.

McWilliams, Carey. *Factories in the Field*. Boston: Little, Brown, 1939.

Osborn, Marijane. "Participatory Parables: Cinema, Social Action and Steinbeck's Mexican Dilemma." In *A Political Companion to John Steinbeck*, edited by Cyrus E. Zirakzadeh and Simon Snow, 227–46. Lexington: University of Kentucky Press, 2013.

Parini, Jay. *John Steinbeck: A Biography*. New York: Henry Holt & Co., 1995.

Shillinglaw, Susan. *On Reading* The Grapes of Wrath. New York: Penguin, 2014.

Stein, Walter. *California and the Dust Bowl Migration*. New York: Praeger, 1973.

Steinbeck, John. "About Ed Ricketts." Appendix, *The Log from "The Sea of Cortez."*

———. "Dubious Battle in California." *Nation* (12 Sept. 1936) 302–4.

———. *The Grapes of Wrath.* 1939. New York: Penguin Books, 1999.

———. *The Grapes of Wrath: Text & Criticism.* Edited by Peter Lisca, updated with Kevin Hearle. New York: Penguin, 1977.

———. "The Harvest Gypsies." *San Francisco News,* 5–11 Oct. 1936. Reprinted in *The Harvest Gypsies: On the Road to the Grapes of Wrath.*

———. *The Harvest Gypsies: On the Road to the Grapes of Wrath,* edited with introduction by Charles Wollenberg. Berkeley, CA: Heyday Press, 1988.

———. *In Dubious Battle.* 1936. New York; Penguin Classics, 1992.

———. *The Log from "The Sea of Cortez."* 1941. New York: Penguin, 1955.

———. *The Moon Is Down.* In *The Short Novels of John Steinbeck,* introduction by Joseph Henry Jackson, 211–69. New York: Viking Press, 1953.

———. *Of Mice and Men.* New York: Covici-Friede, 1937.

———. "Starvation Under the Orange Trees," *Monterey Trader,* 15 April 1938. Reprinted as "Epilogue: Spring 1938," in *Their Blood is Strong,* 31–33.

———. "Statement" in *Writers Take Sides.* Quoted in DeMott, "Introduction," liv n12.

———. *Steinbeck: A Life in Letters.* Edited by Elaine Steinbeck and Robert Wallsten. New York: Viking, 1975.

———. *Their Blood Is Strong.* San Francisco: Simon J. Lublin Society of California, 1938.

———. *Working Days: The Journals of The Grapes of Wrath.* Edited by Robert DeMott. New York: Penguin, 1990.

Taylor, Paul, and Dorothea Lange. *An American Exodus: A Record of Human Erosion.* New York: Reynal & Hitchcock, 1939.

Timmerman, John H. *John Steinbeck's Fiction: The Aesthetics of the Road Taken.* Norman: University of Oklahoma Press, 1986.

Wald, Alan M. Review of *A Political Companion to John Steinbeck,* edited by Cyrus E. Zirakzadeh and Simon Snow. *ALH Online Review Series II,* 1–4.

———. "Steinbeck and the Proletarian Novel." In *The Cambridge History of the American Novel,* edited by Leonard Cassuto, Clare Eby, and Benjamin Reiss, 671–85. Cambridge: Cambridge University Press, 2011.

Walther, Louis. "Oklahomans Steinbeck's Theme." San Jose *Mercury Herald,* 8 Jan. 1938, 12.

Wartzman, Rick. "John Steinbeck in the 1930s: Living Under the Gun." In *Political Companion to John Steinbeck*, edited by Cyrus E. Zirakzadeh and Simon Snow, 1–7. Lexington: University of Kentucky Press, 2013.

———. *Obscene in the Extreme: The Banning and Burning of John Steinbeck's* The Grapes of Wrath. New York: Public Affairs, 2009.

Windschuttle, Keith. "Steinbeck's Myth of the Okies." *The New Criterion* 20, no. 10 (June 2002), http://www.newcriterion.com/articles.cfm/ steinbeck-windschuttle-1941.

Wollenberg, Charles. Introduction to Steinbeck, *The Harvest Gypsies: On the Road to the Grapes of Wrath*, v–xvii.

Wyatt, David, ed. *New Essays on* The Grapes of Wrath. Cambridge: Cambridge University Press, 1990.

Steinbeck Reviews

Birney, Earle. "A Must Book." Review of *The Grapes of Wrath*, by John Steinbeck. *Canadian Forum* 19 (June 1939): 94–95. Reprinted in *Critical Essays on Steinbeck's* The Grapes of Wrath, edited by John Ditsky, 29-30. Boston: G. K. Hall & Co., 1989.

Cowley, Malcolm. "An American Tragedy." Review of *The Grapes of Wrath*, by John Steinbeck. *The New Republic* 98, no. 1274 (3 May 1939): 382–83.

Davis, Joseph. "*The Grapes of Wrath* is a Great Proletarian Novel." *Daily Worker*, 4 April 1939, 9.

Hicks, Granville. "Steinbeck's Powerful New Novel." Review of *The Grapes of Wrath*, by John Steinbeck. *New Masses*, 2 May 1939, 22–24.

Hoffman, Frederick. *The Modern Novel in America, 1900–1950*. Chicago: Henry Regnery Co., 1951.

March, Fred T. "*In Dubious Battle* and Other Recent Works of Fiction." *New York Times*, 2 Feb. 1936, BR7.

McCarthy, Mary. "Minority Report." Review of *In Dubious Battle*, by John Steinbeck. *Nation*, 5 March 1936, 226–27.

Roosevelt, Eleanor. "My Day." *New York World Telegram*, 28 June 1939.

Shockley, Martin. "The Reception of *The Grapes of Wrath* in Oklahoma." *American Literature* 15 (Jan. 1944): 351–61. Reprinted in *The Grapes of Wrath: Text and Criticism*, ed. Lisca, 490–501.

Wilson, Edmund. *The Boys in the Back Room*. San Francisco: Colt Press, 1941.

Wright

Burnshaw, Stanley. "Wallace Stevens and the Statue." *Sewanee Review* 69 (Summer 1961): 355–66. Reprinted in *A Stanley Burnshaw Reader* as "Stevens' 'Mr. Burnshaw and the Statue,'" 22–32. Athens: University of Georgia Press, 2010.

Crossman, Richard H., ed. *The God that Failed*. New York: Harper & Row, 1963.

Davis, Alfred. "The Story of a Winner: Richard Wright, Negro WPA Writer, Wins Nation Fiction Contest; 600 Competed for $500 First Prize." *Daily Worker*, 25 Feb. 1938, 7.

Ellison, Ralph. "Remembering Richard Wright." In *The Collected Essays of Ralph Ellison*, edited by John F. Callahan, 663–79. New York: Modern Library, 2003.

———. "Richard Wright's Blues." In *The Collected Essays of Ralph Ellison*, edited by John F. Callahan, 128–44. New York: Modern Library, 2003.

Fabre, Michel. "Richard Wright, French Existentialism and *The Outsider*." In Hakutani, *Critical Essays on Richard Wright*, 182–98.

———. *The Unfinished Quest of Richard Wright*. New York: William Morrow, 1973.

———. *The World of Richard Wright*. Jackson: University of Mississippi Press, 1985.

Foley, Barbara. "The Politics of Poetics: Ideology and Narrative Form in *An American Tragedy* and *Native Son*." In *Richard Wright: Critical Perspectives*, ed. by Gates and Appiah, 188–99.

Gates, Henry Louis, Jr. and K. A. Appiah, eds. *Richard Wright: Critical Perspectives Past and Present*. New York: Amistad, 1993.

Hakutani, Yoshinobu, ed. *Critical Essays on Richard Wright*. Boston: G. K. Hall, 1982.

Herndon, Angelo. "Negroes Have No Stake in This War." Interview with Richard Wright. *Sunday Worker*, 11 Feb. 1940, 7.

Howe, Irving. "Black Boys and Native Sons." In his *A World More Attractive: A View of Modern Literature and Politics*, 98–122. New York: Horizon, 1963.

Kinnamon, Keneth, ed. *Critical Essays on Richard Wright's* Native Son. New York: Twayne, 1997.

———. *The Emergence of Richard Wright: A Study in Literature and Society*. Urbana: University of Illinois Press, 1973.

———, ed. *New Essays on* Native Son. Cambridge: Cambridge University Press, 1990.

———. "Richard Wright: Proletarian Poet." In Hakutani, *Critical Essays on Richard Wright*, 243–51.

Margolies, Edward. *The Art of Richard Wright*. Carbondale: Southern Illinois University Press, 1969.

McCall, Dan. *The Example of Richard Wright*. New York: Harcourt, Brace & World, 1969.

"'Native Son' Author Backs Ford, Browder: Richard Wright Hails Ford's Leadership in Fight for Peace." *Daily Worker*, 30 Sept. 1940, 1.

Rowley, Hazel. *Richard Wright: The Life and Times.* New York: Henry Holt, 2001.

Siegel, Paul N. "The Conclusion of Richard Wright's *Native Son.*" In Hakutani, *Critical Essays on Richard Wright,* 94–103.

Webb, Constance. *Richard Wright: A Biography.* New York: Putnam's, 1968.

Wright, Richard. "Almos' a Man" [first version of "The Man Who Was Almost a Man"]. In *O'Henry Award Prize Stories of 1940,* 289–305. New York: Doubleday, 1940.

———. "A.L.P. Assemblyman Urges State Control of Price of Milk." *Daily Worker,* 8 Nov. 1937. Reprinted in *Byline,* 33–34.

———. *American Hunger.* In *Richard Wright: Later Works,* edited and notes by Arnold Rampersad, 4-365. New York: Library of America, 1991.

———. "Bates Tells of Spain's Fight for Strong Republican Army." *Daily Worker,* 1 Oct. 1937. Reprinted in *Byline, Richard Wright,* ed. Bryant, 112–15.

———. "Between Laughter and Tears." Review of Zora Neale Hurston's *Their Eyes Were Watching God. New Masses,* 5 Oct. 1937, 22, 25.

———. "Big Boy Leaves Home." In his *Uncle Tom's Children,* 17–61.

———. *Black Boy.* 1945. New York: Harper & Brothers, 1945; Harper Perennial, 1993.

———. "Blueprint for Negro Writing." *New Challenge* 11 (1937): 97–106; http://thirtiesculture.files.wordpress.com/2011/10/wright-blueprint.pdf.

———. "Bright and Morning Star." In his *Uncle Tom's Children,* 221–63.

———. *Byline, Richard Wright: Articles from the* Daily Worker *and* New Masses. Edited with introduction by Earle V. Bryant. Columbia: University of Missouri Press, 2015.

———. "Down by the Riverside." In his *Uncle Tom's Children,* 62–124.

———. "The Ethics of Living Jim Crow." In his *Uncle Tom's Children,* 1–15.

———. "Fire and Cloud." In his *Uncle Tom's Children,* 157–220.

———. "High Tide in Harlem: Joe Louis as a Symbol of Freedom." *New Masses,* 5 July 1938. Reprinted in *Byline, Richard Wright,* ed. Bryant, 157.

———. "How 'Bigger' Was Born." Afterword to *Native Son.* Restored edition, 433–62.

———. "I Tried to be a Communist." *Atlantic Monthly,* pt. 1, Aug. 1944, 61–70; pt. 2, Sept. 1944, 48–56.

———. Introduction to *12 Million Black Voices* (condensed version). In *Coronet,* April 1942, 78.

———. *Lawd Today!* In *Richard Wright: Early Works*, edited and notes by Arnold Rampersad. New York: Library of America, 1991.

———. "Long Black Song." In his *Uncle Tom's Children*, 125–56.

———. *Native Son.* New York: Harper & Brothers, 1940.

———. *Native Son.* Restored Text ed. Introduction and notes by Arnold Rampersad. New York: Harper Perennial Classsics, 1993.

———. "Not My People's War." *New Masses*, 17 June 1941, 8–9, 12.

———. *The Outsider.* 1953. New York: Harper Perennial Modern Classics, 2003.

———. "Richard Wright's Statement Supporting Browder, Ford." *Daily Worker*, 30 Sept. 1940, 5.

———. *12 Million Black Voices: A Folk History of the Negro in the United States.* Photo direction by Edwin Rosskam. New York: Viking Press, 1941.

———. *Uncle Tom's Children.* Restored text ed. with introduction by Richard Yarborough. New York: Harper Perennial, 1993.

Wright's Poetry

"Ah Feels It in Mah Bones." *International Literature* 4 (Apr. 1935): 80.

"Between the World and Me." *Partisan Review* 2 (July–Aug. 1935): 18–19.

"Child of the Dead and Forgotten Gods." *The Anvil* 5 (March–April 1934): 30.

"Everywhere Burning Waters Rise." *Left Front* 1 (May–June 1934): 9.

"Hearst Headline Blues." *New Masses* 19, 12 May 1936, 14.

"I Am a Red Slogan." *International Literature* 4 (April 1935): 35.

"I Have Seen Black Hands." *New Masses* 11, 26 June 1934, 16.

"King Joe." *New York Amsterdam Star News*, 18 Oct. 1941.

"Obsession." *Midland Left* 2 (Feb. 1935): 14.

"Old Habit and New Love." *New Masses* 21, 15 Dec. 1936, 29.

"Red Clay Blues." With Langston Hughes. *New Masses* 32, 1 August 1939, 14.

"Red Leaves of Red Books." *New Masses* 15, 30 April 1935, 6.

"A Red Love Note." *Left Front* 1 (Jan.–Feb. 1934): 3.

"Rest for the Weary." *Left Front* 1 (Jan.–Feb. 1934.): 3.

"Rise and Live." *Midland Left* 2 (Feb. 1935): 13–14.

"Spread Your Sunrise!" *New Masses* 16, 2 July 1935, 26.

"Strength." *The Anvil* 5 (March–Apr. 1934): 20.

"Transcontinental." *International Literature* 1 (Jan. 1936): 52–57.

Untitled poem. In *Richard Wright: A Biography*, by Constance Webb, 357. New York, 1968.

"We of the Streets." *New Masses* 23, 13 April 1937, 14.

Wright Reviews

"Bad Nigger." Review of *Native Son*, by Richard Wright. *Time*, 4 March 1940, 72.

Cowley, Malcolm. "Long Black Song." Review of *Uncle Tom's Children*, by Richard Wright. *New Republic*, 6 Apr. 1938, 280.

Davis, Benjamin, Jr. "Richard Wright's 'Native Son' a Notable Achievement." *Sunday Worker*, 14 April 1940, 4, 6.

Farrell, James T. "Lynch Patterns." Review of *Uncle Tom's Children*, by Richard Wright. *Partisan Review* 4 (May 1938): 58.

Ford, James W. "A Disservice to the Negro People: The Case of Richard Wright." Response to "I Tried To Be a Communist." *Daily Worker*, 5 Sept. 1944, 6.

Gannett, Lewis. "Uncle Tom's Children by Richard Wright." *Book Union Bulletin*, Apr. 1938, 2.

"A Garbage Can Book" Review of *Uncle Tom's Children*, by Richard Wright. *Jackson (Miss.) Daily News*, 26 April 1938, 6.

Gold, Mike. "Dick Wright Gives America a Significant Picture in *Native Son*." *Sunday Worker*, sec. 2, 7.

———. "Open Letter to a Fighting Dentist and to a Famous Author." *Daily Worker*, 29 Sept. 1940, 8.

———. "Still More Reflections on Richard Wright's Novel, 'Native Son,'" *Daily Worker*, 29 April 1940, 7.

Hicks, Granville. "Richard Wright's Prize Novellas." *New Masses*, 29 March 1938, 23.

Locke, Alain. "The Negro: 'New' or Newer—A Retrospective Review of the Literature of the Negro for 1938." *Opportunity* 17 (Jan. 1939): 8.

Maltz, Albert. "What Shall We Ask of Writers?" *New Masses*, 12 Feb. 1946, 20–21.

———. "Moving Forward." *New Masses*, 9 Apr. 1946, 8–10, 21.

Marsh, Fred T. "Hope, Despair, and Terror." Review of *Uncle Tom's Children*, by Richard Wright. *New York Herald Tribune Books*, 8 May 1938, 3.

Poore, Charles. "Books of the Times." Review of *Uncle Tom's Children*, by Richard Wright. *New York Times*, 2 Apr. 1938, 13.

Roosevelt, Eleanor. "My Day." *New York World-Telegram*, 1 Apr. 1938, 25.

Schneider, Isador. "One Apart: 'Black Boy' by Richard Wright." *New Masses*, 4 Apr. 1945, 23–24.

Sillen, Samuel. "The Responses to 'Native Son.'" *New Masses*, 23 Apr. 1940, 25–27.

———. "Richard Wright in Retreat." Response to "I Tried To Be a Communist." *New Masses*, 29 Aug., 1944, 25.

Van Gelder, Robert. "Four Tragic Tales." Review of *Uncle Tom's Children*, by Richard Wright. *New York Times Book Review*, 3 Apr. 1938, 7, 16.

Hemingway

Baker, Carlos. *Ernest Hemingway: A Life Story.* New York: Scribner's, 1969.

———. "The Spanish Tragedy." *In Ernest Hemingway: Critiques of Four Major Novels.* New York: Charles Scribner's Sons, 1962.

Barea, Arturo. "Not Spain But Hemingway." Reprinted in *Hemingway and His Critics*, edited by Carlos Baker, 202-212. New York: Hill & Wang, 1961.

Beevor, Antony. *The Battle for Spain: The Spanish Civil War 1936–1939.* New York: Penguin, 2006.

Benson, Jackson J., ed. *New Critical Approaches to the Short Stories of Ernest Hemingway.* Durham, NC: Duke University Press, 1990.

Carr, Virginia Spencer. *John Dos Passos: A Life.* Evanston, IL: Northwestern University Press, 2004.

Cohen, Milton A. "Beleaguered Modernists: Hemingway, Stevens, and the Left." In *Key West Hemingway: A Reassessment*, edited by Kirk Curnutt and Gail Sinclair, 77–90. Tallahassee: University of Florida Press, 2009.

———. *Beleaguered Poets and Leftist Critics: Stevens, Frost, Cummings, and Williams in the 1930s.* Tuscaloosa: University of Alabama Press, 2011.

Cowles, Virginia. *Looking for Trouble.* New York: Harpers, 1941.

Donaldson, Scott. *Fitzgerald and Hemingway: Works and Days.* New York: Columbia University Press, 2009.

———. "The Last Great Cause: Hemingway's Spanish Civil War Writing." In his *Fitzgerald & Hemingway: Works and Days*, 372–451.

Dos Passos, John. *The Big Money.* 1936. New York: Mariner Books, 2000.

———. "The Death of José Robles." *New Republic*, 19 July 1939. Reprinted in his *Travel Books*, 623–25.

———. "Farewell to Europe!" *Common Sense*, July 1937. Reprinted in his *Travel Books*, 618–22.

———. "The Fiesta at the Fifteenth Brigade." April 1937. Reprinted in his *Travel Books*, 472–77.

———. *The Fourteenth Chronicle: Letters and Diaries of John Dos Passos.* Edited by Townsend Ludington. Boston: Gambit Inc., 1973.

———. *1919.* 1932. New York: Mariner Books, 2000.

———. *Travel Books and Other Writings 1916–1941.* New York: Library of America, 2003.

———. "The Villages Are the Heart of Spain." May 1937. Reprinted in his *Travel Books*, 478–88.

Edgerton, Larry. "Nobody Ever Dies: Hemingway's *Fifth* Story of the Spanish Civil War." In Benson, *New Critical Approaches*, 331–40.

Ehrenburg, Ilya. *Memoirs: 1921–1941*. Cleveland: World Publishing Company, 1964.

Graham, Helen. *The Spanish Republic at War: 1936–1939*. Cambridge: Cambridge University Press, 2002.

Hemingway, Ernest. *Across the River and Into the Trees*. New York: Scribner's, 1950.

———. "The Barbarism of Fascist Intervention in Spain." *Pravda*, 1 Aug. 1938. Reprinted in "Humanity Will Not Forgive This: The *Pravda* Article." *Hemingway Review* 7, no. 2 (Spring 1988): 114–18.

———. *By-Line: Ernest Hemingway: Selected Articles and Dispatches of Four Decades*. Edited by William White. New York: Simon & Schuster, 1998.

———. *Complete Short Stories of Ernest Hemingway*, Finca Vigía edition. New York: Scribner's, 1998.

———. *Death in the Afternoon*. 1932. New York: Charles Scribner's, Sons, 1960.

———. "The Denunciation." In his *The Fifth Column and Four Stories*, 89–100.

———. "Dying Well or Badly." *Ken* 1, no. 1 (7 Apr. 1938): 68–71.

———. "Ernest Hemingway Says Aid to China Gives U.S. Two-Ocean Navy Security for Price of One Battleship." *PM*, 15 June 1941, 6.

———. "False News to the President." *Ken* 2, no. 5 (8 Sep. 1938): 17–18.

———. *A Farewell to Arms*. 1929. New York: Scribner's, 1957.

———. *The Fifth Column and Four Stories of the Spanish Civil War*. New York: Scribner Paperback Fiction, 1998.

———. *For Whom the Bell Tolls*. 1940. New York: Scribner Classics, 1996.

———. "Fresh Air on an Inside Story." *Ken* 2, no. 6 (22 Sept. 1938): 28. Reprinted in his *By-Line*, 294–95.

———. *Green Hills of Africa*. 1935. New York: Charles Scribner's Sons, 1963.

———. "The Heat and the Cold." *Verve* 1, no. 2 (Spring 1938): 46.

———. "Hemingway's Spanish Civil War Dispatches," edited with introduction by William Braasch Watson. *Hemingway Review* 7, no. 2 (Spring 1988): 4–92.

———. "His Majesty's Loyal State Department." *Ken* 1, no. 6 (16 June 1938): 36.

———. *In Our Time*. 1925. New York: Scribner's, 2003.

———. "The Last Commander and the Unpublished Letters." *American Dialog* 1 (1964): 10–11.

———. "Mussolini: The Biggest Bluff in Europe." Reprinted in his *By-Line*, 61–65.

———. "Night Before Battle." In his *The Fifth Column and Four Stories*, 110–39.

———. "Old Man at the Bridge." *Ken* 1, no. 4 (19 May 1938): 36. Reprinted in his *Complete Short Stories*, 57–58.

———. "Old Newsman Writes: A Letter from Cuba." *Esquire*, Dec. 1934, 25–26. Reprinted in his *By-Line*, 179–85.

———. "On the American Dead in Spain." *New Masses* 30, 8 (14 Feb. 1939): 3. Reprinted in *New Masses Anthology*, 306–08.

———. "A Program for U.S. Realism." *Ken* 2, no. 3 (11 Aug. 1938): 26. Reprinted in his *By-Line*, 290–93.

———. *Selected Letters 1917–1961*. Edited by Carlos Baker. New York: Scribner's, 1981.

———. "The Snows of Kilimanjaro." In his *Complete Short Stories*, 39–56.

———. *The Sun Also Rises*. 1926. New York: Scribner's, 1970.

———. *To Have and Have Not*. 1937. New York: Charles Scribner's Sons, 1965.

———. "Treachery in Aragon." *Ken* 1, no 7 (30 June 1938): 26.

———. "Under the Ridge." In his *The Fifth Column and Four Stories*, 140–51.

———. "Who Murdered the Vets?" *New Masses* 16, 17 Sep. 1935, 9–10. Reprinted in *New Masses Anthology*, 181–87.

———. *Winner Take Nothing*. New York: Charles Scribner's Sons, 1933.

———, and Max Perkins. *The Only Thing That Counts: The Ernest Hemingway/Maxwell Perkins Correspondence 1925–1947*. Edited by Matthew Bruccoli. New York: Scribner, 1996.

——— (collaborator). *The Spanish Earth* [film]. Directed by Joris Ivens. Contemporary Historians, Inc., 1937.

Herbst, Josephine. *The Starched Blue Sky of Spain and Other Memoirs*. Boston: Northeastern University Press, 1991.

Ivens, Joris. *The Camera and I*. New York: International Publishers, 1969.

Jackson, Gabriel. *The Spanish Republic and the Civil War, 1931–1939*. Princeton, NJ: Princeton University Press, 1967.

Josephs, Alan. "Hemingway and the Spanish Civil War or the Volatile Mixture of Politics and Art." In *Rewriting the Good Fight: Critical Essays on the Literature of the Spanish Civil War*, edited by Frieda S. Brown et al., 180–83. East Lansing: Michigan State University Press, 1989.

Kinnamon, Keneth. "Hemingway and Politics." In *The Cambridge Companion to Hemingway*, edited by Scott Donaldson, 149–69. Cambridge: Cambridge University Press, 1996.

Knightley, Phillip. *The First Casualty: From the Crimea to Vietnam: The War Correspondent as Hero, Propagandist, and Myth Maker*. New York: Harcourt Brace Jovanovich, 1975.

Koch, Stephen. *The Breaking Point: Hemingway, Dos Passos, and the Murder of José Robles.* Berkeley, CA: Counterpoint Press, 2005.

Matthews, Herbert. *The Education of a Correspondent.* Westport, CT: Greenwood Press, 1946.

Mellow, James R. *Hemingway: A Life Without Consequences.* Cambridge, MA: Perseus Publishing, 1992.

Meyers, Jeffrey. *Hemingway: A Biography.* New York: Harper & Row, 1985.

Molesworth, Charles. "Hemingway's Code: The Spanish Civil War and World Power." In Sanderson, *Blowing the Bridge,* 83–97.

Moorehead, Caroline. *Gellhorn: A Twentieth Century Life.* New York: Holt, 2003.

Morris, James McGrath. *The Ambulance Drivers: Hemingway, Dos Passos, and a Friendship Made and Lost in War.* Boston: Da Capo Press, 2017.

Nelson, Cary. "Honor and Trauma: Hemingway and the Lincoln Vets." In his *Remembering Spain,* 19–39.

———, ed. *Remembering Spain: Hemingway's Civil War Eulogy and the Veterans of the Abraham Lincoln Brigade.* Urbana: University of Illinois Press, 1994.

Orwell, George. *Homage to Catalonia.* New York: Harcourt, 1938.

———. *Politics and the English Language and Other Essays.* Oxford: Benediction Classics, 2010.

Payne, Stanley G. *The Spanish Civil War, the Soviet Union, and Communism.* New Haven, CT: Yale University Press, 2003.

Regler, Gustav. *The Great Crusade.* Translated by Whittaker Chambers and Barrows Mussey. New York: Longmans, Green, 1940.

———. *The Owl of Minerva.* Translated by Norman Denny. New York: Farrar, Straus & Cudahy, 1959.

Reynolds, Michael. *Hemingway: The 1930s.* New York: Norton, 1997.

Sanderson, Rina, ed. *Blowing the Bridge: Essays on Hemingway and* For Whom the Bell Tolls. New York: Greenwood Press, 1992.

Shi, David E. *Matthew Josephson: Bourgeois Bohemian.* New Haven, CT: Yale University Press, 1981.

Shoots, Hans. *Living Dangerously: A Biography of Joris Ivens.* Translated by David Colmer. Amsterdam: Amsterdam University Press, 2000.

Solow, Herbert, "Substitution, at Left Tackle: Hemingway for Dos Passos." *Partisan Review* 4 (Apr. 1938): 62–64.

Solow, Michael K. "A Clash of Certainties, Old and New: *For Whom the Bell Tolls* and the Inner War of Ernest Hemingway." *Hemingway Review* 29, no. 1 (Fall 2009): 108–9.

Vernon, Alex. *Hemingway's Second War: Bearing Witness to the Spanish Civil War.* Iowa City: University of Iowa Press, 2011.

Veterans of Abraham Lincoln Brigade (VALB). "Open Letter to Ernest Hemingway." *Daily Worker*, 22 Nov. 1940, 7.

Watson, William Braasch. Introduction to "Hemingway's Spanish Civil War Dispatches." *Hemingway Review* 7, no. 2 (Spring 1988): 4–13.

———. Introduction to "Humanity Will Not Forgive This: The *Pravda* Article." *Hemingway Review* 7, no. 2 (Spring 1988): 114–16.

———. "Joris Ivens and the Communists: Bringing Hemingway into the Spanish Civil War." In Sanderson, *Blowing the Bridge*, 37–57.

Wolfert, Ira. "Hemingway Off to Spain to Write About the War." *New York Times*, 28 Feb 1937, 30.

Hemingway Reviews

Bessie, Alvah. "Hemingway's 'For Whom the Bell Tolls.'" *New Masses*, 5 Nov. 1940, 25–29.

———. "A Postscript" [to review]. April 1970. Reprinted in *The Merrill Studies in* For Whom the Bell Tolls, edited by Sheldon Grebstein, 13. Columbus, OH: Merrill, 1971.

Chamberlain, John. "Books of the Times." Review of *Green Hills of Africa. New York Times*, 25 Oct. 1935, 19.

Cowley, Malcolm. "A Farewell to Spain." Review of *Death in the Afternoon. New Republic*, 30 Nov. 1932, 76–77.

———. "Hemingway: Work in Progress." Review of *To Have and Have Not. New Republic*, 20 Oct. 1937, 305–06.

Eastman, Max. "Bull in the Afternoon." Review of *Death in the Afternoon. New Republic*, 7 June 1933, 94–97.

Fadiman, Clifton. "Letter to Mr. Hemingway." Review of *Winner Take Nothing. New Yorker* 9 (28 Oct. 1933): 74–75.

Forsythe, Robert. "In This Corner, Mr. Hemingway." *New Masses*, 27 Nov. 1934, 26.

Gold, Mike. "The Great Tradition: Can the Literary Renegades Destroy It?" Review of *For Whom the Bell Tolls. Sunday Worker*, 8 Dec. 1940, 5, 6.

Gregory, Horace. "Ernest Hemingway Has Put on Maturity." Review of *Winner Take Nothing. New York Herald Tribune Books*, 20 Oct. 1933, vii–5.

Hicks, Granville. "Bulls and Bottles." Review of *Death in the Afternoon. Nation*, 9 Nov. 1932, 461.

———. "Small Game Hunting." Review of *Green Hills of Africa. New Masses*, 19 Nov. 1935, 23.

Kazin, Alfred. "Hemingway's First Book on His Own People." Review of *To Have and Have Not. New York Herald Tribune Books*, 17 Oct. 1937, 3.

Matthews, T. S., "Fiction by Young and Old." Review of *Winner Take Nothing. New Republic*, 15 Nov. 1933, 24–25.

McManus, John T. "Realism Invades Gotham." Review of *The Spanish Earth*. *New York Times*, 22 Aug. 1937, 3.

———. "'The Spanish Earth' at the 55th St. Playhouse is a Plea for Democracy." *New York Times*, 21 Aug. 1937.

Meyers, Jeffrey, ed. *Hemingway: The Critical Heritage*. London: Routledge & Kegan Paul, 1982.

Rahv, Philip. "The Social Muse and the Great Kudu." Review of *To Have and Have Not*. *Partisan Review* 4 (Dec. 1937): 62.

Schneider, Isador. "The Fetish of Simplicity." *Nation*, 24 Jan. 1931, 184–86.

Shields, Art. "Hemingway's Travesty on Spain's Fight for Freedom." *Sunday Worker*, 8 Dec. 1940, 4.

Stephens, Robert O., ed. *Ernest Hemingway: The Critical Reception*. New York: Burt Franklin & Co., 1977.

Trilling, Lionel. Review of *For Whom the Bell Tolls*. *Partisan Review* 8 (Jan. 1941): 63–67. Reprinted in Meyers, *The Critical Heritage*, 334.

Troy, William. "Mr. Hemingway's Opium." Review of *Winner Take Nothing*. *Nation*, 15 Nov. 1933, 570.

Wilson, Edmund. "Ernest Hemingway: Gauge of Morale." *Atlantic*, July 1939, 36–46. Reprinted in Meyers, *The Critical Heritage*, 308–9.

———. "Letter to the Russians about Hemingway." Review of *Green Hills of Africa*. *New Republic*, 11 Dec. 1935, 135.

———. "Return of Ernest Hemingway." *New Republic*, 28 Oct. 1940, 591.

Wolff, Milton. "Hemingway's 'On the American Dead in Spain.'" In Nelson, *Remembering Spain*, 7–17.

62, 63, 70, 93, 167, 168, 298–99, 301; initial enthusiasm, 56; initial aim, 56–57, 67, 70, 94; joins Party, 4, 63, 322*n*10; protests closing of John Reed Clubs, 64, 65; Wright's separation from cell, 4, 7, 53, 69, 70. *See also* Wright, works: "I Tried to Be a Communist"; *The Outsider*

Daily Worker, reporter for, 5, 53, 54, 70, 71, 72, 83–86, 88, 89, 90, 95, 168, 169, 296, 299, 324*nn*33,42

Federal Theatre Project, publicist for, 67–68, 322*n*13

Federal Writers' Project, writer for, 67, 68, 69, 71, 72, 75, 90, 95, 168

and "negro nationalism": defined, 323*n*18; Party's opposition to, 65, 74; Wright's practical expression of, 74, 94, 171, 232–33, 297, 323*n*25, 339*n*21; Wright's theoretical opposition to, 73, 94. *See also Native Son*, thematic ambivalence in, defiance of communist ideology in; Wright, works: "Blueprint for Negro Writing"; *Uncle Tom's Children*, "negro nationalism" in

and New York branch of Communist Party: conflict between cell's expectations and Wright's creative needs, 54, 88, 95, 169, 233–34, 299; renewed relationship with, 4, 53, 54, 70, 71–72, 90, 95, 168; Wright's international views determined by, 5, 7, 85–86, 88, 94–95, 169, 266, 297–98, 310, 313, 324*n*43, 346*n*74. *See also Native Son*: reviews of

Party's attacks on Wright after public separation, 7, 8, 304–05

separation from Communist Party, 7, 302, 304; Party's negative criticism of *Native Son*: see

Native Son, reviews of; Wright's resentment at being censored by Party, 7, 299–300, 310, 346*nn*74,75 (*see also* Wright, works: "Not My People's War"); Wright's anger at Party for abandoning black cause, 7, 300–01, 313–14

turns from poetry to fiction, 54, 65, 64, 68, 69

and South Side Writers' Group, 67, 68

See also John Reed Clubs: and Richard Wright

Wright, works

"Almos' a Man," 69, 322*n*15

articles for *Daily Worker*, 5, 83–86, 88; articles on Joe Louis, 87–88, 91

"Big Boy Leaves Home." *See* Wright, works: *Uncle Tom's Children*

Black Boy or *American Hunger*, 76, 302, 321*nn*1,3, 323*n*23; communists' response to, 304–05

"Blueprint for Negro Writing," 72–75, 81, 94, 232, 233

"Bright and Morning Star." *See* Wright, works: *Uncle Tom's Children*

"Down by the Riverside." *See* Wright, works: *Uncle Tom's Children*

"The Ethics of Living Jim Crow," 75–76, 77, 323*n*20

"Fire and Cloud." *See* Wright, works: *Uncle Tom's Children*

"How 'Bigger' Was Born," 50, 91, 92–93, 171, 209, 210, 211, 212, 216, 223, 224, 230, 231, 232, 233, 297. *See also Native Son*: Bigger's characterization

"I Tried to Be a Communist," 53, 54, 55, 56, 62–67, 69, 70, 91, 223–24,

232, 297, 302–04, 307, 321*nn*1,3;
communists' response to, 304;
unreliability of, 53–54, 321*n*4
Lawd Today! (or "Cesspool"), 61, 68,
69, 73, 90, 322*n*15; communists'
opposition to, 65, 322*n*12, 323*n*23
leftist poetry, 54, 56, 57–62, 93, 167,
321*n*5
"Long Black Song." *See* Wright,
works: *Uncle Tom's Children*
"Not My People's War," 7, 298, 299
The Outsider, treatment of
communists in, 300, 303, 305,
306–08, 321*n*2
"Silt," 69, 75
12 Million Black Voices, 6, 265,
346*n*77
Uncle Tom's Children, 69, 74, 75, 170,
232, 322*n*20; "Big Boy Leaves
Home," 58, 68–69, 75, 76–77;
blacks fighting back in, 77–78,
93; breakthrough success of,
54, 81, 89–90, 168; "Bright and
Morning Star," 69, 77, 78, 80–81,
323*n*24; "Down by the Riverside," 69, 77; "Fire and Cloud,"
54, 58, 69, 77–79, 80, 323*n*25,
wins *Story* magazine prize, 54,
75; "Long Black Song," 69, 77,
79; "negro nationalism" in, 74,
80–81, 323*n*25; reviews of, 78,
81–83, 294; Social Realism in,
78, 79, 80; violence against blacks
in, 76–77
See also Native Son
Wright, Dhimah Rose Meidman, 264
"Writers Take Sides," 9, 36, 316*n*7. *See
also* League of American Writers